Theology Matters

Theology Matters

Answers
for the
Church
Today

In Honor of Harold Hazelip

Edited by
Gary Holloway,
Randall J. Harris,
Mark C. Black

COLLEGE PRESS PUBLISHING COMPANY • JOPLIN, MISSOURI

International Standard Book Number: 0-89900-813-5

CONTENTS

Preface

This book has two purposes.

First, it is designed to be of value to the churches of Christ as they face a new millennium. As editors, we chose topics we believed would be particularly relevant to the understanding and practice of the Christian life. The authors intend this to be a volume for the church, not a collection of scholarly essays. Although the book can be profitably studied individually, it will have greater value when discussed in small groups or church classes. We do not expect most people or groups to study a book of this length from cover to cover. Instead, the book is arranged so people can begin with the introduction and then study the topics and questions that interest them most.

Secondly, this volume is published to honor Harold Hazelip. Harold has served the church as a minister, a television evangelist, a writer, and a university president. This volume particularly recognizes his contributions as a teacher. All the contributors to this volume have two things in common. All are faithful servants of Christ and his church and all have been greatly influenced by Harold Hazelip (with one exception, all are his former students). Harold thus embodies the instruction of Paul to Timothy: "And the things you have heard me say in the presence of many witnesses entrust to reliable men who will also be qualified to teach others" (2 Timothy 2:2).

The writers honor Harold as a faithful teacher who formed us as teachers of God's word. His influence is seen in the lives of these writers, in the essays they write, and in his own writings.

Appropriately, this volume ends with a brief biography of Harold Hazelip and a bibliography of his writings.

Many people worked hard to produce this volume. Carl McKelvey and the Lipscomb University administration supported it from the beginning. Each writer contributed hours of prayerful thought and work. Michael Moss and Sam Wallace gave computer assistance. Deb Holloway helped proofread.

The editors pray that God will use this book to produce reflection on the depth of his love for humanity as expressed in the giving of his Son. We pray it will contribute to unity among those who wear the name of Christ. We pray it gives a deeper insight into the will of God revealed in Scripture. We pray God will raise up more faithful followers like Harold Hazelip to lead the church in a new millennium.

Introduction

Does Theology matter?

What you heard from me, keep as the pattern of *sound teaching*, with faith and love in Christ Jesus. Guard the good deposit that was entrusted to you — guard it with the help of the Holy Spirit who lives in us (2 Tim. 1:13-14).

In the presence of God and of Jesus Christ, who will judge the living and the dead, and in view of his appearing and his kingdom, I give you this charge: Preach the Word; be prepared in season and out of season; correct, rebuke and encourage — with great patience and careful instruction. For the time will come when men will not put up with *sound doctrine*. Instead, to suit their own desires, they will gather around them a great number of teachers to say what their itching ears want to hear (2 Tim. 4:1-3).

There is an old piece of advice that is given to aspiring writers of western novels, "Always shoot the sheriff in the first paragraph." Somehow, I'm not sure the reader is going to be immediately grabbed by being told that this is a book of theology. You may have heard these only slightly tongue-in-cheek definitions of a philosopher and a theologian:

- A philosopher is a blind man in a dark alley looking for a black cat that isn't there.
- A theologian is a blind man in a dark alley looking for a black cat that isn't there, and who thinks he has found it.

Indeed, in Churches of Christ the mere word "theology" creates suspicion. This suspicion, of course, is not entirely without basis. Some serious pastoral and biblical malpractice has been committed under the auspices of "theology."

Unfortunately, today, in many quarters, even the word doctrine is not welcome. "Doctrine" is associated with intolerant, mean-spirited sectarianism that leads to witch hunts, hard feelings, and division. And many have had their fill of that. So perhaps we need to be reminded of Paul's instructions to Timothy quoted above which emphasize the necessity of sound doctrine, especially when people lose their desire for it. But why is doctrine so important?

Let me offer three reasons. First, it is only by understanding doctrine or theology that we are able to give reasonable answers to those who inquire of us. I once had a person who had a religious background but who was now quite hostile to faith ask the following:

> I was with a bunch of Christians one night and they all got to praying. They said things like "God, we know you are here because we can feel your presence." What I want to know is, how does that *feel*? Is it like when you go out with your bowling buddies and have a few beers? Is that what it feels like?
>
> And by the way, how do you put your hand in the hand of the man from Galilee?

The questions may seem profane or absurd, but we must not miss the point. We ought to be able to provide answers for questions about what we say we believe.

In the above case, sloppy thinking may lie behind the sloppy language. Do we understand our own faith deeply enough to be able to explain it in ways an outsider can understand?.

What if we are asked about how the death of Jesus saves us? Is the end of the world coming soon? If prayer can make sick people well, why do Christians die? Do we really believe grape juice is the blood of Jesus? What makes one church better than another? I'm a good person, do you really think I'm a sinner going to hell? And the questions go on and on. Non-Christians deserve good answers when they inquire about faith:

> But in your hearts set apart Christ as Lord. Always be prepared to give an answer to everyone who asks you to give the reason for the hope that you have. But do this with gentleness and respect . . . (1 Pet. 3:15).

Second, doctrine or theology is important in making us spiritually healthy. This is what Paul means by sound doctrine in the passages quoted above. Does our doctrinal diet produce health or disease? What one believes does matter, especially at those times when life is confusing or oppressive.

I have from time to time discussed the old doctrine of "providence" in Bible classes at various congregations (this topic is discussed in chapter six of this book). When I asked people about their understanding of God's "providing," especially during the Persian Gulf War, they would often talk about how God provided protection in dangerous circumstances. Or others would talk about how God had granted health in answer to prayer against all medical odds. This is all fine, but I wonder what it says to the person who lives uprightly and prays passionately only to have a child die? If at times like these we are not doctrinally healthy (sound), we could produce some serious spiritual diseases. People can have their spiritual lives destroyed by bad teaching.

Third, doctrine is important because it helps us "think God's thoughts after him." It helps us draw closer to the one we claim embodies all truth. We generally consider it pitiful when people live their lives based on lies. We aspire to sound doctrine not because it makes our lives work better, but because it corresponds to the way things really are.

In a world of so many viable religious alternatives (some of which are increasingly bizarre) it is imperative that we attempt to find our way by the light of truth, not by the most interesting or entertaining fad of the moment. Even among proponents of "Christianity," the teaching often strays far from the biblical witness. For a people who claim to be guided by the truth of Scripture, there is no shame in putting forth our best effort to get it right, fallible as we are.

So, here you have a book of theology or doctrine. In different ways, all of the writers attempt to contribute to sound doctrine by providing answers to questions people ask, by giving us an understanding of our faith that will sustain us, and by drawing near to the truth of things as embodied in our God.

But I would issue a warning to you, reader, before you proceed. No one writing in this book claims the last word on his topic. The point is to stimulate you to understand your faith. You must finally answer for yourself on each topic. The pursuit of a true, full, spiritual life is the responsibility of all Christians, not just professional teachers and preachers. Of course the time will come when all will be more clear, when every knee will bow and tongue confess that Jesus is Lord, when God will be all in all. Amen. Come Lord Jesus!

But in the meantime...

SECTION ONE
QUESTIONS ABOUT GOD

All theology, of course, begins with God. In orthodox Christianity throughout the centuries that has meant confessing God the Father, God the Son, and God the Holy Spirit. In this opening section, our writers consider questions related to the Godhead.

In the opening article Ron Highfield takes on that most puzzling of all theological doctrines, the Trinity. Some have thought this doctrine so obscure and beyond human understanding that it is worthy of little consideration. While not attempting to unlock the mystery of the Trinity, Highfield does show that the doctrine is both biblical *and* significant.

In the second article the subject is no less baffling. How can Jesus be both God and man? Barry Blackburn takes on the question of the humanity of Jesus. He not only asserts the full humanity of Jesus but contends there are important implications involved in confessing that Jesus was "one of us."

The third article involves questions no less vexing. How are we to identify and appreciate the work of that least understood member of the Trinity, the Holy Spirit? Mike Cope challenges us with these issues.

I suppose these articles show that any God that can be contained in the box of human rationality is less than the God of Scripture. While not attempting to reduce God to the size of our minds, we do attempt to understand more deeply the one in whom we place our trust. For in coming to see him more clearly, we come to love him more dearly.

Chapter One

Does the doctrine of the Trinity make a difference?

Ron Highfield
Pepperdine University
Malibu, California

The word Trinity doesn't flow naturally from the lips of the heirs of Alexander Campbell and Barton Stone. We hesitate to embrace it, not because we reject the doctrine of the Trinity or consider it trivial. Confessing our faith, worshiping and praying in a Trinitarian vocabulary trouble us, for the most part, because we don't find such language in the Bible.

Campbell and Stone led a movement to restore New Testament Christianity, Christianity as it was before the development of non-biblical creeds and confessions of faith. A key element in their strategy to reconstitute the church and unite all Christians was the pioneers' determination to confess their faith in biblical language alone, to "call Bible things by Bible names." They observed that many of the divisions within the Christianity of their day were due, not so much to differences in faith, as to stubborn adherence to different systems of humanly contrived theological terms.

It has been our practice, therefore, to confess, proclaim and teach the Christian faith whenever possible in the words of Scripture. We've not hesitated to confess God as "Father" (Matt. 6:1-32; Rom. 8:14) and Jesus as "Christ" (Mark 8:30; 1 John 5:1), "Lord" (John 28:20; Acts 10:36; Phil. 2:11; Rev. 19:16), "God" (John 1:1; 28:20; Rom. 9:5; Titus 2:13; Heb. 1:8; 1 John 5:21), and "the Son of God" (Matt. 3:17; John 1:14; 3:16; 1 John 4:9).

In view of Matthew 28:19, we've baptized believers "in the name of the Father and of the Son and of the Holy Spirit." The Word, we've acknowledged, existed with God before creation, acted as God's agent in creation and became flesh in Jesus Christ

(John 1:1-14; Heb. 1:1-4; Col. 1:15-20). In sum, we've not hesitated to embrace enthusiastically every biblical text that states, illustrates or implies the supernaturalness of our Lord Jesus Christ. Nevertheless, we have hesitated to incorporate into our worship, teaching and evangelism language referring to God as Holy Trinity or God in three persons.

The Biblical Teaching Supporting the Doctrine of the Trinity

Do the Scriptures support the doctrine of the Trinity? To answer this question the Church Fathers, who lived in the second through the fifth centuries, A.D., developed a twofold strategy. First, they showed that the Scriptures acknowledge each member of the Trinity, Father, Son and Spirit, as God. They accomplished this by demonstrating that Father, Son and Spirit are each (1) addressed by divine names, (2) acknowledged as having divine attributes, (3) shown as engaging in divine actions and (4) recognized as worthy of divine worship. Second, the Church Fathers argued that Scripture makes distinctions among the members of the Trinity. The Father is distinguished from the Son, and the Spirit is distinguished from the Father and the Son. In this way, the Church Fathers explained the deity, the unity and the distinctions among the Father, Son and Spirit, using the term Trinity to summarize and unify these different biblical affirmations.

The Deity of the Father, Son and Spirit

The Father

The deity of God the Father is so clearly attested in Scripture that it hardly occurs to anyone to argue the point. Jesus addresses God as Father (Matt. 5:45), and Paul salutes the Galatians in the name of "God the Father" (1:3). God the Father is holy (John 17:11); he is "Lord of heaven and earth" (Matt. 11:23). The Father is all-powerful (Mark 14:34), created all things (1 Cor. 8:6), and raises the dead (John 5:21). God the Father must be worshiped in "spirit and truth" (John 4:23). We are to pray to our "Father in heaven," asking him for that which only God can give.

The Son

In contrast to that of the Father, the deity of the Son has been disputed often through the centuries. In the fourth century, it became the center of a controversy that led first to the Council of Nicea (A.D. 321) and then to the Council of Constantinople (A.D. 381) which issued the Niceno-Constantinopolitan Creed, the classic formulation of the doctrine of the Trinity. It's not an exaggeration to say that the doctrine of the Trinity grew out of the attempt to answer the question Jesus asked Peter, "Who do you say I am?" (Mark 8:29).

The mountain of data in Scripture relevant to the Son's deity looms so massive that a serious study would demand multiple volumes; in one way or another, it includes every verse in the New Testament and much of the Old. We can only survey the general landscape here. Dividing the material in the four categories described above (divine names, attributes, actions and worship), we will map out the bare bones of the argument for the Son's deity.

First, Scripture addresses the Son by names that rightly belong to God alone. The Gospel of John begins with the startling affirmation, "In the beginning was the Word, and the Word was with God, and the Word was God" (John 1:1). Thomas, the skeptic, confronted with the risen Jesus, cried out, "My Lord and my God" (John 20:28). Jesus accepted Thomas's confession and blessed all who would believe likewise in the future (v. 29). "The fullness of the Deity lives in bodily form" in Christ, according to Colossians 2:9. Paul extols God's grace that teaches self-discipline and patience while we wait for the appearing of "our great God and Savior, Jesus Christ" (Titus 2:13). The writer of Hebrews, after declaring the Son to be "the radiance of God's glory and the exact representation of his being" (1:3), applies Psalm 45:6 to the Son, "Your throne, O God, will last for ever and ever" (v. 8). The First Epistle of John declares, "We know also that the Son of God has come and has given us understanding, so that we may know him who is true. And we are in him who is true — even in his Son Jesus Christ. He is the true God and eternal life" (1 John 5:20).

Jesus is also called Lord, a title that links the incarnate Son to the Lord God of the Old Testament and sets him in opposition to the false "Lord" Caesar and the Greco-Roman pantheon. "No one," declares Paul, "can say, 'Jesus is Lord,' except by the Holy Spirit"

(1 Cor. 12:3). The one who was in the "form of God" became human, died on the cross and has been exalted to heaven. He's been given the "name that is above every name." Every creature must bow to the name of Jesus and confess that "Jesus Christ is Lord, to the glory of God the Father" (Phil. 2:5-11). Jesus is "the Lord of glory" (1 Cor. 2:8), the "Lord of all" (Acts 10:36), "the King of kings and Lord of lords" (Rev. 17:14; 19:16).

Second, Scripture acknowledges the Son as having attributes that belong exclusively to God. The Son exists eternally (John 1:1; 8:58; 1 John 1:1; Col. 1:17). In his risen state, the Son is capable of being with his followers wherever they are as long as the world shall last (Matt. 28:20; also 18:20; Heb. 13:8). In the Gospel and letters of John, the Son embodies life, light, and truth (John 1:4,5; 3:19; 11:25; 14:6), attributes that are elsewhere recognized as God's (1 John 1:5).

Third, we find in Scripture the Son doing works that only God can do. Through the Son, all things were created (John 1:3; Col. 1:16; Heb. 1:10), and in the Son all things are held together (Col. 1:17; Heb. 1:3; 1 Cor. 8:6). The Son can forgive sins (Mark 2:7) and shall save his people from their sins (Matt. 1:21). The Son of God will raise the dead in the last day (John 5:28,29; 6:39,40). The Son can reveal the Father. Jesus instructs Philip, "If you really knew me, you would know my Father as well. . . . Anyone who has seen me has seen the Father" (John 14:7-10). "No one has ever seen God, but God the only Son, who is at the Father's side, has made him known" (John 1:18, 1978 edition NIV). Who but God can reveal God?

Fourth, Scripture honors the Son as worthy of worship. Jesus did not reject the worship of his disciples after the miracle of calming the sea (Matt 14:33). Everyone must "honor the Son, even as they honor the Father" (John 5:23). In John 14, Jesus encouraged his disciples, "Trust in God; trust also in me" (14:1), a blasphemous command if the Son is not also God. In the throne room scene in Revelation 4–5, every creature in Heaven sings out, "To him who sits on the throne and to the Lamb be praise and honor and glory and power for ever and ever!" (Rev. 5:13). Baptism, surely an act of worship, is administered in the name of the Son, as well as of the Father and of the Spirit (Matt. 28:19; Acts 2:38; 19:5). The Apostles performed miracles in the name of Jesus (Acts 3:6; 4:10; 16:18). And, as a final example, many of the apostolic blessings in the New Testament letters are given in the names of "God our Father and our Lord Jesus Christ" (Rom. 1:7; 1 Cor. 1:3; 2 Cor. 1:2; 13:14; Gal. 1:3; Eph. 1:2; Phil. 1:2; 4:23).

The Spirit

The deity of the Spirit did not become the focus of controversy until well after the main lines of Trinitarian doctrine had been hammered out. Only in the later part of the Fourth Century did the Church Fathers need to reflect deeply on the divinity of the Spirit. They followed the same line of argument they had in proving the deity of the Son: the Spirit is called by divine names, acknowledged as having divine attributes, does divine works, and is honored as worthy of divine worship.

Scripture understands the Spirit to be "the Spirit of God" or "God's Spirit" (Num. 24:2; Ezek. 11:24; Matt 3:16; 12:28; Rom 8:9; 1 Cor. 2:11; 12:3). The Spirit is the "Holy Spirit" (Matt. 1:18; Mark 3:29; Acts 2:38; 13:2; Eph. 4:30; 2 Pet. 1:21), the "Spirit of Christ" (Rom. 8:9; 1 Pet. 1:11), the "Spirit of truth" (John 14:17; 15:26; 16:13; 1 John 4:6), and the "Spirit of grace" (Heb. 10:29). God refers to the Spirit as "my Spirit" (Gen. 6:3; Joel 2:28; Isa. 44:3).

Scripture acknowledges the divine attributes of the Spirit. Christ offered himself for our sins through "the eternal Spirit" (Heb. 9:14). The Spirit of God knows all things, "even the deep things of God" (1 Cor. 2:10, 11). "Where can I go from your Spirit? Where can I flee from your presence?" asks the psalmist in a psalm praising God for his infinite knowledge and limitless presence (Ps. 139:7).

Scripture proclaims the works accomplished by the Spirit as God's own work. Jesus casts out demons by the Spirit whom he calls "the finger of God" (Luke 11:20). The Spirit reveals "the deep things of God" (1 Cor. 2:10, 11). The Spirit makes us children of God who are able to cry, "Abba Father" (Rom. 8:14-16) The Spirit has set us free from the "law of sin and death" (Rom. 8:2), and will raise our mortal bodies from the dead (Rom. 8:11). The Spirit sanctifies believers (Rom. 15:16; 2 Thess. 2:13; 1 Pet. 1:2) and performs miracles (Matt. 12:28; Luke 1:35; Acts 2:4).

Scriptural texts that witness to the Spirit as being worthy of divine worship are scarce and indirect. Perhaps this is because the Spirit's work is not to "speak on his own" but to bear testimony to the Son and impart knowledge of the Father (John 16:12-15). The focus in Scripture is not so much on worshiping the Spirit as on the necessity of having the Spirit as a condition of true worship. "God is spirit, and his worshipers must worship in spirit and in truth" (John 4:24). Believers should "worship in the Spirit" (Phil. 3:3), "pray in the Spirit" (Eph. 6:18; 1 Cor. 14:15,16), and "be filled with the Spirit," so we can "speak to one another with psalms, hymns and spiritual songs. . . . always giving thanks to God the Father for everything, in the name of our Lord Jesus Christ" (Eph. 5:18-20). Notice the Trinitarian implications of this last verse. Being filled with the Spirit is the condition by which we are able to worship God the Father rightly, in the name of Jesus Christ.

The Distinctions among the Father, Son, and Spirit

Recognizing the scriptural distinctions among the Father, Son, and Spirit is as important in assessing the doctrine of the Trinity as recognizing their unity in the divine nature. Focusing on the unity without the distinctions might lead to the conclusion that the Father, Son and Spirit are one and the same, merely different names for different appearances of the one God. Equally dangerous would be approaches that focus on the distinctions but downplay the unity. Such thinking might lead to the conclusion that Father, Son, and Spirit are three distinct Gods. Accordingly, without forgetting the unity, we now examine a few passages that bring out the distinctions among Father, Son and Spirit.

The account of Jesus' baptism by John the Baptist is the classic text of differentiation (Matt. 3:13-17; Mark 1:9-11; Luke 3:21,22; cf. John 1:31-34). The Spirit, in the form of a dove, descends from heaven on the Son as the Father announces, "This is my Son, whom I love; in him I am well pleased." Throughout his earthly ministry, Jesus prays to the Father (Mark 1:35; Luke 5:16; 9:18; 10:21-23; John 11:41,42; 12:27,28). In the garden of Gethsemane on the night of his betrayal Jesus prayed earnestly to his Father: "*Abba*, Father, everything is possible for you. Take this cup from me. Yet not what I will, but what you will" (Mark 14:36).

The Gospel of John, which contains the clearest testimony to the unity of the Father and the Son in the divine nature, witnesses also unambiguously to the difference between them. In an extended discourse in John 5, Jesus differentiates himself from the Father. The Father is working "and I, too, am working" (v. 17). "The Father loves the Son and shows him all he does" (v. 20). The Father does not judge, but "has entrusted all judgment to the Son" (v. 22). The Father sent the Son and has "himself testified concerning me" (v. 37). In John 8, while defending himself before his adversaries, Jesus argues, "In your own Law it is written that the testimony of two men is valid. I am one who testifies for myself; my other witness is the Father, who sent me" (vv. 17,18). "My Father is greater than I," said Jesus in chapter 14, clearly distinguishing himself from the Father (14:28).

The Son also differentiates himself from the Spirit. In view of his approaching departure, Jesus promises his distraught disciples "another Counselor," one who will never leave, the "Spirit of truth" (John 14:16). The Father will send the Counselor in the name of the Son. The Spirit, says the Son, "goes out from the Father" and "will testify about me" (John 15:26). The Son is going away, but the Counselor is coming. "Unless I go away, the Counselor will not come to you; but if I go, I will send him to you" (John 16:7). In Matthew 12, Jesus declares that one who blasphemes the Son can be forgiven, but one who blasphemes the Holy Spirit can never be forgiven (v. 32).

Thus we see that Scripture amply documents the unity of Father, Son, and Holy Spirit in the divine nature and yet equally evinces the distinctions among them. I hope we are beginning to understand how, to hold these two lines of scriptural thought together, the Church Fathers could be justified in developing the doctrine of the Trinity into its classical form. But being justified in developing the doctrine does not explain why the Church Fathers actually did so. To find this explanation, we must rehearse a bit of history. This history lesson will disclose not only why the Church Fathers developed the doctrine of the Trinity, but also why they had no choice but to do so.

From Jerusalem to Constantinople[1]

Perhaps, the post apostolic Christians need not have worked so diligently to understand how the Christian teaching about Father, Son, and Spirit can be harmonized with the Old Testament faith in the one God. Perhaps, they could have been satisfied simply to confess their faith in the words of Scripture alone. Despite our speculations about what might have been, however, many in the church did in fact develop theories about the relationships among the

21

Father, Son and Spirit, some of which were clearly destructive of the New Testament faith itself. Notwithstanding their attempts to do so, the Church Fathers discovered they could not answer these destructive theories effectively in the words of Scripture alone.

Subordinationism and Modalism: Two Opposite Reactions[2]

The Church of the post apostolic era, for the most part, simply continued to worship God and confess faith in Jesus Christ in the language of Scripture. They baptized in the name of the "Father, Son, and Spirit" without reflecting deeply on the formula's significance. Some thinkers, however, out of their concern for the biblical message of the unity of God, wanted to make it clear how the Christian teaching about Christ did not compromise this vital truth. Several theories may be grouped under the general heading of Subordinationism. Characteristic of these theories is the fear that admitting the full deity of the Son and the Spirit would mean acknowledging three gods.

Subordinationist theories, in one way or another, argue for the inferior status of the Son and the Spirit. They begin by emphasizing such passages as John 14:28, in which the Son says, "My Father is greater than I," and 1 Cor 15:28 which says, "When he has done this, then the Son himself will be made subject to him who put everything under him, so that God may be all in all." They interpret the passages we discussed above in our argument for the Son's deity by the half-light of their subordinationist proof texts, Proverbs 8:22, John 14:28 and 1 Cor. 15:28.

According to one subordinationist theory, Jesus was not God but a man filled with the power of God's Spirit. This theory interprets the texts that seem to indicate the Son's deity as referring, not to the person of the Son who is a mere man, but to the presence of God that indwells and empowers the Son. In another theory, the Word, an attribute of God, came to rest on the man Jesus because of his sinlessness, making him the greatest of the prophets. The Son, for the proponents of this theory, was not in his own person the incarnate Word. A third subordinationist theory, that of Arius (A.D. 250-336), a deacon in Alexandria, is so important that it deserves special attention; however, let us first take note of Modalism, the opposite reaction.

Modalist theories attempt to preserve the unity of God by arguing for the full deity of the Son and the Spirit at the expense of the distinctions among the Father, Son, and Spirit. In Modalism, the Father takes on the form of the Son and the Spirit to accomplish particular tasks in the history of salvation. The Son is the Father, and the Father is the Son. The Spirit is the Father, and the Father is the Spirit. Father, Son, and Spirit are merely modes or ways the one God acts. The texts that assert the deity of the Son and Spirit are accepted at face value, while those that assert differences among Father, Son, and Spirit are interpreted away.

The Councils of Nicea and Constantinople

One of the greatest challenges to the Christian Faith came with the subordinationist theory of Arius. According to Arius, the Word of God existed before the creation of this universe but was, nevertheless, not eternal as the Father is eternal. God the Father created the Word as his first and highest creature, and through the Word, God created the world. That Word replaced the human soul of Jesus at his conception by the Holy Spirit. The key textual basis of Arius's theory was the great wisdom text, Proverbs 8, especially verse 22: "The Lord created me at the beginning of his work, the first of his acts of long ago" (NRSV). The church had used this chapter to prove the preexistence of the wisdom that became incarnate in Jesus. Now Arius used it to limit the Word to a created existence.

Arius's theory caused such controversy that the newly converted Roman Emperor Constantine (d. A.D. 337) convened the Council of Nicea (A.D. 325) to settle the issue and restore peace to the church. Arius and his followers were hard to defeat because they could plausibly interpret every biblical text as in harmony with their views and confess their faith in biblical terms that sounded orthodox. Arius agreed that Jesus was the Word of God, the Son of God, the Lord, and the Christ. But Arius understood these biblical terms within the framework of his own theory. The biblical words were there, but they had changed meaning, frustrating all attempts to expose the dangers inherent in Arianism.

Finally, the Emperor himself proposed that believers confess the Son as "having the same essence" as the Father. Arius and his disciples refused to confess the Son in these words. With this, it became evident that Arius, though he did not mind using the words of

Scripture, did not accept the faith taught in those words. Accordingly, Arius and five others who refused to sign were banished by the Emperor.

Another fifty years of controversy followed the Council of Nicea. At times, it seemed as if the Arians were going to win after all. Various compromises were offered, the most famous being from Eusebius of Nicomedia (died about A.D. 342). Eusebius proposed that the church confess the Son as of "like essence" to the Father, but not of "the same essence" as the Father. The controversy was put to rest only with the Council of Constantinople (A.D. 381). The Council issued what has come to be called the Niceno-Constantinopolitan Creed. The portions relevant to the doctrine of the Trinity, as they appear in the text and translation of the Anglican Book of Common Prayer, read as follows:[3]

> I believe in one God the Father Almighty; Maker of heaven and earth, and of all things visible and invisible. And in one Lord Jesus Christ, the only-begotten Son of God, begotten of the Father before all worlds, [God of God], Light of Light, very God of very God, begotten, not made, being of one substance [essence] with the Father; . . . And [I believe] in the Holy Ghost, the Lord and Giver of Life, who proceedeth from the Father [and the Son]; who with the Father and the Son together is worshipped and glorified. Amen.

Evaluation and Conclusion

What shall we make of all this? Does the doctrine of the Trinity make a difference? I'm afraid some of us within the Restoration Movement have taken the attitude of Edward Gibbon, the skeptical eighteenth-century English historian. In his vast study of the Roman Empire, he commented on the silliness of the fourth century dispute over the Trinity. He wryly remarked, "The profane in every age have derided the furious contests which the difference of a single diphthong excited between them."[4] Gibbon referred to the one letter difference between the Greek words at the center of the debate, *homoousios* (of the same essence) and *homoiousios* (of a like essence). Evidently, the skeptic can afford to dismiss such disputes as having nothing more at stake than words.

I hope you can see that Gibbon's dismissive attitude is unacceptable for people who, as did the Church Fathers, take the revelation recorded in Scripture seriously. To confess the Son as being "of like essence" with the Father leaves the Arian interpretation as a live option. One can understand any creature as having some likeness to God its Creator. Only by confessing the Son as "of the same essence" as the Father can you rule out the Arian interpretation of the Son as a creature. The difference of one Greek letter, the difference between *homoousios* and *homoiousios*, turns out to be the difference between Christianity and Paganism, a difference worth fighting for.

Some may argue that the whole controversy could have been avoided had everyone concerned shunned speculation and been satisfied to confess their faith in the words of Scripture alone. This objection is misguided in two ways. First, the Church Fathers tried to limit themselves to the language of Scripture, until it became obvious that Arius and his disciples could continue indefinitely to twist the language of Scripture to fit their theory. The Church Fathers had the choice of allowing the Arians to destroy the faith or of finding a word that would bring the true nature of the Arian heresy out into the open for all to see. Second, the Niceno-Constantinopolitan Creed is not speculative, but conservative. The creed functions not as a speculative philosophy about things beyond our abilities, but as a way to preserve the Bible's balance between the unity of the Father, Son and Spirit in the divine nature and their differences. *Homoousios* is the only nonbiblical word in the creed.

Being a Restorationist myself and firm believer in the exclusively normative nature of the Bible, I'm not saying that contemporary Christians must confess their faith with the postbiblical Trinitarian vocabulary. I'm not even saying that a Christian must raise the question of the Trinity, i.e., of how the Bible's message about the Father, Son, and Holy Spirit can be understood in a way that preserves the unity of God as well as the difference among Father, Son and Spirit. But I am saying that if you do raise the subject, if you do form an opinion on the relationship among the Father, Son and Spirit, you'd better come up with something like the historic doctrine of the Trinity. The two logical alternatives, Subordinationism and Modalism, have been tried, thoroughly examined and found sorely wanting.

Endnotes

[1]In this historical section, I have relied on two authorities, Jaroslav Pelikan, The Christian Tradition Series, and Reinhold Seeberg, *Text-Book of the History of Doctrines*, trans. Charles E. Hay, (n.d., reprint, Grand Rapids, MI: Baker Book House, 1977).

[2]I have relied on Otto Weber for this twofold classification. See Otto Weber, *Foundations of Dogmatics*, trans. Darrell. L. Gruder (Grand Rapids, MI: Eerdmans, 1981), 1:365-368.

[3]Philip Schaff, ed., *The Creeds of Christendom*, 6th ed., revised, David S. Schaff (New York: Harper and Row, 1931; reprint, Grand Rapids, MI: Baker Book House, 1990), vol 2, *The Greek and Latin Creeds*, 58, 59.

[4]Quoted in Pelikan, vol. 1, 209.

Chapter Two

Was Jesus really human?

Barry Blackburn
Atlanta Christian College
East Point, Georgia

"Was Jesus really human?" To some this may sound like a peculiar question. Especially since the rise of science and of philosophies that exalt systematic doubt, the critical question has been, "Was Jesus really divine?" It was taken for granted that, for whatever else he may or may not have been, he was human.

Against the background of the modern struggle over the divinity (or deity, if you prefer) of Christ, it may seem strange to learn that the church of the second through the fourth centuries was forced by heretics to assert and defend the full and complete human nature of Jesus. Various Gnostic Christian sects, working from the notion that there can be no real union between the divine and that which is physical/material, argued either 1) that Jesus only *seemed* to be a human being, or 2) that there was a divine Christ-spirit that descended upon and inhabited the man Jesus, but only temporarily (from the baptism of Jesus to some point prior to his suffering and crucifixion).

The first alternative reminds us of Abraham's angelic visitors, whom he mistook as humans (Gen. 18); the second notion has Old Testament parallels in those stories of how the Spirit of the Lord would temporarily come upon selected individuals to make them channels of divine revelation or to equip them to accomplish a difficult task. Either way, there are biblical analogies to which the Gnostics could point. The church, on the other hand, found itself forced by the evidence of New Testament Scripture and apostolic tradition to argue that the preexistent Son of God, or Word, had assumed genuine human nature in the person of Jesus of Nazareth.

In biblical language, "the Word became flesh" (John 1:14). The incarnation of the Son of God in Jesus was a *new* work of God, and no Old Testament model could adequately express the truth about Jesus.

Fully Human

Present-day Christians have no problem in believing that Jesus possessed a genuinely physical, human body. After all, the Gospels make it clear that Jesus' body was like ours and that he was subject to the same constraints that our bodies place on us. He was limited to being in one place at one time and had to travel from one location to another. His body required food, drink, rest, and sleep. Therefore, according to the Scriptures, when deprived, he suffered hunger (Matt. 4:2), thirst (John 19:28), and exhaustion (John 4:6). Even the *risen* Christ can assure his disciples that his body is real and not an apparition: "See My hands and My feet, that it is I Myself; touch Me and see, for a spirit does not have flesh and bones as you see that I have" (Luke 24:39, NASB). Finally, as Thomas Oden says, *"The most decisive proof of his humanity is simply that he died."*[1] The violence of the crucifixion was simply too much for his body to bear, and so his body succumbed to the same forces of death that will eventually overpower us. There can be no doubt that Jesus possessed a genuinely human body.

However, the early church, especially during the third through the fifth centuries, faced a more difficult issue when it came to the matter of Jesus' soul, or mind. During this period of time it was attractive for some Christians to believe that while Jesus' body was human, his soul (the seat of reason and will) was nothing other than the preexistent Son of God, or the Word (as he is described in John 1:1-14). To this way of thinking, God the Son became incarnate as he clothed and veiled himself with flesh, so that Jesus is (or was?) really God (the Son) dwelling in a human body. One can understand how such an interpretation might arise, especially from the prologue of John, and no doubt a number of Christians today understand Jesus in this way.

Nevertheless, under the influence of some of its greatest teachers the church as a whole was driven to the conclusion that Jesus' human nature included soul as well as body. This is what is meant when the church confessed that Jesus was "fully man," as well as "fully God."[2] As expressed by Augustine (fourth century), in Jesus "nothing was lacking that belongs to human nature."[3] The author of Hebrews puts it this way: "he [Jesus] had to become like his brothers and sisters in every respect" (2:17). This means that Jesus was as fully human "on the inside" as he was "on the outside."

The church was constrained to adopt and defend this judgment, not because of any desire to detract from the deity of Jesus, but largely because of scriptural details of Jesus' life appearing in the Gospels. For example, the Gospel narratives make it clear beyond all doubt that Jesus was not omniscient, that is to say, in possession of all knowledge. This is perhaps clearest in Matthew 24:36, according to which Jesus affirmed that he, along with the angels, did not know the day or hour of the Second Coming. In some cases Jesus asks questions whose only apparent purpose was to gain information. Thus he asked the father of the demon-possessed epileptic lad how long his son had been having frightful seizures (Mark 9:21). According to Mark 5:9, Jesus demanded that the demonic horde possessing the Gerasene demoniac reveal its name. Finally, one recalls instances where the Gospels attest that people behaved in ways that *surprised* Jesus. He was surprised at the great faith of the centurion of Capernaum (Matt. 8:10), just as he was astonished at the lack of faith by the people of his home village (Mark 6:6). Surely one with omniscience would never be surprised or amazed.

That Jesus had a human soul, and was *fully* human (as well as fully divine) is demanded by the fact that he offered to God the worship due him by every rational creature. Like us, Jesus offered to God prayers filled with praise, thanksgiving, and petition (for example, John 6:11; Matt. 11:25-26; John 17:1-26; and Matt. 26:39). Thus we can imagine Jesus' prayers including every element of the so-called Lord's Prayer except the request for the forgiveness of sins. Jesus not only attended synagogue worship on the Sabbath, but also actively participated by reading the prescribed prophetic text and by delivering the homily/teaching that would normally follow the readings from the Law and Prophets (for example, Mark 1:21-28; Luke 4:16-28). In addition, the Gospel of John in particular attests that Jesus regularly traveled from Galilee to Jerusalem in order to worship at the Jewish feasts (2:13; 5:1; 7:10,14; 10:22-23; 12:12,20).

The human will of Jesus clearly manifests itself in the Garden of Gethsemane. Although Jesus had previously prophesied his impending death at the hands of the authorities as the centerpiece of God's preordained act of redemption for Israel and the gentiles (see, for example, Matt. 16:21), in the garden Jesus staggered as the prospect of the cross loomed before him: "My Father, if it is possible, may this cup be taken from me. Yet not as I will, but as you will" (Matt. 26:39). Here Jesus states his own will, concedes that it may not be the Father's will, and expresses his willingness to submit to the latter even if it is alien to his own desire.

In light of the foregoing paragraphs, we should be prepared to accept the texts that speak of Jesus' emotions as testimonies to a life of genuinely *human* feelings. Such emotions included not only the positive ones of love (Mark 10:21; John 13:1) and joy (Luke 10:21; John 15:11; 17:13), but also those which entail suffering, to one degree or another, for those who experience them: compassion (Matt. 9:36; 14:14), indignation (Mark 10:14), anger (Mark 3:5), and distress and sorrow (John 11:33,35,38; Matt. 26:37-38). In other words, Jesus experienced the full range of human emotions (except for emotions associated with the guilt of sin).

Implications

In light of the preceding considerations, one can easily see why the church eventually felt compelled to confess that Jesus was genuinely human, both in body and soul. The church views Jesus' humanity as a fact. Now of course many facts are totally, or at least relatively, insignificant to us. But not this one. The significance of Jesus' humanity is profound and multifaceted.

First, the humanity of Jesus, among other things, qualifies him to be the *human* Messiah prophesied in the Old Testament and expected by first-century Jews. Not only would the Messiah be a man — to be born in the village of Bethlehem according to Micah 5:2 — but specifically a descendant of David (especially 2 Sam. 7:12-13,16; cf. Luke 1:32-33). Thus Paul can declare that his gospel concerns God's Son, "descended from David according to the flesh" (Rom. 1:3). Jesus Christ, a genuine human being descended from David via Joseph, is therefore fully qualified to be "great David's greater Son."[4]

Second, Jesus' full humanity enables him — in his life, death, resurrection, and present intercession — to act as our saving *representative* before God. As *one of us*, our great High Priest, Jesus offered to God a complete life of total obedience to God's will, a self-offering that vicariously becomes ours. Likewise, as *one of us* he was able to draw down upon himself God's wrath against human disobedience so that, again, his death might vicariously become our own. In spite of death, however, God raised Jesus, our God-*man*, from the dead to become the first, and therefore the representative, of a new, redeemed humanity, a Second Adam as Paul puts it in Romans 5:12-21. As the glorified God-*man*, Christ is able to communicate to us, by means of the Holy Spirit, the perfect human nature that he possesses. (This healing of our fallen nature, though begun in this life, will not, of course, be finished until our own glorification at the End.)

Finally, the author of Hebrews encouragingly reminds us that with Jesus as our great High Priest, now enthroned at God's right hand, we have one who can with full sympathy represent and help us since he is intimately familiar with our weaknesses, trials, and suffering (2:17-18; 4:14-16). To carry out his priestly work of representing us, the children of God, before the Father, it was necessary for Jesus to be like us in every way. It is for this reason that, amazingly, Jesus can speak of us without falsehood or shame as his brothers and sisters; conversely, we address him as our "elder brother" (2:10-17).

Third, when we look at the life of Jesus as portrayed in the Gospels, we catch a glimpse of human life as God intended it to be. Like beasts slogging about in the swamp of sin and fallenness, we peer up at one who was perfectly related to himself, to the other humans about him, and to his God. Here is one who so intensely relied on the companionship and strength of his heavenly Father that he was *always* able to choose God's way, even in those situations when the price he paid was staggering (Matt. 26:39). Here is one who, in following God's will, became "the man for others."[5] Here is one who never suffered from the racking accusations of his conscience, who never had to despair over harm inflicted on others, who never had to feel shame before his God. It is most natural that Christians have always viewed Jesus' life as a kind of model to be emulated. It is precisely this notion that undergirds *The Imitation of Christ* by Thomas à Kempis, *In His Steps* by Charles Sheldon, and the contemporary practice of wearing bracelets inscribed with the letters "WWJD," "What would Jesus do?" Naturally, there are various details of Jesus' life which we need not or cannot emulate, but

31

in a general way Jesus' life surely does give us sorely needed guidance in how to live authentically human lives.

Fourth, God's assumption of human nature in the person of his Son, Jesus Christ, lies at the root of one of the most powerful motivations, if not *the* most, for becoming and remaining a Christian, the amazingly costly and sacrificial love lavished upon us by the three-in-one God. For the incarnation of the Son of God necessarily thrust him rudely into our "vale of tears." Even earthly life at its best in its present fallen condition is filled with countless sufferings: disappointment, rejection, emotional trauma, injury, illness, bereavement, and of course death. In Jesus' case, however, he voluntarily suffered massive and vehement rejection by his own countrymen, which led in turn to an execution whose humiliation, degradation, and physical torment leave us reeling. The incarnation of the divine Son, with all the sufferings that it entailed, overwhelms us with his love and reduces our arrogant pride to tears of repentance. It was such "divine humility," motivated by radical love, that evoked from Charles Wesley the well known words,

Amazing love! how can it be
That Thou, my God, shouldst die for me?[6]

Fifth, and finally, the incarnation of the Son of God is a potent comfort in the face of the hideous and mind-numbing pain and suffering that from time to time erupts with such fury and madness that it threatens to snuff out our trust in a good and loving God. Christian theologians as diverse as Augustine and C. S. Lewis have long wrestled with the problem of evil with limited success. But in the last analysis we simply have to admit that we do not have the intellectual prowess to *solve* this mystery. Christians, however, *do* have the assurance that our God has not remained aloof from our predicament, but rather has plumbed the depths of pain and sorrow. In the person of Jesus Christ, He has swallowed the bitterest dregs of evil that he might rescue us from the shadowlands of the present and bring us into fair and sunny Jerusalem Above where tears and the pains that cause them will be forever banished. In the depths of our own grief and in the face of apparently absurd and meaningless evil, we may recline against the chest of one who himself entered the fray and won the costly victory which will soon transform our night to glorious day.

Recently, Joan Osborne recorded a popular song entitled, "One of Us." She asks,

> What if God was one of us,
> Just a slob like one of us,
> Just a stranger on the bus
> Trying to make his way home?

I cannot claim to know what interpretation the lyricist would put on these words, but I do know the Gospel answer to this question; in Jesus Christ God *was one of us*, and that has made all the difference!

Endnotes

[1]Thomas C. Oden, *Systematic Theology*, The Word of Life, vol. 2 (San Francisco: Harper & Row, 1989), 123.

[2]Irenaeus, *Against Heresies* 4. 6. 7 (late second century).

[3]Augustine, *Enchiridion* 10. 34 (translation found in Albert Outler).

Augustine: Confessions and Enchiridion, Library of Christian Classics, vol. 7 [Philadelphia: Westminster Press, 1955], 360).

[4]A phrase found in James Montgomery's hymn entitled, "Hail to the Lord's Anointed."

[5]The title of a book on Jesus by John A.T. Robinson.

[6]From his hymn entitled, "And Can It Be?"

Chapter Three

How does the Spirit work in the Christian?

Mike Cope
Highland Church of Christ
Abilene, Texas

The functional creed for many Christians, as Gordon Fee points out, could be stated something like this: "I believe in God the Father; I believe in Jesus Christ, God's Son; but I wonder about the Holy Ghost."[1]

My religious upbringing was full of concern about heretics who taught that the Holy Spirit works "separate and apart from the Word of God" or that the Spirit literally indwells a Christian. How foreign that thinly disguised deism was from the Spirit-drenched reflections of the first-century Christ-followers.

The New Testament never develops a carefully prepared doctrine of the Spirit. However, its pages are filled with the life-changing experiences of the early Christians that the God who had been present among them in Jesus Christ was still present in his Holy Spirit. They knew they had received the gospel message with joy inspired by the Holy Spirit (1 Thess. 4:8). They understood that they, the people of God, had become the temple in whom God through his Spirit dwells (1 Cor. 3:16-17). They recognized that only through the Spirit's power were they able to live holy lives commensurate with their calling (1 Thess. 4:3-8).

Life apart from the presence and work of the Spirit was unimaginable. As Paul put it, "If anyone does not have the Spirit of Christ, he does not belong to Christ" (Rom. 8:9). Before his conversion, the apostle saw the world clearly divided into two groups: Jews and Gentiles. After receiving God's grace, he saw humanity separated between those "in Christ" (which to him meant those with the Spirit) and those not in Christ (and, therefore, without the Spirit).

So common was their experience of God's Spirit that Paul could ask the Galatians, "Did you receive the Spirit by observing the law, or by believing what you heard?" (Gal. 3:2). The argument he constructs in Galatians 3 stands or falls on this, their recognition that the Spirit had come powerfully into their lives at conversion and had continued to work in them to produce the character of Christ.

No New Testament writer set out to develop a formula for the Trinity, yet Trinitarian language abounds, for that was the early church's experience in salvation. The one God had entered the world through his Son, Jesus Christ. And when that Son "left," he still remained through "another Counselor" (John 14:16 — which implies that Christ, too, had been their Comforter or Counselor).

The benediction at the end of 2 Corinthians is typical. It doesn't attempt to argue the case for a Trinitarian understanding of God, but it uses Trinitarian language to describe their experience, "May the grace of the Lord Jesus Christ, and the love of God, and the fellowship of the Holy Spirit be with you all" (2 Cor. 13:14). The Christians had experienced the love of God (which had been poured into their hearts by the Holy Spirit, Rom. 5:5), the grace of their Lord which gave expression to the Father's love, and the participation in the Spirit which made that love and grace present in the church.

In their encounter with the gospel, they learned what the people of Israel had not known about their one God, that he existed in eternal relationship as God the Father, God the Son, and God the Spirit.

The prophets of Israel had looked forward to a day when God would pour out his Spirit. Through the preaching of Ezekiel, for example, God had said:

> I will give you a new heart and put a new spirit in you; I will remove from you your heart of stone and give you a heart of flesh. And I will put my Spirit in you and move you to follow my decrees and be careful to keep my laws. . . . I will put my Spirit in you and you will live, and I will settle you in your own land (Ezek. 36:26-27; 37:14).

Luke, who was concerned to show that such promises to God's people had indeed been fulfilled (Luke 1:1), reports that John the Baptist told the crowd around him that while he was baptizing in water, Jesus would baptize them with the Holy Spirit and with fire

(3:16). Shortly before his ascension, Jesus told his followers to stay in Jerusalem and "wait for the gift my Father promised, which you have heard me speak about. For John baptized with water, but in a few days you will be baptized with the Holy Spirit" (Acts 1:4-5).

On Pentecost, this promise was fulfilled. The disciples, hearing the howling of a violent wind and seeing what looked like tongues of fire, were filled with the Spirit (Acts 2:1-4). Peter explained that God's people were experiencing the fulfillment of Joel's prophecy:

> In the last days, God says,
> I will pour out my Spirit on all people.
> Your sons and daughters will prophesy,
>   your young men will see visions,
>   your old men will dream dreams.
> Even on my servants, both men and women,
>   I will pour out my Spirit in those days,
>   and they will prophesy.
>   Joel 2:28ff; Acts 2:17-18

But was this gift of God's Spirit only for a few leaders? No! Peter told those who were listening that they too, upon repentance and baptism, would receive this gift (2:38).

Various groups have taught that the baptism in the Holy Spirit is a gift that comes to some Christians at a later point in their spiritual journey. But the New Testament writers considered it the normal experience of all believers at their conversion. Because of their common experience of baptism in water and in the Spirit, Paul could argue for Christian unity by saying, "For in the one Spirit we were all baptized into one body — Jews or Greeks, slaves or free — and we were all made to drink of one Spirit" (1 Cor. 12:13, NASB).

The early church believed the Spirit was much more than some intangible, impersonal force or attitude. They welcomed the Spirit as the indwelling presence of God himself, a presence that had been promised long before. They thankfully recognized that God had delivered them "through the washing of rebirth and renewal by the Holy Spirit" (Titus 3:5).

But they also believed that the Spirit had done more than take up residence in them. They knew that God was doing something powerful among them (just as he continues to do something powerful among his people today) through this Spirit.

The Deposit of the Spirit

Everyone needs a place where they can set their watch. In my hometown, Pet Milk was the ultimate authority. People in Neosho, Missouri, could set their watches by the noon whistle. It was an authority that wasn't to be questioned, although there always lingered the uncertainty of where the whistle-blower at Pet Milk set his watch!

I like the tradition of a church in Abilene. Every April when it's time to set clocks forward an hour — so that non-church-attenders don't notice it while church-attenders are punished (since they have to finish their sleep in hard pews!) — this church waits until they meet the next morning. They get their full night's sleep. Then together they roll their watches forward from 10:00 to 11:00.

Paul would have approved of this picture, a church gathered on Sunday to make sure everyone knows what time it is. So much of what Christians do in their times together is to help each other recalibrate their time frame.

Our two central reference points are the ones communion underscores each week: "For whenever you eat this bread and drink this cup, you proclaim the Lord's death until he comes" (1 Cor. 11:26). Our first reference point is the death and resurrection of Jesus; the second is the future return of Jesus. The first is the pivotal event of all history. The second is the inevitable culmination of that event.

The Apostle Paul was quite familiar with the apocalyptic time frame, that following this evil age there would be the age of God. But while his language is similar, it also has a unique twist. To Paul the end has already begun. In other words, there is an overlap of the two ages, and it's in this overlap that God's people live.

The old age is one marked by sin. It is the world of death, of pride, of lust, of disregard for God. It is the place of despair and hopelessness. It's a time when old prejudices are savored and hurt feelings are cherished.

The new age is the one marked by grace and by freedom from sin. It is where life is oriented around God and his rule. It is the realm where humans are freed from the evil forces that previously kept a gun to their heads with bullets like fear, anxiety, and meaninglessness.

God's people already are a part of this new age. We already have eternal life. We already have forgiveness. We have already been delivered from our sins and passions.

37

But we have not yet fully experienced the new age. While we have been saved from sin, we still struggle with sins. While we have already been forgiven, we still need forgiveness. While we have been raised to walk in new life, we still face death.

Especially in Paul's letters, it is evident that the key to the early church's "already, but not yet" perspective on history was the Spirit. They received the gift of Christ's Spirit as a sign that the age to come had already broken into this age. They were Spirit-filled, Spirit-gifted, and Spirit-led people who lived out in this world the life of the messianic age.

Paul makes that point through three metaphors. First, he calls the Spirit a down payment (2 Cor. 1:21f; 5:5; Eph. 1:14). On the one hand, this image highlights the "already" of our salvation, since the Spirit had been a promise of God's future age, and on the other hand, it underscores the "not yet-ness" by pointing toward the full "redemption of those who are God's possession" (Eph. 1:14).

Second, he refers to the "firstfruits of the Spirit" (Rom. 8:23). In the Old Testament, God instructed his people to bring the first of their harvest to God. This "first fruit" was representative of the whole crop which would soon be ready for harvest. Likewise, God's Spirit serves as a mighty sign of power for the kingdom that has been inaugurated but not yet consummated.

Third, the Apostle Paul calls the Spirit a seal of ownership (2 Cor. 1:21f; Eph. 1:13; 4:30). Just like the seal that was stamped on wax or clay to prove authenticity or ownership, so the indwelling of the church by the Holy Spirit points to God's ownership. He is the one who has redeemed us and who will finally one day fully redeem us (Eph. 4:30).

We are now a people who hope (Rom. 8:24), wait (Phil. 3:20f), long (Rom. 8:19), and groan (Rom. 8:22f, 26). We don't fall into the pit of despair or try to leap to the peak of final triumph.

All of this is possible because the Spirit dwells in us as a fore-taste of heavenly glory. Therefore, Paul could write the Christians in Rome: "May the God of hope fill you with all joy and peace as you trust in him, so that you may overflow with hope by the power of the Holy Spirit" (Rom. 15:13; cf. 8:23-25).

God's Spirit helps us wait in hope. Even more, the Spirit empowers us to live out the future that's already broken in through the death and resurrection of Christ.

The Transforming Power of the Spirit

Living with anticipation of the appearing of Jesus leaves no room for resigned tolerance of the ways of this world. Rather, the Spirit-indwelt people of God are called to live holy, hopeful, joy-filled lives.

Leonard Allen is right on target when he writes:

> But far from leading us out of the world into other-worldly glories, far from spiriting us away from struggles in the worldly arena, the Spirit always directs us to the Crucified One and thus into the way of the cross. The Spirit forms in us the character traits required to follow that way. The Spirit implants in our hearts the strength to follow the way of weakness, the power to receive and care for the powerless, the peace to endure and absorb hostility.[2]

God, in his mercy, has declared us to be righteous through the atoning death of his Son. In that sense, we have already been saved. But salvation is much more. It is the continual deliverance from the power of sin. It is the Spirit-produced transformation into the likeness of Christ. We are expected to work out our own salvation "with fear and trembling" since it is God (through his Spirit) who is actually working in us (Phil. 2:12f).

The Holy Spirit empowers us to live lives that are appropriate for the new age that has broken in. The responsibility of a Christ-follower, boiled down, is this, to walk by the Spirit (Gal. 5:16). Failure to do so by limping along with the ungodly, community-destroying thinking and behaving of this world is tantamount to grieving the Holy Spirit (Eph. 4:30).

The great struggle is between the Spirit, God's power for the new age, and the flesh, the weak, transitory sphere of the old age that is so vulnerable to sin (though, apparently, not sin itself):

> To set the mind on the flesh is death, but to set the mind on the Spirit is life and peace. For this reason the mind that is set on the flesh is hostile to God; it does not submit to God's law — indeed it cannot, and those who are in the flesh cannot please God (Rom. 8:6-8, NRSV).

Those who live in the flesh are the unconverted, those without the Spirit who have to rely on weak, human resources. For such people, sin always gets the upper hand. Their minds, rather than being renewed like those with the Spirit (Eph. 1:17; Col. 1:9; Rom.

12:1-2), are focused on the flesh, which leads to death (Rom. 8:5).

Life in this realm of the flesh has a predictable outcome: "Sexual immorality, impurity and debauchery; idolatry and witchcraft; hatred, discord, jealousy, fits of rage, selfish ambition, dissensions, factions and envy, drunkenness, orgies, and the like" (Gal. 6:19-21). When Paul adds "and the like," he indicates that this list of sins is typical of living in the flesh but not exhaustive.

This weakness of the flesh is related to the conflict between the Spirit and the law in Romans and Galatians.

While Paul recognized the divine origin of the law (Rom. 7:14), its holiness (7:12), its ability to identify sin (7:7), its glory (2 Cor. 3:7), and its ultimate preparation for Christ (Gal. 3:24), he also believed that the law itself was powerless to help God's people in their quest for holiness. It stirred up a recognition of what was right but was not able to assist in carrying that out (Rom. 7:14-24).

A person under the law could only conclude: "with my mind I am a slave to the law of God, but with my flesh I am a slave to the law of sin" (Rom. 7:25, NRSV).

Since the real problem with the law was its inability to empower God's people, Paul celebrated a new "law," "the law of the Spirit of life in Christ Jesus" that has set us free from the law that produced sin and death (Rom. 8:2).

We are no longer subject to the power of sin, for we have a greater power, God's Spirit. Though the New Testament writers didn't believe we'd achieve perfect living before the appearing of Christ, they also didn't believe we are helpless. The Spirit who prays, "*Abba*, Father" on our behalf, testifying that we are God's children (Rom. 8:15-16; Gal. 4:6-7), is also the one who produces in our lives the righteousness of God.

The Holy Spirit leads us into and empowers us for a certain kind of life, the life that promotes the attitudes and actions of Christ. He begins by leading us to the confession that "Jesus is Lord," a confession that cannot be made without his guidance (1 Cor. 12:1-3).

And what exactly does the Spirit-filled life look like? "The fruit of the Spirit is love, joy, peace, patience, kindness, goodness, faithfulness, gentleness and self-control. Against such things there is no law" (Gal. 5:22-23). Again, when Paul adds the phrase "against such things," he hints that the list of fruit isn't exhaustive. The life of the Spirit begins in love (Col. 3:14; Gal. 5:13f) and then spreads throughout a believer's life to produce Christlikeness. The Spirit radically transforms us over time into the image of Christ "with ever-increasing glory" (2 Cor. 3:18).

Christians no longer live by law-keeping, though the Torah is still very much a part of their story and still has great value in their lives. Rather, they "live by the Spirit" (Gal. 5:25).

No one should understand that this leaves them without responsibility in ethical formation, however. As God's people whose minds have been renewed, we must daily choose to "keep in step with the Spirit" (Gal. 5:25). We must decide to "be filled with the Spirit" (Eph. 5:18). Hearts of obedience are still essential. What's new is that God's Spirit puts desires for obedience in us and then empowers us to live them out in Christ-honoring ways.

God's Spirit is producing a people who are like him. The focus is not on individual believers, per se, but on the community. Therefore, Christians have a responsibility to help one another to walk in the Spirit. If a brother or sister is trapped in a sin, "those who are spiritual" are to restore them gently. In this sense, we help carry one another's burdens (Gal. 6:1-2).

The Illumination of the Spirit

I remember as a teenager being warned about a song in our hymnal with the line "Beyond the sacred page, I seek thee Lord." Finally, an approved hymnal came out that righted all such doctrinal wrongs, changing the lyrics to "Within the sacred page, I seek thee Lord."

With some modification, that warning still has value. For it is *primarily* in Scripture that God's Spirit speaks to us. Through many writers and in a variety of ways, God has used the Spirit-inspired Scriptures "for teaching, for reproof, for correction, and for training in righteousness, so that everyone who belongs to God may be proficient, equipped for every good work" (2 Tim. 3:16-17, NRSV).

> Scripture is one aspect of the Spirit's mission of creating and sustaining spiritual life. He both authors and speaks through the Bible, which is ultimately the Spirit's book. By means of Scripture he bears witness to Jesus Christ, guides the lives of believers, and exercises authority in the church.[3]

But while the Spirit speaks first and foremost in Scripture, the New Testament writers believed that his guidance of believers would go "beyond the sacred page."

41

When, for example, Paul prays that God will "give you the Spirit of wisdom and revelation, so that you may know him better," he's asking for much more than for copies of the New Testament (an anachronistic thought) to be distributed (Eph. 1:7). He wanted God to open their eyes through the Spirit's illumination so they might grasp gifts like the hope to which they had been called, the riches of God's inheritance, and the incomparable power he offers those who believe (1:18-19).

Exactly *how* God chooses to do this never seems to concern Paul. A still, small voice? Guided instruction? Inner promptings? He never says. But he is convinced that God will, through his Spirit, fill us "with the knowledge of his will through all spiritual wisdom and understanding" (Col. 1:9).

Before Paul could address questions that came to him from the church in Corinth, he had to challenge an anti-Christian view of wisdom that was creeping in. It was the wisdom that puts confidence in powerful rhetoric and human reasoning rather than in the weakness of the cross (1 Cor. 1:18–2:5).

The apostle reminded the believers that his ministry had been Exhibit A. His preaching of the crucified Christ hadn't been delivered with wise, persuasive arguments, "but with a demonstration of the Spirit's power," so their faith would rest on God's power rather than on human wisdom (2:2-5).

The wisdom that centers on a cross can never be figured out by human logic. So how had they come to understand? "God has revealed it by his Spirit" (2:10).

> For the Spirit searches everything, even the depths of God. For what human being knows what is truly human except the human spirit that is within? So also no one comprehends what is truly God's except the Spirit of God. Now we have received not the spirit of the world, but the Spirit that is from God, so that we may understand the gifts bestowed on us by God. And we speak of these things in words not taught by human wisdom but taught by the Spirit, interpreting spiritual things to those who are spiritual. . . . Those who are spiritual discern all things, and they are themselves subject to no one else's scrutiny. "For who has known the mind of the Lord so as to instruct him?" (1 Cor. 2:10-13, 15-16, NRSV).

In this remarkable text, Paul argues that only the Spirit can know the mind of God. Humans, bound by the limitations of the flesh and the attacks of sin, could never grasp his mysteries. So, the

Spirit is the only way by which our minds may be illuminated to understand. "We have the mind of Christ" (2:16) precisely because the Spirit of Christ is guiding us.

As interested as we may be in exactly how the Spirit illuminates us, we should probably settle for believing that he is guiding us. As we grow in our understanding of God, his redemptive actions, and his purposes in the world, there is no room for self-congratulation. Rather, we should thank God, who reveals himself to us in, and beyond, the pages of Scripture.

The Gifts of the Spirit

A central concern of the Holy Spirit is the unity of God's family. "Make every effort," Paul wrote, "to keep the unity of the Spirit through the bond of peace" (Eph. 4:3).

This desire for unity is at least partly behind the distribution of spiritual gifts. Every believer, upon conversion, receives at least one spiritual gift (*charisma* in Greek) that is to be used to serve others (1 Pet. 4:10). These gifts aren't for the spiritually elite, as sometimes taught by modern Spirit-focused movements, but for all.

> To be a Christian is to be a charismatic. There is no division between charismatics and non-charismatics, between "haves" and "have-nots" in the one-class community of Christ. All alike are charismatics; for all alike are eternally in debt to the sheer *charis* of God who sought us, rescued us, equipped us with varying gifts, and shared his own loving nature with us through the Spirit which he has lavished upon every one of us who are in Christ.[4]

The church in Corinth, seriously deficient in the central way of love, tended to exalt the most spectacular gifts. Paul's response is to tell them that any sense of pride comes from a misunderstanding and misuse of the Spirit's gifts. Humans aren't to be credited, for it is the Spirit who distributes gifts as he sees fit (1 Cor. 12:11). These spiritual gifts have been given for the common good, for the mutual building up of the body of Christ (12:7).

The list of gifts in 1 Cor. 12:7-11 varies from other New Testament lists (Rom. 12:3-8; 1 Cor. 12:28-30; Eph. 4:11-12), indicating that none of them are exhaustive. But whichever ones the Spirit chooses to give are an offering of grace to be used for the community, for "we were all given the one Spirit to drink" (1 Cor. 12:13).

The conversation Paul imagines the body members having, points out that each believer is equally important for the functioning of the body and is equally dependent upon others (12:14-26).

As crucial as these gifts were for the ministry and edification of the church, Paul never would have imagined an end to spiritual gifts until Christ appeared on the day of consummation, though this doesn't necessarily mean he expected all gifts to continue (1 Cor. 1:7; 13:10).

Conclusion

The reason we stumble so much in understanding the pivotal role of the Holy Spirit in a Christian's life is that we've been trained to view the world through a secular lens. We've often unwittingly bought into a closed worldview where we feel uncomfortable with God's continued intervention.

How different was the worldview of the writers of Scripture who knew that "our struggle is not against flesh and blood, but against the rulers, against the authorities, against the powers of this dark world and against the spiritual forces of evil in the heavenly realms" (Eph. 6:12). If a person understands that, they can then appreciate how important the sphere of the Spirit is in this time just before the Lord appears. They will learn again the importance of praying "in the Spirit on all occasions with all kinds of prayers and requests" (Eph. 6:18).

Though the New Testament does record some spectacular actions prompted by the Spirit, the greater focus is on his quiet movement in our lives that molds us into the likeness of Jesus. But it is in those quiet, daily movements of the Spirit that great battles for the kingdom are won.

Endnotes

[1]Gordon Fee, *Paul, the Spirit, and the People of God* (Peabody, MA: Hendrickson Publishers, 1996), 37.

[2]C. Leonard Allen, *The Cruciform Church* (Abilene, TX: ACU Press, 1990), 163.

[3]Stanley J. Grenz, *Theology for the Community of God* (Nashville: Broadman and Holman Publishers, 1994), 495.

[4]Michael Green, *I Believe in the Holy Spirit* (Grand Rapids: Eerdmans, 1975), 196.

SECTION TWO
QUESTIONS ABOUT THE WORK OF GOD

Our questions about God eventually lead us to ask questions about how God relates to us. Our God is not the God of Greek philosophers who will have nothing to do with the world because it is beneath his dignity.

All talk about the work of God in our world begins with God's work in Christ. In the first two articles, Stacy Patty and John Mark Hicks address questions about how Jesus' death is atoning. We commonly talk about how Jesus died for us, but what really happened in our relationship with God through the work of Christ?

The second two articles by Gary Holloway and Randy Becton raise questions about the continuing work of God in the world. Holloway's article wrestles with the difficult questions of providence, how God answers prayer, and the possibility of the miraculous. Can we expect God to intervene in our lives, or has God's intervention in the world essentially ended at the close of the first century?

While Holloway struggles with God's presence in the world, Becton engages God's apparent absence. How can we explain the huge amount of suffering in our world and how much of it comes to Christians who have done nothing to deserve it? Has God abandoned his people?

The biblical understanding of God is always relational, and so these articles that address how God relates to us are at the very heart of biblical theology.

Chapter Four

How are we saved through Jesus' death?

Stacy Patty
Lubbock Christian University
Lubbock, Texas

Those who know Harold Hazelip likely recall his famous sermon on "The Impossible Dream." In the sermon he retells the story of a determined Don Quixote whose commitment and idealism cause him to search for a full, rich, and exemplary life. Quixote, we are reminded, may have been viewed as crazy and difficult, but in fact his focused vision and uncompromising dedication to excellence provide for us examples similar to Jesus' call that we strive for maturity.

Introduction

Both the story and the sermon are memorable in part because they remind us of our need to become better people with higher, nobler goals and actions. But in so reminding us, they also make clear a universal truth: frequently we fail at being the kind of persons that we should be. All too often we ignore the calls to be holy and to live mature Christian lives. We sin, and despite our penitent attitudes, we continue to fall into patterns of sinful behavior.

Encumbered with this knowledge of our own sinful behavior, we long for a lasting release from guilt, an enduring peace and happiness, and a life both abundant and eternal. In a word, we seek salvation. As Christians we profess that this salvation comes through Jesus Christ. Since Jesus died for our sins, we can be saved. Because of him, we are new creations, free from the bondage to guilt, sin, and death. But what does all of this really mean? How did Jesus die for our sins? How are we saved through his death? And what clearly is "salvation"?

Christ as Victor

Throughout history, theologians have addressed these questions with studies of the doctrine of atonement. Three basic theories, all of which have biblical support, have been given. How then are we saved through Jesus' death? A first theory emphasizes rescue and deliverance from the grasp of the "principalities and powers" of evil (Eph. 6:12).

Because "all have sinned and fall short of the glory of God" (Rom. 3:23), humans are caught in what appears to be an endless cycle of sin. Thus, Irenaeus, a second-century theologian, argued that since the power that has entrapped humans is a personified and deceptive Satan, God's reasonable response was to redeem us by the real, human Jesus, offering him to the devil. On the cross Jesus "gave himself as a ransom for all" (1 Tim. 2:6).

This view often is termed the "Christ as Victor" theory, after the classic text by the Swedish theologian Gustav Aulen (1931). Aulen emphasized that Christ's entire earthly life was a conflict with sin, death, and the devil, and that this battle culminated with his death on the cross and ultimate victory. Similar themes about captivity, ransom, and victory are found throughout Christian history. One of the more colorful descriptions comes from Gregory of Nyssa, a fourth-century church leader. He compared Satan to a greedy fish that had taken the bait (Jesus) and had thereby been "hooked" by God's divine plan to redeem sinners from their captivity.

This ransom and rescue view has been popular throughout the history of the Christian church, both because it expresses biblical truths and because it appeals to a very basic condition of many humans. Believers often have suffered under various powers of evil, including persecuting governments, paralyzing plagues, and numerous social and moral injustices. To these sufferers, the message that Jesus has fought the evil one and has won brings great encouragement. Jesus thus becomes both the liberator from present bonds of sin and evil, and ultimately, for all who believe, the Savior from the eternal guilt of sin.

Even though today the guises of evil may have changed, the powers of Satan seem very strong and captivating. Who can rescue us from a host of addictions, physical and spiritual illnesses? Who can give us the victory from the guilt of sin? Who can free us to live abundantly and responsibly with assurance for an eternal future of goodness? Only Jesus can provide such a rescue! Only Christ is such a Savior!

Yet strangely, this Christ as Victor theory carries with it one troubling matter, it seems to assign very great power to the devil. The focus of the need for redemption is not primarily human sinfulness. Rather, it is Satan's powerful dominance over all of humanity. Since the ransom is "paid" to Satan, a critic might ask, who then really releases humans from bondage? Is God or Satan in control?

Christ as Substitute

From concerns surrounding questions like these, theologians have articulated a second major theory, rich with both biblical support and practical meaning. This view stresses that we are saved not through some kind of deal or trick made with Satan, but instead because Jesus has satisfied the necessary demands of the justice of God. To be sure, a price is paid for our sinfulness; however, it is paid not to the devil but to God. In our sins, we fail to meet the ethical and spiritual demands of a holy, just, and honorable God. A breach has developed, and no human endeavor can repair it. Yet neither can any sort of cheap grace; God's own identity and justice make such an "easy forgiveness" impossible. The only sufficient satisfaction would be one who was both God and man. Thus Jesus becomes "a curse for us" (Gal. 3:13), dying in our place for our sins (1 Cor. 15:3; 2 Cor. 5:21).

Popularized by Anselm, a medieval monk from eleventh-century Britain, this view is often identified as the substitutionary theory. In his classic text, "Why God Became Man," he stressed that Jesus had to die for humanity because of the extreme great weight of sin. Neither any "payment" nor any simple pronouncement of forgiveness would do. God's holiness and righteousness demanded more than an assurance of forgiveness; it called for a satisfactory, human substitute. And only Jesus could be "good enough to pay the price of sin." Therefore, "God made him who had no sin to be sin for us, so that in him we might become the righteousness of God" (2 Cor. 5:21).

If the first major theory addresses the inevitability of sinful behavior — the trap that we alone seem unable to escape — then this second theory speaks to the seemingly eternal problem of human guilt. Nothing that we can do will alleviate our internal strife; nothing will give us peace of mind so that we can effectively serve and follow Jesus. It is only by God's sheer grace that we obtain such a salvation. With this realization, we begin to understand something truly marvelous about God's own heart: While the holy righteousness of God demands a just sacrifice, the love of God makes that sacrifice possible through the substitutionary atonement of the one Savior, Jesus the Christ. Oh, what a Savior!

An added strength of this view is that it does not emphasize the role of the devil. There is no honor for Satan here, no question of whether the devil has any real control. Instead, "Christ Jesus, who, being in very nature God, . . . made himself nothing . . . and became obedient to death . . . on a cross" for us (Phil. 2:5-8). Yet, modern thinkers sometimes question this model as too "neat" and mathematically calculated. They say that its theological formulation reflects Anselm's own medieval Europe, where insecurities and uncertainties about God, the authoritative church, and eternal damnation were met with sophisticated systems of logic and codes of honor and tradition. Contemporary Christians, it is assumed, simply cannot relate to such a premodern worldview.

Such thinking, however, seems quite naive itself. While today's world is certainly more scientifically advanced, patterns of behavior and systems of mass entertainment mirror a humanity equally encumbered by feelings of guilt and failure. Despite our technological successes, we cannot forget our misuses of these technologies. Even while we view and communicate globally in "real-time chatrooms," we churn inside ourselves over the paucity of genuine human contact we practice, even with our loved ones. Guilt remains, and only a guiltless, human one can save us. Only Jesus!

Christ as Example

But can we say more? Are there still other aspects involved in what happens on the cross? A third theory answers positively, but with a radically different perspective. Both ransom and substitutionary theories emphasize what occurred *for* us; they are identified as "objective views." The third model stresses what happens *in* us when we understand the atonement: When we see what great love God has for us — that Christ would die for us — we become compelled to imitate this love. Because of the radical nature of this love, we receive the power to follow Christ. As Douglas Hall suggests in his book *Professing the Faith* (1993), the typical human "incapacity to realize that one's very life is enfolded in transcendent love may be the most devastating thing that could be said about human existence" (p. 429). Yet, this incapacity does not have to remain. Jesus, by his very example, saves us from such impotence and ignorance. He provides us an example, a "way" of salvation that has very real and immediate practical implications.

Peter Abelard, a contemporary of Anselm, first stressed this "moral example" theory, but it did not become popular among Christian theologians until modern times. While he affirmed the aspect of sacrifice as present for us, he stressed the biblical emphasis of our own subjective responses to Jesus' sacrifice. Everyone, he says, is able to become "more righteous" after the death of Christ because the "realized gift inspires greater love than one which is only hoped for." Thus, our redemption through Christ's suffering "not only frees us from slavery to sin, but also wins for us the true liberty of the sons of God, so that we do all things out of love rather than fear" (*Exposition on Romans*, p. 283). As Paul states, "Live a life of love, just as Christ loved us and gave himself up for us as a fragrant offering and sacrifice to God" (Eph. 5:2). We are saved, therefore, not simply because Jesus pays the price for us, or becomes the perfect substitution for us, but also because he teaches us how to love. And, in teaching us how to love, Jesus teaches us how to *live*.

Conclusion

Certainly the biblical witness affirms truths stressed in each of these three views. Often the ransom and substitutionary models are deemed more important, no doubt in part because they are "objective." Truthfully, they do make clear that Jesus' death is necessary because of the weakness of all human beings. The language may trouble us; theories that stress cosmic battles and substitutionary sacrifice seem so archaic and irrational to some. Yet the central truth is unmistakable, even to the most skeptical among us: No matter how much we try, we cannot save ourselves; we are incapable either to pay an appropriate ransom or to provide an adequate substitute for our own inconsistencies and failings. It is only by the grace, power, and sacrifice of God through Jesus Christ that we receive freedom from guilt and forgiveness of sins. How then are we saved through Jesus? Simply put, we are saved through him because he freely provides the only possible avenue to reconciliation with God.

Yet the importance of the third theory should not be overlooked. While we may begin to understand objectively what happens in the death of Jesus, we may not quickly sense its effect on our daily lives. We may come to realize that we are saved through Jesus' death, and we might then believe and profess that we have security with regard to our place in heaven. However, we may not comprehend how Jesus' action on the cross affects us in the way we live our *present* lives. To put it another way, Jesus' death saves us not only by making possible eternal life, but it saves us by exhibiting the way of abundant life. Through Jesus' death we are saved from the curse of eternal damnation, but we also are saved from the kinds of immature, dissatisfying lives that human-centered agenda tend to promote. We are given an example of enduring love, selfless service, and truly joyous and full living. Such an example provides an answer for many persons of yesterday and today. Such a model makes possible the fulfillment of our own various quixotic quests. For "whoever wants to save his life will lose it, but whoever loses his life for [Christ] will save it" (Luke 9:24).

Chapter Five

What did God do to sin and death through Jesus Christ?

John Mark Hicks
Harding Graduate School of Religion
Memphis, Tennessee

"He was delivered over to death for our sins and was raised to life for our justification" Romans 4:25.

Atonement means reconciliation (at-one-ment). It is God's work whereby he provides the basis for and accomplishes the goal of reconciliation between himself and sinful humanity. Reconciliation is God's redemptive act whereby he fulfills his original intention of communion between himself and his creatures.

God created the human community in order to share the loving fellowship of his own triune community (Father, Son and Spirit). By creation God brought others into the fellowship of his own life. In much the same way that parents bear children in order to express and share their love, so God created out of his self-giving and other-centered love. God created others to share what he already possessed, the fellowship of a loving community (John 17:24-26).

But sin alienates God and humanity. God's holy communion cannot embrace ungodliness any more than light can embrace darkness. There is no darkness in God and there is no communion with sin in his light. Light dispels darkness because they cannot coexist at the same time and in the same place. Therefore, sin separates God and humanity (Isa. 59:2). The holiness of God's community is at stake. The holy God cannot dwell among the wicked (Ps. 5:4). Thus, God excluded his original children from the Garden (Gen. 3:23-24), excluded wicked Israel from his presence (2 Kgs.

17:22-23), and will one day banish the ungodly from his eternal communion (Rev. 21:6-8).

Yet, just as parents yearn for their children, so God yearns for his people. Even when Israel was a rebellious child, God compassionately longed for their fellowship (Jer. 31:20; Hos. 11:8). Even when Israel was an unfaithful wife, God pursued her as a husband yearns for reconciliation with his beloved (Hos. 1–3). Even while we were yet enemies, God demonstrated his love for us in that Christ died in order to restore fellowship (Rom. 5:6-11). In Jesus Christ, God first loved us before we loved him (1 John 4:7-12).

The holy God, then, takes the initiative in reconciliation. God invites us into his fellowship and seeks a renewed communion (1 John 1:3). The holy God wants to dwell with his people. In Israel, he gave them his holy presence as he dwelled among them in the tabernacle (Lev. 26:11-12). In the church, he gives us his holy presence as his Holy Spirit dwells in us (2 Cor. 6:16; 1 Cor. 3:16-17; 6:19-20). In the new heaven and new earth God will fully dwell among his redeemed people (Rev. 21:3-4).

But how can the holy God dwell among unholy people? Must he not exclude unholy people from his presence? Can he commune with ungodliness? Can God tolerate evil without denying his own integrity?

Atonement means that God makes a "holy place" for himself by removing sin from his people so that he dwells among them in his transforming, life-giving presence. Atonement accomplishes a reconciliation between God and his people so that they dwell together in a loving, holy fellowship.

God accomplished this mighty act of atonement through Jesus Christ. The earliest Christian confession is (1) that Christ died for our sins, (2) that he was buried, (3) that he was raised on the third day, and (4) that he appeared to Cephas (1 Cor. 15:3-5). The gospel, in its most basic form, is proclaimed in those four facts. Jesus really died (as his burial verifies) and he was really raised (as his appearance to Cephas verifies). But these are not mere facts; they have meaning. They accomplished something. The death and resurrection of Jesus are God's mighty act whereby he reconciled the world to himself (Rom. 5:9-11; 2 Cor. 5:18-19). God removed sin and offers his life-giving presence through the gospel. God destroyed both sin and death through Jesus Christ.

Christ Died for Our Sins

Paul's summary of the gospel locates the importance of Christ's death in the idea that Christ died "for our sins" (cf. Gal. 1:4). In other places, Paul characterizes this divine work as Christ's death "for us" (cf. Rom. 5:8; 2 Cor. 5:15; Gal. 2:20; 3:13). The mystery of the atoning function of Christ's death lies behind these two motifs, that is, that Christ died (1) for sin and (2) for us.

This is not simply Paul's version of the mystery, but it is the witness of the whole New Testament. Peter writes, "Christ died for sins once for all, the righteous for the unrighteous" (1 Pet. 3:18; cf. 2:24). Hebrews describes both the expiatory significance of Christ's death ("to take away the sins of my people," Heb. 9:28; cf. 2:17; 7:27; 10:12) and its substitutionary character ("he might taste death for everyone," Heb. 2:9). John also testifies that Jesus' death was "for our sins" (1 John 2:2; 4:10) as well as "for us" (1 John 3:16). Matthew records Jesus' teaching that his death was both "for the forgiveness of sins" (Matt. 26:28) and "for many" (Matt. 20:28).

But what does it mean to say "Christ died for sin" and "for us"? If this is the most basic Christian confession, why are so many Christians plagued with ambiguity and inept in their articulation of its fundamental meaning? What does it mean to confess that "Christ died for our sins"? Four points summarize its meaning.

First, God himself removed sin from his people through Jesus Christ. This is the basic idea of atonement. The death of Jesus removed sin. It took away sin. As a result of his death, sin no longer exists as a barrier between God and humanity. God reconciled himself to sinful humanity by removing sin.

This was the function of the Levitical sacrifices. They removed sin from the presence of God's people and created a "holy place" where God could dwell. The "blood of the covenant" sanctified the people, the tabernacle, the altar and the scroll. The law required "that nearly everything be cleansed with blood" (Heb. 9:22). Through sacrifice, through the removal of sin, God made "holy space" for himself so that he could dwell among his people in a holy communion.

This was also the function of the death of Jesus. Since sin has been removed through Jesus, God has created a holy place in our hearts for the indwelling of his Holy Spirit. We are now God's holy temple in which he dwells through his Spirit (Eph. 2:18-22). We are

God's saints, his holy ones. God lives within his holy people instead of merely in a holy temple. Indeed, the Levitical sacrifices were inadequate for God's ultimate purpose. They were provisional and patterned after God's own design in Jesus Christ (Heb. 9:1–10:18). In the eternal mind of God sin is only removed through Jesus (Heb. 9:15) though provisionally offered to God's people under the old covenant.

But in what sense did the death of Christ remove sin? Paul offers several metaphors. One is commercial. God canceled the debt of sin. He nailed it to the cross. Paul writes that our certificate of indebtedness, our "I owe you," was canceled at the cross (Col. 2:14). By whatever means, God forgave our debt through the cross and removed sin from our account. The ransom was paid and we were freed from indebtedness.

Another metaphor is legal in character. God no longer charges us with sin. The indictment has been revoked and we have been declared "not guilty." God reconciled himself to the world by "not counting men's sins against them" (2 Cor. 5:19). In Jesus Christ, God no longer "imputes" sin (Rom. 4:8) and, therefore, there is no "condemnation" for those who are in him (Rom. 8:1).

Yet, how can the holy God remove the sin of a depraved people? How can God declare the guilty "not guilty"? How can God forgive a debt that is justly owed? God removes sin, but on what basis? We need to say more.

Second, God identified himself with sinners in Jesus Christ. God did not distance himself from his fallen, sinful people. Rather, he came near. He joined them in their fallenness. The holy God entered the fallen world and shared its shame, pain and death.

God's first act of identification was the incarnation. God joined us in our fallenness by sharing our flesh, our sickness, our fatigue, our hunger and our death. God became a slave for our sakes by becoming one of us. Jesus Christ "did not regard equality with God as something to be exploited, but . . . . he humbled himself" by "being born in human likeness" (Phil. 2:6-8; NRSV). God did not send a sympathy card. He came and sat with us on the mourner's bench in order to groan with us in our shame and pain.

Jesus also identified with sinners when he was baptized. Jesus underwent a rite designed for those who (a) repent of sin; (b) confess their sin; and (c) are immersed for the forgiveness of sins (Mark 1:4-5). The righteous one submitted to a ritual designed for sinners. The righteous one joined sinners in an act of humility and submission.

The cross, however, is the moment of God's ultimate self-humiliation. There Jesus was "numbered with the transgressors" (Luke 22:37). There Jesus "became sin" for us (2 Cor 5:21). There "he humbled himself and became obedient to death — even death on a cross" (Phil. 2:8). There he became a "curse" for us (Gal. 3:13). There he "bore our sins in his body" (1 Pet. 2:24). There one who knew no sin became one with sin as he died "for us."

But what does it mean for Christ to identify with sinners? How does he become "sin" for us? How does this remove sin? We need to say more.

Third, God substituted himself for sinners in Jesus Christ. The Cross is not fundamentally a *human* sacrifice. It is God in the flesh sacrificing himself for humanity. God himself assumes the substitutionary role. One of the triune community, the Word become flesh (John 1:14), represented the Godhead in this act of self-humiliation and offered himself for sinners. The triune community experienced the hideousness of sin through the Godforsakenness of the crucified one. The triune community risked its own life, community and fellowship for the sake of reconciliation with the world it loved.

God acted against sin in Jesus Christ. He punished sin. But he did so within his own life rather than externalizing that punishment by tormenting sinners. God himself experienced the torment of the sin rather than inflicting that torment on us. God in Jesus Christ became sin for us (2 Cor. 5:21). The Lord of glory cried, "My God, My God, why have you forsaken me?" (Mark 15:34). The triune community suffered rather than inflicting that suffering upon us. The triune community internalized the horror and punishment of sin rather than punishing us with eternal wrath. God saved us from the "wrath to come" by experiencing that wrath himself in his own triune life through Jesus Christ (1 Thess. 1:10). This is the love of the Father that sent his Son into the world as a "propitiation" for sin (1 John 4:10).

The Cross is the moment of God's self-substitution. God substitutes himself in such a way that it is just for God to "justify the ungodly" and "not impute sin" to sinners. God substituted himself in that he experienced and internalized within himself the wrath that was due us. Jesus Christ, as one of the triune community, experienced the curse we deserved, paid the debt we owed, and suffered the eschatological death we earned.

But why did God substitute himself? Why did he not just "forgive" without substitution? Why did anyone have to "pay"? We need to say more.

Fourth, God satisfied himself in Jesus Christ. We do not satisfy God. We do not live up to his holiness and emulate his character. We are unworthy servants even if we are obedient (Luke 17:10). We cannot deal with our own sin or make up for our mistakes. We cannot pay the ransom for our own iniquities. Only God could pay it.

To whom or what did God pay it? Some believe he paid it to Satan as if God owed Satan something. Some believe he paid it to some principle of justice to which he was obligated as if there is a law that stands above God to which he must submit. God does not satisfy a law higher than himself. God is not subservient to some higher principle. On the contrary, God's character is the highest principle in the universe. He does not owe anything to anyone (Job 41:11; Rom. 11:35).

Instead, God acts consistently with his own character. God does not deny himself (2 Tim. 2:13). God acts in character and with integrity. This is God's own faithfulness. He is faithful to himself. He could not do otherwise and remain who he is. So God decided to redeem sinful humanity in a way consistent with his character. Therefore, out of his mercy and because of his great love God determined he would justify the ungodly, but in a just way. Because he loved his creation and yearned for their fellowship, he decided to offer mercy through his own self-satisfaction.

The cross is the moment of God's self-satisfaction. God purposed to set forth Jesus Christ as the means of averting his just wrath. The first chapters of Romans are replete with references to God's wrath and just condemnation (1:18,32; 2:2,3,5,8,12,25; 3:8-10,19-20,23). God's solution is to demonstrate his righteousness by a propitiation so that he could remain righteous and at the same time declare believers righteous. The clear implication of Romans 3:25-26 is that God could not have been just in declaring the ungodly righteous if Jesus had not been offered as a propitiation. God's own self-satisfaction was necessary if God was to remain both just and justifier. God's work in Christ is a divine self-propitiation whereby the triune community absorbs the eschatological wrath due us. Because of this self-propitiation with regard to our sins God may now justify the ungodly (Rom. 4:5). God's wrath is averted, not by anything we have done, but by his own righteous act in the gospel wherein the righteousness of God is revealed (Rom. 1:16-17).

This understanding of the atonement has been criticized as unintelligible to the modern mind. It appears to value human sacrifice and thus sounds mythological and hideous. But the principle of inner moral conflict whereby one sacrifices himself in self-giving love rather than compromising hallowed principles is still valued. We see it in parents who are torn apart with conflicting emotions when their children go astray. They long to forgive, but not in such a way that condones or encourages the wrongdoing. True forgiveness is costly. It cost God something. God decided to deal with sin by taking it up into his own life where he destroyed its power. God offers himself as a substitute in order that his holiness might meet his love for the sake of his people. The triune community sacrificed its own unbroken bliss so that others might join their communion. The triune community laid its own life on the line in order to save us from sin. God in Jesus Christ experienced Godforsakenness for the sake of his people. In that act God destroyed sin. I am not sure we can say much more.

Ultimately, the mystery of the atonement lies beyond the images and metaphors Scripture offers. The mysterious reality which lies behind the fact that "God was in Christ reconciling the world" (2 Cor. 5:18) and "God made Christ to be sin for us" (2 Cor. 5:21) is beyond our finite minds. We will spend eternity not only worshiping God and the Lamb, but also exploring the mystery that inspires our worship. The atonement is more than an example of martyrdom. Christ died for sin. He did something to sin. He removed it, canceled it, and destroyed it. We will never fathom the mystery of that relationship, but it speaks volumes about who God is (faithful, holy love), what he has done (humbled himself) and how he has loved us (substituted himself in self-propitiation).

Christ Was Raised for Our Life

While we often describe the death of Christ as "for us," we rarely say this about his resurrection. We more readily speak of rising "with Christ" — and this is the dominant language of the New Testament (cf. 2 Cor. 4:14; Rom. 6:5-8; Col. 2:12; 3:1). However, it is also appropriate to say that Christ was raised "for us." Jesus was raised for "our justification" (Rom. 4:25) so that we might be saved by "his life" (Rom. 5:10). In much the same way that Christ died for us, he was also raised for us. Indeed, Paul explicitly says this in 2 Corinthians 5:15 (NRSV): "And he died for all, so that those who live might live no longer for themselves, but for him who died and was raised for them."

Just as with the death of Christ "for us," so we must ask what it means to say that Christ was raised for us and for our life. But before we can answer that question, we must address what the resurrection meant for Jesus. Then we can apply its meaning to us.

On the cross Christ experienced the Godforsakenness of the sin he bore. Through that suffering the Son of God experienced shame and condemnation. Jesus suffered on a "tree" and therefore suffered the curse of God (Gal. 3:10-13). Consequently, the cross was a stumbling block for Jews because the cross represented the curse of God (1 Cor. 1:23). God's Messiah could not hang on a "tree" (Acts 5:30; 10:39). The Messiah was a conquering hero, not a crucified servant. Rather than confessing, "Jesus is Messiah," unbelieving Jews would say, "Jesus is cursed." While the cross in our post-Christian culture is an object of love, gratitude and appreciation, to first-century culture it was an object of horror, curse and humiliation.

The preaching in Acts, however, accentuates the importance of the resurrection. While the Jewish leaders crucified Jesus, "God raised him from the dead" (Acts 2:23-24; 3:14-15; 4:10; 5:30; 10:40; 13:26-31). If Jesus' life had ended on that tree, he would have been an accursed servant. But the resurrection of Jesus is his justification. When God raised him from the dead, he reversed the curse and vindicated his just one. God reversed the judgment of death. The "mystery of godliness," according to 1 Timothy 3:16, is that God appeared in the flesh (incarnation and death), but was "vindicated by the Spirit" (resurrection).

Death did not win. Satan was defeated. God's anointed one was not left in Hades, but God raised him from the dead and proclaimed him Lord (Acts 2:24-28). The accursed one was justified. The resurrection of Jesus proclaims God's victory over sin and death. The resurrection of Jesus destroys death.

He was, in fact, raised "for our justification" (Rom. 4:25). His victory is our victory. His resurrection is our resurrection. His justification is our justification. There are at least three ways in which this is true.

First, our resurrection with Jesus is the presence of God's transforming Spirit. Since Christ died to sin and we are dead to sin in him, we are now alive to God. "Count yourselves dead to sin," Paul exhorts, "but alive to God in Christ Jesus" (Rom. 6:11). The life we now live is not our own — it is the resurrected life of Jesus. We have been crucified with Jesus, and we have been raised with him. So the life we now live is his (Gal. 2:20). We live in the power of the life-giving Spirit who has given us "new life" in Christ.

The presence of the Spirit is God's gift by which he transforms us into the image of his Son. The work of the Spirit is sanctification (1 Pet. 1:2; 2 Thess. 2:13). God's Holy Spirit empowers our sanctification (Eph. 3:16-17), and God transforms us "into his likeness with ever-increasing glory" (2 Cor. 3:18). God calls us to live holy lives and he gives us his Holy Spirit as a transforming power.

This power is the vigor of a resurrected life that is lived out in the present as we anticipate the fullness of that power in the resurrection of the body. Paul makes this point in Romans 8:10-11: "But if Christ is in you, your body is dead because of sin, yet your spirit is alive because of righteousness. And if the Spirit of him who raised Jesus from the dead is living in you, he who raised Christ from the dead will also give life to your mortal bodies through his Spirit, who lives in you." Thus, the present experience of the transforming power of the Spirit by the fruit he bears in us is but a foretaste of our full redemption by the power of the Spirit in the resurrection.

Consequently, the sanctified life we now live is by the power of the life-giving Spirit who gave life to the dead body of Jesus Christ. By his work of atonement God has made "holy space" for himself in the bodies of his redeemed people (1 Cor. 6:19-20). We are called to be holy, then, because God has given us his Holy Spirit (1 Thess. 4:3-8).

Second, our resurrection with Jesus transforms our experience of death. Since God has defeated death, we no longer fear its hostile grip. His resurrection has destroyed death so that the keys of Hades are in the hands of Jesus (Rev. 1:18). His resurrection is a revelation of our future resurrection because he is the "firstfruits" of the harvest to come. The resurrection of Jesus actually belongs to the end of time (*eschaton*), but God raised him in the midst of history as a revelation of the end. God raised Jesus in order to show us what the end of history is. He gave us the "firstfruits" in order to assure us of the coming harvest in which we will participate. We know what the end is because God raised Jesus from the dead. The gospel has brought the light of resurrected immortality into the darkness of this fallen world (2 Tim. 1:10).

Consequently, our experience of death is transformed from hope-lessness, fear and despair into hope, expectation and anticipation. We comfort each other with this hope (1 Thess. 4:13-18). We no longer fear death though we hate it. We hate it because it is God's enemy (1 Cor. 15:26), but we do not fear it because God in Christ has conquered it. As the writer of Hebrews notes, Jesus "shared in [our] humanity so that by his death he might destroy him who holds the power of death — that is, the devil — and free those who all their lives were held in slavery by their fear of death" (Heb. 2:14-15).

Third, our resurrection with Jesus in our "spiritual" bodies enables full communion with God in the eschaton. Since God has raised Christ with a "spiritual body," we yearn for our spiritual bodies when we will experience the fullness of God's Spirit in the new heaven and new earth. Indeed, the indwelling Spirit is our promise that we will be raised, and the power of the Spirit that now works for sanctification will transform our vile bodies into the glorious body of Jesus Christ (Rom. 8:11; Phil. 3:21). Our present mortal, weak, and fallen bodies will be transformed into immortal, powerful, and glorious bodies. We will have "spiritual bodies," that is, bodies energized and empowered by the full transforming presence of the Spirit of God (1 Cor. 15:42-44).

The present work of the Spirit which offers us daily renewal (2 Cor. 4:16) will bear its full fruit in the resurrection when the Spirit will sanctify our whole person (body and soul; cf. Rom. 8:23). The Spirit who now sanctifies us will animate our bodies throughout eternity. The Holy Spirit will complete his work of sanctification through the resurrection so we can abide in the presence of God forever by his power and holiness. God will fully dwell among his people when they are fully sanctified by his Spirit in the new heaven and new earth. That work is still in process and not yet complete. The indwelling Spirit is God's promise that he will complete that work as we continue to trust in him (Eph. 1:13-14; 2 Cor. 1:22; 5:5).

Just as the death of Christ is the culmination and representation of all that is fallen in the world, so the resurrection is God's pledge to restore the world to its original goodness. God decisively reversed the effects of Good Friday. The resurrection is God's pledge of an eschatological reversal in a new heaven and a new earth. The resurrection is a new day of creation/redemption and signals the defeat of God's enemies, especially the last enemy which is death.

Conclusion

The death and resurrection of Jesus are God's two mighty acts of reconciliation. The cross is God's self-humiliating participation in human suffering in order to substitute himself for the sake of his own self-satisfaction. The resurrection is God's justification of Jesus through which we presently experience the power of a sanctified life, live with hope in the face of death, and expect our full sanctification by God's Spirit in the *eschaton*.

Indeed, the death and resurrection of Jesus are both eschatological events where Christ suffered eschatological wrath "for us" and God justified his Son in eschatological victory "for us." While we will experience death, we will not experience wrath because Jesus suffered it for us. While we will experience death, we will nevertheless live through our resurrection with Jesus.

Jesus Christ suffered with us and for us. He did not distance himself from our suffering, but joined us in it. He did not succumb to sin, but overcame it in his life and ministry. He did not leave us in our sin, but destroyed it through his death. He did not leave us in our death, but justified us through his resurrection.

Atonement destroys sin and restores life. It cancels the debt of sin and gives back the life that sin stole. In Jesus Christ, God reconciles the world to himself. He fulfills his goal for creation. He again communes with humanity and he will restore the Garden of Eden (Rev. 22:1-6).

Atonement is God's work. The gospel is what God has done in Jesus Christ. We do not "do" the gospel. We believe the gospel, trust the gospel, respond to the gospel and obey the gospel. But the gospel is God's work of atonement whereby he reconciles us through submissive faith. God is the actor and we are the receiver. God accomplishes redemption and we accept his gift. We are saved by grace through faith (Eph. 2:8).

Just as he created, so he has redeemed. God created out of his self-giving, self-sacrificing love, and he has so redeemed. God has made atonement and overcome the barrier that separated him from his creatures. His self-humiliating, self-sacrificing, self-substituting love has defeated sin and empowers our holy, hopeful and immortal lives. In Jesus Christ God atoned for sin and death, and now we are called to receive his gift and emulate the one who loved us.

Chapter Six

How does God work in the world and in the life of the Christian?

Gary Holloway
Lipscomb University
Nashville, Tennessee

The scene is a hospital room late at night. Your ten-year-old daughter lies in the bed. Cancer. Inoperable. The doctors have no hope. As a Christian, what do you do?

There's a knock at the door. A stranger enters. He introduces himself as Brother Welch and claims to have the gift of healing. Laying his hands on your daughter, he begins to mumble a prayer then grows louder and louder until he shouts, "Come out of her! Be healed."

The next day your daughter opens her eyes and says, "I'm hungry." Her color is better. The nurses are amazed. The doctor orders tests. No cancer. None. He orders more tests. Still no cancer. Your daughter goes home healthy.

How would you explain it? Did the faith healer have the power? Did God work a miracle? Is the healing a result of God's providence? Did he work through natural law to cause a spontaneous remission of the cancer? Or is the remission just a coincidence? Or is it all a complete mystery?

Suppose the scenario is the same, your daughter has inoperable cancer, but instead of a faith healer, your family and church pray for her recovery. The next day the cancer is gone. What then is your explanation?

Or suppose a brilliant physician tries an experimental procedure on your daughter and cures the cancer. What part does God play in that healing?

Or suppose you pray as you've never prayed before and your daughter dies. Where is God?

How does God work in the world?

Take a more mundane example. You've been offered a job in another city. You're not sure whether you should take it. You pray. How do you expect God to answer you? Will he give an audible or visible sign? Or will he provide an inward conviction that you should go or stay? Or are you left on your own to make the best decision you can?

How does God work in the world? How bold can we be in prayer? What kind of guidance can we expect from God? Is he active in our lives?

The Biblical Story of an Active God

When we turn to the Bible and ask, "How does God work in the world?" the answer seems clear. He works miraculously and dramatically, breaking into the world with acts of judgment and grace. Think of Noah and the flood, the call of Abraham, the destruction of Sodom, the Ten Plagues, the destruction of Jericho, the strength of Samson, and the wonders done by Elijah and Elisha. Most dramatically and personally, he worked through his Son made flesh. In Jesus and the apostles, we see God at work making the lame walk and the blind see, multiplying loaves and fish, and even raising the dead.

When we read the Bible, it looks as if there is a miracle on every page.

But such a view may be misleading. The miracles of Scripture tend to cluster around God's acts of salvation: creation, the exodus, prophetic warnings, and the ministry of Jesus. There were times, even in the Bible, when God did not act so dramatically. For example, when the boy Samuel hears the voice of God, he does not recognize it because, "The word of the LORD was rare in those days; visions were not widespread" (1 Sam. 3:1, NRSV). Most of God's people even during "Bible times" did not hear audible voices or witness spectacular miracles. Still they trusted God and believed he cared for them.

Yet many did witness miracles and received special power from God. In the New Testament, Jesus through the Spirit gave the apostles and others miraculous powers of healing, tongues, and prophecy. Does God still work that way today? Are there people today who have the power the apostles had or have miracles ceased?

It is hard to answer this question directly from the Bible. There is not a passage that clearly says, "Soon after the death of the last apostle, miracles will cease." Some believe 1 Corinthians 13:8, "But where there are prophecies, they will cease; where there are tongues, they will be stilled; where there is knowledge, it will pass away," is such a passage. This cessation of prophecy and miracle will occur "when perfection comes" (1 Cor. 13:10). However, Bible students are divided over what "perfection" means in this passage. Is it when the New Testament is completed, or when the church matures in love, or at the end of time?[1]

In short, it is not completely clear that any New Testament passage promises the end of miracles. However, many argue for the cessation of miracles based on the purpose of miracles and the role of the apostles. Some say the sole or primary purpose of miracles was to confirm the word of the apostles and other eyewitnesses to Jesus. Since we now have their word in written form in the New Testament, there is no longer need for miracles. Others object that confirming the word was not the only purpose of miracles; other purposes include gaining attention for God's message and showing compassion to the suffering. Such purposes are still needed today.

However, there are few Christians around today who claim there are still apostles in our midst who have the power to heal with their shadow or their handkerchiefs (see Acts 5:15; 19:22). Some argue it thus follows that God does not heal through empowered individuals as he did through the apostles.

The Witness of History

If Scripture speaks of a God who is dramatically and miraculously active in the world, then why do many Christians believe miracles have ceased? In addition to the logical arguments from the Bible just discussed, many point to the witness of church history.

Claims to the power of prophecy and miracle among Christians are relatively rare from the middle of the second century until the beginning of the twentieth. Many of those who claim such power during this time period are condemned as heretics by the church. Throughout this time period until the seventeenth century, there is the widespread conviction that God still does miracles — from making the sun rise, to producing a good crop, to healing the sick — but he does not empower individuals to work miracles.

That attitude toward miracles begins to change with the Enlightenment of the seventeenth and eighteenth centuries. It was during this period that the terms most often used to describe God's work in the world, "miracle" and "providence" began to change their meaning. Many phenomena considered "miraculous" in the Middle Ages were shown to be the result of natural processes. Miracle was defined as a violation of natural law and relegated to the biblical past. More and more, any belief in miracle (even biblical miracles) was thought of as superstition.

It was during this period that many Christians became more comfortable with the term "providence" to refer to God's work in the world. "Providence" is a particularly slippery term. One can argue it is a biblical concept, but not a biblical word. "Providence" became a popular way to describe God's activity in the age of rationalism and deism. That age believed providence to be God's "ordinary" work in creation and was not to be confused with miracle. They said God now works only through natural law.

Although many today use "providence" to describe the work of an active God, there are some who use it to practically deny God's healing and wonder-working power. Today, some in our churches avoid both "miracle" and "providence," hardly speaking of God's present action, assuming he completed his work in Bible times. They pray as an obligation, not because they think God will actually "do" something. Or if they do expect him to act, they expect he will in normal scientific and technical ways. They shackle God with the chains of science, making him a "God-of-the gaps" who does something only when science and medicine cannot.

Thus, there is a distinction in the history of the church between God's miraculous actions after the second century and the claim of some to supernatural power. In the modern period since the Enlightenment, there is the tendency to reject miracle on the basis of a misunderstanding of natural law. Some think belief in miracle means we must abandon the idea of an orderly universe of cause and effect. But natural law simply refers to the regularity we see in nature. Regularity, however, does not mean uniformity. If God enters an event as cause, we still have cause and effect. In other words, we should look for regularity not in nature itself, but in the God who made nature.

Those who believe individuals today are miraculously empowered can also make a historical argument for their position. They

admit there are few throughout church history who have miraculous gifts, but they explain the lack of gifts as a lack of faith and
knowledge. At the turn of the twentieth century with the Pentecostal
revival, many Christians rediscovered the biblical promise of spiritual gifts and claimed them by faith. Therefore, they say, we now
live in the age of signs and wonders just as the New Testament
Christians did.[2]

Arguments from Experience

If the Bible does not clearly say miracles will end and if the message of history is ambiguous, then where do we go to answer the
question, "How does God work in the world?"

We usually rely on experience. This is true whether one thinks
miracles have ceased or one thinks they occur daily. If you are sure
God does not work miraculously today, then what evidence would
convince you otherwise? If your best friend said, "I've seen someone raised from the dead," would you believe him? No, you would
explain it away as an illusion. What if you personally witnessed
someone miraculously healed. Would you believe it? No, you'd say
it was a trick, or you were under a great deal of stress, or give any
explanation except the miraculous one. If you are completely convinced God will not work a miracle, then no amount of evidence
will convince you otherwise.

By the same token, if you are certain there are miracles today, no
one can dissuade you. "I saw it with my own eyes," you say, and
no one and nothing can convince you otherwise.

What both of these groups have in common is their complete
assurance that they know how God works in the world. One side
knows God does not do miracles today. The other side knows he
does. In both cases how they read the Bible shapes their experiences. If you know the Bible says miracles have ceased, you are not
likely to see one. If you know the Bible promises miracles, then you
expect to see one. It sometimes works the other way, also. If one
sees a miracle, one understands that the Bible promises them. If
one has never seen a miracle, one knows the Bible says they will
cease.

Are these the only alternatives, "No miracles" or "Expect a miracle"? No. It seems to me that there are many faithful Christians
who believe in a good and powerful God who works his way in

the world but who are rightly skeptical of many claims of miracle. They believe God works, but can't say exactly how. Some call that work "providence," and some call it miracle.

Imagine a conversation among three devout Christians: an older man named Empiricos, his granddaughter Miracula, and his son Bob.

EMPIRICOS: I don't know why anyone would even ask how God works in the world. It's clear from the Bible that the age of miracles ended with the New Testament. All these "faith healers" are really "fake healers" preying on people's gullibility. Just let one of them bring your grandma back from the dead, and then I'll believe.

BOB: Would you really, Dad?

EMPIRICOS: You betcha. But it ain't gonna happen. I've never seen a miracle. Have you?

MIRACULA: Of course I have, grandpa! Don't you remember how we prayed for Aunt Sadie and she miraculously got well?

EMPIRICOS: That was no miracle; she just had a good doctor. Isn't that right, Bob?

BOB: She did have a good doctor, but I believe the prayer helped, too.

EMPIRICOS: Of course it did. God worked providentially through natural law to bring her to health.

MIRACULA: Is that all he did? Don't you think he did something special? Don't you believe in prayer, Grandpa?

BOB: Of course he does!

EMPIRICOS: Of course I do!

MIRACULA: But why pray if God does only what happens naturally? Hasn't God promised to hear our prayers and act powerfully on our behalf? Didn't he hear the prayer of Daniel and shut the lions' mouths? Didn't he guide Paul? Doesn't he guide us today? "Guard, guide, and direct our ways," I've heard you pray that, Grandpa.

EMPIRICOS: I never thought I'd see the day. What have you been teaching this girl, Bob? We pray because we are commanded to. God guides us providentially. Next thing you know, you'll be telling me God speaks to you.

MIRACULA: He does! I hear his voice every day. He tells me what choices to make. He opens up parking spots for me when I'm late to school. He fights the power of darkness I face each day. I know he works in my life because I see his actions each moment of every day. Right, Dad?

BOB: I'm not so sure, sweetheart. I believe God is at work in our lives, but I'm not sure he opens up parking spots for us. What if someone else needs that spot? I pray and I believe God heals, but I'm not sure how he does it. I think he guides me, but I don't hear audible voices. I believe he can raise the dead, but I've never seen him do it.

MIRACULA: Oh Daddy, you don't know much, do you?

EMPIRICOS: You can say that again.

BOB: I don't know all the ways of God, but I do think he works miracles. I'd even define a miracle as an event that would not have happened had we not prayed to God and God had not acted.

EMPIRICOS: That's not a "miracle;" it's providence.

MIRACULA: So you do believe in miracles!

What Difference Does It Make?

How does God work in the world? Is this just a theological argument, perhaps between generations, never to be settled? Is it a silly question, one that causes division and hurt feelings? Should we avoid discussions like the one above?

No. The question has important practical implications for how we live as Christians. It raises other significant questions. How bold can we be in praying for the sick? How certain can we be that a particular event is an answer to prayer? Has God abandoned us? How does his will work with our own? Are we puppets or robots in the hands of God, or are we the complete masters of our own destinies?

Those who think they know exactly how God works in the world are on dangerous ground. Those who know there are no miracles today are prone to deny all of God's activity in their lives. If God works providentially, only through natural law, it is hard to see what difference he makes in our lives. These Christians have little, if any, assurance that something happens in response to their prayers that would not have happened naturally. They cannot boldly claim that God did something in answer to prayer. Some even go so far that they claim prayer is a mere obligation, one that may affect us psychologically but does not affect the will of God.

Such Christians seem very alone in the world. Their spiritual well being is completely up to them. They make decisions based on their best judgment, perhaps shaped by Scripture, but with no divine guidance. They rely solely on science and medicine for health. They serve a God who was active in the biblical past but is active no longer. They tend to rely on their ability to understand and keep God's law instead of having a relationship with a living, active Savior.

Many who are certain God directly intervenes in their lives face other dangers. They may trivialize God. Some think God directly guides them in every choice in life including picking vanilla over chocolate at the ice cream stand. It is true that there is no aspect of our lives as Christians that is too trivial for God's interest. There might also be good reason for God to lead us to pick vanilla (the chocolate may be contaminated). But expecting God's direct guidance in every aspect of life easily leads us to demand that God respond to us on our terms and on our timetable. He becomes little more than a genie in a bottle, there to grant our every wish.

Christians who expect God always to intervene in dramatic ways have an endangered faith. Like Jesus' contemporaries, they may seek the sign instead of the Savior. What happens when the miracle doesn't come? What happens when the loved one sickens and dies instead of being spectacularly healed? What happens when the path God chooses for you ends in utter disaster? Those who clearly see God's miraculous work in every event have great difficulty handling disappointment. Their faith may be in the good gifts they receive, not in the Sovereign Lord whose will must be done.

Those who accept almost every claim of God's action may lack spiritual discernment. They fail to test the spirits and may fall prey to those who are false prophets. Having put their trust in teachers who claim to be anointed with God's power, they may lose their faith in God when those teachers spiritually fail.

He Works His Will, Not Ours

So if we are not certain God never does miracles today yet we do not expect daily miracles, then how does God work in the world? The answer is, "Any way he wants to." This is not a flippant answer, but a serious one. God is the sovereign Lord of the Universe. He is in control. We are not. His ways are not ours. He works his will any way he chooses. He doesn't will everything that happens to us, but in everything that does happen, he wills our good.

But how can we see his will at work? Only by faith. Like "Bob" in the dialogue above, I find it more difficult than some to see God's hand in my life. But unlike others I believe he is actively at work in our world, sometimes in dramatic, wonderful, even "miraculous" ways. I believe we see his guidance most often in hindsight. We pray for guidance, but hear no voices. Still we know God cares for us and guides us. Sometimes in looking back at the crossroads of our lives we can see how he guided our paths, many times in unexpected ways. At other times, we cannot see his loving hand at work but we trust it is there.

By faith we see God at work and by faith we can approach his throne of grace with boldness. We pray for the sick. We pray they will be healed. God may lead them to find good doctors with good medicine. He sometimes heals through doctors and medicine. But he also sometimes heals without them. Perhaps you have witnessed a dramatic healing. I have not, but I believe God can and does heal in any way he chooses.

Sometimes he chooses not to heal. We don't know why. When I was twelve, my mother passed away after a fight with cancer. Many righteous Christians prayed for her healing. Why didn't God answer? People gave me all kinds of explanations: he wanted her with him in heaven; he knew the challenges she would face if she lived; we just didn't pray with enough faith. The ultimate answer is in the mystery of the will of God. I don't know why he did not heal my mother. I do know he is a loving Father. Although I do not always understand him, even though his will is not always mine, I trust his love.

So, back to our opening illustrations. What do you do when your daughter lies in the hospital at death's door? I would not call for a faith healer who claims to have the power to heal. I would call for devout Christians to pray to the One I am certain has the power to heal. He can heal any way he wants, with or without medicine and science. We can pray boldly to our God because he is a loving father who promises good gifts. But he is God, not a genie. He has his own will, and we must conform to it. Not the other way around.

What about guidance? How do we know whether we should take the new job? Because we pray confidently for guidance. God guides through Scripture, through circumstance, through brothers and sisters, through strangers, and even through dramatic wonders. I've never heard an audible voice that tells me what to do. Perhaps you have. I have witnessed, usually in hindsight, his direction in my life. He works his will in whatever way he wants.

Which brings us to a final answer. How does God work in the world? He works his will, not ours. When we ask this question we usually mean, "How does God give me what I want — healing, guidance, assurance, excitement, parking spaces?" How does he answer our prayers?

If we pray as Jesus taught us, "Not my will but your will be done," then the Father answers every time. This is the prayer that cannot fail. God is at work in the world and in our lives. He works in his own way, to shape us into his image, not always to give us what we want. His will, not ours. How can we know his will? How can we see his work?

Paul says:

> I appeal to you therefore, brothers and sisters, by the mercies of God, to present your bodies as a living sacrifice, holy and acceptable to God, which is your spiritual worship. Do not be conformed to this world, but be transformed by the renewing of your minds, so that you may discern what is the will of God — what is good and acceptable and perfect (Rom. 12:1-2, NRSV).

This is Paul the apostle who had miraculous power from God. He says to seek God's will not through signs and wonders but from spiritual sacrifice and transformation. This is Paul who asked the Lord three times to remove his thorn in the flesh. The Lord did not remove it. He did say, "My grace is sufficient for you, for my power is made perfect in weakness" (2 Cor. 12:9).

How does God work in the world? He works to show us grace. That grace may take the form of marvelous experiences. Grace may mean healing and guidance and victory. But grace also means cross and sacrifice and pain. We are called not to expect miracles, but to trust the God of miracles. We are called not to box God in by our views of nature and providence, but to trust he is at work in our lives. When darkness veils his loving face, when we do not know how he is at work, we trust in his unchanging grace, we believe he is at work in the world.

Endnotes

[1]For a list of views on this passage see Richard E. Oster, Jr., *1 Corinthians*, The College Press NIV Commentary Series (Joplin, MO: College Press, 1995), 320-321.

[2]See Jack Deere, *Surprised by the Power of the Spirit* (Grand Rapids: Zondervan, 1993) for a popular defense of modern-day miracles and a rebuttal of cessationist arguments.

Chapter Seven

How can a loving God allow suffering?

Randy Becton
Herald of Truth
Abilene, Texas

Pascal once described an important key to understanding human suffering. He wrote: "Not only do we only know God through Jesus Christ, but we only know ourselves through Jesus Christ; we only know life and death through Jesus Christ. Apart from Jesus Christ we cannot know the meaning of our life or our death, of God or of ourselves."

Pascal, in short, believed Jesus Christ is the answer of God to human suffering. In my library there are perhaps more than one hundred titles dealing with "theodicy" or the love of God and the problem of human suffering. I pick up two or three more every year. Most recently Peter Kreeft, professor of philosophy at Boston College, wrote *Making Sense Out of Suffering* (Servant Publications). His chapter seven, "The Clues Converge: Jesus, the Tears of God," is the finest short form theodicy I've ever seen.

Kreeft speaks of Jesus, the tears of God in a way that shatters the thesis of a more popular book, *When Bad Things Happen to Good People* by Harold Kushner. Kushner forces a choice between an all-powerful God and an all-loving God inviting sufferers to be comforted by God's loving concern even as we are compassionate toward God for not having power to stop "bad things" happening to us.

Peter Kreeft argues that the New Testament writers believed "it was God there on the cross." Jesus did three things to solve the problem of suffering: (1) he came and suffered with us, (2) in becoming man he transformed the meaning of our suffering, and (3) he died and rose again, paying the price for sin, opening heaven to us, and in rising he transformed death from a hole into a door, from an end into a beginning. Kreeft says it well: "Jesus is the tears of God."

In 1988 I published *Does God Care When We Suffer and Will He Do Anything about It?* I wrote about the biblical picture of God as one involved with us, not aloof from us: "God participated in his suffering world and suffered as a real human being in Jesus."

Harold Hazelip graciously wrote an expanded preface for my book. In his preface he wrote these words:

> The suffering of believers is heightened by our need to reconcile our personal pain with the goodness of God. If we do not believe God loves us, suffering would not be a profound philosophical or religious problem. We would simply say, "This is the way life is. What else can we expect?" A child who has a cruel or uncaring parent and can honestly admit this can then go on to build his life without the parent. But the child who must pretend to himself that his father loves him, while deep in his heart he knows this is not true, may be crushed. Christians love God, trust him, and believe he is in control of the world.

I wrote that the final and best proof of an all-loving and all-powerful God comes from God himself, what he has said and what he has done. The New Testament writers affirm God's complete identification with a suffering world. The apostle John says it best when he says God became flesh and dwelt among us. Wayne Oates, in *The Revelation of God in Human Suffering*, says: "The core of truth in the revelation of God is that He, in Jesus Christ as Lord, has Himself entered the arena of human suffering." The Christian affirmation is that, far from being aloof, God participated in his suffering world and suffered as a real human being.

God tells us about himself when we look Jesus squarely in the face, for God reveals in Jesus' life, ministry, death, and resurrection that "His supreme intention is for the redemption of mankind."

The Gospels tell us that Jesus brought God's final message — that *he is with us* — and that his loving power rescued us as he gave himself for us, conquering sin, suffering, and death. He overcame the rule of Satan, healing those who were oppressed by the devil, "for God was with him" (Acts 10:38).

> Jesus enters this world enslaved by Satan with the authority of God, not only to exercise mercy, but above all to join battle with evil . . .

76

[his victories] over the power of evil are not just isolated invasions of Satan's realm. They are more. They are manifestation of the dawn of the time of salvation and of the beginning of [the end] of Satan. (See Mark 1:23-28; 5:6-10.)

For all those burdened with sin and its inevitable result, suffering, the good news is "God has intervened"; salvation is here through the forgiveness of sins; "God wants to be near you." God has disclosed his nature dramatically as *loving* and in the resurrection makes a powerful display to emphatically pronounce himself "for us."

Edward Schweizer in *Jesus* says, "It was revealed in Jesus that God is really a God on the side of man." In their book *In His Image*, Dr. Paul Brand and Philip Yancey underline the truth that if we want to discuss the effect human suffering has on God, we must "center on the Incarnation, when God Himself lived among us."

Because we see and understand God best when we look into the face of Jesus, we can accurately answer "How does the suffering of people affect God?" by seeing how it affected Jesus. The Gospel writers show how deeply touched Jesus was by people's pain and grief. A major aspect of his ministry was the healing of the sick (Luke 4:18; 7:22). He dealt with his own pain as we do, praying in the Garden of Gethsemane, "Father . . . remove this cup from me," and crying out his feelings of abandonment on the cross. "My God, my God, why hast thou forsaken me?" (Luke 22:42; Mark 15:34, KJV). We cannot read the story of Jesus' crucifixion without thinking about God's pain in that event.

When suffering people talk to me about feeling alone and ask me where God is, I always think about where he was when his Son died. He was right there, identifying with mankind, going through death for us.

Nineteen hundred years later came the Holocaust, when more than six million Jews were murdered. In Elie Wiesel's *Night*, an account of his boyhood experiences in Nazi death camps, he said he would never get over "the first night in camp, which turned my life into one long night, seven times cursed and seven times sealed. Never shall I forget that smoke [of the crematorium] . . . never shall I forget those flames which consumed my faith forever . . . never shall I forget those moments which murdered God and my soul and turned my dreams into dust."

He tells of a young boy being tortured and hanged by the guards. Just before the hanging, he heard someone behind him whisper, "Where is God? Where is He?" After the prisoners had watched the half-hour-long hanging of the boy, the voice asked, "Where is God now?" Wiesel's heart spoke out within him: "Where is HE? Here He is — He is hanging here on the gallows." He added, "I was alone — terribly alone in a world without God and without man. Without love or mercy."

What does God announce in the face of horrible suffering? The instructions were given: His name shall be called Immanuel, meaning, "God is with us." But if God in Christ suffers with the world, and I believe he does, how can we feel that suffering presence?

The answer is the cross of Jesus Christ. That's where we feel it, see it, and embrace it for our own suffering.

God fully revealed how he feels about our pain, and we see this by watching Jesus' feelings and actions, even his own suffering and death. But there is a mystery here. There will always be mystery in our faith.

The Cross of Jesus and Our Suffering

In the face of the most agonizing misery, such as Elie Wiesel depicts so graphically, we ask, "Does Christian teaching have anything that speaks meaningfully to it?" Another who suffered during the Nazi regime was the German pastor Dietrich Bonhoeffer. Bonhoeffer, was a part of the Christian resistance to Hitler. He rejected an opportunity to flee his country and teach theology in a prestigious American university, choosing instead to stay and suffer with his people. He was arrested, imprisoned, and later put to death by the German authorities.

His *Letters and Papers from Prison* and other writings show his own clear understanding of and abhorrence for the Nazi horror; but his determined Christian faith led him to a radically different conclusion from those voiced by Elie Wiesel about God's relationship to anguished people. Bonhoeffer believed in a suffering God who suffered on behalf of and with his people. "It was a good thing to learn early that God and suffering are not opposite but rather one and the same thing and necessarily so; for me the idea that God Himself suffers is far and away the most convincing piece of Christian doctrine."

Bonhoeffer believed that in some difficult-to-comprehend way it was God himself who came into the world and died. He believed

Paul's statement: "in Christ God was reconciling the world to himself" (2 Cor. 5:19).

Centuries earlier the prophet Isaiah had foretold the coming of a Messiah who would be a suffering servant:

> He was despised and rejected by men, a man of sorrows, and familiar with suffering. Like one from whom men hide their faces he was despised, and we esteemed him not. Surely he took up our infirmities and carried our sorrows, yet we considered him stricken by God, smitten by him, and afflicted. But he was pierced for our transgressions, he was crushed for our iniquities; the punishment that brought us peace was upon him, and by his wounds we are healed. We all, like sheep, have gone astray, each of us has turned to his own way; and the LORD has laid on him the iniquity of us all (Isa. 53: 3-6).

If we understood how sin separates us from the God who wants fellowship with his special creation — man — then perhaps we'd understand more about the tension between his wrath and love, his justice, and his mercy. Maybe then Elie Wiesel could understand that God was on the gallows with that young boy as sinful men displayed their inhumanity.

A striking statue of Jesus stands high, 2,310 feet, above the city of Rio de Janeiro in Brazil. Called the Christ of Corcovado, it is visited not only by tourists, but also by poor Brazilians from the *favelas,* or slums of Rio. They seek consolation and help by religious devotion, seeming to plead, "Come down with us, Jesus, into our destitution and poverty and help us. Be concerned. Do not remain aloof in your splendor up here. Come and restore our faith." Yet the cry of the poor has been heard. As Jesus said, "I came down from glory. I have lived among you and I do live among you. I have demonstrated my love through pouring myself out for you. I know of your tribulation, but be encouraged; take heart. I have overcome the world" (cf. John 1:14; 16:33).

John Stott says, "I could never myself believe in God, if it were not for the cross. In the real world of pain, how could one worship a God who was immune to it?" Even Rabbi Kushner accepts that "Christianity introduced the world to the idea of a God who suffers."

Close your eyes and visit Calvary for a moment. You see a rejected, writhing, abandoned figure on that cross. Nails cruelly pierce his hands and feet. His body has been severely beaten; he is bruised and bleeding. Blood drips from the jagged thorns circling his fore-head. But he hangs there willingly (John 10:18).

This is an involved God. From now on all human suffering must be understood in the light of his suffering; it is the source of meaning, hope, and new life for sufferers. When someone cries out, "He doesn't care. He's immune to pain," he is brought to the foot of the cross to see for himself. "Perhaps suffering poses the fundamental test for theology in our time." If that is true, then God's self-giving, in the cross of Jesus and in his resurrection from the dead, is the place where the test is effectively met.

The cross and resurrection hold the key to the mystery of suffering, and while all doesn't become immediately clear, something occurs there that forever affects human suffering. "The God disclosed to the disciples in Jesus Christ was victorious over all evil. The suffering love that they had encountered in him had triumphed over sin, pain, and death. The ultimate power in the universe is the love of God, and fulfillment of his righteous will is on the way."

In Jesus, God "broke the power of death and showed us the way of everlasting life" (2 Tim. 1:10, LB). Because God is good and his power is stronger than death, believers can have confidence that produces the ability to endure and offers a purposefulness to their suffering experiences.

In *Dark Threads the Weaver Needs*, Herbert Lockyer encourages believers because of God's action in his Son, not to "forget that the pattern we fail to see of our perplexities is up there — a pattern fashioned by divine love and wrought out by divine wisdom." Now, when we don't understand, we can trust because we know who God is and that he is for us.

Once I drove to a small Texas town to attend the funeral of the father of a valued coworker. The man died unexpectedly, and the sudden loss was especially hard on his family. I listened as the minister spoke words of comfort to the family.

"We know John is all right because God loves him so much. God knows we're experiencing great pain because we don't have him with us. But John will have a new body the next time we see him. His was worn out and hurt. His new one won't experience sadness, won't know sorrow, will not encounter pain. We know this because that's what God promised, and we know he'll keep his promises because of what Jesus did for us."

I was witnessing real consolation. The minister obviously knew John and understood the family's grief and loss. He also knew God and had great confidence in who God is. He knew God cared. He knew God was going to do something about it; in fact, he already had dealt decisively with death. He was a compassionate man with a compassionate message that was not only comforting, but true!

Why is God silent? Why doesn't he intervene? He has. He has spoken, and he has acted. We still experience personal tragedies and calamities that force us to cry from the depths of our heart, but in the midst of our cry we can know that he is present. Our redemption has been secured. We and all creation groan in our suffering as we await God's new day (Rom. 8:18-25). Yet we can know that "God is at the helm of the universe . . . there is firm basis for belief in the sustaining power of God's sacrificial love and in the future to which He leads us."

I believe strongly in personal responsibility — the power of choices. That's why I emphasize that each of us chooses how we will respond when suffering touches us. We can rebel, which leads to cynicism and despair. We can passively resign and wait to die. Or we can trust and affirm the God who has loving purposes. Because of Jesus Christ's life, death, and resurrection I am choosing trust, even in the dark days.

After Jesus cried out, "My God, my God, why . . . ?" he said, "Father, into your hands I commit my spirit" (Mark 15:34; Luke 23:46). In his deepest anguish he called God "Father." His disciples had run away; God had abandoned him; he was dying one of the cruelest deaths ever devised. Yet Jesus still trusted his Father and his purposes in all this.

Remember C.S. Lewis's statement in *The Problem of Pain*: "God speaks to us in our pleasures, speaks to us in our conscience, but shouts in our pain; it is His megaphone to rouse a deaf world." If I could be allowed to disagree with a revered source like Lewis, I would say that God's way to rouse a deaf world is by offering his own pain in the death of his Son; and his megaphone announces that he is the risen Lord. When we're hurting badly and hear this news about God, we are drawn to him. Receiving our comfort from him, we then comfort others who are racked by life's hurts.

Dr. Paul Brand, physician to lepers, courageously suggests, reflecting on Hebrews 2:10:

Instinctively, we want a God who not only knows about pain. but shares in it and is affected by our own. By looking at Jesus, we realize we have such a God. He took onto Himself the limitations of time and space and family and pain and sorrow.

Suffering a New Way

The apostle Paul, who wrote more of the New Testament than anyone, bore his suffering as an honor. In the course of his life Paul was robbed, shipwrecked, beaten, and imprisoned. He was exposed to hunger and cold and was threatened with death. Yet he bore his suffering as a badge of honor so that the "life of Jesus" could be seen by others. He was thankful that his message about Jesus was backed up by a credible life (2 Cor. 4:10-12).

In a sense Paul went through what all believers go through. He learned the paradoxes that all Christians learn by dying to self, that we rejoice in suffering — not because it's good, but because of what God does in and through it in our lives.

From Jesus' resurrection forward, suffering doesn't stop, but it is looked at differently by those who believe. There is a power in suffering and a victory over suffering that Christians experience. It is not easy to understand what I've just said. But it's true, nevertheless.

The Scottish minister and university professor at Edinburgh, James Stewart, was well known for his compassionate preaching to sufferers. Building on Hebrews 5:9, he reminded suffering people of some values or uses to which they could put their adversity. "And be very sure of this — no sorrow will have been wasted, if you come through it with a little more of the light of the Lord visible in your face and shining in your soul . . . the creative attitude toward suffering . . . [is to] develop your own character [and] become a source of blessing and of strength to others."

Furthermore, he says, "because of the cross, God is in it [suffering] with you . . . . When I look upon the cross [I see] the sufferer hanging there is not just another martyr dying for his faith, but God incarnate." Thus, believers can "count it all joy" when they experience trials because they relate them to their faith in God as Father (Jas. 1:2). Or as Paul says, "In all these things we are more than conquerors through him who loved us" (Rom. 8:37).

Paul says that nothing (trouble, hardship, famine, nakedness, danger, or sword) can separate us from the love of God.

Believers can look to this God who keeps his promises, especially that "in everything God works for good with those who love him, who are called according to his purpose" (Rom. 8:28, RSV). That's why William Barclay encouraged troubled Christians to pray, "Help me to be very sure that, whatever happens, I do not have to face it alone."

Paul told Christians in Thessalonica that when they were heavy with grief over the death of loved ones, they grieved differently than those who had no hope. They grieved in light of what God had done in Jesus, with a heavy but not hopeless heart.

Living in the In-Between

The Spirit himself testifies with our spirit that we are God's children. Now if we are children, then we are heirs — heirs of God and co-heirs with Christ, if indeed we share in his sufferings in order that we may also share in his glory.

I consider that our present sufferings are not worth comparing with the glory that will be revealed in us. The creation waits in eager expectation for the sons of God to be revealed. For the creation was subjected to frustration, not by its own choice, but by the will of the one who subjected it, in hope that the creation itself will be liberated from its bondage to decay and brought into the glorious freedom of the children of God.

We know that the whole creation has been groaning as in the pains of childbirth right up to the present time. Not only so, but we ourselves, who have the firstfruits of the Spirit, groan inwardly as we wait eagerly for our adoption as sons, the redemption of our bodies (Rom. 8:16-23).

God has our time in his hands, and because we have confidence that he is working his plan, we patiently wait. We long to be with him to celebrate the victory as his children. But we are living *between* the *accomplished fact* of redemption and the time when that redemption will be *fully made known*. We anticipate. We live with real hope. We live by the power of his Spirit, which is God's gift to his children. But we live with the *not yet*. What is ahead for us outweighs the afflictions of the present.

Paul says:

(1) Creation groans because evil, though defeated, still produces suffering. It's in its last gasp. God is going to redeem it fully so it will respond fully to his purposes (cf. 2 Pet. 3:13).

(2) Christians are God's children and have his spirit, but there is so much more in store for them. "The body of humiliation will be transformed into the likeness of Christ's glorified body, when the whole personality will finally experience the benefits of His redemptive work."

(3) Christians must wait in this hope, "accept the trials of the present, so that by patient endurance they may win their lives."

(4) In today's afflictions God's spirit intercedes to help believers. Paul knew his hardships had helped further God's work and his pains "were the means by which the power of Christ rested upon him" (2 Cor. 12:9 ff.). Everything was affected negatively by the fall of man through sin — everything is being restored because of Christ. Dr. Everett Harrison says, "Scripture does not tell us much of *what* that glory will be, but it assures us *that* it will be." We're given just a glimpse, but one that excites and draws us toward it.

I remember Nannie Lewis Frith, a severely affected multiple sclerosis patient. Her days were filled with limitations because her gnarled hands and legs wouldn't allow her freedom of movement. However, I remember her not for her limitations and physical appearance but for her expectant, soaring spirit. If anyone should have despised the present moment, it should have been Nannie; but she would have none of that. For her the present was a time of purpose, even in the midst of anguish. Her God was a God who, because he guaranteed the future, was powerful enough to fill the present with purpose and joy. She looked confidently to the future when the shackles on her body would be broken, but she believed that the "present time is of the utmost importance" (Rom. 13:11, Phillips).

For others, like Carol T., physical pain is complicated by mental anguish. She told me, "My husband and teenage children ignore me because I'm sick and can't do anything for them. They use the house as a stopover place for quick meals and changes of clothes. Their lives go on. They are ashamed of what has happened to me, and they no longer treat me like I have a mind or feelings at all. How can I stand this rejection? I'm no good to God or anybody else." The pain of her waiting is incredibly agonizing. The hours of the day are seemingly endless times in which she wonders, "Why do I have to wait? Where is God's will? There's nothing here but utter darkness."

I spent hours in Carol's living room talking about possible reasons for her suffering. I tried to comfort and console her by telling her how much God loved her, how Jesus would see her through. She dismissed this rather quickly until I finally said, "Carol, I believe God sent me to you today as a visible symbol of his love. I believe also, as one who has suffered only a little, that it comes down to this: you've made a decision of your will to trust God, and you are being overwhelmed with feelings of isolation, loneliness, and lack of purpose. Now I'm going to ask you to go a step beyond your own situation. I want to ask you to encourage a cancer patient in Texas who feels the way you do. Send her a short note, and ask God to ease her pain. Be God's person for her time of need, Carol. You can do this while you wait on God for your own needs."

At first she looked at me sternly; then a smile came to her face and she said, "I'll try."

Today Carol is still living in the in-between, still living with enormous ,rejection; yet she is trying to give love *until* . . . . Life's challenging and draining experiences call believers to depend on the resources of God's spirit to help them wait purposefully until God's *kairos* — his eternal timetable — is given.

Helen Keller believed that "so long as you can sweeten another's pain, life is not in vain." This is what we do when we find ourselves, as Bernhard Anderson writes, "living in the interim between the inauguration of God's kingdom and its final realization, between the first break of dawn and the full light of day."

Jesus as Teacher and Example

Jesus was made like us in every respect, so he understands the sufferings of flesh and blood people (Heb. 2:17). He experienced the kind of life situations that caused him tears, and he prayed in those depressing and distressing times of his life (Heb. 5:7). Thus, sufferers can fix their eyes on Jesus because he knows how to be faithful during hard times, and he'll help them endure as they run to win life's race (Heb. 12:1-7).

We can look to Jesus both as mentor and model as we face life's losses. He's not an outsider giving advice; he has been a human being. He really cares. He knows that resources are available to us to help us make it. The late E.H. Ijams loved to say that Jesus gives us "power to survive and surpass." Jesus knows about being reject-ed by people who used to think we were great. He knows how to deal with people who only want to be with us in order to use us.

He knows how to nurture the inner life of the human spirit while our physical bodies are facing limitation and pain. He knows how to return good for evil. He knows what it feels like to pray when we're so anxious that we're sweating. He knows all about the "cup of suffering." He not only knows how to live, he knows how to die. And he is willing to teach those who ask him.

Lewis Cassals, in *The Real Jesus*, says that Jesus knew how to trust God and to wait in trust for God to accomplish his purposes. Now he offers each follower a special relationship with God similar to his own. There's no better teacher than someone who (a) knows what he's talking about; (b) has been through it; (c) loves you and is eager to work with you until you can do it well too. That's why Jesus is looked to as the perfect teacher about suffering.

Dr. Neil Lightfoot, in *Jesus Christ Today*, describes the Christians to whom Hebrews is addressed as people in need of encouragement. They had suffered many losses and "hope itself was fading from view." Some felt God had forgotten them and could not be counted on to keep his promises. But, the writer agues, Jesus came to earth to identify with us. He suffered because it was appropriate that a Savior suffer with suffering people. When believers suffer hardships, they have a Savior who really understands what they are going through. He's not like someone who is unable to sympathize with their weakness; he has been through the fire of trials and temptations (Heb. 4:14). In fact, "although he was a son, he learned obedience from what he suffered" (Heb. 5:8). "Although a Son, He still had to suffer. This was consequence of His incarnation and an essential qualification of leadership." He can lead us because he is especially qualified. He knows how to do God's will through submission in hard times, even when he'd prefer to do something else. He accepted a terrible bitter death, the worst suffering, as his Father's will. And because of his willing suffering, Jesus now has the power to be the source of salvation to us (Heb. 5:9).

Paul said, "Therefore God has highly exalted him and bestowed on him the name which is above every name that at the name of Jesus every knee should bow, in heaven and on earth and under the earth, and every tongue confess that Jesus Christ is Lord, to the glory of God the Father" (Phil. 2:9-11, RSV). So Jesus, who offered himself willingly as sacrifice for man's sin, is Lord. He understands the human situation totally. Lightfoot writes that the Hebrew writer, "purposely exposes the grim reality of Jesus' sufferings. He points to Gethsemane; for if ever there was a time when Jesus was surrounded with weakness, it was there. There he urgently prayed that death's cup might be withheld. But if this had been granted, he would not have been like his brothers [us] in all respects."

Jesus didn't have it easy. He knew severe suffering. He cried out for relief. "He suffered as few men have been called upon to suffer." He trusted God when it was dark, and he didn't fully understand. That's why I accept him fully as my teacher and my example in many areas, but especially in suffering. He knows the secrets to endurance. That's why I'm carefully studying him.

Peter told suffering Christians, who certainly felt life was unfair, that the way Jesus suffered was an example to them:

> . . . Christ suffered for you, leaving you an example, that you should follow in his steps.
> He committed no sin . . . .
> When they hurled their insults at him, he did not retaliate; when he suffered, he made no threats. Instead, he entrusted himself to him who judges justly. He himself bore our sins in his body on the tree, so that we might die to sins and live for righteousness; by his wounds you have been healed (1 Peter 2:20-24).

I have received letters like the following from cancer patients who feel they are suffering unjustly.

> I can't understand why I am in this condition. And other people in the world are free, drinking, gambling, and other wrong doings, not being Christian and never sick. *Charlene P.*

> I know the pain and depths [that] despair and hopelessness can throw us into. Especially when it seems our battles are endless. . . . I want to shake my fist at God and say, "Why? Why do you let your servants suffer? We who love you and are so loyal. You have the power to protect us. Why don't you? Why?" *Julie T.*

> I shook my fist at God for standing quietly by while the substance of my life was squeezed from me like the squeezing of the inside from a grape. I was angry because the heart of my life was gone. I despaired because the taking was permanent. *Jim V.*

What do we say to them? I say, God understands how you feel. Innocent suffering drains the life from all of us. But God cares about your suffering and the suffering of those you love, and he has done something about it. Trust him. God will vindicate you. He will do justice as his plan comes to full development. Look to Jesus. He will give you the grace to make it through. He will show you a way through your suffering. He suffered and died not only to provide salvation, but to establish *a way to live* in a suffering world.

(1) God knows you are innocent and suffering unjustly.

(2) Jesus' suffering is a model or pattern to be copied.

(3) Yes, it is unjust, but you can trust that God will make it just one day.

(4) Don't retaliate. Control your tongue and trust. The innocent must also be patient.

(5) Remember, Jesus died for you to be able to live this way.

I don't know many suffering believers who have it all together, in the sense that they don't struggle from time to time with doubts. However, my reading of the Psalms and the life of Jesus convinces me that struggling with doubt is far from unhealthy; in fact, it may be a good sign that we are seeking an honest, reliable faith.

I also want to add a word of encouragement to those who sometimes feel, "It's not true," or "God isn't here." Don't be shocked by your wavering. Admit it. God isn't shocked, and I'm convinced that he isn't disappointed in you. Wrestle with your faith and your doubts honestly. Keep seeking. Remember what I said earlier: God can deal with the full range of human emotions.

Disappointment in God isn't a terminal condition. You will come out on the other side after your horrible pain recedes some. You will believe again. Why? Because in the midst of suffering we *know* that God our Father truly loves us.

SECTION THREE
QUESTIONS ABOUT SALVATION

It hardly needs to be said that the doctrine of salvation (soteriology) plays a critical role in theology. By addressing different issues, these three articles form a coherent progression of questions about salvation that must be answered.

First, Waymon Hinson asks us to consider the human condition. Are we basically good or evil? Are we in need of salvation? By comparing the biblical view of human beings with other philosophical, psychological, and sociological views, he calls us to a realistic evaluation of our situation before God.

Mark Black then leads us on an examination of the role of grace and works in our salvation and subsequent life. Can we do anything for ourselves? Or is it entirely in God's hands? Are good works the result or the cause of salvation? What would the absence of obedience mean?

The section is then brought to a close by Mike Moss who asks whether Christians can be sure of their salvation. Must we live in constant fear of damnation for a misdeed or impure thought, or is there a way to find security without encouraging more "sins that grace may abound"?

The old joke about the cheer going up at judgment day on the discovery that "Wednesday nights don't count" is a grim and not very funny reminder of the unease about salvation that underlies much of our activity. Hopefully, these articles will provide some insight that will lead to joyful discipleship.

Chapter Eight

What does it mean to be human?

Waymon R. Hinson
Abilene Christian University
Abilene, Texas

Jean Valjean, thief, victim, and saint in Victor Hugo's *Les Misérables*, leaves prison, steals from a priest who forgives his misdeed, and eventually becomes both mayor of Montreuil and a successful entrepreneur. His life is complicated by a host of characters including Fantine and her illegitimate child, Cossette, but most of all by Javert, an incorruptible and obsessive policeman who seeks to punish Valjean for his past. In his former life Valjean symbolizes the dark side of humanity, but in his new life he represents the good in people as he rescues the downtrodden, endows a hospital, protects a parentless child, and avoids the relentless pursuit of Javert. Javert, the symbol of law and order who is tormented by his own demand for perfection, eventually commits suicide while Valjean dies in the presence of those whose lives he has blessed. The contrast between the two characters is striking; one man evolved from thief to saint, while the other went from rigid orthodoxy to despair and suicide.

Victor Hugo was not alone in his quest to explore the nature of human beings. Literature, television, the movie theater, and everyday life remind us of the struggle between good and evil in both human societies and individual human hearts. Stories of horror haunt the history books and the six o'clock news. The ethnic cleansing of the Holocaust costs six million innocent Jews their lives. Over one million innocent people are murdered in Rwanda. Teenagers are gunned down in a Kentucky school, as are the middle schoolers and their Christian teacher in Arkansas. Off the screen the husband assaults his wife, the uncle sexually abuses his niece, and the aunt sells drugs to her nephew.

And yet, despite the ugliness, good Samaritans are everywhere. Thousands participate in Make a Difference Day: the elderly volunteer at the local hospital, one offers a cup of cold water in the name of the Lord, a prayer is uttered or a card mailed to a grieving person, a Christian bathes the fever-racked body of a person with AIDS, and a woman leaves her warm bed and goes immediately next door upon hearing that her neighbor's nephew has been killed.

What are we to make of these conflicting pictures of human beings? People, both individually and collectively, are indeed rather mysterious, possessing capacities for rationality and irrationality, civil behaviors and acts of savagery, warm and engaging friendships and heated and distant hostilities; people are the ultimate of God's creation and creation's worst enemy. It is too simple to say that some people are good and some are bad. Good and evil wage a war in the heart of each individual. Paul's self-revelation fits all, "I do not understand what I do. For what I want to do I do not do, but what I hate I do" (Rom. 7:15).

In order to unravel the mystery of the human contradiction, we must ask and answer several questions: What does it mean to be a human? Do Adam, Eve, and the Garden inform us of our humanity? Does contemporary psychology have any perspectives from which we can learn? Is human nature essentially good, bad, or some paradoxical mixture of the two? And finally, once we decide upon a view of human nature, what then are our moral obligations? To answer these questions, we must compare several theories about the nature of humanity.

Theories of Human Nature:
Contemporary and Not-so-contemporary Perspectives

Theories are not facts, but they do help us organize and interpret the information we have at hand. Some theories of human nature are plausible, and others are rather far-fetched. According to Leslie Stevenson in *Seven Theories of Human Nature*, rival theories about human nature have five key themes in common. First, each theory places a claim on how to view the universe. Second, each attempts to describe the essential nature of people, both individually and collectively. Third, each attempts to diagnose what is wrong with humankind. Fourth, each provides different answers to the woes of human life. And last, each has an organization that claims authority on the teachings and the practice of that theory.

While sacred and secular theories may clash, it is foolish to think that the scientist studying animals can tell us nothing about human nature; on the other hand, it is absurd to think that Genesis and other passages of Scripture can tell us nothing of who we are as human beings. Secular perspectives, while reflecting partial truths, will not go far enough and will be incomplete, inaccurate, or misleading.

Some perspectives of human nature are optimistic. They suggest that we have a spark of the divine, are naturally immortal, ethically good, and evolving into higher levels of perfection with each passing generation. On the other hand, some views of humankind are pessimistic, such as the one epitomized by Mark Twain when he called man "the only animal that blushes or needs to." Others have said that man is "what he eats," a "being unto death," and "a useless passion." Dostoevsky once commented that to describe humans in terms of "bestial cruelty" was an insult to animals, because animals are never so "artistically cruel."

On a fundamental level, the problem is that most attempts to explain human nature begin with *anthropos* (humanity) rather than *theos* (God). Beginning with God allows a perspective that originates in creation, defines the spiritual nature of our existence, gives meaning and purpose to life, and allows for the consideration of various contemporary perspectives. Even the best perspectives that begin with humanity will reflect only partial truths rather than a complete definition of human nature. Such limited views may contribute to the knowledge and understanding of people, but will ultimately fail to provide a meaningful context for viewing the person as a whole.

For instance, Plato, a Greek philosopher and student of Socrates living in Athens in the fourth century B.C., subscribed to the theory of dualism, a perspective which asserts that the immaterial, or the soul, exists apart from the body and pre-existed birth. He described a human nature that divided the soul into three parts: appetite, reason, and spirit. All three parts exist within each person, and the manner in which the person lives reflects the degree to which the person is dominated by a particular part. According to Plato's theory, defects within humans reflect defects within society and vice versa. The ills of humanity could be fixed by organizing a perfect society in which classes are clearly defined, harmonious, and stable. Since Plato believed that the body is material and bad, but the spirit is immaterial and good, he claimed that the control of the physical body, the appetite, would solve the evils found in human societies.

Karl Marx developed a different theory of human nature. A German living in the nineteenth century, Marx was born Jewish, converted to Christianity, and later abandoned all religion. His philosophies still serve as the dominant principles for communism. He believed that learning is a social phenomenon, and we acquire those behaviors that keep us alive and the species propagating. A person is different from an animal in that the person is designed to produce that which keeps him or her alive rather than conquering it, as animals do. According to his theory, if people are not able to produce what they need, the resulting lack of fulfillment alienates them. Since Marx believed that private ownership is a sign of this type of alienation, then the solution to the problems of humanity is to destroy everything and to rebuild a system in which private ownership is eliminated. Thus, according to his theory, human nature is, at its core, communal.

Another theorist, Sigmund Freud, is considered to be the father of modern day psychiatry. Living in Austria in the nineteenth century, he based his worldview on the tenets of atheistic evolution and determinism. According to Freud, nothing is accidental, not even slips of the tongue. The unconscious mind contains information not available to the conscious mind, and it uses psychic energy to influence activities. He suggested that a person's problems originated either from internal conflicts, or from conflicts between the person and the external world. His explanation of human nature, then, is pessimistic; a person's actions are determined by unconscious forces, and are therefore instinctive. The result is unpredictable behavior.

B.F. Skinner, an American-born and educated psychologist, avowed atheist and evolutionist, wed the scientific method and technology to the study of human behavior in developing another theory of what it means to be human. Very much of a materialist, Skinner insisted that only observable behaviors are appropriate to study, but that humans and animals are valid subjects for the methods of scientific research. Humans, who are creatures of time and space, can be investigated and interpreted with scientific rigor in an attempt to reduce multiple aspects of the human being to simple explanations. Skinner ignored mental events or thoughts, because they are not observable or quantifiable. He maintained that the same laws govern both human and animal behavior, and his theory of operant conditioning assumes that the environment actively reinforces behaviors that will be repeated. Thus, the study of rats or pigeons can inform scientists of human behaviors, because the human condition is behaviorally determined. According to this theory, we have very little freedom to make individual choices, although we act as if we are free to do so. What is the remedy for human ills according to the behaviorist? Change the social environment and you change human behavior. Human nature, then, is predictable, determined, and biological. We are very much like the animals.

On the other extreme, Jean Paul Sartre, a twentieth-century French philosopher, denied any such thing as human nature, insisting that one's existence is that which precedes what he called "essence." Not created for any specific purpose, Sartre says that we "simply find ourselves existing, and then have to decide what to make of ourselves." Freedom is unlimited, and our moods are how we perceive the world. Sartre described the human's moment of awareness of existence and self-hood as "anguish" and insisted that bad faith is the attempt to escape anguish by pretending to believe that we are not free and deluding ourselves with the notion that poor choices are the result of bad character rather than simply poor choices. Sartre offered no specific cure for the ailments of the human condition.

According to these human-oriented perspectives, what, then, does it mean to be human? Plato pointed to the physical and non-physical aspects of human nature, Marx insisted that we must be defined within a community, and Freud asserted that people have a mental aspect of our nature that determines and predicts what we do and who we are. Skinner wrote that we are biological creatures and therefore controllable, and Sartre pointed to the experiences of our humanity as we live in an unpredictable world. Each theory explains a part but not the whole. Yes, we are biological, spiritual, emotional, and relational. But is there more?

A Biblical Perspective on Human Nature

What, by comparison, does the Word of God present about the nature of human nature? The Bible contains no detailed, well-thought-out theology of humankind. Scripture reveals and reports aspects of human nature in a variety of ways, occasions, and time periods, not merely for its own sake, but in order to explain our relationship with God.

Themes of Creation

Developing a biblical perspective of human nature begins with the Old Testament and the creation story. The divine drama begins as the world and persons are created, allowing us a fuller picture of the goodness and creativity of God. Genesis reveals the solidarity of human life with God, with other human beings, and with the natural world. First, God creates all other living things, which makes them "creatures." All are created from nothing, and God is both generous and welcoming in his creativity. Creation is God's choice, his gracious gift in keeping with his character. God gives life without any hint of deficiency that would compel him to seek fulfillment through the act of creation. He is complete and self-sustaining, and as creatures, we are ignorant unless God acts to make himself known to us.

Second, there is the interrelatedness of God and the world he created. Nothing can stand alone. Both existence and relationship are gifts. A human-centered theology would say, "We were necessary," but a God-centered theology would assert, "We might not have been, so, our very existence is a gift from One beyond ourselves."

Third, creation, with all of its imperfections, limitations, and inadequacies, is pronounced good. God is good, and all that he creates is good (Genesis 1:10, 18, 21, 25, 31). Attempts to categorize that which is good and that which is bad fail. All of creation demands respect. "Good" does not suggest the denial of evil, however, nor does "good" deny fallenness and the necessity of reconciliation.

Themes of the Fall

The Fall also has its themes. First, people are created, like the rest of creation; but unlike the remainder of creation, we possess a mind and the freedom to determine our own course and destiny. We often reveal our freedom in the willfulness which sets the stage for the decisions we make that are in opposition to God's will. Secondly, at the Fall the first couple tested their relationship with God and experienced temptation by Satan. The Fall compels us to examine our own willful rebellion, Satan's efforts to tempt us, and our cooperation with those efforts. Third, their fall for Satan's schemes led them to see that God is indeed truthful, that if they ate, they would die (Gen. 3:3). Finally, the first couple's sin was not an isolated, private act but rather one lived out before God and all of history. It was both their literal, individual story of sin as well as the narrative of all people.

A Hebrew Perspective of Human Nature

By comparison to either ancient or contemporary views of human nature that emphasized various aspects of the person, the ancient Hebrews viewed the person as a whole. Accordingly, person and personality are one and the same, and thus no division of mind, body, and spirit exists. Hebrew writers describe humanity in the physical sense using terms such as body, dust, and breath, but they acknowledge human superiority over the animals. Mind and emotion are linked to the body as people think with their hearts, feel with their bowels, and long for God with their flesh. Thus, any artificial Platonic division of the material (flesh) as evil, and the immaterial (soul or mind) as good is absent.

Image of God

Genesis 1–3 reveals the who and the why of creation. People are the creatures, God is the creator, and we are different from God. Hierarchy is established: God is over us and we are over creation. Movement, activity, conflict, triumph, fidelity, and rebellion are all there at the beginning. Creation, when understood from God's perspective, suggests that the relationship between creator and created provides meaning and significance. God actively created and actively maintains that relationship with both the persons and the world he created.

How, then, are we to understand God's directive, "Let us make man *in our image*, in our likeness, and let them rule . . ." (Gen. 1:26)? There are several possible interpretations. Some suggest a *physical resemblance* in a depiction of God that uses human images (Gen. 3:8ff); however, Exodus 20:4 forbids images of the divine. Religious writers of the seventeenth century asserted that man has the *capacity to reason*, believing that humans participate in the divine image by the very reason that created the world. However, this perspective elevates intellect and often neglects the emotional or physical dimensions of human existence.

Others believe that humans and God are alike in their *ability to exercise dominion* over the earth. Humans serve in a manner parallel to God in exercising power and authority over creation, and the Bible clearly spells out the pattern of hierarchy of God over humankind and humans over the natural world.

Yet another possibility is the concept of *human freedom*. God's creativity is reflected in qualities seen in people: creative freedom, self-determination, and self-transcendence. A final interpretation of humanity's likeness to God is based on the necessity of *human life in relationship*. God is a God of interpersonal relationships, relating to Himself as Father, Son, and Holy Spirit from the very beginning with "let *us* make man in *our* image;" thus, God has historically related to people as God the Father, God the Son, or God the Holy Spirit. Likewise, God designed humans to function in relationships. Sexuality, expressed as male and female ("male and female created He them"), is an intimate aspect of relationship as each partner helps to complete that which God created. Humans as social beings in community round out the possible definitions of human nature.

Humanity's creation in the "image of God" indicates a unique relationship with God that transcends that of other created things. Along with God's image comes an ethical, moral, and spiritual responsibility to make good choices (Gen. 2:15-17; 3:1-7). A curious set of paradoxes exists for humans. People are both created and given a position "little lower than the heavenly beings" (Ps. 8:4). We are both aware of our dependence upon God as Creator and yet willful enough to rebel against our creatureliness. We possess the image of God, and although we cannot be God, we pretend to be more than we are. Our self-centered willfulness, and the sins that result, are at the center of our assertion that we are the end within ourselves rather than part of a greater whole.

However, this "image" with which we are stamped is not a permanent stamp but an imperfect image that we possess of that which we are ultimately to reflect. Only Jesus of Nazareth is the fullest expression of what God intended for humanity to be. He alone bears the full expression of the image of God. Scripture makes this clear when it says that Jesus is the "image of God" (2 Cor. 4:4) and calls Him "the image of the invisible God, the firstborn over all creation" (Col. 1:15).

The Entrance of Sin and Its Effects

Human beings, far from being afterthoughts, were planned for, willfully and lovingly created, and pronounced, as part of the entirety of creation, as "very good" when "God saw all that He had made, and it was very good" (Gen. 1:31). Adam and Eve realized that they were the objects of God's affection and adoration and that He asked for a covenant with them. Adam and Eve were to live as worthy partners with God. They failed and lost much in the process. Choosing to ignore God's instruction to obey Him by staying away from the tree in the middle of the garden, they willfully disobeyed, and "the eyes of both were opened" (Gen. 3:7). The image of God in human form, though perhaps not destroyed, had become somewhat tarnished. Humanity no longer bore the image in its fullness. The intimate relationship with God was broken by sin.

The tragedy of the human condition is clear (Ps. 88), and the appropriate response is lament (Ps. 51:5). The question is not simply, "Why did I do that?" but *Who am I* that I did that? *Who am I* to want to do that?" We, therefore, experience ourselves as sinners, living without the cross, desperately in need of redemption and reconciliation.

Adam and Eve, realizing they were naked, went into hiding (Gen. 3:6-10) in an attempt to quiet their anxiety and guilt. Guilt is a natural reaction to both sin and the awareness of one's sinful state. The fear led to hiding. Their desire was for autonomy, or separateness from God, and their sin achieved that end. They were alone. Prior to their sin, they were secure, loved, and confident in their relationship with God. Before the sin, no effort was needed to be who they were created to be.

With the temptation to be like God, Adam and Eve fell, and a split developed between what they were intended to be, and what they had become. Aware of the gap between the ideal and the real, they experienced anxiety in relation to the threat of God's wrath. Their sin, then, made them objectively guilty as they stood before God.

Four dimensions of estrangement occurred at the Fall. First, persons became separated from other persons by a self-centered and loveless decision. Second, we became estranged from our true selves by pursuing fragmented and inauthentic goals that excluded God. Third, we became isolated from God in a feeble attempt at self-sufficiency. And fourth, we distanced ourselves from nonhuman nature by denying the inherent value of nonhuman creation. All sin, therefore, is "a violation of relatedness."

The creation story, then, is one of contradiction and paradox, image and rebellion. Reflections of the image of God — and what we consider kind, gentle, orderly, and exhilarating — are juxtaposed with post-Fall behavior, or that which we judge to be evil, painful, cruel, and self-serving. Inescapable conflict defines the creation and the Fall, both between God and Satan and between God and humanity. Even now, after the Fall, not every moment reflects the battle. Not every thought and feeling is detestable; and yet something has been irrevocably changed. Willful humanity is not content to remain simply the created, standing in a unique relationship with God. We are not content to be merely human. We desire to go beyond God's original design for us. This dichotomy between the ideal and the real must figure in to any comprehensive conception of what it means to be human.

Pre-Fall humanity lived in God's presence with a clear sense of identity, a positive evaluation by God, and an intimate relationship with each other. Post-Fall humanity lives with anxiety and insecurity, guilt and shame, and a division emotionally, physically, and spiritually from God and each other. Only eventual restoration in Christ could remedy such a division.

What, then, are our choices, since we live with our "post-Fall condition"? We can become like the animals, getting rid of tensions via sins of aggression or sensuality. Or we can become our own "god," falling into sins of pride, seeking elevation to places where we do not belong, seeking security in power, intellectualism, materialism, or social relations. Or we can become persons of faith, fully aware of our humanity but relying on God.

One theologian wrote that sin is "inevitable but not necessary." We are responsible for our choices, but the deck is stacked against us. Thus, three paradoxes exist when we consider the goodness of creation as determined by God himself and the seriousness of sin. First, sin, though a universal condition, is an act we choose and one for which we are responsible. Second, sin sometimes masquerades as something good. And last, sin corrupts the individual as well as actively and powerfully infecting public life.

There are three basic ways to describe sin based on the biblical depiction of humanity. The softest description is a social one, that we live in a bad world in which evil abounds, and we are disadvantaged because of Adam. The hardest is that we have inherited guilt, with the sin of Adam being passed on to us - that we are born sinful via our biology. A more moderate description is that we have an inherited tendency, that we are "ontologically tainted," or stained in our character, and as a result we are different from the pre-Fall Adam, but we have not inherited the sin of Adam. We are free to choose.

Biblical Words for Human Nature

The quest for a biblical understanding of human nature is further complicated by the many terms for various aspects of human nature found in Scripture. Are we dichotomists who believe in body and mind and their separateness? Or, are we trichotomists who believe in the division of the human being into three parts: body, mind, and spirit? Perhaps we believe in the wholeness of human nature. The following biblical terms help to clarify the biblical view of human nature.

Nephesh. The person is a "living being" (Gen. 35:18; 1 Kgs. 17:21), like cattle or any other animal, in that we eat, breathe, reproduce, and die. This word most frequently refers to the concrete, physical individual, the total life of a person, with his or her own biology and inner emotional/mental life.

Ruach. Translated "spirit" or "breath" (Gen. 6:17), *ruach* refers to that which God breathes into the dirt to give it life, creating in the process a living person, not merely a thing.

Psyche. "Psyche," or "soul," refers to a person's internal spiritual being or personal life (1 Thess. 2:8; 5:23; Rom. 13:1) rather than serving as a description of a third separate part of human nature.

Pneuma. This word, translated "spirit," may simply indicate the self, the whole person, a person's higher nature which is neither good nor bad, but which is capable of defilement (2 Cor. 7:1) or of consecration (1 Cor. 7:34). The spiritual person is one who is wholly dependent upon God.

Kardia. "Heart" is used primarily to describe the emotional and volitional aspects of the person (Rom. 10:10; 2 Cor. 4:6; Eph. 1:18). The heart in which one's spiritual life is rooted influences one's moral conduct and can only be changed through Jesus Christ (Eph. 4:16-19).

Nous. The "mind," or intellect, is not exalted above the person. Each person possesses a mind which has both intellectual aspects and aspects that can be renewed by conforming to God (1 Cor. 2:16). Renewal of the mind follows Christian conversion as the believer is equipped to discern God's will more accurately than before.

The Wholeness of Humanity

Both the Old and New Testaments present humans as whole beings. Rather than any arbitrary division into parts, a theology of the wholeness of humanity allows one to hear Jesus tell the questioner in Matthew 22 to "love the Lord your God with all your heart and with all your soul and with all your mind" as a command to "love God with your entire being" (verse 37). Also, Paul's admonition in I Thessalonians 5, to keep the "whole spirit, soul and body . . . blameless at the coming of our Lord Jesus Christ" (verse 23) is viewed as a piling up of attributes of the whole person, not as an indication of internal division.

Spirituality: A Missing Dimension

A theology of spirituality is only occasionally added to the descriptions of human nature. David Benner outlines three subtypes of spirituality. "Natural spirituality" is that which all of us have by nature of being a human being in a big world. We possess a "religious spirituality" when we are attached in meaningful ways to an organized effort to approach God. But the third type, "Christian spirituality," reveals itself in an intentional relationship with Jesus Christ. Broadly speaking, spirituality suggests that we yearn for something greater than ourselves. It is both our yearning and our response to God's call to a relationship with him. We look beyond ourselves and surrender our will to his. In *Addiction & Grace*, Gerald May asserts that God created us by love, in love, and for love. As his creation, we have within us a space that only God can fill. In our wanderings through life, we pursue objects, behaviors, or relationships in an attempt to fill that space. By doing so we become idolaters, thus "addicted," or sinners, and in need of "recovery" and Jesus Christ. True healing occurs when we surrender our chosen attachments, which are actually counterfeits. God then frees us to seek him and him only. We move from a willful, self-centered life to one in which we invite God to do the leading.

What Humanity Should Be: Jesus Christ

A theology of human nature is incomplete without an understanding of the incarnation of Jesus Christ. Jesus as the one perfect, undistorted image of God models what a true human being should be (Col. 1:15-20). He confronts us, pushing us to be transformed (Rom. 12:1, 2). He both restores creation and reconciles humanity to God at the same time. Taking humanness upon himself, he became like us in order to redeem us. In Jesus, God, the creator, redeems those whose relationship with him had been shattered, reclaiming those who were created to be his own. The church facilitates that transformation by our participation in it.

In Jesus we know what it means to be human as humanity was intended to be. Our brokenness affects our relationship with God, ourselves, and other human beings. Jesus claims authority over us, calls us to rebirth, and insists that we reenter into a new definition of humanity. He is the vicarious substitute for our sins, and "by his wounds we are healed" (Isaiah 53:5).

A definition of human nature informed by Jesus Christ and the cross insists that we recognize the seriousness of sin and its effects upon humanity. Humankind, the pinnacle of God's creation, became self-centered, sinned, and created a chasm of estrangement between us and God. God's choice was to reconcile us to himself through the cross.

A nontheological view of human nature leaves humans holding the final word. However, a theological view of human nature begins with God and incorporates the person to whom God has revealed himself. Humanity must come under the radical grace of God. Jesus is himself the turning point for a true theology of human nature. The cross weaves together God, sin, and human createdness. When Jesus hangs on the cross, sin is confronted as an aberration of what God intended for people and relationships to be. God's expectation for atonement is realized. Jesus of Nazareth is crucified, and Christ the Lord is resurrected.

What, Then, Is Human Nature? Good? Evil? Both?

Scripture presents a set of curious paradoxes about human nature: we are created in the image of God but are lost sinners (Gen. 1:27; Rom. 3:10-12); we were ejected from the Garden but pursued by the Loving Father (Gen. 3:23; Luke 15:11-32)); we have been admonished not to live by the works of the flesh but by the fruit of the Spirit (Gal. 5:16-26); and like Peter we have denied Jesus (John 18:27) but we have been instructed, like Peter, to follow him (John 21:19). Like Jean Valjean and Javert in *Les Misérables*, we are all both good and bad, behave lovingly and disrespectfully, serve both God and ourselves with equal intensity, and possess instincts to bless and to curse. Our most important decision is to surrender to Jesus, to die to ourselves.

What, Then, Is Our Obligation?

A theological view of human nature demands a response. When we know that we are created in the image of God, even though we are fallen, self-centered, and self-seeking, then we are free to act. The biblical view of human nature makes our obligations clear. We must subdue the natural world God created and treat it respectfully, live graciously with other human beings, live under the cross as redeemed persons, and call other people to surrender to Jesus the Christ. By doing so we can understand what it means to be a human, created in the image of God, in a world which is estranged from God but never forgotten by the creator.

Chapter Nine

Are Christians saved
by grace, faith, or works?

Mark Black
Lipscomb University
Nashville, Tennessee

The Problem

Are Christians saved by works? At first reading, James and Paul appear to give opposite answers. Paul writes, "For by grace you have been saved through faith; and this is not your own doing, it is the gift of God — not because of works, lest any man should boast" (Eph. 2:8-9, RSV). James almost seems to reply to Paul when he writes, "You see that a man is justified by works and not by faith alone" (Jas. 2:24, RSV). How can both be right? More to the point, how can Paul be right? James' argument seems to make more sense.

The natural human assumption is that we are and should be judged by our actions. After all, the effective and productive worker gets the promotion. It is the most competent athlete who gets to play. The student with good grades gets the scholarship. Furthermore, we have little sympathy for those who fail because they put forth no effort or, even worse, break the rules. Some workers deserve to be fired. Some players deserve to sit on the bench. Some students deserve to fail. Shouldn't those who live by God's standards be rewarded, and shouldn't those who don't be punished?

There are many biblical passages, even in the New Testament, which associate salvation with good works. Earlier in the passage cited above James writes:

> What does it profit, my brethren, if a man says he has faith but has not works? Can his faith save him? If a brother or sister is ill-clad and in lack of daily food, and one of you says to them, "Go in peace, be warmed and filled," without giving them the things needed for

the body, what does it profit? So faith by itself, if it has no works, is dead (Jas. 2:14-17, RSV).

James is in good company when he takes this view. Jesus also clearly links salvation with "doing," when he says:

> And every one who hears these words of mine and does not do them will be like a foolish man who built his house upon the sand; and the rain fell, and the floods came, and the winds blew and beat against that house, and it fell; and great was the fall of it (Matt. 7:26-27, RSV).

Similarly, in Matthew 25:31-46 it is those who have fed the hungry, clothed the naked, cared for the ill, and visited the imprisoned who are invited into his presence. Those who failed to do these good works are cast out. In other words, doing God's will (often called simply "obedience") is a necessary part of the Christian life.

Even Paul seems to suggest on occasion that people will be judged by their actions. In Romans 2:6 he writes, "God 'will give to each person according to what he has done.'" Seven verses later he writes, "It is not those who hear the law who are righteous in God's sight, but it is those who obey the law who will be declared righteous." However, these are not Paul's most typical comments relative to works and the law.

Paul's most common perspective on works is that expressed in Romans 3:20: "For no human being will be justified in his sight by works of the law" (RSV). Paul makes it quite clear in many passages that all are sinful and therefore lawbreakers. Even the most conscientious and best of people fall far short of the standard. ". . . I have already charged that all men, both Jews and Greeks, are under the power of sin" (Rom. 3:9, RSV).

Paul is not alone in his perspective on works. The point of Jesus' parable of the Pharisee and the tax collector (Luke 18:9-14) was to warn "some who trusted in themselves that they were righteous and despised others" (RSV). The self-acknowledged sinner "went down to his house justified," not the Pharisee who fasted, tithed, and did not steal or commit adultery. The parable of the prodigal son teaches the same lesson: God forgives and accepts those who realize their own failure to live up to the standard. Those who trust in their own ability to do God's will refuse to accept God's forgiveness. They want righteousness the old fashioned way, by earning it.

Saved by Works?

The confusion surrounding the grace and works discussion is understandable. There would appear to be New Testament passages on both sides of the argument. Yet salvation by grace excludes salvation by works, doesn't it? Is it possible that the New Testament writers disagree on this question? Or is there some other solution?

One solution might be to distinguish between "works of the law," such as circumcision, and "good works," such as caring for orphans and widows and keeping oneself unstained from the world. Perhaps Paul is really saying that the ritual laws of Moses can never save. However, Paul nowhere makes this clear distinction between ritual and moral laws, and he points out that the law itself is "holy and just and good" (Rom. 7:12). Paul believes no one can live up to the high moral standard of the law. He uses the example of coveting (a "moral" law) in Romans 7:7-11 when discussing human inability to keep God's law. He is himself the great proof of the point, being the one who lived in all good conscience and yet persecuted the church of God. Even as a Christian, he knows that he comes up short of the standard (Phil. 3:12-14).

Another solution might be to argue that Christians are initially saved by grace but are kept saved by doing right. However, Paul attacked this exact view when he wrote to the Galatians, "Are you so foolish? After beginning with the Spirit, are you now trying to attain your goal by human effort?" (3:3) A close reading of Paul's letters will convince the reader that he meant just exactly what he appeared to be saying. There is absolutely no room for boasting in any human achievement, before or after conversion. No one will be saved by good works or righteousness. Paul was quite serious when he wrote that he wanted to be "found in [Christ], not having a righteousness . . . that comes from the law, but that which is through faith in Christ — the righteousness that comes from God and is by faith" (Phil. 3:9).

At the same time, few matters are more important for Paul than doing what is right, keeping the law's demands, being obedient (Rom. 2:15; 8:4). He knew that God desires good works. He knew the utter tragedy brought about by evil works and disobedience. In fact, as we will later see, Paul even argues that we are created to do good works. How can Paul argue both for and against good works?

It is helpful to ask at this point, "How are people motivated to do what is truly good?" The common sense answer is, "People need rules (standards), supported by rewards and punishments." However, Paul argues that common sense (human thinking) is not God's thinking. Paul's inspired teaching was that rules do not and cannot create righteousness for a number of reasons. First, humans are completely sold into sin. They are incapable of doing what is right apart from the Spirit of God. The true standard is far above human ability to grasp, much less abide by. Even the aging and mature Paul himself knew that he had not reached the standard of the self-giving love and goodness of Jesus Christ (Phil. 3:12-14). Only the least introspective Christian with the shallowest understanding of the standard set by Jesus could claim to meet that standard.

A second problem with the rule-keeping approach is that human sinfulness perverts the rules themselves (no matter how holy and good the rules). The rules then become a source of pride, arrogance, and independence from God, all the epitome of sin. This is how Paul describes himself in his pre-Christian days:

> If any other man thinks he has reason for confidence in the flesh, I have more: circumcised on the eighth day, of the people of Israel, of the tribe of Benjamin, a Hebrew born of Hebrews; as to the law a Pharisee, as to zeal a persecutor of the church, as to righteousness under the law blameless. But whatever gain I had, I counted as loss for the sake of Christ. Indeed I count everything as loss because of the surpassing worth of knowing Christ Jesus my Lord. For his sake I have suffered the loss of all things, and count them as refuse, in order that I may gain Christ and be found in him, not having a righteousness of my own, based on law, but that which is through faith in Christ, the righteousness from God that depends on faith (Phil. 3:4-9, RSV).

Finally, Paul argues that the works approach actually increases the amount of sin. Although the law itself is holy, sin uses the law to arouse our passions and lead us to sin. He writes in Romans 7:7-8, "What then shall we say? That the law is sin? By no means! Yet, if it had not been for the law, I should not have known sin. I should not have known what it is to covet if the law had not said, "You shall not covet." But sin, finding opportunity in the commandment, wrought in me all kinds of covetousness" (RSV).

So the rule-keeping approach, even with the highest of standards, cannot produce genuinely good works. We might want to ask Paul at this point, "Are humans even capable of doing what is right? And, if not works, what do people contribute to their salvation?" Surely, we must do something.

Saved by Grace?

Paul argues that since we cannot merit our salvation by doing right, then salvation can only be received as a gift. The ground or basis of justification, therefore, is pure grace. It is important here that we distinguish between the ground, or basis, of salvation, and that which accompanies salvation or is a result of salvation. Paul contends that humans can do nothing to contribute to the basis on which salvation is given. Salvation is based on righteousness, but it is not our righteousness but rather that of Jesus Christ. It is given purely as a gift, the gift we call grace.

As radical as this sounds, this is the teaching of Paul. It is precisely the radical nature of this teaching that led some who heard him to argue that Christians should "go on sinning, so that grace may increase" (Rom. 6:1). Paul, of course, denies that this is the logical conclusion of his doctrine of grace, but he nowhere dilutes the doctrine. He writes in Galatians 2:21, "If justification were through the law, then Christ died to no purpose" (RSV).

If this is true, what does it imply about good works? Does God save irrespective of a person's efforts to be good? And what is the role of human faith? Are we not saved by our faith? Surely, we must do something.

Saved by Faith?

Grace is a completely free gift, but it must be accepted; it is forced upon no one. The acceptance of the gift is simply called faith. Faith has an objective and a subjective element. It is belief that Jesus died for sins and was raised, and it is trust that our sins have been removed. In other words, faith is our recognition that we have nothing to offer God and that we have no hope outside that offered because of the righteousness of Jesus Christ. It is also our complete confidence that God accepts us on the basis of the death and resurrection of Jesus.

Faith is the human side of the salvation equation. While we thus "do something," Paul contrasts this something with works: "Faith . . . not works, lest any man should boast" (Eph. 2:9). Faith by definition is a claim to be without meritorious good works. But faith is not meritorious either. It is our confession of our utter lack of merit.

Theologians debate whether or not faith is also a gift from God. Churches of Christ have traditionally maintained that faith is truly a human response. Note, however, that there is some mystery involved, that it is wholly a response to God's initiative and that it is not a thing of "merit." One can no more boast of faith than of works. And yet there can be no salvation apart from the acceptance of salvation through faith.

What Role Do Works Play?

This brings us back to our original question; if grace is God's free gift and faith is simply our response of acceptance, then what role do works play? Works must not be seen as either the basis of salvation or the means to salvation. However, good works are a necessary part of the salvation equation. It is for this reason that the New Testament can make so many statements associating good works with salvation. There are a number of ways in which the New Testament associates works with salvation.

Works are, first of all, a *response* to the gift of salvation. Many have used the grammatical terms, indicative and imperative, for Paul's approach to grace and works. The indicative, "You are saved," must come first. Only then does the imperative come into play: "Now live as one saved by a holy God." In 1 Corinthians 5:7 Paul encouraged the Corinthians to become (in their lives) the new batch of yeast which they really were (in the sight of God because of the work of Christ). Another way of stating Paul's doctrine is that grace is a gift, and works are gratitude. In Luke 7, Jesus told Simon, the Pharisee, that the sinful woman who washed his feet with tears and dried them with her hair responded correctly to the gift of forgiveness. She, unlike Simon, understood the depth of her sins and responded with good deeds. Similarly, in the Gospel of John works follow grace, so that love is the reason for obedience: "If you love me, you will keep my commandments" (John 14:15, RSV).

Good works are also one of the purposes of the gift of salvation. Paul writes in Ephesians 2:10, "We are . . . created in Christ Jesus to do good works." The believer who has accepted the gift is freed from the self-concern of having to earn salvation. As Paul says in

1 Corinthians 13:1-3, any motivation for good works other than love is worthless. Good works done for less than good reasons cease to be good. Even giving away all that one has is not truly good if the goal is to score points with God rather than to show love to those who receive. In Christ therefore the true meaning of the law may be seen and lived. Paul writes that, "the whole law is fulfilled in one word, 'You shall love your neighbor as yourself'" (Gal. 5:14, RSV).

One must not think, though, that freedom from self-concern alone gives sufficient power to enable good works. Paul writes that Christians are able to do what is truly good because we have been given a completely new identity and a new orientation, having been encountered by the love of God. We also have been given a new source of power for doing what is right, the Spirit of God (Rom. 8:3-8). We are created to do good works, but good works follow rather than precede the gift of salvation. Paul thus writes, "For we are his workmanship, created in Christ Jesus for good works, which God prepared beforehand, that we should walk in them" (Eph. 2:10, RSV).

It is this understanding which explains the often-misunderstood Philippians 2:12, concerning the need for Christians to "work out" their "own salvation." Paul does not mean that salvation is the result of works, but that Christians should work in light of their salvation that has been given to them. The next verse makes this plain: "It is God who works in you to will and to act according to his good purpose."

Works are, finally, a *sign* of salvation. Simply put, there is no clearer sign that one has been saved than the good works of obedience that define his or her life. Calvin wrote, "It is faith alone which justifies, but the faith which justifies is not alone." That is, good works will always accompany the one who truly understands and accepts the grace of God. Christians who fail to fill their lives with righteousness and good works have failed to comprehend their own sinfulness and the cost of God's gracious gift.

And so we return to James, who is concerned about those who profess faith but whose lives show that their faith is not real. In fact, it is dead. James knows that trusting belief is the means to the free gift of God's grace. But he also knows there will always be those who profess to have faith but really have none. And the clearest sign of a false or lifeless faith is the absence of good works.

Like James, Paul is very much in favor of humans making the effort to do what is good. He speaks of straining, pressing on, running the race, buffeting his body, and the like. He knows that this can only be done through the power of the Holy Spirit and that it cannot be done perfectly. But Paul knows that right living and obedience will always accompany salvation. For this reason, Paul can make the statements referred to earlier, such as, "Each will give an account for the deeds done in the body." Faith will produce goodness every time. For this reason Paul uses the phrases, "the obedience of faith" and "work produced by faith" (Rom. 1:5; 1 Thess. 1:3).

What about Baptism?

A word needs to be said about the place of baptism and similar acts of obedience in Paul's writings. Baptism in Paul's thinking is the place where one "puts on Christ" (Gal. 3:27; Rom. 6:1-14) and where one receives the Holy Spirit (1 Cor. 12:13). Perhaps we should argue, therefore, that baptism is one thing people do which does ensure salvation.

The problem with such thinking is that it looks at baptism as a meritorious act that a person does in order to be saved. Nothing could be further from the truth. For one thing, baptism is passive by design. Christians do not baptize themselves; they are baptized, implying their passive role. God is the one "working" in baptism. More importantly, baptism must be categorized as an act of faith rather than as an act of personal merit. Baptism, like the faith that leads to it, is a confession that a person has nothing to offer God. It is a believer's expression of utter helplessness apart from the blood of Jesus, in whose death the believer is placing all his or her trust.

Conclusion

Paul's entire understanding of grace, faith, and works can only be explained in a relational sense. It is difficult to find an adequate illustration, but perhaps the following is at least helpful. A young orphaned teenager faces continual struggles with foster parents, school authorities, and the police. He has been given rules, only to break them. He has been promised rewards for better conduct, only to fail to receive them. He has been lectured, threatened, and punished. His constant failures have convinced him that he doesn't deserve any better than his hopeless life.

However, after several years of trouble, a concerned judge

declares him "not guilty" of the latest charge against him and places him in a loving home, where he is soon adopted. The new parents love him unconditionally, discipline him with love, and rejoice with every victory. They not only teach him, discipline him, and reward him, they also help him succeed in every possible way, and they call him their own. He knows that his position with his parents is not based upon his ability to live up to their standards. Although he never fully escapes his past, he grows to be like his parents more and more each passing year. Their goal for him has always been more than simply to provide him with a good life. It is also to mold him into a person who will do what is right and make the world a better place. Over time, he becomes that person.

Therefore, the ground of our salvation is grace. "None is righteous, no not one." We receive salvation by our trusting relationship with God. "We are saved by grace through faith." A primary goal of salvation is good works. "We are created in Christ Jesus for good works."

Chapter Ten

How can I be sure I'm saved?

C. Michael Moss
Lipscomb University
Nashville, Tennessee

"But, Lord, sometimes I don't feel saved!" Unfortunately that is the plight of many Christians. The harsh reality of the human circumstance forces Christians to face their own failings and inadequacies before God. One must be conscious that falling from the grace of God is a possibility and, at the same time, feel secure in relationship with God. Walking that tightrope will never be easy.

Jack Exum described an experience that illustrates that dilemma. While holding a meeting in a small town in Ohio, he went to the little restaurant next door to the motel where he was staying. The proprietor of the motel assumed that, since he was a preacher, he was bound to have a great deal in common with a minister from one of the denominations in the town. So he introduced the two men. Jack, who is known for his candor, began the discussion by saying, "Oh yes, you are from a denomination that teaches once saved always saved." "Yes, that's right," replied the minister. "No, that's wrong," retorted Jack. Not to be out done, the minister said, "I assume then that you are from a religious body that teaches 'never really sure you're saved.'" After considerable thought, Jack reluctantly responded, "Yes, I suppose that's right." Back came the rejoinder, "No, that's wrong."

Over two thousand years ago, Aristotle said, "Perfection is the golden mean." The difficulty is that the pendulum has a tendency to swing from one extreme to the other. In correcting one problem, we often create another. The perspective of the Bible is not "once saved always saved," else how does one explain the warnings of the epistles regarding the possibility of apostasy (cf., Rom. 6:1-14; 1 Cor. 10:1-13; Heb. 6:1-12)? One can never grow cocky about his status, or he may find himself slothful about service. Grace and God's protection can never mean license. Likewise, the perspective of the Christian ought not to be "never really sure you're saved" (cf., 1 John 5:13). Many Christians respond to the question, "Are you saved?" with "I hope so," "If I don't commit some terrible sin," "I guess I won't know until the judgment day," or "I don't know." Is it any wonder that with such an attitude one would have real difficulty in living the Christian life with excitement and zeal?

John was writing to first-century Christians who were facing a similar problem. Someone or something (the heresy John's church was facing) was producing a lack of confidence regarding their salvation. John, near the end of his first epistle, tells his readers, "I write these things to you who believe in the name of the Son of God so that you may know that you have eternal life" (1 John 5:13). John has given his audience a benchmark by which they can examine their lives and, thus, their relationship with God.

Martin Luther met his servant early one morning. The servant asked, "Master, do you feel like a child of God today?" Luther replied, "No, I can't say that I do, but I know that I am." That is where the Christian should take his stand.

I came to grips with this idea as a junior in college. While home from school, college students at my home congregation would conduct devotionals at the homes of shutins. One week we were discussing Christian security. The good sister in whose home we were meeting said, "If I were to back out of my driveway and someone were to crash into my car, and if I were to curse that person or think some terrible thought before being killed, I am convinced I would go straight to Hell!" Oh, what a miserable situation! The Christian is always just one sin, one slip, one mistake away from eternal damnation.

Everyone is familiar with the deadly game Russian roulette. Someone toying with life simply puts one bullet in the cylinder of a gun and spins the cylinder. He then puts the gun to his head and pulls the trigger. He has a one in six chance that the bullet will be in the chamber in front of the hammer. He never knows for sure where that bullet is or what will be the outcome when he pulls the trigger. That is the way many view their Christian lives. It is no more than a calculated gamble.

Imagine a sheet of paper with a line down the middle with one side labeled "lost" and the other "saved." Every person begins on the lost side. Upon becoming a Christian, that person moves to the saved side of that ledger. In this view, as a Christian I would face the following plight; the first time I sin, I move to the lost side of the ledger. I penitently ask God for forgiveness, and he graciously forgives me. Again I am on the saved side of the ledger. It is not long before again I fail to live up to God's rules, and I sin. Again I move to the lost side. I ask God for forgiveness, and I am back on the saved side. And so goes my life — saved, lost, saved, lost, saved — back and forth and back and forth. I must simply hope that I die on the right side of that imaginary line, or hope that there is no bullet in the chamber in front of the hammer. Is it any wonder that, when the Christian life is viewed in this way, there is no security?

In chapter one of 1 John, John sets the stage for a solution that he offers throughout the remainder of the book. This article will examine 1 John 1:1–2:11 and some of the recurring themes which inform our understanding of Christian security.

Direction in Life: Lifestyle

John begins his epistle with a classical introduction, a prologue, in which he addresses several issues pertinent to the teaching of the false teachers in his day. In verse 5 he contrasts light and darkness, a metaphor that runs throughout both John's gospel (John 1:49; 3:19-21; 5:35; 8:12; 9:5; 11:9-10; 12:35-36, 46) and his first epistle (1 John 1:58; 2:8-10). God enlightens and enlivens. In him there is nothing sordid. If I am his, my life will be like his.

One of the bywords of John's opponents was apparently, "We have fellowship with God." That was another way of saying, "We are saved." Although the opponents of John made these claims for themselves, the claims did not produce action. Their lifestyle was characterized by darkness. Is it not interesting how prominent religious leaders and vocal church members often have the same difficulty? "Ah, yes. I am enlightened. I have the Spirit. My failings? Oh, they don't make any difference. Dishonest business dealing? Sexual immorality? Skimming contributions for personal use?"

The word fellowship (*koinōnia*, in Greek) is used to indicate what two persons or groups hold in common. The Christian's fellowship with God indicates that he or she and God share something special.

116

If one claims to have fellowship with God, lifestyle will either verify or deny that claim.

John calls Christians to recognize that fellowship with brothers and sisters in Christ is linked to fellowship with God. That fellowship makes Christians a body, a family. This relationship with the Father, which grows out of the saving blood of Jesus, is what really matters.

John is not as concerned about what the believer did last as he is about where the believer is headed. Notice the following phrases: walking in the darkness, practicing truth, and walking in the light. The picture of the Christian life is not spiritual Russian roulette. As long as I am headed the right direction, the blood of Jesus continues to cleanse me from my sin. I am not gambling on ending up on the right side of that saved/lost line. God knows my mind. He loves me. He wants me to be saved. He understands my failings. He is a God who is sometimes portrayed as holding the Christian as a spider on the end of a spider web over the fires of hell, bouncing it, attempting to make that poor spider fall. I am not that spider.

God is not out to get me. He knows my heart. Jesus' blood continues to cleanse me of my sin. That is what grace is all about. John has given his audience the first clue for examining their relationship with God. I can know that I am saved, forgiven, by examining my direction in life, my lifestyle. Where am I headed? Toward closer communion with God, a life of appreciation for the work of Jesus? Or am I walking in darkness? I can be lost by turning my back on the Lord. Nothing and nobody can separate me from God; that is, nobody but me. I can head the wrong way and walk away from the saving blood of Jesus.

A Confessional Lifestyle

John's opponents had convinced themselves that sin was not something one did or committed. They had somehow moved beyond such a mundane thing as sin. They now knew something that made them above sin. At its worst, what most would call "sin" was no more than a bodily act for these enlightened souls; their minds, what was of real importance anyway, had not engaged in that act. They were above sin.

Sin is real. Due to human predicament we have sin in our lives (1:8); we have sinned in the past with an abiding present consequence. The word "sin" means literally "to miss the mark." That point was brought home to me when translating a passage in Plato's *Apology*, his account of Socrates' final defense. Socrates described a man who took aim with his bow and arrow at a target. The man "sinned," that is, he missed the target. All fall short; they miss the target.

John is concerned that his audience might take sin too lightly. Doing so would make life no more than a long stream of sins with no growth. John tells his audience that anyone who claims to have no sin in his life is deceiving himself, and the truth is not in him. His opponents might claim that they were beyond sin, that they knew the grand mysteries, the truth, and that they had fellowship with God. In reality, that simply was not the case. They needed to confess their sins.

"Wait just a minute! Did you not earlier say that the Christian life was not a vicious game of Russian roulette? Did you not claim that it was not a chain made up of 'I am lost as an alien sinner, I am baptized, I am now saved, I sin, I am lost, I confess that sin and pray for forgiveness, I am again saved, I sin, I confess that sin and pray, I am saved,' etc.? Is that not what John is saying here? John does say that if we confess our sins God will forgive us. Does this not suggest I am moving back and forth across that imaginary saved/lost line?"

Remember John's opponents. They were people who would contend that they did not sin. They now knew the mystery of the universe, and sin was simply ignorance of this truth. Sin, they would say, was not a part of their lives. The Christian who was struggling to overcome shortcomings in his life would not have this understanding of sin. Guilt could plague his life.

The word translated "confess" means literally "to say the same thing." It can also be translated "to acknowledge." In our context, that is the better understanding. If these Christians will acknowledge sin in their lives, they can find forgiveness. The blood of Jesus will continue to cleanse them from their sins (1:7b).

If one will not admit that he has sinned and is indeed deserving of the consequences of those sins, how can God shower his grace upon that person? To claim that one has no sin is to say that God is a liar. Why? Because God has been acting from the beginning to deal with a problem which then is not a real problem. The word of God recounts the story of sin, its consequences, and God's plan to deal with it.

Today people do not claim they are above sin in the same way John's opponents did. There is, however, still a problem with taking ownership of sins. "My boss forced me into a position where I had to . . ." "I could not . . . because of my wife." "If I am to survive and provide for my family in a society like ours today . . ." "But all of my friends at school are . . ." "You know the old devil really has a hold on me and . . ." "Sin really is irrelevant, as long as I don't hurt someone else . . ."

The Christians to whom John was writing, as well as his opponents, had sin in their lives (1:8). It was a present reality. They also had sinned in the past and would bear the consequences of those sins if they did not acknowledge that they were sinners (1:10). Or as Paul would say, "All have sinned and fallen short of the glory of God" (Rom. 3:23). Is that not the universal human predicament? All have sinned and carry the consequences of past sin. The guilt hangs on. Some people, however, have found the cure for the malady in the blood of Jesus. God is faithful, utterly dependable. He is just; he will do the right thing.

John in no way wants Christians to minimize the significance of sin. He tells them that he was writing that they might not sin, that is, that sin would not be their way of life. He wants them to direct their lives in the light. John says with Paul, "Shall we continue in sin, that grace may abound? God forbid" (Rom. 6:1, ASV).

Here again John's concern is lifestyle. That lifestyle is clearly confessional. One must own up to sin in one's life if one is to be pleasing to God and to have access to the grace that issues from the blood of Jesus. The structure of verses 7-10 is very much like a poem with an A B A B pattern:

> A — "if we **are walking** in the light"
> B — "if we *claim* that we have no sin"
> A — "if we **are confessing** our sins"
> B — "if we *claim* that we have not sinned"

The tense of the verb "confess" indicates "keep on confessing." The structure indicates that the life lived in the light will be a life that owns up to brokenness. The issue is neither saying out loud, "I have sinned," nor coming down the aisle during an invitation song, nor telling someone about your sinful deeds or thoughts. John is concerned about the contrite heart.

The idea of a command being issued is not only unappealing; it is repugnant. When Maynard G. Crebs, sidekick of Dobey Gillis in the sixties television sitcom, would hear that dirty word "work," he would cringe and cower. Some Christians are tempted to respond in kind when they hear their dirty word, "obey."

As Americans we focus on the rights of the individual; we are not interested in hearing about responsibilities or duties. In religion, some proclaim a real conflict between salvation by grace and any call to obedience. John helps his audience to see that obedience does have a place in the life of a Christian and that such obedience is not grievous.

Most translations render 2:1b, "If anybody does sin . . . ." That is a very literal translation of the Greek text. If one remembers what John has just said, he is forced to understand the text as follows, "If any one sins, and he will, we have an advocate with the Father, Jesus Christ, the Righteous One."

The term "advocate" is a special word for John. He used the same Greek word to describe what Jesus said of the coming Holy Spirit in John 14 and 16. Jesus tells his disciples that he must leave so that the Father will send another Advocate (note that Jesus says "another"). The Greek word is *paraclētos* (cf. our word "paraclete"). The KJV translates this word as "Comforter." The root meaning of this word is "one called alongside to help." The term is sometimes used of an attorney. The NIV renders it as "Counselor," while the NASB chose "Helper."

When we do sin, if we acknowledge those sins, we have someone who will come to our aid, Jesus the Messiah. God had planned this event, Messiahship, before the foundation of the world. That promise is the single thread that holds the Bible together. Jesus comes to our aid. It is he who is the propitiatory sacrifice for our sins.

Propitiation is a bad word according to many theologians today. They argue that it has lost its original meaning and substitute a more neutral term, "expiation," or the phrase, "atoning sacrifice." The Greek word behind propitiation originally was used to refer to a sacrifice that would somehow avert the wrath of gods. Admittedly, it sometimes amounted to bribery; however, that idea is foreign to all of Scripture. While expiation is the handling of sin, propitiation is the handling of wrath. The wrath of God is a legitimate idea that runs through the whole Bible. His wrath is not a temper fit that so often characterizes human beings. It is righteous indignation. Unlike sacrifices people made to the gods, the propitiation of God could not be accomplished by humans. God himself had to act to avert his own anger. He became the propitiatory sacrifice (2:2); he himself was the propitiatory altar or mercy seat (Rom. 3:25). It is by the grace of God that God's wrath is averted.

Jesus Christ is the Righteous One. There is no other. He has met head-on our problem with sin, not ours alone, but the problem which plagues the whole world. Sin has been dealt a fatal blow in Jesus. My security rests there. That in no way minimizes my struggle for a Godlike, God-pleasing life. Sin cannot be my lifestyle. But, Jesus is my advocate.

An Obedient Lifestyle

Again we see the bywords of the "bad guys" who are destroying the security of John's audience. "We know"; "we know him"; "we possess the truth"; "we are perfect (mature)"; "we are in him." John wants his audience to know who really knows God, who really is mature, who really has fellowship with Christ.

The obedience for which John is calling also indicates a lifestyle. John uses a construction to indicate that the one who knows God continues to keep his commandments. John is not calling for sinless perfection or perfect obedience. He has already told his audience that anyone who claims such is making God a liar. John is calling Christians to ask questions about their lives. "Is my aim to please God, to fulfill his will? Can I characterize my life as one of obedience or of self-seeking? I will fall. I will break commandments. But where am I headed? Is the direction of my life God-ward?"

Those who claimed special knowledge and relationship with God but lived lives of rebellion were liars. Lifestyle cannot be divorced from relationship. The "religious person" today who claims to possess blessings from God but lives a life characterized by sin is a liar.

In verse 5 of chapter 2, John speaks of "the love of God." That phrase is ambiguous in most English translations as it was in the original Greek. One must decide from the context whether John is talking about God as the one who loves or the one who is loved. In the present context, John's concern is the Christian's love for God. He is answering the question, "How can one detect the love of God in a Christian's life?" John suggests a simple solution; mature love produces an obedient lifestyle.

An important word for John is the word often translated "perfect." The KJV has translated verse 5, "But whoso keepeth his word, in him verily is the love of God perfected . . ." Perfect, for us, normally means without flaw or fault. The Greek word here, however, carries the idea of wholeness or completeness, of reaching an intended goal. The Christian's love for God that has reached maturity can be easily identified; it produces an obedient life. If John has in mind, not the Christian's love for God, but God's love for his people, he has indicated that God's love reaches its intended goal when the believer is obedient to God's will. Either way, John is echoing what he heard Jesus say:

> If you love me, you will obey what I command (John 14:15).

> He who does not love me will not obey my teaching (John 14:24).

> Now remain in my love. If you obey my commands, you will remain in my love (John 15:910).

For the disciples to claim that they loved Jesus and yet live a life that was defiant with regard to his teaching was in itself contradictory.

One is led to obey out of love, God's love for him and his love for God. Children often respond to their parents out of fear. Initially the slap on the leg or the scolding may be the stimulus that will produce the correct behavior in the worship assembly. Fear is not, however, an effective long-term motivator. Unfortunately many Christians have stagnated at that point. Most of us initially responded to the gospel out of fear; we did not want to go to hell. Preachers have sometimes reinforced that stagnation by attempting to motivate the Christian to act, be, and evangelize with a steady diet of fear. But too soon the "hellfire and brimstone" sermon wears off. Other Christians have difficulty moving beyond habit as motivator. They may worship every Sunday, and they may not do so out of fear. It provides no joy and no growth in fellowship with Father and brother or sister. But in contrast consider the sister who has learned to appreciate what God has done for her and the brother who knows who he is because of who Jesus is. Their obedience may look like the person motivated by fear, but that obedience is drastically different.

That obedient lifestyle can best be seen in the life of Jesus him-self. "Whoever claims to live in him must walk as Jesus did." Generally when we think of the life of Jesus, we think of his sin-lessness, of his miracles, of his parables, and of his power. We may move to contemplate the suffering and death of the Savior. Seldom, however, do we think of Jesus as the paradigm for obedience because, after all, he is God. Yet that is John's emphasis here.

The bad guys could claim to be in God's favor, but if their lifestyle did not demonstrate love for God, they were not his. The Christians who were struggling with insecurity could look for this mark of salvation in their own lifestyles.

A Loving Lifestyle

When Jesus said, "Love one another," the disciples might well have replied, "Lord, that's a tall order. My brother isn't always lov-able." By his teaching, especially his parables, Jesus answered, "Neither are you."

Our society has a twisted perspective on what love really is. The problem is compounded because, when we talk about loving our brother, we do not always have a clear understanding of love as it is used in the New Testament. We often use the term in an empty fashion. We can use "love" to talk about ice cream, one's mate, a child, or, for that matter, anything that gives pleasure.

The early Christian writers began to use the term *agapē* to fill a special need. This term came to be used when speakers and authors were describing God's love for us — a love that does not expect anything in return, one that places someone or something ahead of self.[1] John will clarify that definition in chapter 3 when he further defines the word for his readers.

Agapē indicates putting a thing or person above other things or persons. It is not primarily an emotion but involves action. One cannot command emotions. You can tell me, "Like canned spinach," but I will still not like it. I might eat it, but I will not like it. *Agapē* is something you can command. Paul says, "Husbands, love your wives" (Eph. 5:25). That is a command. A husband might go to a counselor and say, "I don't love my wife anymore." Some counselors say, "Go home and love her." They have issued an instruction, a command. "Treat your wife with respect and honor, putting her needs ahead of your desires."

One cannot command another person to like his or her enemies. Yet Jesus commands us to love (*agapaō*) our enemies. In fact, if I am honest, I must admit that there are some, even among my brothers and sisters, with whom I have major differences. We may have personality conflicts. We may be at odds. That is not to be preferred, but it is all right as long as I love them. Loving my brothers and sisters means putting their welfare ahead of my own, no easy task. John tells his audience and, in turn, us, that loving fellow Christians is one of the marks of a saved person.

In verse 7 John clarifies this love by describing it as both an old commandment and a new one. "New commandment . . . old commandment . . ." should sound familiar to the reader who is familiar with John's gospel.

> Little children, I am with you a little while longer. You shall seek Me; and as I said to the Jews, I now say to you also, "Where I am going, you cannot come." A new commandment I give to you, that you love one another, even as I have loved you, that you also love one another. By this all men will know that you are My disciples, if you have love for one another (John 13:33, NASB).

Does that not sound like our passage? Jesus' admonition is very much alive for John. But why does he say that this commandment is both a new commandment and an old commandment? What made it new when Jesus gave it in John 14? The commandment is old because to love one another, to love your neighbor as yourself, goes back to the book of Leviticus. It is new because Jesus provides a new perspective. He defines how that love will behave by demonstrating it in his own life. It is the "as I have loved you" that makes the commandment new.

A most important mark of the saved person for John is to be found in the question "Do I love my brother?" Loving one's brother is a recurring theme throughout this epistle.

One who hates brother or sister is in the darkness. Again John's concern is not a single act but a direction. The word for hate in the original language indicates a continued action. Such a one is walking in the darkness and is headed the wrong way. Those who hate do not know where they are going because the darkness has blinded their eyes.

The lesson Jesus taught his disciples in John 13–15 that last fateful night had sunk deeply into the life of John. Legend says that the old man John was carried around on a litter and would reach out to pat the folks on the head and to say, "Love one another, my little children."

Love is not easy to practice. It stretches the Christian. Going the second mile and turning the other cheek will never be easy.

In the remainder of the book, John will return to these themes and provide a few more interesting twists. One can respond to doubts and insecurity by recognizing that the blood of Jesus covers sin, guilt, and failings as long as one's life is headed in the right direction.

John would have his audience to examine their lives and come to assure their hearts that they are among God's saved ones. They must ask some simple questions:

1. "What direction am I headed? How can I characterize my lifestyle?"
2. "Do I own up to my own shortcomings and sins?"
3. "Am I really striving to be an obedient child of God?"
4. "Do I really love my brothers and sisters in Christ? Am I seeking their welfare?"

John really wants his audience to feel secure in their relationship with God, to know they have eternal life. Although the struggles for the modern day believer differ in many ways, they are similar in many more. Today we too are plagued with guilt and insecurity. As a Christian today I am still called to examine my lifestyle, to acknowledge my own sins, to make every effort to obey, and to be diligent to love as Jesus loved. I can know that I "have eternal life."

Endnotes

[1]The word *agapaō*, the verb form of *agapē* is not always used in a positive light in the New Testament (cf. 2 Pet. 2:15; 1 John 2:15). In such passages *agapaō* still carries the idea of setting one person, thing, or goal ahead of another.

SECTION FOUR
QUESTIONS ABOUT SCRIPTURE

A deep commitment to Scripture has always marked Churches of Christ. Since we claim to be "a people of the book," our understanding of the Bible will always be central to our identity. In the following articles, the authors lead us to a deeper understanding of what it would mean to be truly biblical.

David Young raises questions that have been fundamental to Christian faith from the time it became clear that Christianity was not just another Jewish sect. How shall we read the Old Testament and understand our relationship to the Law and Judaism? He wrestles with Paul's twin affirmations that the law is "holy, right, and good" yet cannot be the basis for salvation, and leads us to a more profound appreciation for the role of the Old Testament in our lives.

Allen Black examines the contemporary attacks on the reliability of the Gospels, asking whether we can still have confidence in the picture of Jesus that is painted there. If the Bible is not trustworthy with regard to its portrayal of the Jesus of history, we can hardly claim it to be the "word of God."

To conclude the section, Paul Pollard asks how Scripture applies to us today. In answering this question he grapples with the difficulties of trying to understand an ancient document from another culture for our time and place. How do you understand what is eternal and what is only cultural and temporary?

All three writers lead us to see that being "a people of the book" is not just a matter of memorizing verses, but seeing that all of life is informed by the living word of God.

Chapter Eleven

How is the Old Testament
relevant to Christians?

David M. Young
North Boulevard Church of Christ
Murfreesboro, Tennessee

When the Apostle Paul returned to Jerusalem from his third missionary journey, the elders of the Jerusalem church warned him of a crisis brewing among the church members there. A rumor had been circulating, they reported, that accused Paul of teaching Jewish Christians to turn away from Moses, to cease circumcising their children, and to abandon the customs of the Jews. The rumor was false, and in order to prove that Paul himself was living in obedience to the Old Law, the elders requested that Paul join in the purification rites for certain Jewish Christians who had taken upon themselves an Old Testament vow. Paul proved that he was faithful to the Old Testament the very next day by initiating the ritual at the Jewish temple and attempting to offer a sacrifice (Acts 21:17-29).

This incident in the life of Paul, carefully recorded by his companion Luke, reveals Paul's lifelong respect for the authority of the Old Testament. That respect is demonstrated throughout the last part of the book of Acts, as Paul, in trial after trial, argues that he is a faithful Jew who has been faithful to the Law. His remark to the Pharisees in the Sanhedrin, who could find no fault in him, reveals his loyalty to the Law: "I am a Pharisee, the son of a Pharisee" (23:6). This claim was made years after his conversion to Christianity.

Paul's allegiance to the Old Testament in the book of Acts raises questions for those who may believe that the Old Law was entirely "nailed to the cross." Why does Luke take such pains to affirm that the Jerusalem church and the Apostle Paul were "zealous for the

Law" (Acts 21:20)? Was Paul being deceitful when he vowed to offer a sacrifice at the temple to show that he obeys the Old Law? Isn't it Paul himself who argues in his epistles that "circumcision is nothing" (1 Cor. 7:19)? What does Paul mean when he says that Christians have "died to the law" (Rom. 7:4)?

The "Problem" of the Old Testament

What is the proper relationship between the Christian and the Old Testament? At first glance, the New Testament, as in the case of Paul, may seem to reflect two positions at once.

On the one hand, the New Testament teaches us that the Old Testament rightfully belongs to our Bible as a source of authority for Christians. Paul affirms that Old Testament Scripture is inspired of God, is profitable for teaching, rebuking, correcting, and training in righteousness, and is capable of thoroughly equipping God's child for every good work (2 Tim. 3:16-17). Jesus promised that the "law and the prophets" would not pass away as long as heaven and earth abide until all is fulfilled. He condemns those "in the Kingdom" who disobey the Old Testament or who teach others to disobey it (Matt. 5:17-20). In Acts Luke defends the early Christians from accusations that they were disobedient to the Law (21:17-26; 22:12; 25:8). In Romans 3:31 Paul argues that through faith in Christ the Christian ought to "uphold the law," and James suggests that Christians ought to "fulfill" the law (James 2:8-11, quoting three times from the Pentateuch). Further, in his letters Paul often uses the Old Testament as a source of authority for developing Christian doctrine (see, e.g., 1 Cor. 9:8-9; 14:21; 1 Tim. 5:18). Indeed, Paul remarks that "the law is holy, just, and good" (Rom 7:12), and the law was "written for us (Christians)" (Rom. 15:4; 1 Cor. 10:11). The entire New Testament assumes a knowledge of the Old Testament and is filled with citations from the Old Testament, as the New Testament draws heavily upon Old Testament theology to teach Christians how to be children of God.

On the other hand, the New Testament teaches that in some sense the Old Testament has been changed, spiritualized, or rendered nonbinding under the Christian system. The Jerusalem Council reminded Gentile Christians that they were not bound to keep the law (with a few exceptions, Acts 15:5, 28-29). Paul compares the law to a schoolmaster whose job is to bring us up to

Christ, concluding that we are "no longer under the supervision of the law" (Gal. 3:23-25). He suggests that the law and its ordinances have been taken away uniting Jews and Gentiles in Christ (Eph. 2:14-18) and flatly states that "we have died to the law" (Rom. 7:4). He points out that "works of the law" do not justify the child of God (Rom. 3:27-28) and that the written word is insufficient for rendering in us the image of God, which requires instead the Spirit of God (2 Cor. 3:7-18). The Hebrew letter develops its entire argument about Christ's supremacy by comparing Him to various aspects of the Old Covenant, showing that the New Covenant is superior to the Old in every way (see Heb. 3:1-19; 4:1-13; 5:1–7:28; 8:1-13; 9:1–10:18).

The New Testament obviously grants some authority to the Old Testament, but at the same time restricts that authority. Exactly how the Old Testament exercises authority over the Christian, and how the Christian should use the Old Testament, has been a matter of debate in the church for centuries.

Past Approaches to the Old Testament

Some have simply chosen to ignore the Old Testament. The second-century Gnostic, Marcion, who was declared a heretic by the early church, believed that the God of the Old Testament was an evil, earthly god, who was unworthy to be considered the same as the God of the New Testament. Marcion deleted the Old Testament from his Bible entirely, even cutting out New Testament references to the Old Testament. Though the church quickly rejected Marcion's views, they have occasionally reemerged in various forms — in the theologies of a few twentieth century antisemitic German scholars and, at least in practice if not in theory, among a few members of the churches of Christ who have ignored the Old Testament.

Others have acknowledged that the Old Testament possesses a certain authority for the Christian, but have argued that this authority is valid only when the Old Testament is allegorized with a Christian meaning. This was the approach of many of the church fathers, some of whom agreed with Marcion that the Old Testament has much, when read literally, that is crude or even ungodly. To save the Old Testament from these literal readings, then, the allegorists devised philosophical and mystical meanings for every text of the Old Testament. The allegorists reread Joshua 2–6, for example, to show that Rahab in this passage is actually a reference to the church, the three [sic] spies are the Trinity, and the scarlet rope is the blood of Christ. Whenever allegorists read of Jerusalem in any Old Testament context they understood that it might refer to the heart of the believer, to the church, or even to heaven, but it rarely meant a city in Judea.

A third answer to the question of the Christian's relationship to the Old Testament offered by the church has been simply to bind the Old Testament upon Christians. This was the effect of John Calvin's view of the Old Testament. Calvin sought to create a Christian state, and since the New Testament does not provide the necessary legal or political foundations for such a state, Calvin was forced to go to the Old Testament in order to create his system. Though Calvin did not literally bind every part of the Old Testament upon the Christian, his general tendency was to see no significant difference between Old and New Testaments. Calvinist churches have often tended to blur the distinction between the Testaments.

Still others have advocated a fourth approach to the Old Testament: one that reassesses portions of the Old Testament in light of the New, rejecting those sections that seem morally weak, historically inaccurate, or simply irrelevant. A number of liberal Protestants of the nineteenth and twentieth centuries have held that the task of the Bible student is to discern those parts of the Old Testament which are "fit" for Christians by virtue of their ethical, moral, or social values. Measuring these against the teachings of Jesus, Christians should keep only those sections of the Old Testament that aspire to Jesus' values, such as the prophetic calls for justice and mercy.

New Testament Perspectives

Of course the New Testament does not present contradictory positions regarding the proper use of the Old Testament, but the previous discussions should remind us that the New Testament view is somewhat complex. Further complications in discerning the New Testament approach to the Old arise from certain semantic and lexicographic difficulties. One of these is the confusion created by the variety of terms used in the New Testament for "Old Covenant," "Old Law," and "Old Testament Scripture." Generally in the New Testament, "Old Covenant" refers to the total relationship God developed with the Jewish people, solemnized at Sinai after the Exodus. The New Testament commonly uses the Greek word *diatheke* to refer to this Covenant in contrast to a New Covenant God has made with us through Jesus Christ (see 2 Cor. 3:6-18; Gal. 4:24; Heb. 8:1-13). To govern the Jews in that Covenant, God gave them the "Law" (Greek = *nomos*), which term in the New Testament often refers to the legal regulations of the Old Covenant. The collection of thirty-nine books that describes both the Old Covenant and its legal restrictions — called the "Old Testament" by many of us — is generally called "the Law and the Prophets" or "the Scriptures" by New Testament writers.

Interpretive problems arise when we fail to distinguish between the Old Covenant, the Old Law and the Old Testament Scriptures. Unfortunately, it is not always easy to make the distinction because the New Testament occasionally uses its terms interchangeably, especially the word "law."

Another semantic problem arises from misconceptions about the meaning of the New Testament word "fulfill" (Greek = *pleroun* or *teleioun*). Occasionally it is assumed that when the New Testament speaks of an Old Testament text as being "fulfilled" this actually means that it is "annulled," "abrogated," or "brought to an end." But the word "fulfill," both in English and in Greek, has the primary meaning of "satisfy, " "achieve," or "fill up." To "fulfill" a law is not to abrogate it; it is to obey it or satisfy it. To "fulfill" a passage of Scripture is to "satisfy" it or to "give it full meaning." In this way the Old Testament can be "fulfilled" many times — indeed, it is fulfilled every time it is properly satisfied. Jesus himself says this, when he tells us that he did not come to abolish the Law or the Prophets, but to "fulfill" them (Matt. 5:17-20). Notice that "fulfill" here is the opposite of "abrogate."

The term "fulfill" is critical to our understanding of the Christian's use of the Old Testament, since the New Testament so often speaks of Christ, the church, and Christians "fulfilling" Old Testament Scripture. In what sense can it be said that Christians "fulfill" the Old Testament?

"No one is justified by observing the law."

The Bible clearly teaches that Christians are not bound by the Old Law in the same way as were the Jews before Christ. The Old

Covenant that gave the context for the Old Law, was explicitly made between God and the Jews, not between God and the Gentiles or God and the church. Since the Old Covenant was made between God and the Jews, strictly speaking, only the Jews were expected by God to keep its Old Law.

Through their constant sin, however, even the Jews showed that they were unable to live righteously under this Old Law. They continually broke their part of God's covenant, and the sacrifices provided under that Covenant were not sufficient to atone for their guilt (Rom. 2–3; 7:1-12; Gal. 2:21; 3:10-11; Heb. 10:4). Consequently, the Old Law, which was intended to keep the Jews righteous in their covenant with God, proved unable to justify anyone before the eyes of the Lord.

For this reason, God promised, even to those under the Old Covenant, that he would soon make a New Covenant with his people (Jer. 31:31ff.). The New Covenant would not be written on stones or with ink, but on the hearts of those who come to God through the instrument of the Holy Spirit (2 Cor. 3; Heb. 8; Gal. 3:17). Further, the New Covenant would be far more inclusive than the Old, welcoming anyone who would come to God in faith, and creating a new, spiritual Israel.

In two senses, then, the New Testament limits the authority of the Old Testament. First, the New Testament is adamant that the legal regulations of the Old Testament, the Old Law, are unable to save us. We must not seek justification in the Old Law, which, due to our own sinfulness, is only able to prove that we are unjust but is never able to save anyone. We are saved instead by grace acting through faith in Jesus Christ; it is in this sense that Paul can say that we have "died to the law" (Eph. 2:14-18; Gal. 5:1-15). Second, the New Testament shows us that the Old Covenant that God made with the physical Jews has been replaced with a New Covenant. This New Covenant is marked by the Spirit of God, not by tablets of Stone, and its salvation comes through faith in Christ, not through works of the law. The glory of the New Covenant is such that it renders the Old Covenant "faded" (2 Cor. 3:4-18).

"The Law is holy, just, and good."

The Old Covenant was not made with Christians, and the Old Law proved unable to provide salvation for anyone. This does not mean, however, that the Old Testament *Scriptures*, which give us our record of the Old Covenant and its Law, have no authority for the Christian. Rather, as Paul so clearly says, the Old Testament Scriptures are indeed profitable for equipping the Christian in every good work.

The authority of the Old Testament Scriptures is twofold. First, the Old Testament has the authority to teach us what sin is and, therefore, what righteousness is. Without the Law, for example, we would not understand what it means to covet; through the Law we learn both the sinful nature of coveting and the consequences of coveting (see Exod. 20:17; Josh. 7; Rom. 7:7). The Law has the authority, then, to teach us the difference between right and wrong. In this way, even for Christians the Law is holy, just, and good (Rom. 7:7-12; 10:4).

Second, the Old Testament Scriptures have the authority to point us to Jesus Christ as God's Chosen One. This they do by first showing us our sins and thereby proving our need for a Savior, and second by promising that Jesus would come as the One who can make us righteous. The New Testament reads these two themes throughout the entire Old Testament, and therefore it concludes that the whole Old Testament actually speaks of Jesus (see, among many references, Matt. 2:5-6,14-15,17-18; Luke 4:18-19; 24:44-49; John 1:45; 5:39; Acts 26:22-23; Rom. 10:4). By speaking of the need for a Savior and showing Jesus to be that Savior, the entire Old Testament actually addresses the followers of Christ, whether Jew or Gentile. This is what leads Paul to say that the Old Testament Scriptures were actually written for us (1 Cor. 10:11; Rom. 15:4).

"By this faith . . . we uphold the law."

But how should Christians use the Old Testament Scriptures if we are no longer under the Old Covenant and if its Old Law cannot save us? The answer lies in understanding the spiritual nature of Old Testament Scripture. The Old Testament is more than just a list of the legal requirements that God gave to the Jewish people. Instead, the Old Testament is an inspired revelation of eternal truths about the nature of God, of God's expectations from humans, and our proper response to him. In other words, there are spiritual principles and realities reflected in the Old Testament that are true and valid for all times, irrespective of their being recorded in a document originally given only to one people. The Old Testament teaches us the truth regarding such principles as love, holiness, justice, worship, obedience, and faithfulness. It also teaches us about the love of God and his desire to bring us into union with him. The Christian realizes that the Old Testament contains spiritual principles that are universal in quality because they came from God himself.

But this raises another question. How does the Christian find the spiritual truths contained in the Old Testament? The New Testament answer is simple, the whole of the Old Testament is to be interpreted "through Christ." Repeatedly, the New Testament shows how Christ fulfills passages of Old Testament Scripture — even where we may not have noticed messianic overtones. The Gospels show that Jesus is the fulfillment of Old Testament prophecy. Even deeper than this type of fulfillment, the Gospels reveal that Jesus is the Lord of the Old Testament with all its institutions. He is the one who is capable of giving a proper interpretation of Scripture. He is the true teacher of the Law. He is the one who shows us that the real meaning of Scripture is a matter of the heart, not of the letter.

This explains the meaning of the Sermon on the Mount, where Jesus declares that he did not come to abolish the Old Testament but to "give it full meaning" (Matt. 5:17-20). Reminding those "in the Kingdom" of the need to "practice and teach" the Old Testament commands, Jesus proceeds to quote from the letter of the Law, only to challenge his followers to achieve a "surpassing righteousness" by obeying not its letter, but its spirit. The Law forbids murder, but its spiritual truth is that we shouldn't even call our brother evil names (5:21-26). The Law forbids adultery, but its spiritual truth is that we should control our evil desires for others (5:27-30). The Law protects those whom we divorce, but its spiritual meaning is that we should preserve the family by not divorcing (5:31-32). The Law forbids swearing by God's Name, but its spiritual meaning is that our word should be honored without any need for oaths (5:33-37). The Law forbids cruel and excessive punishment with its "eye for eye" principle; its true meaning is that we should love our enemies (5:38-48).[1] By going beyond the letter of the law in each case, the righteousness of the Christian "surpasses" that of the teachers of the law (5:20). By going to the spiritual truth reflected within the Law, we actually uphold the righteousness the Old Testament really intended.

136

Jesus' approach to the Old Testament is maintained throughout the rest of the New Testament as well, where the spiritual truths of the Old Testament are constantly brought to Jesus Christ for reinterpretation. Indeed, the rest of the New Testament expands upon this theme, teaching us that even Old Testament institutions, such as the priesthood, the temple, and the sacrificial system, are actually "copies" (Greek = *hypodeigmata*) of spiritual realities now properly understood in Christ (see, e.g., Heb. 8:5; 9:23; 10:1; cf., also Col. 2:17, where "shadow" means something like "primitive copy"). Distinct from the allegorists' approach to the Old Testament Scriptures, the New Testament acknowledges a literal level of truth to the Old Testament, but seeks to show the Christian that the more important level of truth is the spiritual level.

In Romans 2–3, Paul reveals his spiritual understanding of the Old Testament, as he uses it to show that "all have sinned and fall short of God's glory." Quoting the Old Testament as his authority that "all have sinned," Paul argues that the Old Law itself could not justify us. Here again, notice that the Old Testament has the authority to show us what sin is and that we need a Savior, but it does not have the authority to save us. Rather, Paul points out, the Old Testament makes known to us a new righteousness, one which comes through faith in Jesus Christ (3:21-22). By believing in Jesus, to whom the Old Testament points, our faith actually upholds the Old Law, and we Christians actually become the ones who truly fulfill the Old Law (3:31). Thus, Paul can remind us that a "true Jew" is not a physical or literal Jew, but a spiritual Jew, one who has submitted to the spiritual truths of God as understood in Christ. He declares that "true circumcision" is not of the flesh, but of the heart and by the Spirit (2:28-29). When we accept the spiritual truths recorded in Old Testament Scripture, which ultimately means living by faith in Jesus Christ, to whom the Scriptures point, we Christians prove ourselves to be the true heirs of the Old Testament Scriptures. Through faith in Jesus Christ, then, Christians "fulfill" the spiritual truths of the Old Testament Scriptures.

Various other texts show how Christians live under the authority of the spiritual truths recorded in Old Testament Scripture. For example, in 1 Corinthians 9:9, Paul quotes Deuteronomy 25:4 in an effort to establish the Christian principle of supporting gospel preachers. Deuteronomy 25:4 states that one must not muzzle the ox that treads out the grain. Paul argues that the spirit of this text applies to Christian preachers of the gospel, who deserve to be financially supported by those among whom they work. "Is it about oxen that God is concerned? Surely he says this (i.e., Deut. 25:4) for us, doesn't he? Yes, this was written for us . . . ." (See also 1 Tim. 5:17-20 for another way this text is "fulfilled.") In 1 Corinthians 10:1-22 Paul argues that God's punishment of Israelites who drifted into idolatry was actually recorded in Old Testament Scriptures for us Christians "on whom the fulfillment of the ages has come." This punishment was to teach *us* that even we Christians can fall from God, and that He will punish us if we do. The book of Hebrews, as has already been pointed out, makes an elaborate argument for the supremacy of Christ by pointing out that in Christ the various institutions of the Old Covenant find their true meaning.[2] Even where it is not explicitly stated, the New Testament reflects extensively upon Old Testament Scriptures, as interpreted spiritually through Christ, to establish Christian doctrine.

The New Testament use of the Old operates in at least three different ways. First, in many instances, the spiritual values of the Old Testament are obvious and merely need to be understood in Christ. For example, several New Testament writers reassert the importance of the Leviticus command to love others as a central command for Christians as well (Rom. 13:8-10; Jas. 2:8). The command to love has not changed, but Jesus' love for us surely gives that command fullness of meaning. Second, in some cases the truths in the Old Testament are cast in a literal, time-bound form. In these cases the New Testament writers perceive the spiritual or moral meaning behind the literal form (without denying the historical truthfulness of the literal!). For example, the Old Testament Law commanded the Israelites to keep their clothing fabrics pure (Lev. 19:19); the New Testament teaches us to put on purity of heart for our clothing (Col. 3:1-17). Third, the New Testament occasionally spiritualizes the Old Testament Scripture to the point that it reverses its literal meaning. For example, the Old Law had taught the Jews not to eat certain unclean foods (Leviticus 11); Jesus explains that what really makes us unclean is what comes out of the heart, not what goes into the stomach, thereby declaring all foods clean (Mark 7:1-21; note that Jesus is using Isaiah 29:13 to interpret Lev. 11). In every case, Christians are able to see how in Christ the Old Testament Scriptures find their fullness of meaning, and we are able, by following the true spirit of the Scripture, to develop a righteousness that surpasses that of the scribes and Pharisees.

Conclusion

The Christian thus uses the Old Testament spiritually, to learn about the nature of God, sin, worship, faithfulness, and, ultimately, Jesus Christ. We understand that though the Old Testament Scripture was written for us, the Old Covenant with its regulations and ceremonies was never intended for anyone other than the Jews, so we do not seek to go back to what has faded in value. Even if we were Jews, the New Testament forcefully reminds us that no one could ever flawlessly keep all of the laws recorded in the Old Testament. We do not seek our salvation from the Old Law. Rather, we seek salvation by grace through faith in Jesus Christ.

Nevertheless, Christians do accept the Old Testament Scriptures as our book, intended, when understood through Christ, to guide us in godliness. We understand that by honoring the spiritual dimensions of the Old Testament Scriptures, we become spiritual Jews (Rom. 2:28-29) who practice a spiritual circumcision. We still believe the Old Testament commands to love God and others as the basis of godly living (Mark 12:29-31), and in this sense we still obey the "royal law" (Jas. 2:8). As Gentile Christians, instead of worshiping at the literal temple, we understand that the church is now God's temple (1 Cor. 3:16-17) or our bodies are the temple of the Spirit (1 Cor. 6:19-20). Instead of offering lambs and bulls, we realize that Christ is our spiritual sacrifice (Heb. 9:11-14). We no longer have a Jewish high priest; Christ is our High Priest. Our Sabbath rest is not of this earth, but comes to us in heaven. We do not follow Moses, but Christ, a greater Moses.

When we read the Old Testament Scriptures through Christ, he opens our minds to understand them, as he did the disciples after his resurrection (Luke 24:45). By accepting the spiritual authority of the Old Testament Scriptures, Christians gratefully acknowledge that they are "able to make [us] wise for salvation through faith in Christ Jesus" (2 Tim. 3:15). By accepting that "everything that was written in the past was written to teach us," Christians may, "through endurance and the encouragement of the Scriptures," have hope (Rom. 15:4).

A Christian Method for Reading the Old Testament

Three fundamental steps can aid Christian interpretation of the Old Testament Scripture. These steps assume a basic spiritual unity between the Old and the New Testaments found in Jesus Christ.

The **first step** for a Christian in reading the Old Testament Scripture is to uncover what the Old Testament meant in its historical, grammatical, and literary context (this is what the word "exegesis" means). Here the Christian seeks to understand the "plain," "literal" meaning of the Old Testament text. The Christian, like any other responsible reader, brings to this task whatever knowledge is useful in uncovering what any given text meant in its original context. Historical, linguistic, and literary data all help the Christian understand what a text was trying to say.

The **second step** for the Christian in reading the Old Testament is to uncover the religious significance underlying any given Old Testament text. Here, like the Jew before him, the Christian recognizes that the material in the Old Testament was written for *religious* reasons, not just historical reasons, and that the Old Testament presents deep spiritual truths for God's people. A number of spiritual truths are often reflected in every text.

The **third step** for the Christian in reading the Old Testament is to bring this spiritual truth to the New Testament for its "full meaning." Knowing that the entire Old Testament is "filled with meaning" only in Christ, the Christian seeks to uncover what the Old Testament *still means* (where the first step uncovered what it *once meant*). Most often the New Testament will reach beyond the "letter" of the Old Testament to bring to light its spiritual truth for the Christian. Sometimes the Christian meaning of an Old Testament text will be similar to its literal meaning. Other times, the Christian meaning will be the moral or spiritual equivalent of a literal reading. Occasionally, the teachings of Jesus will so thoroughly modify the literal meaning of the Old Testament text that the latter really only serves as a contrast to the former.

Many Old Testament texts are explicitly interpreted for the Christian in the New Testament. The Christian should always check the references on any Old Testament text to see what the New Testament has said about that text, if anything. Those Old Testament texts not explicitly mentioned in the New Testament still present spiritual truths that Christians should embrace through their knowledge of Jesus Christ.

Endnotes

[1]Remember that the "eye for eye" law was not intended to authorize cruel punishment, but to prevent it (Exod. 21:24). It did this by limiting punishment to fit the crime. You cannot take a man's eyes, ears, and hands if he takes your eye; you are limited to only to taking his eye. Jesus thus rightly perceives that this law is really about compassion for one's enemies.

[2]This also seems to be Paul's meaning in Romans 10:4, usually translated "Christ is the end of the law," but also legitimately translated "Christ is the goal of the law."

Chapter Twelve

Can we still believe in the Jesus of the Gospels?

Allen Black
Harding Graduate School of Religion
Memphis, Tennessee

From the beginning of Christianity, there have always been skeptics. Matthew 28:11-15 provides the first report of an alternative explanation to the resurrection of Jesus: the disciples stole the body while the guards were asleep. Skeptical explanations have continued unabated for almost two millennia.

Nevertheless, there is something different about the approach of skeptics during the past two centuries, since the beginning of the so-called "Quests for the historical Jesus."[1] During this period various scholars have not just denied the credibility of the Gospels, but also have offered scholarly reconstructions of what they suppose Jesus really did and said. The first of many such works was the 1778 (postmortem) publication of a work by H.S. Reimarus, a German Deist. One of the more recent and better-known attempts is the work of the "Jesus Seminar," which has published the Gospels using a color-coded system to indicate which sayings in the Gospels they believe Jesus actually said.[2]

Contemporary Christians can come into contact with skeptical views of the Gospels in a variety of ways. They are taught on many university campuses. Popular magazines like *Newsweek* and *Time* carry articles on the "Jesus Seminar" and other skeptical projects, especially (and ironically) in their Christmas and Easter issues. Evangelistic Christians find themselves trying to answer questions raised by well-read friends.

This essay provides a defense of the historical reliability of the four Gospels. In it, I will be approaching the Gospels simply as ancient documents and asking the same kind of historical questions we might ask of other ancient documents.

For example, in the late first century A.D. a Jew by the name of Josephus wrote an account of *The Jewish War* of A.D. 66-70. In assessing the historical reliability of his work, we ask questions like: Do our copies of it contain what Josephus originally wrote? Did Josephus himself really write it? Was he present for any of what he reports? Does what he says agree with what we know about the circumstances and places he describes? Do other writers confirm or disagree with his story? We then draw conclusions about the historical reliability of Josephus's report.

We can ask similar questions about the Gospels. Positive answers to such questions can demonstrate that the Gospels should be taken seriously as historical documents. What the evangelists tell us about Jesus should not be placed in the same category as the legends about Paul Bunyan or ancient heroes like Hercules. They should be placed in the category of historical reality.

Do We Have Reliable Copies of the Gospels?

The first question to ask about any ancient document is whether the ancient handwritten copies available to us are faithful replicas of the original. Before Gutenberg's invention of the printing press in the 1450's, all books were hand-copied. We do not have the originals of the Gospels or virtually any other important piece of literature from the ancient world. In many cases we have very few copies and they are several centuries later than the original composition. We often have serious questions about how much they have been changed.

But all scholars, even the most skeptical, agree that our copies of the Gospels are very close to the originals. We have fragments of the Gospels from the first half of the second century, copies of large sections from about A.D. 200, and full copies beginning in the fourth century. We also have many quotations from Christians writing from the early second century forward and ancient copies of translations into Latin, Syriac, and Coptic.

Of course, we do not have perfect copies of any ancient book. Everyone who owns a twentieth century translation of the Bible knows that there are a few texts in our Gospels about which we are uncertain. By far the most notable are the "long ending" of Mark (16:9-20) and the story of the woman caught in adultery in John (7:53–8:11). Neither of these texts contains insights into Jesus that we could not learn from the rest of the Gospels. The New Testament documents are by far the best-attested books from antiquity. Classical scholars would love to be as confident about the text of other ancient books.

When Were the Gospels Written?

In the mid-1800s the German scholar F.C. Baur claimed that Mark and John were not written until at least the middle of the second century. Such opinions have now been forever laid to rest. Even during the 1800s scholars such as J.B. Lightfoot proved to the satisfaction of all that we have reliable copies of books written by Christians who lived in the first half of the second century and who refer to our Gospels. Some would argue that the late first century author Clement of Rome knew at least one of our first three Gospels. Several authors from the first half of the second century refer to them. The early 1900s saw the publication of a fragment of John that dates to the first half of the second century. Even skeptics agree that our Gospels were written during the first century, within thirty to less than seventy years after Jesus' death.

Who Wrote the Gospels?

The fact that they were written by men who lived during the lifetimes of eyewitnesses bolsters the reliability of the Gospels as historical documents. This would be true even if we did not know whether any of the evangelists themselves were eyewitnesses.

Skeptical scholars often reject the traditional views that two of the Gospels were written by apostles (Matthew and John) and the other two by associates of the apostles (Mark and Luke). But the evidence supporting these traditional views is strong.

One important piece of evidence is the titles (e.g., "The Gospel according to Matthew") which name the authors. The authors did presumably not write the titles themselves. But we have every reason to believe that these titles come from the first century and the earliest days of the circulation of these books, days when their authorship would still be known. As soon as there were several circulating Gospels, there would have been a need to distinguish them. There are no competing titles.

Our earliest indication that these titles were known is from Papias, a bishop from Asia Minor, who in roughly A.D. 120–30 refers to the discussions of a man of a generation prior to his (the elder John). Papias's comments indicate the elder John probably knew the Gospels by the titles that are known in the later second century.

Second century authors affirm all four of the traditional authorships. The affirmations of Mark and Matthew are as old as Papias's reference to the elder John. The affirmation of Luke is found in several works of the last third of the second century. Among those who affirm John's authorship is Irenaeus, who in an interesting letter to Florinus states that he had personally heard Polycarp (who was martyred in the mid-second century at the age of 86) speak of his (Polycarp's) personal acquaintance with the apostle John. Here we are in contact with a direct line of information, John the apostle to Polycarp to Irenaeus.

John's Gospel has internal indications of having come from an eyewitness. The disciple Jesus talked to Peter about in John 21:20-23 is "the disciple who is bearing witness to these things, and who has written these things; and we know that his testimony is true" (John 21:24, RSV). Even those who deny that one of the apostles wrote John usually feel compelled to offer some explanation for this statement, often suggesting that the testimony of the apostle lies in some sense behind John's Gospel, even though they believe he did not write it.

The main reason for denying the tradition of authorship is the belief that Jesus did not work miracles; therefore, the Gospels must be distorting the truth; therefore, eyewitnesses or their close associates cannot have written the Gospels. It will be necessary to take up the question of miracles as our inquiry proceeds.

Even skeptics agree that men who lived in the days of eyewitnesses wrote the Gospels. Many consider the traditional authors to be correctly identified. This would mean that two of them were eyewitnesses, and the other two were close associates of eyewitnesses.

Do the Gospels Intend to Be Read As History?

The Gospels are not stories about things that happened in Never-Never Land or in a far away galaxy. They do not include mythological features like Hercules' Cyclops or Paul Bunyan's giant blue ox.

The Gospel of Luke sets the story of Jesus within the framework of ancient history:

> In the fifteenth year of the reign of Tiberius Caesar, Pontius Pilate being governor of Judea, and Herod being tetrarch of Galilee, and his brother Philip tetrarch of the region of Ituraea and Trachonitis, and Lysanias tetrarch of Abilene . . . (Luke 3:1, RSV).

Skeptics cannot argue that the evangelists intended their books to be viewed as completely fictional. But some do argue that each Gospel was (to a varying extent) intended to be viewed as a mixture of history and fiction. There are in fact no statements in the Gospels that support such a claim and there are several to the contrary. In his purpose statement Luke says:

> Inasmuch as many have undertaken to compile a narrative of the things which have been accomplished among us, just as they were delivered to us by those who from the beginning were eyewitnesses and ministers of the word, it seemed good to me also, having followed all things closely for some time past, to write an orderly account for you, most excellent Theophilus, that you may know the truth concerning the things of which you have been informed (Luke 1:1-4, RSV).

In his purpose statement John says:

> Jesus did many other signs in the presence of the disciples, which are not written in this book; but these are written that you may believe that Jesus is the Christ, the Son of God, and that believing you may have life in his name (John 20:30-31, RSV).

Both evangelists intended to be taken seriously as telling facts, not fictional stories.

Skeptical scholars argue that the Gospels are heavily laced with myth. They have drawn this conclusion primarily because of the miracles described in the Gospels. However, even if the miracles of the Gospels were fictional, that would not prove that their authors did not believe, and intend their audiences to believe, that they actually happened.

One way this issue of intent is sometimes addressed is to argue that since the evangelists were writing theology, they could not have been writing history. This fallacious either/or argument would surprise every ancient reader and most modern ones. Historians often write history in order to teach philosophical or theological truths.[3]

Are the Gospels Accurate with Respect to Information in Other Sources?

One important way to examine the reliability of any ancient story is to check items that are verifiable from other sources. Many items in the Gospels can be verified from other ancient information concerning geography, the military, governments, coinage, religious practices, famous people, etc.

The Gospels fare well in this arena. For example, the above quotation from Luke 3:1 refers to five officials and their titles. The first four are easily verifiable. Their names and titles are correct, and they all were in office at the appropriate time. Some have accused Luke of a mistake concerning the fifth official (Lysanias tetrarch of Abilene) because they believe Luke refers to a Lysanias put to death by Mark Anthony in 36 B.C. However, Josephus mentions another Lysanias whom he identifies as tetrarch of Abilene, apparently confirming Luke's identification.

In a few cases the Gospels have information that seems to conflict with other sources. For example, according to our best ancient copies, Mark 5:1 places the demoniac Jesus heals in "the country of the Gerasenes." But Gerasa was thirty miles from the shores of the Sea of Galilee. Some ancient manuscripts read "Gedarenes." But Gedara was about five miles from the edge of the Sea — still a significant distance for the comment of verse 14 that the swineherds ran into the city and the inhabitants ran out to the Sea. To solve this problem, some would opt for a less well-attested ancient reading "Gergasenes" and associate the site with a set of ruins on the northeast side of the Sea known as Kursi.[4]

In a discussion focused on general historical reliability (rather than inspiration) it should be pointed out that even for those who (mistakenly) conclude that Mark made a mistake, an occasional mistake of this sort would not undermine the basic trustworthiness of his Gospel. We do not discard the historical value of other generally trustworthy ancient and modern histories because of a few mistakes. In fact in uninspired books, we expect them.

Do the Gospels Contradict Each Other?

Since we have four accounts of the story of Jesus, their reliability may be judged not only by comparison with other ancient sources, but also by how they relate to each other.

Many of the supposed contradictions between the Gospels can be resolved satisfactorily by correcting some basic misunderstandings about their nature. Modern readers often read these ancient books with expectations that do not fit what their ancient authors apparently intended.

One error modern readers may commit is to assume that the Gospels intend to portray a strict chronological order. From this viewpoint Matthew and Luke would appear contradictory when they describe the last two temptations of Christ in two different orders. And Matthew would appear to contradict Mark and Luke when he places the raising of Jairus's daughter in a different position in his Gospel. But all of the Gospels give evidence of some amount of thematic order mixed in with chronological order.

Furthermore, it is a mistake to assume that the Gospel writers intended to report the words of Jesus or others with the exactitude of a transcript or tape recorder. To begin with, Jesus and those he conversed with probably spoke primarily in Aramaic, not Greek. Furthermore, when the Gospels are compared, it is apparent that they contain more paraphrasing than literal translation of Jesus' words. Examples can be found in virtually every parallel passage. For example, in addressing his disciples did Jesus ask, "Who do men say that the Son of man is?" (Matt. 16:13), or "Who do men say that I am?" (Mark 8:27), or "Who do the people say that I am?" (Luke 9:18)? If we grant that the Gospels intend to be paraphrasing, the differences are insignificant.

And even though it may seem more difficult for modern readers to accept, the Gospel writers also seem to "paraphrase" the flow of certain stories, retaining what is significant for their purposes and omitting details which modern authors would usually not omit. For example, Matthew omits the emissaries used by the Capernaum centurion (Matt. 8:5-13; cf. Luke 7:1-10), and Mark omits James's and John's mother's role in asking for the places of honor beside Jesus (Mark 10:35-37; cf. Matt. 20:20-21). With further reflection such "paraphrasing" of events may not seem so odd. Most readers of Mark 15:15 ("having scourged Jesus, [Pilate] delivered him to be crucified") would assume Pilate himself did not do the scourging, but ordered a soldier to wield the whip. A modern news reporter may say, "Today the President said . . ." with reference to something said by the President's press secretary.

Space does not permit examination of even a representative set of apparent contradictions between the first three Gospels or between them and John. The vast majority are soluble along the three lines suggested here: the Gospels use other principles of order in addition to chronology, they usually paraphrase the teachings of Jesus, and they sometimes "paraphrase" even the events in a particular incident.

The general historical reliability of the Gospels would not be fundamentally undermined even if some problems of harmonizing the Gospel accounts resisted explanation. It is no different in other cases where there are several accounts of various events in antiquity and even in modern times.

What about the Miracles in the Gospels?

Throughout the over two hundred years of modern criticism of the Gospels the driving force in denying their credibility has been the problem of Jesus' miracles. Raymond Brown, who has written several internationally respected volumes on various aspects of the Gospels, has recently written an overview of research on "The Historical Jesus." In it he correctly observes that "from the beginning the application of historical research to Jesus was mixed with rationalism (touted as scientific but actually very lacking in objectivity) that *a priori* denied the possibility of the supernatural."[5]

Some scholars believe that modern science has shown miracles to be impossible. Others believe that although they are not scientifically or philosophically impossible, there is not enough evidence to warrant belief in any miracles — those of Jesus or any others.

I will assume that modern science has not proven that miracles should be ruled out of court without looking at the evidence for particular cases. The real issue is whether in the case of Jesus there is adequate evidence to justify belief that he performed miracles. If there is not, then the Gospels would obviously contain a large percentage of erroneous assertions. If there is, then the Gospels can stand up under stringent historical examination.

The critical miracle is the resurrection. If Jesus was raised from the dead and made postresurrection appearances to hundreds of men and women, then it is not so difficult to believe that he could have performed miracles demonstrating his power over disease, demons, nature, and even death. If he was not, then as Paul correctly states, our preaching and faith would be in vain (1 Cor. 15:12-19).

The fundamental argument for the truth of the resurrection of Jesus is the witness of hundreds of men and women who said they saw him and who had little to gain, but everything, even their lives, to lose. That these witnesses existed is not questionable. In addition to the Gospel accounts, other books of the New Testament and a few non-Christian sources testify to their existence.

Of particular importance are the letters of Paul. Even skeptical scholars believe that Paul wrote 1 Corinthians and that he wrote it in the early fifties.[6] In 1 Corinthians 15:1-8 Paul testifies to Jesus' appearances to various persons, even "to more than five hundred brethren at one time, most of whom are still alive, though some have fallen asleep." This is within roughly twenty years of Jesus' death.

Paul himself and many others among these witnesses accepted martyrdom for their belief. If Jesus did not appear to them, did they combine forces to perpetuate a colossal lie? Why did none recant? Why did many suffer and even die for their belief? If we grant that they truly believed, did they all suffer from delusions? Did some even experience a mass hallucination of five hundred at once? Skeptical scholars have a tough time answering such questions.

A good example of a skeptical scholar's approach to this testimony is Rudolf Bultmann, probably the most famous German New Testament scholar of the twentieth century. Bultmann plainly stated, "It is impossible to use electric light and the wireless and to avail our selves of modern medical and surgical discoveries, and at the same time to believe in the New Testament world of spirits and miracles."[7] Specifically concerning the resurrection he asks, "But what of the resurrection? Is it not a mythical event pure and simple? Obviously it is not an event of past history . . ."[8] How, then, does Bultmann explain the rise of belief in the appearances of the resurrected Jesus? ". . . how the Easter faith arose in individual disciples, has been obscured in the tradition by legend and is not of basic importance."[9] At least he realizes the futility of explanations such as Jesus only appearing to be dead or the disciples stealing the body and lying about the resurrection. However, his position that how hundreds of early Christians came to believe they had seen Jesus is indecipherable and unimportant, is based on an *a priori* refusal to accept the one explanation that makes sense of the evidence, Jesus rose from the dead and appeared to many.

An excellent case can be made for believing in Jesus' resurrection. In addition to the historical approach outlined here, most

Christians would also appeal to the explanatory power of the Christian message, which makes sense out of the major puzzles of life's meaning. One can also appeal to Christian experience. Experience alone may seem overly subjective. But in conjunction with various historical and theological arguments, Christian experience adds further testimony that Jesus lives.

Those who are open to the historicity of the resurrection are open to the historicity of the other miracles in the Gospels.

Conclusion

The "Jesus Seminar" and other modern skeptics are wrong about the Gospels. They are blinded by their bias against Jesus' miracles. When the Gospels are examined by the same criteria used for other ancient historical books, they receive high marks.

The Gospels fare well in the areas we have examined. We have reliable copies that are close to the originals. The originals were written during the time that eyewitnesses were alive to challenge or verify their assertions. Two eyewitnesses and two associates of eyewitnesses probably wrote them. They were written to be read as history, not myth. They are accurate with respect to information that can be checked in other ancient sources. They present a generally harmonious portrait of Jesus and his times.

With the exception of the miraculous features, the Gospels pass the tests historians would make of any ancient work. For those who are persuaded by the ample evidences of the truth of Jesus' resurrection, they pass every test.

Of course we can and should still believe in the Jesus of the Gospels.

Endnotes

[1]See the brief overview of the "Quests" in Craig Blomberg, *Jesus and the Gospels* (Nashville: Broadman, 1997), 77-79, 179-185.

[2]Robert W. Funk, Roy W. Hoover, and the Jesus Seminar, *The Five Gospels* (New York: Macmillan, 1993).

[3]Craig Blomberg, "Where Do We Start Studying Jesus?" in *Jesus under Fire*, eds. Michael J. Wilkins and J. P. Moreland (Grand Rapids: Zondervan, 1995), 36-37.

[4]See, e.g., Craig Blomberg, *The Historical Reliability of the Gospels* (Downers Grove, IL: InterVarsity, 1987), 149-150.

⁵Raymond E. Brown, *An Introduction to the New Testament*, Anchor Bible Reference Library (New York: Doubleday, 1997), 817-818.

⁶Clement of Rome, who was himself writing to the Corinthians in the mid-90s, refers specifically to 1 Corinthians as a letter Paul had written to them. See Dunbar, 324.

⁷Rudolf Bultmann, "New Testament and Mythology," in *Kerygma and Myth: A Theological Debate*, ed. H. W. Bartsch, rev. trans. by R. H. Fuller (New York: Harper & Row, 1961), 5.

⁸Ibid., 38.

⁹Rudolf Bultmann, *Theology of the New Testament*, trans. K. Grobel, 2 vols. (New York: Charles Scribner's Sons, 1951, 1955), 1:45.

Chapter Thirteen

How does Scripture speak to our lives?

Paul Pollard
Harding University
Searcy, Arkansas

This essay is written in the hope that it will help inform the person already steeped in hermeneutics and the person, perhaps less informed in the technicalities, yet desiring some insights into how to go about applying Scripture in today's world.

Past Attempts at Application

Attempts to apply Scripture are not new, and through the ages men have sought to use principles that would make the Bible relevant to their times.[1] Rabbi Hillel, for example, is famous for his seven exegetical rules:

> Rule 1 was called "light and heavy" and signified the inference . . .
> from the less to the greater. Rule 2, "equal decision," meant discernment of analogies and comparisons. Rules 3 and 4 were concerned with deducing the general implications from one passage, or from more than one passage; Rule 5 with a more precise statement of the general by reference to the particular, and vice versa; Rule 6 with the use of one passage to interpret another, and Rule 7 with the use of the whole context to elucidate a verse or passage.

Some of these rules can be helpful even today although most have to do with finding the meaning rather than application. Rule 2, for example, is relevant for application since in many biblical texts the situation addressed is not exactly like ours, i.e., Paul's instructions about eating meat offered to idols in 1 Corinthians 8. Some analogies or comparisons may exist between our modern situation and the Corinthians'.

Later in Alexandria, Egypt, the allegorical method became prominent since one could maintain contact with the ancient texts while bringing a fresh message to the contemporary world. Practiced by Philo in the first century A.D., this method of exegesis and application held a firm grip on biblical studies for one thousand years.

During the Middle Ages interpreters emphasized several levels of meaning in Scripture, thus interpretation could be literal, allegorical, moral, or anagogical. For example, Jerusalem could refer to the literal city in Palestine. Allegorically it could mean the church. Morally it could refer to the human soul. By analogy it could refer to the heavenly city. On this schema, the literal meaning is the plain, evident one; the moral sense tells men what to do, the allegorical indicates what they are to believe and the anagogical focuses on what Christians are to hope.

The problem is that while Jerusalem may have some of these meanings indicated above in some contexts, the word does not have all these meanings at the same time. The context dictates meaning and the application one makes. Furthermore, looking for multiple meanings in every word and text led to extreme subjectivism. The text could mean literally anything a person wanted it to mean.

In the sixteenth century Martin Luther and others abandoned the allegorizing method along with the fourfold interpretation of the medieval period, stressing instead the literal or grammatical sense. He also emphasized the role of the Holy Spirit in illuminating the student of God's word. Many of the procedures he advocated are still valuable for contemporary interpretation and application.

Modern Interpretation and Application

Today, the interpreter of the New Testament has many tools and resources available for interpretation and analysis of the text.[2] In addition, the principle derived from the period of the Enlightenment and extending to the present that the biblical documents must be studied and understood like any other set of documents from antiquity is a sound one. But the problem is this, once one discovers the meaning of the text, how can one apply it to contemporary humans? What approaches can the average person use in order to make the Bible speak to his time and problems? What do we do when the Bible does not specifically discuss a problem being faced today such as cloning, AIDS, abortion, etc.?

The situation faced by interpreters is like a bridge, perhaps the Golden Gate in San Francisco. Viewed from the side, the bridge connects two pieces of land separated by water. For the Bible student this bridge represents the assignment at hand. The task of discovering the meaning of the biblical text is at one end of the bridge, while the application to contemporary life is at the other. One cannot get to "how" that text applies to us today without first examining the part dealing with meaning.

Too often people start applying the Bible without first understanding what the text meant to the first readers. Without the "control" of finding what the text first meant one will apply it to situations never envisioned by the original author. When this is done, for example, people start finding Cobra gunships, bar codes and laser beams in Revelation. Such "application" is based on a subjective approach to the biblical text. This extreme subjectivism is avoided if one simple control is utilized — understanding what the text meant and how it applied to the ancient readers. Then and only then can we discover what it means for us.

Some distortion always takes place in our application of biblical texts because we are human and not able to understand totally what a writer may have originally intended. This distortion is compounded unless a serious attempt is made to find out first what the text meant to the original audience. A good rule of thumb is, "no text can mean today what it never meant to the original readers."[3]

Without the control of first finding the meaning for the original audience a text can be made to mean almost anything and will likely be applied in a subjective manner. The essential point here is that serious study must be made of the biblical text — historically, grammatically, and literarily before good judgments can be made about application to modern times.

It is not the intention of this essay to deal at length with how to do exegesis of the text — looking for its meaning(s). That aspect, which is frequently the easiest of the interpretative process, is assumed as a prerequisite for application. Rather, the focus here is the formulation of guidelines (not hard and fast "rules") to help the average person apply what has been learned from primary study of the text itself.

Problems in Application

In making application the student encounters several serious problems (some of which are also faced in the exegetical phase of Bible analysis). One of these is the "third-party perspective." The particular book we may be studying was not written primarily to us but, say, to the Romans or Corinthians, etc. In a real sense we are intruders into the original correspondence. Much information and informal understandings assumed between a writer and his audience are unknown to us. Therefore, when we apply a text we must first know something about both the sender and the recipients of the letter and then about their situations.

Another problem involves language. The Bible was originally written in Hebrew and Aramaic (Old Testament) and Greek (New Testament). When we use an English translation we are actually using an "interpretation" of the original language. It is true that every translation is an interpretation. Thus, as we interpret and apply the English text we are interpreting and applying a secondary "interpretation." Ideally, one needs to work straight from the original language, but this is not possible for most. Translations can help bridge the gap between one language and another, but they can never do so one hundred percent. Unfortunately, working with a translation affects both interpretation and application.

An additional factor in application is the "cultural gap." The Bible was written in one culture, and certain problems occur in applying it to another. Practices at home in Corinth or Jerusalem and understood by the readers of the material addressed to them may be totally unknown in our modern culture. The more distance and time there is between the culture presupposed in a biblical document and our own, the greater difficulty there is in making faithful application to the modern world. An example is women's dress.

What may have been very important in the ancient culture, i.e., wearing veils by women, is not strongly held in our culture. In addition, what do we do today with the ancient practice of the "holy kiss," foot washing, and eating meat offered to idols? How do we know when something is cultural and applicable only to the readers in the first century and when it is not? Such questions about culture impact issues such as the role of women, homosexuality, worship practices, and dress, etc.

The recognition that the Bible was not written directly to any living person today must also be considered when working out a methodology for applying those texts in modern society. How much applied only to them and how much, if any, applies to us today? How do we decide what we should take and leave? Or, does the entire Bible apply to us just as much as it did to the original readers? If so, we are in deep trouble because most of us do not have animals for sacrifice nor may we take Paul's cloak and parchments to him as he commanded. How do we decide what to take for today and how much to leave in the ancient world? Such questions must be answered if we are to apply accurately God's word today.

The Restoration Movement

Before looking at specific principles for applying Scripture today, we will examine some of the application methods commonly used in the Restoration movement of which we are part. There has been extensive usage of commands, examples and necessary inference in the Churches of Christ in both interpretation and application — not interpretation only, as many assume. How do we know what applies to us today from the Bible? Answer: look at the commands where we are told what to do. How do we know what to do and when to do it? Answer: look for examples. Also, what may we infer or deduce from the biblical text that applies to us? Answer: look for necessary inferences. All three of these have, of course, been used with considerable refinement over the years.

Commands

Clearly, not all commands in the Bible are intended for us today. For example, when people in the Old Testament were commanded to worship on the Sabbath, that command was specifically given to those under that covenant and not to us today living under the new covenant. A key question about the function of commands is: who is the command given to and under which covenant (Old Testament or New Testament) was it given? Some commands cannot be applied in Western society today, for example, the command not to eat meat offered to idols, because the situation and issues are totally different. It will be discussed more later, but as a caution we should keep in mind that although some commands may be cultural this does not mean that they are nontransferable.[4]

Examples

Not all the examples in the Bible are to be followed. But, if a command is given and then examples of how that command is to be carried out are found, then that type example carries more weight than an isolated one. In Acts 2 the Christians pooled their resources and had all things in common. This is a fine example of Christian love and care, but not one that is binding today, although an example exists of such a practice.

The very difficult issue with reference to examples is what methodology can be used in order to apply examples *consistently*. Thus, why insist on some examples being a part of our church life and not others? How far can we go in insisting that certain examples be adopted as church practice and that people who do not follow these examples are violating Christian principle? Should we "bind" any example?

At times we have examples in the New Testament of a practice, but no command to do it in a certain manner or time. For instance, the Lord's Supper is commanded for Christians as a way to remember the Lord's death, resurrection, and coming. Most all agree that it should be done. But how often? Specific details about time are not commanded — only the act. An example is found, however, in Acts 20:7 of the disciples meeting for what appears to be the Lord's Supper and Paul apparently delaying his trip so he could be present on the first day of the week to take it with them. If it was taken infrequently, is it likely that he would have waited?

So when and how often should Christians take the Lord's Supper today? For me, if the choice in such matters comes down to formulating personally a time and frequency plan for when to take it or else following an example of when it was done in the Bible, why should I not follow the biblical example rather than some human alternative?

Inferences

Inferences from biblical texts may also help us to make applications, but as with both direct commands and examples, great caution must be exercised. This was recognized very early in the Restoration movement by Thomas Campbell who observed that while inferences may be useful, they tended to divide believers. In his judgment, such deductions from Scripture should not be made terms of communion.[5]

Dispensations

The tripartite formula above is not the only way members of the Restoration movement have interpreted and applied Scripture; the three dispensations — the Patriarchal, the Mosaic, and the Christian have also been used. In our movement, the Old Testament has not played a significant role in supporting Christian practice since the belief is held that the New Testament and not the Old Testament will judge us. Emphasis on the dispensations has provided an idea of what is authoritative in each dispensation, what the relationship is between the dispensations, and what might be applied from each to contemporary life.[6]

Study of the Patriarchal and Mosaic dispensations has clearly raised questions about the role of the Old Testament in church life. True, we are not living under the Old Testament, but most recognize that it has value and its influence on the New Testament is seen on almost every page. Recent interest in and appreciation of the Old Testament in the Churches of Christ has posed the question even more sharply of how it should be applied today and in what ways it can be used with profit by modern Christians. The Old Testament is full of intriguing stories, parables, prophecies, and poetry written to help God's people. But how do we use the Old Testament today?[7]

First, we can learn that the stories are not just stories about people who lived in olden times but that they are primarily stories of what God did to and for those people. In each story we should see God's hand and then ask what we can learn that fits our situation.

Second, we should realize that Old Testament stories are not allegories or stories filled with hidden meanings. While some things may be hard to understand, they record the acts of God in history. We must be careful not to read into them mystical views of what are in fact historical accounts. In addition, these stories may or may not have something to say about our situation. Often we can learn what not to do by reading a story about a person. So the lesson to be learned in that case is more negative than positive.

Third, Old Testament narratives usually do not teach directly but only illustrate what is specifically taught elsewhere. As a case in point, when David committed adultery with Bathsheba (2 Samuel 11), no statement is found saying directly that he sinned by having sex with her and in killing her husband. The readers are expected to know that adultery and murder are wrong since they had been taught explicitly already in the Bible (Exod. 20:13-14). The story illustrates in a powerful way the personal disaster such conduct brought into David's life.

Fourth, one must not attempt to apply each individual part of the story but, rather, must look at the whole story for lessons that parallel our situation. The overall story is intended to influence our lives and not the bits and pieces of it.

It is not possible here to give complete guidelines for applying all the different literary types found in the Old Testament such as poetry, prophecy, narrative, parables, etc. But, in a general way Christians should remember the Old Testament is not a covenant we are obligated to keep, and we should not assume that the Old Testament is binding on us. Unless the Old Testament stipulation is renewed in the New Testament, it is not directly binding today. In fact, some aspects of the Old Testament have clearly not been renewed in the New Testament. For example, the Israelite civil laws and ritual laws are not restated or renewed in the New Testament. Such matters only applied to the people of ancient Israel.

Parts of the Old Testament have been renewed in the New Testament such as some of the ethical laws, and they are in that sense, therefore, applicable to Christians today. Thus, the command in Deuteronomy 6:5 to "Love the Lord your God with all your heart, soul and mind" and the words of Leviticus 19:18 "Love your neighbor as yourself" find new applicability in Jesus' teaching (cf. Matt. 5:21-48).

The key is that only what has been explicitly renewed from the Old Testament can be considered part of the New Testament "law of Christ" (cf. Gal. 6:2). A good example of this is that the New Testament restates the Ten Commandments in various ways except for the command to keep the Sabbath day holy. Even here, however, the principle of "rest" inherent in Sabbath day observance could be applied by Christians today (but not the specific command to worship on the Sabbath, i.e., Saturday).

The Problem of Culture

One of the major problems in applying Scripture is deciding what the cultural or time-bound elements are in a passage (i.e., those items intended only for the original readers of either the Old Testament or New Testament) and what are the supracultural or eternal principles. D. A. Carson warns against trying to sort out what is cultural and what is eternal, saying that every truth from God comes in cultural guise — even the language used is cultural. Basically, he is concerned about subjectivity in trying to sort out what is what.[8]

While Carson's caveat should be duly noted, it does remain that some practices — slavery, foot washing, temple feasts, meat offered to idols, the holy kiss, etc. — appear to be distinctly first-century issues and have very little to do with us. Thus, we need to understand which texts are normative and which are not. We must, as Osborne argues, contextualize such first century issues listed above at a "secondary level" since we do not find such practices in our culture.[9]

This secondary level application involves searching for principles imbedded in the original practice that apply today. An example of this is that submission and service could be applied today from the earlier practice of foot washing, but not necessarily the act itself. If, however, in some Third World country today it is still the practice to show hospitality by washing the feet of guests, then the ancient practice could be applied directly without having to find the principle embedded in the action.

Some items in all cultures can be understood and pose no problem for the interpreter. (1) We can, to illustrate this, understand Paul's statements about athletics in his letters with very little difficulty and the same holds concerning his references to economic help provided by various churches. "Common sense" helps us to make application to our day with relative ease. (2) The same is true for "universal" type statements in the Ten Commands which are easy to apply in most cultures since the ideas found in the commands occur among most people, although each culture may have differences in how it defines, for example, murder and adultery. Statements about eating together, loving one's neighbor and many of the Old Testament Proverbs fit into the "universal" cultural category. (3) Statements relating to experiences that are common to all mankind such as "trust," "patience," and events such as illness, death, childbirth, and preparing food are also readily applied. (4) The major difficulty in application occurs when the biblical material is presented in cultural forms specific to the cultural practices of a certain people and they are quite different from ours. As we have seen, however, not all the Scriptural material is given at this "culturally specific, distant-from-us level."[10]

General Rules

What general "rules" then can be utilized to help in making the decision about what is cultural and what is eternal? What guidelines do we have for deciding that something needs to be translated into new settings or simply left in the first century?

First, one must understand the original setting and meaning of a passage before making application. Only then can we look for parallels in our situation with the ancient one. It is, therefore, a major mistake to apply biblical texts to nonparallel contexts. In most cases, if the exegesis has been done well a clear principle emerges which usually transcends the historical particularity addressed in the biblical text. This "principle" does not become timeless, however, being applied at random to every kind of situation. It has to be applied to "genuinely comparable situations."[11] Paul, for instance, forbids Christians from eating pagan meals in the temple based on the "stumbling-block" principle. This teaching is not founded on what merely "offends" another believer but on what will cause that person to be "destroyed" if they copy what another Christian does in good conscience. Beards on preachers may offend some members but will not "destroy" their faith. The same is true of differences over Bible versions and women wearing slacks to worship. The "stumbling-block" principle of 1 Corinthians must only be applied in truly comparable situations.

Second, individual statements must be placed within the broader context of Scripture, meaning that we should not make application on the basis of a single passage. This is not an attempt to do away with obscure or difficult texts. Rather, we must first interpret a text in its own context and then place it within the broader scope of Scripture. Only then should we apply the teaching to our day, for without the "big picture" we may miss the exact meaning and principle found in it. As a sample, the absence of parallels elsewhere in Scripture makes the reference to "baptism for the dead" (1 Cor. 15:29) doubtful as a normative practice for today. Third, we must be aware that different types of biblical material must be interpreted and applied in ways appropriate to that particular material. As an illustration, biblical poetry must not be handled like historical narratives; Old Testament prophecy must not be dealt with in the same way as apocalyptic texts from Daniel or Revelation. The Gospels and Paul's epistles have their own unique characteristics.

Fourth, we should make an effort to distinguish between the central "core" of the message of the Bible and what is more peripheral. This is not to argue for a "canon within the canon" by which some parts of the Bible are seen as authoritative and others are dismissed as unworthy, historically inaccurate, or mutually contradictory. This is also not to reduce the Bible to a handful of "core" matters one must follow to the exclusion of others. It is to recognize, however, that Christ's death and resurrection, his return, etc., are clearly part of the "core" which transcends culture, but the holy kiss, women's head coverings, and foot washing are more peripheral and clearly belong to the first century.

Fifth, one should attempt to distinguish what the New Testament itself sees as inherently moral and what is not. Those matters that are inherently moral are absolute and apply to every culture; those that are not should be left in the first century. For instance, Paul's vice lists never contain cultural items, which are relevant to some cultures and times and not to others. Adultery, drunkenness, homosexual activity, thievery, greed, envy, murder, etc., are always wrong. On the other hand, eating food offered to idols, women wearing head coverings while praying, and Paul's personal preference for celibacy are not inherently moral matters to be observed at all times in all cultures. They become moral issues only by their abuses in certain contexts when such abuses involve hard, disobedient hearts or lack of love.

Sixth, when the biblical text transcends the cultural biases of the author and readers, it is more likely to be applicable for all times. Cases of this include Galatians 3:28 and the issues of slavery, as well as passages related to the universal mission. These are not tied to any specific cultural situation and are universal in application. Although there were those in the first century church who had slaves and saw it as an acceptable part of society, Galatians 3:28

was not limited only to that situation; this text was rightly used in arguments by Christians during the Civil War era against slavery.

Seventh, if a command is totally tied to a cultural situation, then the command is likely cultural and not timeless. But, often it is not easy to determine the extent of the cultural influence on a command. Chery Guth suggests several tests in such cases: (1) Does the author's language contain cultural indicators that might help one to search for broader principles behind the first century situation applicable for today? The language used in 1 Corinthians 11:2-16 about head coverings for women ("scandal," "disgrace," "no other practice," etc.) may be a pointer (but not absolute proof) that this practice is cultural and applies only to the primitive church. (2) Does it point to a local custom or cultural institution? The wearing of headgear was very strongly associated with first century worship (at least in Corinth and likely in other places) much more so than in our time. Perhaps, however, in some Islamic context today it would be best, in keeping with Moslem influence on a culture, for women missionaries to wear a head covering as in the first century. In modern American culture the wearing of a hat or the non-wearing of one by women does not matter. In some cultures today, however, it would matter as it did in the first century. (3) Does the author address only a culture-specific situation or question? Paul gave his views on meat offered to idols because of a specific question mentioned in Chloe's letter. The principle of the weak and strong applies today, but not the specifics (unless we have a similar cultural situation).

Conclusion

Contemporary students of God's word first determine the meaning of the original text and then seek to apply it to present times. In doing this, the student must take care not to be relativistic or legalistic and must guard against forcing the Bible to be relevant. It is already relevant; we must discover in what ways, if we can. In disagreements over what is applicable to every age and what is culturally conditioned, we must be guided above all by the command to love one another (1 John 3:16).

In many ways, the biblical interpreter faces the difficult task of taking information given first in the language, culture, and thought forms of an ancient society and making it connect with his contemporaries. To do this, the interpreter must know first how to get at the original meaning of the biblical text, using skillfully all the rules and principles of interpretation. Yet, as Julius Scott has observed, there is a subjective element involved as we transfer the meaning of texts written originally for one world to another.[12]

No rules are given in Scripture for doing exegesis or for the final stage of application. No "holy" method exists, only human guidelines. We can logically deduce certain principles and use methods that have been applied to other literature with success. But ultimately, human judgments and evaluations have to be made. Other than the integrity of the interpreter, the major safeguard against this subjective application phase is the quality of work done in examination of the text and its original message to the first readers.

But when it is all said and done, the person who applies the word of God must seek the direction and guidance of the Holy Spirit and be open to and submissive to him. Jesus promised the presence of his Spirit to "guide into all truth" (John 16:13). This is not a modern Pentecostal type charismatic "guidance," but true submission before him so that we do not so much interrogate and dissect the Scripture looking for meaning and application, but rather, we ourselves are interrogated by it. Only then can we begin to apply God's word for our day.

Endnotes

[1]This survey is indebted to A. Berkeley Mickelsen, *Interpreting the Bible* (Grand Rapids: Eerdmans, 1972), 21-53.

[2]See the article on recent approaches to interpreting Paul's epistles by G.R. Osborne, "Hermeneutics/Interpreting Paul," *Dictionary of Paul and His Letters*, (Downers Grove, IL: InterVarsity, 1993), 388-397. See also his full text on hermeneutics, *The Hermeneutical Spiral* (Downers Grove, IL: InterVarsity, 1991). Among scores of helpful tools for exegetical analysis see the valuable work by Gordon D. Fee, *New Testament Exegesis*, rev. ed. (Louisville: Westminster/John Knox, 1993) and Gordon D. Fee and Douglas Stuart, *How to Read the Bible for All Its Worth* (Grand Rapids: Zondervan, 1982), hereafter designated as *HRBFW*. For a discussion of philosophical hermeneutics, literary approaches, socio-science approaches and liberationist theologies with reference to biblical interpretation see J. Paul Pollard, "Recent Trends in Biblical Interpretation," *Restoration Quarterly* 34 (Second Quarter 1992): 65-81.

[3]Fee and Stuart, *HRBFW*, 27.

[4]Ramesh P. Richard, "Application Theory in Relation to the New Testament," *Bibliotheca Sacra* 143 (July-September 1986): 212.

[5]Thomas H. Olbricht, "Hermeneutics in The Churches of Christ," *Restoration Quarterly* 37 (First Quarter1995): 13.

[6]Ibid, 15.

[7]The following is a condensation of ideas taken from Fee and Stuart, *HRBFW*, 73-78; 137-139.

[8]D.A. Carson, "Factors Determining Current Hermeneutical Debate," in *Biblical Interpretation and the Church* (Nashville: Nelson, 1985), 19-20.

[9]Osborne, *Hermeneutical*, 327.

[10]Charles H. Kraft, "Interpreting In Cultural Context," *Journal of the Evangelical Theological Society* 21 (December1978): 362-363.

[11]Fee and Stuart, *HRBFW*, 63.

[12]J. Julius Scott, Jr., "Some Problems in Hermeneutics For Contemporary Evangelicals," *Journal of the Evangelical Theological Society* 22 (March 1979): 76-77.

SECTION FIVE
QUESTIONS ABOUT THE CHURCH

It is clear from Scripture that Jesus came not only to save individuals but also to call them into a loving community of faith that we call the church. However, our flesh-and-blood experience in the church often does not correspond to the lofty ideals that we read in Scripture. This has led some to be dismissive of the importance of what they call "organized religion." But the authors of this section see the importance of the church and crucial questions about our "life together."

In the opening article, Ross Cochran does basic "ecclesiology" (doctrine of the church), asking from a real-world point of view what the church is and what it is to do. He calls us to a biblical and dynamic view of the importance of Christian community.

Tom Eddins follows with an examination of the concept that is central to the identity of Churches of Christ, restorationism. We have generally understood our reason to exist to be to "restore the New Testament Church," a concept that has come under scrutiny in the last decade. Eddins leads us to consider the possibilities and problems of a "restoration movement."

Finally, Tom Alexander leads us into a discussion of church leadership. One of the distinguishing marks of Churches of Christ has been leadership by local elders in each church. But Alexander leads us beyond the mere question of local church leadership to a discussion of what kind of leadership churches should have. In a day of big business management techniques, his call for truly biblical servant leadership could not be more timely.

In a day when people can choose churches like restaurants, the call to a deeper, fuller understanding of what it means to be a church of Christ could not be more important.

Chapter Fourteen

Do we really need the church?

Ross Cochran
Harding University
Searcy, Arkansas

This is a big old ship, Bill. She creaks, she rocks, she rolls, and at times she makes you want to throw up. But she gets where she's going. Always has, always will, until the end of time. With or without you.[1]

Situation #1

Robert served the church diligently for many years, as his parents had done before him. Now, however, at the age of 47, his involvement in the church feels like a distant dream. He attends the assembly of the Christians only occasionally, ever since that Sunday afternoon fourteen months ago. If only he had never agreed to serve on that committee! To think of all the hours he invested in those plans for that new ministry proposal only to see his input quickly and completely dismissed by the chairman. How, he wonders, could anyone be so narrow-minded? He knows better now. He's alone, but he'll not be hurt again.

Situation #2

Amanda stares at the half-inch of coffee at the bottom of her cup while her fingers gently stroke its handle. Across the table sits Terri, a friend she invited over with hopes of talking about spiritual matters. But after a courageous attempt to talk to her friend about her soul, Amanda sits quietly now, embarrassed to hear the words that still lay stinging in her ears, "Do you think you people are the only ones going to heaven?"

Situation #3

As Jared sat in the assembly that Sunday morning in February, he paused during the singing and listened. The words sounded familiar, yet also foreign. Did he really believe these lyrics? And who are these people with whom he is meeting? How well does he really know them? For some time now, Jared has sensed his attachment to the church diminishing. His faith feels dormant; his soul numb.

These cases illustrate the need for the church to do the work for which Christ has commissioned it and to do it well. In many of its local expressions, however, the church is plagued by a variety of problems. These problems include (but are not limited to) inadequate vision, insufficient leadership and initiative, superficial commitment on the part of too many members, divisive attitudes, tension stemming from generational and theological differences, and (in some cases) extensive conformity to the values of contemporary culture. In addition, the church is not having as great an effect on the world as it could. The metaphors of *salt* and *light* still sound familiar, but we wonder about the degree to which the church is actually functioning as a change agent in the lives of people.

In North America, within the church as well as outside it, many today sense that the church has lost its fire, its reason for existence. Often, local churches are not held in high esteem by those in their surrounding communities. Worse still, the church is frequently derided by its own members. Critics abound. Perhaps they have a point.

Yet, a tremendously high price was paid — the blood of Jesus Christ — to purchase the church, thus affirming its inestimable worth. The church is of great value to God and exists for the noblest of all causes. Nevertheless, a gap exists between what the church was intended to be and what we often experience it to be. How should we respond to this gap?

The church has always had problems; it always will. But our desire to see the church flourish (even though problem-plagued) prompts the asking of some foundational questions as to the nature of the church and its primary business. This chapter will proceed by responding to a series of questions regarding the nature, purpose and importance of the church.

What is the church?
What is the work of the church?
How do we sustain involvement in the church?
How important is the church?

What is the Church?

Our language reveals that, somewhere along the way, we lost a biblical perspective on the nature of the church. For example, we say, "Let's go to church" or we ask, "Where do you go to church?" The way the question is cast implies that some think of the church as a place. More specifically, some talk as if the building in which we assemble is the church ("Let's go over to the church and set up for the fellowship dinner"). Others misspeak when they ask, "What time does church begin?" Is church a meeting? Is it an event?

In our more thoughtful moments, we would admit, "Of course not." Why then do we speak as if it is? It is a short journey from *speaking* as if the church were a building or a worship assembly to *believing* that it is. When we speak of the church in this way, we miseducate our children and each other, and we reduce the church to something significantly less than its biblical portrait. Christianity becomes going to a location, sitting in a building, and participating in a meeting. Inadvertently, through lazy language, we teach Christians to be passive. We all decry the alarming amount of passivity among Christians. Could it be that our language is partly responsible for it?

We need to reclaim from Scripture a more accurate understanding of the true nature of the church. The English word "church" is a translation of the Greek word *ekklesia*. The basic meaning of that word was "assembly." Paul used *ekklesia* at times to refer to the meetings (or assemblies) of Christians, though he also used it to refer to the Christians whether assembled or not.[2] The term clearly refers to people. The church is a people who metaphorically have assembled around the cross and entered into dynamic, transforming relationships with their Savior and each other.

The New Testament uses several images to convey the nature of the church. It is compared to a building, built on the foundation that is Christ (1 Cor. 3:10-17). It is the spouse or bride of Christ (Eph. 5:24-33). It is a new city (Rev. 21:1-4). It is the family of God (1 Pet. 4:7).

But it is the human body that provides the most powerful and frequently used image for the church. In his letters, the apostle

Paul sees the church as the spiritual body of Jesus (Rom. 12:4-8; 1 Cor. 12:12-31; Eph. 4:11-16; 5:23). Just as the Word of God was incarnated first in the physical body of Jesus (John 1:1,14), it is now incarnated for a second time in the spiritual body of Jesus, the church.[3] Jesus is the head of the Body. Just as in a human being, the body responds to the signals of its head, so also the church enfleshes or incarnates the will of Jesus.

What are some of the implications of this image? First, this means that the church is a Christ-centered people. As I write this, I am aware of what a cliché that has become. However, in the absence of affirming Christ as our central focal point, other things can become our center. Cultural values, the *status quo* of tradition, or even our own desire for comfort or control can gain by default the central place in our identity and thinking, unless we intentionally and consistently reaffirm Christ as our central focus and chief signal caller.

A second implication of the head-body image is that the Gospels become primary texts for understanding the nature of the church. We tend naturally to look at the book of Acts to ascertain the nature of the church, since that is a primary source for learning of the activities of the earliest Christians. When we go to Acts first, however, we ignore the fact that Acts is Part Two of Luke's writings. Part One is Luke's Gospel. But the relationship between Luke and Acts involves more than just sequence. The relationship between these two documents is one of continuity and of cause and effect. Luke states that his Gospel records what Jesus *began* to do and teach (Acts 1:1). From this we can infer that Acts records what some of the apostles (as well as the earliest Christians) *continued* to do and teach. Acts records the continuation of the ministry of Jesus through the church.

The relationship of Luke to Acts is also one of cause and effect. Jesus is the impetus, the early church is the response. Jesus is to the church what the splash is to the ripples. What we see the early church doing in Acts is the fruit of the ministry of Jesus described in Luke and the other Gospels. If we want to experience the fruit of Acts, we must sow the seed of the Gospels. The implication of this relationship of Acts to Luke is that the church must draw its agenda and identity from the Christ of the Gospels, then from the church of Acts. The diagram below depicts this relationship.

172

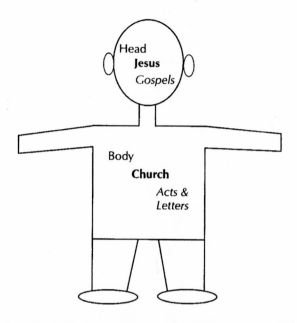

The church is led by Christ, much like our physical head prompts our bodies. How does the church discern the leading of Christ? The answer is, at least initially, through examining the four Gospels. It is from those four documents that we come to understand the primary concerns of Christ. Based on the analogy of the relationship of the body to its head, the concerns of Christ become the primary concerns of the church. Certainly the remainder of the New Testament documents are vitally important, yet we must read them in a way that corresponds with, rather than contradicts, the emphases established by Jesus in the Gospels. For example, Jesus teaches in Matthew that being his disciple is more about treating others with justice and mercy (Matt. 7:12; 22:34-40; 25:31-46) than it is about obedience to technical religious minutia (Matt. 9:9-12; 12:1-14; 23:23). Consequently, it would be a mistake to read the remainder of the New Testament documents in search of tiny details that are only briefly and infrequently mentioned. In order to be a church that truly is *of Christ*, we must allow the contents of the Gospels to assume a place of prominence in our self-definition and to be primary sources for setting the church's agenda.

What Is the Work of the Church?

What did Jesus intend for his church to do? What is the primary business of the church? What are its chief tasks? What activities and dynamics must be present, otherwise the church becomes a lifeless corpse? There are many ways to cast a response to these questions. The figure below attempts to capture in a succinct form the essence of the church's tasks.

The Primary Tasks of the Church

W e
orship
ord
ork
orld

Each of these five W's symbolizes a separate activity that the church must intentionally pursue. *We* stands for the community (or fellowship) Christians should experience with each other. The relationships that Christians strive to develop with each other are best described as supportive, affirming, nurturing, and loving. Even a cursory look at the "one another" texts of the New Testament would call us to a depth of relationship that goes beyond mere acquaintance.[4] The church is the family of God (1 Pet. 4:17), and Christians are to provide for each other the interpersonal support we typically associate with strong, healthy families. We travel best on our spiritual journey when we travel in intimate, loving, and supportive company.

The word *Worship* symbolizes our experience of meeting together to praise God and to encourage one another in Christian life and faith. Scripture teaches that, in one sense, all of life is worship, and every activity we engage in ought to be a sacrifice to God (Rom. 12:1-2; Heb. 12:28–13:10). However, those occasions when we meet together to eat the Lord's Supper and reaffirm our identity as Christians through singing, praying, and hearing God's Word function to rekindle the spiritual fire in our hearts. Just as a lump of coal removed from the fire will soon cease burning, so Christians, if removed from regular interaction with other Christians around the retelling of the Christian Story, will likewise lose their fire. That is why the writer of Hebrews urged his readers to be faithful in their attendance to and participation in the assembly of the Christians (Heb. 10:24-25).

Word stands for our commitment to study Scripture, realizing that it mediates God's Word to us as we reflect on its truths and the applications of its messages to our lives. Bible study and knowledge alone are of little value, however. The Word of God must be obeyed before our commitment to it is complete. We must *live* the Word, in addition to hearing it (Jas. 1:22-25).

Taking its cue from Christ, the church is committed to a variety of expressions of helpfulness to others. Central to the tasks of the church is the **Work** in which it engages to assist other persons, both within and without the Christian community. Sitting up with the sick, bringing food to the bereaved, loading a truck for those who are moving, offering hospitality to newcomers to our communities and assemblies are all important expressions of concern.

Even small acts of care are significant. Jesus said that giving something as simple as a cup of cold water is worthy of reward (Matt. 10:42). Benevolence, ministry, service, and foot washing are all terms which refer to the diligent labor in which we engage in order to "do good to all people, especially to those who belong to the family of believers" (Gal. 6:10).

The church has a love-hate relationship with the **World**. On the one hand, Scripture informs us that the world is to be shunned, even hated (1 John 2:15-17), and it is antagonistic toward the disciples of Jesus (John 15:18-25). On the other hand, the world is loved by God (John 3:16), and we are commissioned to proclaim the Gospel (Matt. 28:16-20; 1 Pet. 2:11-12) and be salt and light to it (Matt. 5:13-16).

How are we to understand our relationship to the world in light of these mixed attitudes towards it in Scripture? We can discern that "world" may refer to the created universe or the people who inhabit the earth. It also may refer to a value system which is opposed to the will of God. Thus, we need to balance doing *ministry* to the world, while simultaneously maintaining an *identity* that is distinctly different from the world. We need the church because it helps us balance these two essential activities. The words of Jesus ring clear: "Be *in* the world, but *not of* the world" (John 17:13-19).

Each of these five W's is important. Something critically significant in the life of the church will be lost if any of them is neglected.

175

In addition, these tasks are interrelated. Our commitment to study Scripture (Word) prompts us to meet together for prayer and praise (Worship) and to fellowship with each other (We). In turn, our time together reminds and encourages us to serve others in the name of Christ (Work) and to witness to lost persons in speech and lifestyle (World) in ways that highlight the attractiveness of the Gospel.

But involvement in the church is not always easy to maintain. Burnout, disappointment, and other debilitating attitudes and experiences threaten to lead us to retreat from active involvement in the community of Christ. We need a way to sustain prolonged involvement in the church.

How Do We Sustain Commitment to and Involvement in the Church?

Unlike Saul who experienced a first-hand, direct encounter with the risen Christ (Acts 9:1-19), each of us came to know Christ indirectly. That is, rather than meeting Christ face to face, we were introduced to Jesus through other Christians. For many of us, these Christians were our family members. The reality is, the church (beginning with our family) provides our initial exposure to Jesus.

Self   Church   Jesus

After we have been in the church for awhile, however, we begin to discover that, though purchased with divine love at substantial cost, the church still has a considerable amount of humanity in it.

Many children identify with the experience of recalling a time when they thought their parents were perfect. Sometime during their early adolescence, however, they made the disappointing discovery that their parents were flawed like all other people.

176

Something similar happens to us after we have been associated with the church for awhile. Soon after entering an adolescent period in our journey with the church, we come to see its imperfections and those of its members. These include (but are not limited to) hypocrisy, immaturity, gossip, divisiveness, politicking, materialism, and superficial levels of commitment. We come to understand the feelings of a writer, unknown to me, who said:

> To dwell above with the saints we love,
> Oh, that will be grace and glory.
> But to dwell below with the saints we know,
> Well, that's another story!

| Self | Church | Jesus |

What happens when we discover problems in the church? Recognizing flaws in the church (or parents, or spouses, or friends, or schools, etc.) does not mean we are being cynical nor unchristian. Certainly Paul recognized problems in the churches with which he dealt. Even a cursory reading of 1 Corinthians will confirm this.

Upon discovering the gap between what the church is called to be and what the church actually is, we must choose how to react to that gap. We could choose to react with cynicism, disillusionment, anger, or frustration. We could get disgusted, discouraged, or depressed. We could bail out, cry out, check out, or drop out. And many have.

Too many are giving up on the church and leaving it. Some who stay disengage emotionally, and though they continue to attend the assemblies, the intensity of their involvement with the church diminishes significantly. As long as our primary relationship is with the church, and we find the church disappointing, we are vulnerable to the possibility of dropping out of it, or at least decreasing to a minimal level our involvement with it.

Some of us have lost our passion for the church and for our ministries within it. How can we come to love the church passionately again? Can anything be done to keep individual Christians from disengaging from the church after they discover its human shortcomings? Is there a way to ensure that no matter how problem-riddled a local church becomes, we will not be disillusioned with it?

We need a change in perspective, a new paradigm, about how we understand our relationship to the church. To gain this, we must imagine our relationship to Christ and to the church in a new way.

The secret is to understand our relationship to the church as secondary rather than primary. Instead of the church being foremost in our experience and our affections, Christ becomes our primary "other." Jesus taught this by imaging our relationship to him as branches attached to a vine (John 15:4-17). When we develop a vital relationship with Jesus, we are attached to him directly. Our relationship with the church is a result of our relationship to him, not the other way around.

We eventually realize that Jesus has not only sent us into all the world. He has also sent us into his church. He commissions us to go into the midst of his people and lay our lives down for them. What a contrast to the attitude that says, "I am not coming to the assembly anymore, because I do not get anything out of it." We do not participate in the life of the church because it is beneficial. We participate because the One from whom we take our orders tells us to do so. Furthermore, it is through loving the church passionately and actively that we show our love to God (Heb. 6:10).

178

What about all the flaws in the church? They are still there. In fact, when we see with the eyes of Jesus, we discover even more imperfections than previously. The difference, however, is that we will anticipate the flaws rather than feel ambushed by them.

Jesus tolerated and served The Twelve, even with all their immaturity. Following his example, consequently, we can love the church just as passionately *after* we become aware of its blemishes as when we were blissfully ignorant of them. When our primary relationship is with Jesus, we will come to the aid of the church as a big brother rescuing his little sister from the cruelties of the neighborhood bully.

How Important Is the Church?

Do we really need the church? If so, why? What is it that the church provides in people's lives? In the world? One way to think about the importance of the church is to ask, "If the church ceased to exist, what activities, dynamics, messages, and ways of being would be lost from people's lives?"

One reason the church is important is because it helps people remain faithful to God. The writer of Hebrews urged his readers to continue assembling with other Christians (Heb. 10:24-25). Ever wonder why? What is supplied in our lives by being together? Simply being in the same room with each other may or may not be helpful. But if everyone intentionally attempted to contribute a word of encouragement to someone else, we would all be helped. An untended fire will slowly, but inevitably, go out. We need the church to tend the fires of our faith.

We need the church to continue the work of Christian education in our lives, in the lives of our children, and in the lives of all Christians. The term "Christian education" is used most often today to refer to the teaching-learning settings we call "Bible classes." More broadly, however, Christian education refers to the entire impact of a church on the life of an individual. In a sense, everything we do as a church is educative, including the songs we sing (and those we do not), the Scripture passages from which we preach (and those we do not), the activities in which the church engages (and those it does not), the people whom we seek to include (and those we do not). A church sends messages to its members and to its surrounding community through the multiplicity of choices it makes, as well as how it makes those decisions.

This educative dimension of the church's life can be described in terms of three ongoing processes: *forming, informing,* and *transforming.*[5] These processes can be symbolized in the following way:

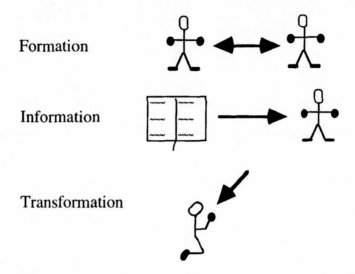

Formation

Information

Transformation

Formation refers to the process of our being shaped spiritually by observing and imitating good models of Christian believing and living. The old adage that "faith is more caught [from others] than taught" got to be an old adage because it contains a significant truth. I learn much about being a Christian father from brothers in the Lord who incarnate well the wisdom of God concerning that role. We are formed in Christian faith and life, even from our childhood, by observing it in, and absorbing it from, other Christians. We recognize the critical importance of the family unit as the primary source of spiritual formation for children during the most impressionable time of life. Likewise, the church is God's tool for shaping, equipping, and maturing his people.

Information refers to the spiritual benefit we receive from studying and applying Scripture to the specific contexts of our lives. More than simply knowing what the Bible says is needed here, however. Jesus himself indicated that it is possible to know the Scriptures but not know him (John 5:38-39). Our knowledge of the Bible should go beyond cognition to a knowing that challenges and shapes our values, our attitudes, our behavior, and our ways of being with others. Transformation of our desires as well as our deeds is the goal. A knowledge of Scripture informs us about the specific outcomes of our transformation.

Transformation symbolizes a work done on believers by God as they open their lives to the possibilities of change while trying to grow in the accuracy and consistency of their imitation of Christ. Paul recognized this process when he said, "And we, who with unveiled faces all reflect the Lord's glory, are being transformed into his likeness with ever-increasing glory . . ." (2 Cor. 3:18). This is also the metamorphosis Paul refers to when he instructed the Christians in Rome to "be transformed by the renewing of your mind" (Rom. 12:1-2).

We need the church because it initiates and sustains a process of spiritual formation in the lives of people. The church is the medium through which persons are formed, informed, and transformed from pre-Christians to Christians and then to mature, mobilized Christians.

We need the church to shape us into a greater likeness of Christ, so that our knowing, doing, and being will become an increasingly more accurate reflection of his image.

We need the church to remind us of what God wants us to be about. Distractions abound. The church helps keep us focused on the central values of our faith.

We need the church to incarnate and proclaim Christ to the world. The church is the syringe that in each generation and culture injects the world with the Gospel.

We need the church, and the church needs us. By working together, the purposes of the church can be realized through us, within us, and between us.

We need the church because it stands beside people throughout their entire life span. As Philip Slate has stated, "In the church we are with people from womb to tomb."

All people need the Lord. To the extent that the church functions as the body of Christ, people need the church.

Endnotes

[1]J.F. Powers, *Wheat That Springeth Green.* Knopf (Random House), 1988, as quoted in Philip Yancey, *Church: Why Bother?* (Grand Rapids, MI: Zondervan, 1998), 17.

[2]See the discussion and support of this in Everett Ferguson, *The Church of Christ: A Biblical Ecclesiology for Today* (Grand Rapids, MI: Eerdmans, 1996), 130-131.

[3]See Rubel Shelly and Randall J. Harris, *The Second Incarnation: A Theology for the 21st Century Church* (West Monroe, LA: Howard Publishing, 1992).

[4]Examples of these "one another" texts include, but are not limited to, Romans 12:10,16; 15:7,14; Galatians 5:13; Ephesians 4:2,32; Hebrews 10:24-25; 1 Peter 1:22.

[5]To my knowledge Thomas Groome was the first religious educator to use the words form, inform, and transform together (see page 8 of his book, *Sharing Faith*). He proposes an approach to Christian education which he terms "Shared Christian Praxis." His most recent and fully developed explanation of his approach is in *Sharing Faith: A Comprehensive Approach to Religious Education and Pastoral Ministry* (San Francisco: HarperSanFrancisco, 1991). A more accessible and concise expression of his approach is available in *Youthworker* 7 (Summer 1990): 20-26.

Chapter Fifteen

Should we call for a
"restoration" of the church?

Tom Eddins
Harding University
Searcy, Arkansas

In his 1992 publication, subtitled *Congress, Term Limits and the Recovery of Deliberative Democracy*, political columnist George Will laments the pitiable state to which the American Congress has fallen, particularly in the public esteem. He is vitally concerned with the recovery of the legislative branch's place of primacy (as he sees it) in our constitutional system, and to this end he proposes a course of action which he thinks holds promise for this very noble end. In his own words, he wants "to restore Congress to competence and respect." Significantly, his book is entitled *Restoration*.

The idea of the recovery of a preexistent, and perhaps "pristine," past is nothing unique to politics or political philosophy. Neither is it unique to time or place in a myriad of other areas. As the *status quo* is perceived to degenerate, there may naturally be a longing for a real or imagined past "Golden Age." At the time of this writing, Americans are looking nostalgically at past, and sometimes fairly recent, decades, longing for what they imagine was a better time. A return to that real or imagined better decade (or shorter or longer era) might or might not bring satisfaction. But the problems of the present seem to make the possibility appealing.

Particularly in religion, *some such concept* has often been suggested as a solution to besetting ills. Whether couched in terms such as reformation, restoration, recovery of primitivism, or other similar terminology, the concept has often held allure. When present conditions are *prima facie* unacceptable, one possible course of action is a return to prior circumstances and conditions, especially those seen as superior or absolutely right. If those conditions are taken to be revealed by God as his own and distinctive way, then all the better.

The problems of the "modern" religious scene are so obvious and graphic as to need no elaboration here. For centuries Christendom has been recognized as having been marred by flaws, both theoretical and practical. Those who hold Christianity dear bemoan the squalor of such a *status quo*. Whether it be the doctrinal aberrations of misguided heresy or the ethical abominations that have blighted mankind from the outset, the need for correction is obvious. Indeed, those who hold to the unique truth of Christianity see its proper practice as the only real hope for a satisfactory life or a meaningful future. Other systems, noble though their intentions might be, are absent certain elements essential for an acceptable life before God. Perverted Christianity is quite clearly exactly what its designation suggests. What then is to be done to bring about the overall desirable and rightly acceptable state of affairs for mankind?

The question to be considered here is, "Should we call for a restoration of the church?" While not holding "the church" as somehow superior to the Savior (for it is simply the body of his people) or suggesting that it is the total "end-in-itself" (since it is of no import without its head), should we see its proper restoration, according to its original design, as a desirable goal? Would such a restoration solve all, or any of, the significant ills (distinctly religious or otherwise) afflicting our world? While recognizing the difficulties inherent in such an approach, the answer to be suggested here is, without hesitation, yes.

Some Preconditions

The call for restoration may be taken as *a priori* axiomatic by many, but more careful reflection will no doubt reveal that it is inoperable or irrelevant apart from certain necessary preconditions. While these conditions *do* obtain, their articulation, and an understanding of them, is important in affirming the desirability of the restoration procedure. These preconditions involve the fact of the static nature of at least some elements of the "primitive/ideal church," as well as a recognition of the loss of at least some of the elements of that static identity over time. To summarize, if there were to be no significant enduring aspects of the church's identity, or if some of these permanent aspects of its identity have not been lost, the call for restoring them becomes either irrelevant or needless.

The Static Nature of "Christianity"

The need for flexibility in a changing world is obvious. A way of life that cannot adapt itself to changing circumstances will sooner or later fall by the intellectual and practical wayside. Of what use is any way of life that cannot give answers to the evolving circumstances and problems of ongoing history? While past systems of thought or ways of life might be interesting matters of historical curiosity, or even beginning points for the construction of future useful systems, if they contain no elements of abiding truth, they hardly qualify as absolute goals for the solving of present or future problems.

The difference between the world of the early church and that of the approaching twenty-first century is evident. Advances that all right-thinking people heartily embrace make our world obviously different from that of the first Christian century. If the development of science is the most significant accomplishment of modern intellectual history, as many maintain, then the adoption of its (modern) solutions surely provides answers for many significant problems. Cultural change, while often debatable as to its advantage, renders many elements of the past no longer the most relevant focus of attention. If the world has changed so much, why call for a restoration of something so possibly antiquated?

Relevant to the question here under consideration is an inquiry about the nature of true religion. For purposes of clarification, two potential "models" of the nature of religion might be considered.

1. One way of conceptualizing religion is to imagine that God's way is "dynamic." According to such a scheme/conception, adaptability becomes not only a strength, but practically a defining characteristic. Here "God's way" becomes simply a function of the supposed "best thinking" of the times. More than this, it is dynamic in that it is marked by continuous change as history "progresses," and the modern intellect is applied to religious, as well as scientific or cultural, questions. Answers (or "positions") of the past are of no particularly *defining* consequence. What was true in the past has no binding consequence in the present or the future. "Truth" abides (if such an expression might be rightly applied

185

here) in a state of flux. Nothing about religion is permanent. A traditional analogy of this view imagines a seed as opposed to a developing plant. While the seed may at one time have been the reality, the growing, developing, constantly changing plant makes ongoing reality quite different. (And an advocate of this view might scoffingly ask, "Who would want only the seed when he might have a beautifully developed rose bush?"

2. The second model of religion might best be described as the "historic" view. While not ignoring the fact of changing scientific and cultural conditions (many of which may ask important questions about religion), adherents of this model posit (at least some) abiding or constant elements in true religion. The exact extent or number of the enduring facets of belief or practice in this approach is irrelevant to the conception. The essential feature is the unchanging nature of what might be described as "the heart of the faith." Whereas the dynamic conception could be counted upon to find no absolute and universal truths, the historic view provides the concept of a core of elements that can be counted upon to remain in spite of the constantly changing nature of society's views and practices. Observe that while it is not intrinsic to this approach to demand that every single practice of the historic entity be emulated, it is a part of the definition that some are. To reject "the core" is to reject the approach, according to this view.

If one were to consider "the church" in light of these two possible models, entirely different conceptions appear. Given the dynamic view, there are no static or enduring elements of the church — indeed, by definition, there could not be. Any continuation of earlier facets of the church's identity would exist by sheer coincidence — they would happen to conform to the evolving entity. The "early church" simply was the way that it was, with no enduring significance for later times, its contemporary characteristics being of no lasting value. On the other hand, given the historic view, it is at least possible that significant and abiding elements appear in the makeup of the primitive church — elements present by God's design and intended by him for later ages of its existence as well. Only on the basis of the historic view would it seem logical to press for a restoration of the church.

A realistic consideration of the New Testament documents can lead one only to the view that the Christian religion is by nature historic. It will perhaps suffice at this point to say that there is a "faith that was once for all entrusted to the saints" (Jude 3). Whatever the significant elements of that faith are, including whatever the static elements of that aspect of it known as "the church" are, they should abide. The evident intentions of Paul to mold the early church according to God's design bear witness to a divine design for the church. The exact nature and extent of the characteristics might be debated, but whatever they are, they need to be preserved. The identity of the church is important. If it is not, "restoration" is irrelevant.

"The Apostasy"

But the static nature of Christianity is only the first of the two preconditions. The significance of the procedure of restoration also presupposes that the identifying characteristics of the entity to be restored have been lost. If they yet remain, "restoration" is needless.

The history of Christianity can hardly be understood to be that of a continuous affirmation of the above-mentioned abiding elements of the Christian system, whatever they are. The jarring, jangling, and contradictory affirmations of a divided Christendom make a mockery of the unity for which Jesus so fervently prayed. Although a total tracing of a departure/apostasy from the original faith can hardly be undertaken here, a few observations are in order.

The New Testament itself can be adduced as a predictor of apostasy. Such passages as Acts 20:28-32, 2 Thessalonians 2:1-12, 1 Timothy 4:1-3, and 2 Timothy 4:1-4 speak eloquently of Paul's expectation of departures from the faith. The exact things to which Paul refers in these passages may continue to be the focus of exegetical questions (e.g., "Exactly who is the 'lawless one' in 2 Thessalonians 2:3?"), but the reality of his expectation is beyond dispute. Further, as history unfolded, no one can deny that apostasy became a reality. Whether it be matters of external or internal characteristics, doctrinal or moral disputes, *et al.*, the purity of the ideal was lost. Only the uninformed would doubt that the medieval Roman institution was in need of reform. The ensuing Protestant Reformation made great gains, but at the price of other theological costs. The fragmented, warring groups that emerged fight one another to this day to the general detriment of the modern religious world. Whether it be spirit, doctrine, or practice, both modern Christendom and the religious world as a whole present a clear departure from the ideals of the primitive Christian ideal.

The Restoration Ideal

Those who affirm and love Christianity are rightly incensed by the turn of events described in the preceding section. While loving the primitive ideal, they abhor the result of two thousand years of human perversion of it! It is therefore logical that they might seek some approach that would allow for the affirmation of the ideal, shedding the accretions of aberrant historical contrivance. It is *in this context* (i.e., with these preconditions) that the ideal of restoration is meaningful.

The call for restoration is nothing more than the call to be Christians in the most proper sense of the term. The church, the body of the Savior's people, the practitioners of his will, is the institution of which they are *de facto* members. It is a body within the proper parameters of which his people function and find fellowship with others of the same faith. When it is constituted as he directs, functions according to his instructions, and molds itself by his expectations, it brings him honor and stands as a witness to the glory of God. When, on the basis of the instruction of the Word of God, Christian people practice the essentials of the Christian faith, the church will emerge restored and pure.

It is not the purpose of this paper to delineate all the particulars of the original Christian system. Indeed, as will be noted below, the discovery/implementation of them may be one of the toughest pragmatic tasks of the modern Christian endeavor. However, should the pristine system be the true way of God, the obviously incumbent task for godly people is to strive to recover/restore that way. In response to the obviously significant question, "What is to be done now?" the truly Christian response is, "Restore the original way."

This *concept* is hardly unique to any particular place and time. While many different terms have been used, the idea of "getting back to the original" has been a theme recurring in a multitude of thinkers/reformers. Indeed, imagining that one has "gotten behind" contemporary perversions and recovered a New Testament thought/practice has been common, even if having truly done so may well be a different proposition! But the ideal of restoration, the goal of the pristine, stands as the meaningful pursuit for Christians in the wake of a past that has seen the abuse of the true way of the Savior.

Some Difficulties

But the articulation of ideals may prove to be relatively easy compared to the realistic attainment of the ends desired. When ancient Israelite religion was perverted in a multitude of ways, the calling voice of the prophets was no guarantee that God's way would be easily recovered in practice. People who should have listened, understood, and responded, chose ways other than those of the God who had so graciously treated them. Whether they turned a deaf ear, failed to understand, or simply chose not to respond, for reasons best known only to them, their ancient faith often continued only in a polluted form.

There are many today who apparently imagine the realization of the ideal of restoration as inherently simple. With faith in the New Testament documents, trust in their clarity, and confidence in their own interpretational abilities, some seem to imply that no intelligent seeker could possibly miss the recovery of the pristine ideal. Even though we are two thousand years removed from the documents that instruct us, even though they do not always *directly* address some issues that must have significance, and even though we are painfully aware of our human intellectual frailties, some scoff at those who suggest the practical difficulty involved in unity among those of faith.

While affirming the importance of the restoration ideal, it seems prudent to at least call attention to some problematic matters. Many of these center around settling the simple-sounding question, "What must be restored?" The initial, and no doubt correct, response, "Only the essentials," simply postpones the giving of a more definitive answer. The idea of "all those things, but only those things, intended by God" would be granted by thoughtful restorationists. But exactly which ones are these?

Two Questions

Perhaps two questions may be taken as focusing certain issues. Each has its own set or types of problems.

1. Exactly which items should be restored?

The "model" of the early church presented in the New Testament is there for all to examine. But which parts of it are restorationists to emulate? Why are certain elements of the model present? Are they all matters of theological significance, or might some aspects be there simply as a result of culture or even coincidence? Did God decree that every facet of the early church's practice be present, or did some facets simply follow in some sort of due course. Surely *some* of the elements of the New Testament church's life are NOT significant. But how does one tell?

2. How does one deal with simple disagreements among advocates of restoration?

This very practical question might seem insignificant at first glance. But it can become a pragmatic hurdle of vast proportions. One has no reason to think that people of differing persuasions are anything but honest in their attempts to understand the documents. When there are simple disagreements about the pattern, are we to be left with dissenters to pursue their own courses to the detriment of Christian unity? Who will exercise forbearance? Are those who feel certain in their interpretations to go their way, leaving others to the exile of disagreement?

Conclusion

The concept of restoration is viable in light of the static nature of "the faith once for all delivered to the saints." It is also necessary in light of the apostasy of the Middle Ages and other times. The pursuit of the primitive church is a beautiful thing in light of God's plan. But great caution must be urged in order to avoid "binding what is not bound" or making one's personal interpretation authoritative for all.

Chapter Sixteen

What kind of leaders are best for the church?

Tom Alexander
Harding University
Searcy, Arkansas

Children's games sometimes speak the language of more mature activities. Baseball was a favorite sport to me and most of my childhood buddies. I was excited when our high school decided to field a baseball team. We had played ball together for years. First there were the games at recess in elementary school, and the pickup games somewhere in town on most Saturdays during warm weather. Then, as we matured, we enjoyed playing on the more organized teams sponsored each summer by local merchants and civic clubs. When we laced up the cleats as the first baseball team in our high school's memory, we were bound together by a tie that reached all the way back to the sandlots of our childhood.

One thing was obvious at every point along the way, our ball teams had their leaders. There were our coaches who showed us how to bunt and field a grounder. They scolded us when we didn't hustle and showered us with "way-to-go's" when we tried hard. For a few months out of the year, we were their children.

And there were others. Both in the backyards of our town and at the ballpark, some of our players emerged as leaders. They would become the captains of our teams. Some were more naturally gifted with athletic skill; we depended on them. Some were students of the game and knew strategy; we listened to them. Others, while not as gifted in these technical dimensions of the sport, had the capacity to encourage us and inspire us by their hustle and desire. All these leaders helped us play well.

But there were times when our leaders let us down. A coach became too overbearing, and his scolding killed our spirit. A good batter, to whom we naturally looked for the clutch hit, would swing for the fence and strike out, when all he needed to do was get on base. A player who knew the game became frustrated with players who were not as sharp, and his criticisms produced resentment. On those occasions, we didn't play so well.

Leaders for the People of God

The people of God are like the baseball teams of my youth. Whenever and wherever God's people have lived, they have had leaders. When those leaders did their jobs well, God's people thrived; but when the leaders lapsed in their duties, the people of God were the worse for it.

After a successful campaign against the Canaanites during a turbulent period of Israel's history, Deborah and Barak sang of the ideals of good leadership. "When the princes in Israel take the lead, when the people willingly offer themselves — praise the Lord!" (Judg. 5:2).

It was a darker day, however, when Hosea the prophet spoke of the accountability of the leaders of Israel as God's punishment of the sinful nation approached. "The more the priests increased, the more they sinned against me; they exchanged their Glory for something disgraceful. They feed on the sins of my people and relish their wickedness. And it will be: Like people, like priests. I will punish both of them for their ways and repay them for their deeds" (Hos. 4:7-9).

The Bible teaches us that what happened to God's people in the past exemplifies what can happen to us in any future period. If the history of Israel teaches us anything at all, it tells us that the success or failure of the church in our time will depend to a large degree on the quality of her leadership. What kind of leadership does the church need?

Organizational Structure

We have often answered this question in terms of organizational structure, pointing out that the church needs leadership that conforms to the model of church polity outlined in the New Testament. Harold Hazelip has reminded us of "what is most needed in religion today — to go back to the teachings of Jesus Christ and his apostles and be true to those teachings in our own service to God."[1] Applying this plea to church organization, he said:

> In New Testament times, Christians were organized into congregations, led in worship and service by elders or overseers who served as shepherds of God's flock. . . . Other men were chosen to be servants of the local church in its various needs; they were called deacons. . . . There was never any suggestion of a hierarchical form of church government; each close-knit group of Christians was self-governing, with its own leadership, subject only to God — never to a pyramid-like structure of institutional government.[2]

This simple congregational form of church organization in which leaders served under the headship of Christ (Col. 1:18; 1 Pet. 5:4) finds solid support in the New Testament.

The apostles were the primary leaders in the first church in Jerusalem (Acts 2:42; 4:35). Eventually there were elders who functioned alongside the apostles (Acts 11:30; 15:2,4,6). The last reference in Acts to leadership in the Jerusalem church mentions only elders (Acts 21:18). The impression is left that the leadership of the Jerusalem church by the apostles eventually gave way to leadership by her elders. After all, the nature of the apostolate was such that their personal leadership of the church would be temporary. As Everett Ferguson has pointed out,

> In the nature of the case, the apostles had an unrepeatable ministry. With their passing, no one else could give the testimony that they could. Their witness to the life, teachings, and resurrection of Jesus made them the foundation of the church (Eph. 2:20). In the reversed imagery of the apostles as laying the foundation (Rom. 15:20; 1 Cor. 3:10), they equally belong to the beginning of the church, for such a task is chronologically limited.[3]

We can assume that the apostles cast a long shadow as the Jerusalem church, under the leadership of her elders, continued to "devote themselves to the apostles' teaching" (Acts 2:42).

Similarly, Paul the apostle understood that in his absence his teaching would be perpetuated in congregations served by their own elders and deacons. These leaders were active in churches that Paul had established in Lystra, Iconium, and Antioch of Pisidia (Acts 14:23), Ephesus (Acts 20:17-35; 1 Tim. 1:3; 3:1-13), Philippi (Phil. 1:1), and on the island of Crete (Titus 1:5-9).

That this arrangement was still more widely recognized in the early church is evident from Peter's exhortation to elders in the churches in Pontus, Galatia, Cappadocia, Asia, and Bithynia (1 Pet. 1:1; 5:1-4).

As we contemplate the leadership needed for the church today, we must reaffirm our commitment to this model over against conflicting systems that are foreign to New Testament authority.

The Function of Church Leaders

More recently attention has moved beyond the organizational pattern for church leadership and has focused more sharply on the nature of the responsibilities of the leaders God has authorized for the church. It is not enough simply to have a plurality of elders in self-governing churches, not a ruling bishop over a diocese. What are the roles of these congregational leaders? And how should they exercise their roles? These are the pressing questions of today.

Harold Hazelip anticipated these concerns when he said that the church's "leaders were elders and deacons; their task was 'ministry.'"[4] Hazelip's statement implies that church leaders do not simply hold office, but perform tasks of ministry or service.

While leadership in the church is carried out by more individuals than the elders of a congregation, it is fair to assume that the success or failure of this group of servants will have significant impact on the welfare of the church. Consequently, Peter's admonition to elders provides a basic lens through which to view the task and the tone of leadership for the church:

> To the elders among you, I appeal as a fellow elder, a witness of Christ's sufferings and one who also will share in the glory to be revealed: Be shepherds of God's flock that is under your care, serving as overseers — not because you must, but because you are willing, as God wants you to be; not greedy for money, but eager to serve; not lording it over those entrusted to you, but being examples to the flock. And when the Chief Shepherd appears, you will receive the crown of glory that will never fade away (1 Pet. 5:1-4).

The task of elders

The term "elder" (Gk. *presbyteros*) does not in itself say much about the function of these individuals. The word fundamentally means "an older man." While chronological age must surely be involved, no minimum number of years is specified to qualify one for the category. He should not be a recent convert (1 Tim. 3:6), so the presumption is that an elder should be old enough to have gained knowledge and experience that naturally command the respect of others. He must at least be old enough to have a family and to have led his children to make their own choices in favor of Christian faith and practice (Titus 1:6). Jack Lewis has observed, "The term 'elder' suggests a leadership built on respect and reverence (cf. Lev. 19:32), a reverence that recognizes ability, service, knowledge, example, and seniority."[5]

Elders as shepherds

Peter calls our attention to the task of elders by his exhortation, "Be shepherds of God's flock" (1 Pet. 5:2). The verb Peter uses here (Gk. *poimaino*) refers to the overall care a shepherd has for his flock. Peter is pointing out that elders have the job of caring for, or tending, the church after the model of the Near-Eastern shepherd, a job that involves at least four aspects.

First, although Peter's exhortation is broader in application than the translation "feed the flock" in the King James Version (1 Pet. 5:2; Acts 20:28), we must acknowledge that a part of the shepherd's work is to provide the sheep with proper food. The apostle Paul teaches us that an elder "must hold firmly to the trustworthy message as it has been taught, so that he can encourage others by sound doctrine" (Titus 1:9; cf. 1 Tim. 3:2). Our spiritual growth depends upon the quality of the spiritual food we eat. Just as a concerned parent sees to it that her children get a balanced diet that will promote their health and growth, good shepherds of God's people learn what spiritual food is best for their congregation. Elders should themselves be capable of either private or public teaching (1 Tim. 3:2; 5:17). They also will see to it that the church has ample opportunities to learn from other capable teachers and will lead the members to accept their personal responsibility in studying the word of God.

Second, the ministry of the word of God carried out by shepherds in a congregation is a tandem task. Not only does it involve the positive feeding of the church with good spiritual food, but it also requires shepherds to protect the flock from enemies who would destroy the sheep.

Jesus referred to himself as "the good shepherd" (John 10:11) and distanced himself from the hired man who abandons the sheep and runs away when he sees the wolf coming (John 10:12). This imagery lies behind Paul's charge that elders must be shepherds of the flock at a time when "savage wolves will come in among you and will not spare the flock," when "men will arise and distort the truth in order to draw away disciples after them" (Acts 20:28-30). Not only must shepherds "encourage others by sound doctrine," they must also "refute those who oppose it" (Titus 1:9), an increasingly important task in today's pluralistic culture.

Third, the shepherd imagery in the Bible is a seeking imagery. One does not soon forget the word picture painted by Jesus in his parable of the shepherd who left the ninety-nine sheep safe in the fold in order to retrieve the one that was lost (Luke 15:3-7; Matt. 18:12-14). Ezekiel the prophet brought God's censure upon the sinful shepherds of Israel, "You have not strengthened the weak or healed the sick or bound up the injured. You have not brought back the strays or searched for the lost" (Ezek. 34:4).

Jesus said that a shepherd "calls his own sheep by name" (John 10:3). This implies that elders of a church should know the individuals under their care well enough to recognize when someone strays from the flock and be willing to seek their return.

Fourth, shepherds of a church should lead their congregation into the areas of ministry it needs to perform. Again, Jesus reminds us that a good shepherd "calls his own sheep by name and leads them out. When he has brought out all his own, he goes on ahead of them, and his sheep follow him because they know his voice" (John 10:3-4). After identifying the avenues of service that God's people are called to perform, shepherds should provide the necessary direction and opportunities for that service. Paul makes it clear that the work of ministry in a church is not the lot of a select group. Ministry is the work of every Christian. However, he points out that "pastors" (the traditional Latinized term for shepherds) function "to prepare God's people for works of service, so that the body of Christ may be built up" (Eph. 4:11-12). It is safe to say that the church will not do well, and God's mission in the world will not be accomplished if church members leave the work of ministry to elders. But it is equally safe to say that the church will not succeed if elders do not catch a glimpse of where God wants the church to be, share that vision with the members of their congregation, and take the lead in enlisting the participation of all in the mission.

Elders as overseers

Peter clarifies further the work of elders by the participle "serving as overseers" (Gk. *episkopeo*). Readers of several English versions will recognize that this expression does not occur in some translations of 1 Peter 5:2. This is due to the fact that the manuscript evidence is fairly evenly divided concerning the presence of this expression.[6] Regardless of how the textual balances ultimately weigh out, the idea of elders serving as overseers is clearly supported in the New Testament.

Paul uses the noun "overseer" (Gk. *episkopos*, also translated "bishop") to designate elders on four occasions. He exhorts the elders from Ephesus to "keep watch over yourselves and all the flock of which the Holy Spirit has made you overseers" (Acts 20:28). He writes to "all the saints in Christ Jesus at Philippi, together with the overseers and deacons" (Phil. 1:1). Paul lists qualifications for an overseer (1 Tim. 3:2ff.) and stresses that "an overseer is entrusted with God's work" (Titus 1:7). He uses a related term (Gk. *episkope*) when he writes, "If anyone sets his heart on being an overseer, he desires a noble task" (1 Tim. 3:1), clearly indicating that this is a task to be performed, not a position to be held.

While this family of words finds usage in Greek literature in a variety of settings, the most fruitful insight into its meaning for church leaders comes from its association with the shepherd terminology. Peter refers to Jesus as "the Shepherd and Overseer of your souls" (1 Pet. 2:25). This provides an appropriate setting for Peter later to write that elders, in carrying out their roles as shepherds of God's flock, function as overseers (1 Pet. 5:2). Paul, reversing the use of the terms, says that elders, who have been made by the Holy Spirit overseers of the flock, should carry out their task by being shepherds of the church of God (Acts 20:17,28).

This association suggests that the nature of the work of an overseer is essentially defined by the pastoral image of the shepherd. We have two expressions that fundamentally underscore the same "watchful, solicitous direction of the congregation."[7]

The tone of elders

It is not only the task of elders that we must understand, but also the tone with which elders should perform their duties. Peter moves us closer to understanding the kind of leaders the church needs by presenting three contrasts which distinguish ways elders should not function from ways they should serve.

First, Peter says elders should serve, "not because you must, but because you are willing, as God wants you to be" (1 Pet. 5:2). The church does not need leaders who accept their roles simply out of a sense of obligation, or because they feel no one else will serve, or because fellow Christians have "twisted their arms" to serve. Grudging service is usually a disappointment both to the server and the served. For an elder who has not freely and willingly accepted the task, any thrill associated with the position is soon replaced by a burden of frustration and guilt when the hard work of shepherding the flock sets in. In addition, the personal spiritual welfare of members of the congregation and the collective effectiveness of the church's ministry are jeopardized by reluctant leadership.

So the church needs leaders whose hearts are willingly set on being overseers (cf. 1 Tim. 3:1); but only if those hearts have been set by the proper motive. James's warning to aspiring teachers is relevant to men who want to be elders: "Not many of you should presume to be teachers, my brothers, because you know that we who teach will be judged more strictly" (Jas. 3:1). While he does not use the more familiar terms elders, shepherds, or overseers, the writer of Hebrews says that church leaders keep watch over Christians "as men who must give an account" (Heb. 13:17). Only men who willingly desire the "noble task" of an overseer (1 Tim. 3:1), not simply a noteworthy position, and are willing to relate to their sheep on a personal level, will meet this high level of accountability.

Second, Peter says elders should not be greedy for money, but eager to serve (1 Pet. 5:2). This admonition makes sense in the setting of 1 Peter only if there was the potential for elders to profit materially from their service. The New Testament world was notorious for philosophical charlatans who lined their pockets at the expense of the people they taught. In light of this, several New Testament passages urge Christian ministers to be discreet in financial matters (cf. 1 Thess. 1:5,9; Acts 20:33-35). It appears that in the early church, elders sometimes received material support for their services (1 Tim.

5:17). Consequently, Peter's admonition that elders should not be greedy for gain is appropriate (cf. 1 Tim. 3:3; Titus 1:7).

In the modern church we only occasionally encounter elders who are paid for their service. Most are not supported by the church. Consequently, they are not likely to be motivated by monetary gain from their churches. However, the principle that underlies Peter's admonition is very contemporary. Today's shepherds must not be self-serving, but eager to serve the needs of others. One is reminded of Ezekiel's condemnation of the shepherds of Israel who only took care of themselves, but did not take care of the flock (Ezek. 34:2-3). In contrast, as guidance for the elders from Ephesus, Paul reminded them of his own unselfish ministry among them (Acts 20:33-34) and the words of Jesus, "It is more blessed to give than to receive" (Acts 20:35).

The church needs leaders who sublimate their own interests to the needs of those whom they lead. Like the good shepherd, perfectly modeled by Jesus, they must be willing to lay down their lives for the sheep (John 10:11). It is trendy in corporate circles to hear individuals call for "servant leadership." Long before leadership principles were outlined for people in today's business world, Jesus spoke of the nature of true leadership when he said, "I am among you as one who serves" (Luke 22:27).

Third, Peter urges that shepherds should serve, "not lording it over those entrusted to you, but being examples to the flock" (1 Pet. 5:3). The expression "lording it over" (Gk. *katakyrieuo*) reminds one of Jesus' response to his disciples who were seeking positions of prominence:

> You know that those who are regarded as rulers of the Gentiles lord it over [*katakyrieuo*] them, and their high officials exercise authority over them. Not so with you. Instead, whoever wants to become great among you must be your servant, and whoever wants to be first must be slave of all. For even the Son of Man did not come to be served, but to serve, and to give his life as a ransom for many (Mark 10:42-45).

Over against leaders who seek to impose their wills on followers and demand compliance through threats, intimidation, the raw use of power, and political maneuvering in the church, the overseers of God's people must function by moral persuasion. It may not be stretching the metaphor too far to say that the good shepherd does not "drive" his sheep, but "leads" them. The sheep follow, not because of the power of the shepherd's powerful position, but because of their trust and confidence in the one who knows them by name and whose voice they know.

The ability of shepherds to lead a congregation grows out of the quality of their lives and their personal faithfulness in the areas they are leading the church to go. Returning to the images of the baseball of my youth, our best coaches were not those who told us what to do and shouted loudly for us to perform. Our most effective coaches were those who had played baseball themselves. They would take the bat in their hands and show us how to hold it and how to position our bodies in the batter's box. They would take the glove and show us how to use both hands when catching the ball. They would take their place on the field and show us how to lead off from first base, take the turn at second, and slide under a tag at third. They modeled for us how the game should be played.

In the same way, the church needs overseers who are examples to the flock. The flock should be able to say when observing the Christian lives of their shepherds, "There is how the game should be played." Wayne Grudem has reminded us:

> Thus all leadership positions in the church should realize that the requirement to live a life worthy of imitation is not optional — it is a major part of the job, challenging though such responsibility may be. Moreover, those who select church leaders should realize that academic excellence and administrative or financial skills do not automatically qualify one for leadership in the church (as they would for leadership in the university or business worlds).[8]

Leaders Who Are Caring Servants

By now the kind of leaders the church needs should be coming into focus. But consider these final thoughts.

Paul writes in 1 Timothy 5:17 concerning "elders who direct the affairs of the church" (KJV "rule"). He uses the same verb (Gk. *proïstemi*) in 1 Thessalonians 5:12 where he speaks of those "who are over you in the Lord." Although Paul does not call these individuals elders, he certainly assumes they were exercising a leadership function. The language may imply that there was some supervisory duty involved. However, what we want to know is not whether elders ever supervise or make decisions regarding the management of a congregation's work, but how they are to go about it.

The context of 1 Thessalonians 5:12 helps us understand that being over other people in the Lord involves something other than "pulling rank." Those who are over you in the Lord are also those "who work hard among you, . . . and who admonish you." The language describes the conduct of individuals who invest themselves in seeking the welfare of others.

In Romans 12:7-8 Paul uses *proistemi* (NIV "leadership," KJV "rule," RSV "give aid") in a list of other gifts that are to be used for service in the church. Its presence with activities such as serving, teaching, encouraging, contributing to the needs of others, and showing mercy helps us to understand better its significance as a gift of service rather than one of domination.

Paul uses this terminology in another passage related to church leaders. After specifying certain domestic qualifications for an overseer, Paul raises the question, "If anyone does not know how to manage [Gk. *proistemi*] his own family, how can he take care [Gk. *epimeleomai*] of God's church?" (1 Tim. 3:5). The association of these terms suggests that management, both in the home and in the church, involves more than setting budgets and arranging furniture.

The verb that refers to the overseer's care of the church (*epimeleomai*) occurs only one other time in the New Testament. Jesus described the conduct of the "Good Samaritan" toward the wounded man in this manner: "He went to him and bandaged his wounds, pouring on oil and wine. Then he put the man on his own donkey, took him to an inn, and took care [*epimeleomai*] of him" (Luke 10:34). The Samaritan gave his own money and told the innkeeper, "Look after [*epimeleomai*] him" (Luke 10:35). Today the church needs leaders who treat the people of God in the same unselfish, compassionate manner.

There is one other passage that needs to be explored. Hebrews 13:17 does not refer specifically to elders, but it is reasonable to think that the verse applies to them in principle. Christians are admonished to obey and submit to their leaders (Gk. participle of *hegeomai*). Since this participle is used elsewhere when we are told that Pharaoh made Joseph "ruler over Egypt and all his palace" (Acts 7:10), and since related nouns are used to designate various political rulers (cf. Luke 3:1; Matt. 2:6), it has sometimes been erroneously inferred that church leaders exercise a rule in the church.

Throughout this essay the words and example of Jesus have been resorted to in order to clarify the nature of church leadership. The terminology for church leaders that appears in Hebrews 13:17 occurs in one of Jesus' most significant sayings concerning leadership among his people:

> The kings of the Gentiles lord it over them; and those who exercise authority over them call themselves Benefactors. But you are not to be like that. Instead, the greatest among you should be like the youngest, and the one who rules [*hegeomai*] like the one who serves (Luke 22:25-26).

Again, the emphasis is not on an office in which one wields an authority of powerful position. Instead, the stress lies on a ministry in which a man humbly serves.

Conclusion

The popular movie "Field of Dreams" tells the fictional story of Ray Kinsella, a young Iowa farmer who grew up hearing his dad tell him about baseball greats from the past. One of the best was "Shoeless Joe" Jackson whose career had been cut short when he was implicated in a gambling scandal in the 1919 World Series. Kinsella would have liked to have seen him play.

One day Kinsella heard a voice that said, "If you build it, he will come." After repeated encounters with "the voice," Kinsella concluded it meant that if he would build a baseball diamond in his cornfield, "Shoeless Joe" would come back and play there. Well, he built it, and Joe came; and that was the beginning of a whole series of exciting experiences in the life of the farmer and his family.

This article has not addressed the responsibilities members of a congregation have to their leaders: respect them, and hold them in the highest regard in love (1 Thess. 5:12-13); obey them and submit to them (Heb. 13:17); be submissive to them (1 Pet. 5:5). Neither has it described specific methods that may be employed in leading a church, nor particular ways in which effective leadership will manifest itself. However, what has been discovered through this examination of the nature of leadership in the church suggests that positive responses should naturally come from good-hearted people when leaders function as the New Testament says they should.

We have heard a voice far more substantial than a mythical

voice from an Iowa cornfield. We have heard the voice of the One who has the words of eternal life (John 6:68). This voice says to us, "If shepherds lead, the sheep will follow." A positive response from us will be the beginning of a whole series of exciting experiences for the church.

Endnotes

[1]Harold Hazelip, "The First Century Church Revisited," Herald of Truth Radio and Television Programs, No. 362 (Abilene: Highland Church of Christ).

[2]Ibid.

[3]Everett Ferguson, *The Church of Christ: A Biblical Ecclesiology for Today* (Grand Rapids: Eerdmans, 1996), 306.

[4]Harold Hazelip and Batsell Barrett Baxter, "Is First-Century Christianity Possible Today?" Herald of Truth Radio and Television Programs, No. 513 (Abilene: Highland Church of Christ).

[5]Jack P. Lewis, *Leadership Questions Confronting the Church* (Nashville: Christian Communications, 1985), 18.

[6]For a discussion of the evidence see Bruce Metzger, *A Textual Commentary on the Greek New Testament* (London and New York: United Bible Societies, 1975), 605-696.

[7]Lewis, *Leadership Questions*, 25.

[8]Wayne Grudem, *The First Epistle of Peter: An Introduction and Commentary*, The Tyndale New Testament Commentaries (Grand Rapids: Eerdmans, 1988), 189-190.

SECTION SIX
QUESTIONS ABOUT WORSHIP

I suppose no question has generated more discussion and tension in our churches over the last decade than the one about public worship. Too frequently, battle lines have been drawn, and blood has been shed over questions of worship style. Indeed, our worship life is basic to our Christian walk. That is why such discussions always seem to be for "high stakes" and why these questions merit their own section in this book.

Dan Dozier begins with a general theology of worship upon which all other questions must depend. He insists that before "how-to" questions can be asked, the more fundamental question of "why worship at all?" must be addressed.

Ken Neller then takes us into the heart of some of our bitterest disputes, the topic of church music. Going beyond the question of instrumental music, Neller asks us to consider what kind of songs we should sing. Having discovered the wide variety of tastes in our local congregations — from classical, to Stamps-Baxter to contemporary — the question of which songs to sing can become vexing and even hostile.

Finally, the section concludes with Randy Harris's reflections on the two central rites of the church, baptism, and the Lord's Supper. Intended as symbols of unity but now points of contention throughout the Christian world, they continue to be the anchors of our spiritual identity.

As the Psalmist says, "Only the dead do not praise Yahweh." Worship is what Christians do even in times of despair. This section calls us back to the first commandment, "Thou shalt worship the Lord thy God."

Chapter Seventeen

How should we worship God?

Dan Dozier
Community Church of Christ
Hendersonville, Tennessee.

In recent years there has been a heightened interest in worship, a genuine yearning to express more heartfelt praise to Almighty God. There is no more important question than "How should we worship God?" How may we come into God's presence, declaring the wonder of his grace? How can we show him our gratitude for his goodness and our thankfulness for his love? What are the ways that enable us to express meaningfully our feelings with both reverence and celebration? Is it possible to respect the time-honored traditions of worship and still find fresh ways of declaring our adoration to our King? How does God desire to be worshipped?

Why Worship?

This chapter does not address the technical "how-to's" of worship, such as the types of songs to sing or where to place the Lord's Supper in the order of the service. Neither is there an attempt to unravel all the controversial issues concerning contemporary worship styles. Although the inquiry, "What should we do and not do in worship?" is an extremely important one, the more significant question is "Why worship at all?" Discussions about the elements and styles of worship usually end up focusing on matters of personal opinion, either on what we do like or do not like. This chapter centers on the "why" of worship. It is concerned with internal matters of the heart more than with external details of the event. It focuses not on our personal tastes, but on the nature of God himself. If we want to engage in right worship, we must make sure that

God is squarely at the center of it. What we believe about God determines how we worship him.

We must avoid two extremes as we answer our earlier questions. One extreme is to pursue worship that seeks exclusively warm and exciting emotional feelings. Such worship is often sentimental and weak and may not be founded on biblical truth at all. We must be sure we worship God in truth (John 4:24). The other extreme is to come to worship in a purely intellectual, legalistic manner. Such an approach is not only cold and lifeless, but also equally false and harmful. Emotions and knowledge must meet in proper balance in a strong faith and fruitful Christian life. A sound understanding will correct a tendency toward unbridled emotionalism, and a sincere, heartfelt expression will keep worship from becoming a dry intellectual game.

If our view of God is incorrect, our worship of God will also be misguided. If we believe God is a vengeful, angry being who is anxious to punish, we will either try to avoid him or try to appease him. If we see him as a permissive, sleepy old grandfather, we will not take him seriously. If we view him as a rule-giver who demands perfect obedience, we will approach him legalistically and without joy. But if we understand the Lord as a Father and a personal God who loves us and longs to enjoy fellowship with us, we will seek to know him in personal relationship.

Why praise God? Because he deserves it. He is complete in righteousness and justice. He is unlimited in power and grace. He is unequaled in kindness and goodness. He is the only true god. Our God is absolutely sinless, totally awesome, and clothed in matchless holiness. He is entirely perfect and wholly unlike any thing or anyone else that exists. That is why the hosts of heaven fall on their faces in the presence of God and cry out, "Holy, Holy, Holy is the Lord God of Hosts" (Isa. 6:3; Rev. 4:8). He is worthy of all honor and glory and praise. God's holiness prohibits us from approaching him flippantly (Heb. 12:38-29).

In contrast to God, we are unholy, impure, unrighteous, imperfect, and common. When we become aware of God's holiness and our sinfulness, we, too, like Isaiah, will fall to our knees in worship and announce that God is holy. We are amazed that such a holy God would want our worship, yet he does. One of the greatest paradoxes in the universe is that the all-holy God is also the all-gracious God whose love is so incomparably great toward us in

Christ Jesus that we may come into his presence with confidence (Heb. 4:14-16). He permits us to call him, "Abba, Father" (Rom. 8:15; Gal. 4:6). He allows us to participate in his divine nature (2 Pet. 1:4). Through the Holy Spirit we have access to the Father (Eph. 2:18; Rom. 5:2). Through Jesus' death and precious blood which he shed to pay the penalty for our sins, we can come before God with full assurance of faith (Heb. 7:25; 10:19-22; 1 Pet. 3:18). God made this possible by taking the initiative. God is seeking worshipers (John 4:23). That means that God is active in worship. He loved us first (Rom. 5:6-8; 1 John 4:10-19), and we respond with adoring worship. Because of his unspeakable love, he saved us by his grace (Eph. 2:4-5). The gospel brings reconciliation, and reconciliation is at the heart of all true worship.

All this compels us to worship. Worship fulfills the purpose for which we were created. Made in God's image, we long to be in fellowship with him. We yearn to worship. Our hearts beat in rhythm with the Psalmist who wrote, "As the deer pants for streams of water, so my soul pants for you, O God. My soul thirsts for God, for the living God" (Ps. 42:1-2). The primary purpose of life is to adore God. True worship can get lost amidst all the activity of our churches. Too often our congregations major on ministry and minor on adoration. Like Martha, we can become so deeply entrenched in activity that we miss the real priority of life, which is kneeling at the feet of our Lord in genuine praise (Luke 10:38-42). The well-known shorter catechism of the Westminster Assembly states, "The true end of man is to glorify God and enjoy him forever." Paul also informs us that we have been chosen in Christ and destined to live *for the praise of his glory* (Eph. 1:4-6). Our bodies are temples of the Holy spirit, and we, therefore, are to glorify God even in our bodies (1 Cor. 6:9-20). The apostle Peter tells us that we "are being built into a spiritual house to be a holy priesthood, offering spiritual sacrifices acceptable to God through Jesus Christ" (1 Pet. 2:5). Peter also wrote, "But you are a chosen people, a royal priesthood, a holy nation, a people belonging to God, that you may *declare the praises of him* who called you out of darkness into his wonderful light" (1 Pet. 2:9).

The word *worship* comes from the Anglo-Saxon *weorthscipe*, which was later developed into *worthship* and then into *worship*. It means to attribute worth and honor and dignity to an object. Why do we worship God? Because he deserves it and because we long to honor him. As we worship God we ascribe to him supreme worth. He alone is worthy. "Ascribe to Yahweh, O families of nations, ascribe to Yahweh glory and strength. Ascribe to Yahweh the glory due his name; bring an offering and come into his courts" (Ps. 96:7-8). "Worthy is the Lamb who was slain, to receive power and wealth and wisdom and might and honor and glory and blessing" (Rev. 5:12, RSV).

Wonder, Awe, and Reverence

A necessary factor in real worship is a sense of wonder at God. In other words, unless we truly marvel at God's greatness, unless we are filled with a sense of amazement at all he does for us, we are not going to be able to praise him from the depths of our being. Regrettably, however, there is a terrible lack of the sense of mystery and wonder in many of our worship assemblies. Many of us have been careful to practice the correct *acts* and *forms* of worship; we have not been nearly as concerned about the *spirit* and *experience* of worship. True servants of God were always aware that it was the spirit of worship that gave meaning to the rituals and that the spirit was more important than the acts. It is not that the ritual acts of worship were unimportant. It is that God has always been more concerned with the heart than with mere ritual accuracy.

When we begin to understand God's majestic holiness, we are filled with awe and reverence (Isa. 6:1-5). There is a mystery surrounding God that leaves us in a state of wonder. William Quayle wrote, "When wonder is dead the soul becomes a dry bone." Thomas Carlyle captured the thought most concisely when he wrote, "Wonder is the basis of worship." Carlyle's words come to life in several New Testament passages. When the shepherds returned from seeing the newborn Jesus, they were "glorifying and praising God for all the things they had heard and seen" (Luke 2:20). After Jesus healed the paralyzed man and the people saw him walking, the Scripture says, "Everyone was *amazed* and gave praise to God. They were *filled with awe* and said, 'We have seen remarkable things today'" (Luke 5:26). On another occasion when Jesus was healing many people, we read that "the people were *amazed* when they saw the mute speaking, the crippled made well, the lame walking and the blind seeing. And they praised the God of Israel" (Matt. 15:31). On yet another occasion Jesus raised to life the dead son of a widow from the city of Nain. Luke reports that the people "were all *filled with awe* and praised God" (Luke 7:16).

The point is that a sense of awe and wonder naturally leads us to worship. Without a sense of wonder, there can be no true worship. It is hard to amaze people anymore. With heart-lung transplants, space walks, and Star Wars special effects, we have become somewhat callous in the amazement department. We witness technological wonders daily that would have shocked our ancestors beyond belief. Therefore, unless we continually encounter the amazing God in his word, we may also discover that we are not too impressed with him anymore either. That is a horrifying thought, but it has become a reality in the lives of countless millions of people. Mark this down, you will never praise God as you should until you rediscover a sense of wonder at who God is and what he has done and what he continues to do.

When we deal with the matters of wonder, reverence, and awe, we also must deal with the issue of emotion in worship. What we do in public worship should occur somewhere between the extremes of total passivity and unbridled enthusiasm. It has been suggested that in worship we need to intellectualize our emotions and to emotionalize our intellect. Obviously, what is needed is balance. Many of us who are modern descendants of the American Restoration Movement were taught to treasure a rational understanding of Scripture, but to question personal spiritual experiences that involve our emotions. That's unfortunate because it creates an imbalance. In an 1834 letter to Alexander Campbell, John Rogers expressed a concern that is not restricted to the nineteenth century. He wrote, "Many of us in running away from the extreme of enthusiasm, have on the other hand, passed the temperate zone, and gone far into the frozen regions. There is, in too many churches a cold-hearted, lifeless formality, that freezes the energies." Even Campbell, who championed a rational approach to religion, raised similar concerns on a few occasions. Religion certainly is an intellectual matter, he wrote in 1837, "but religion dwelling in the heart, rooted in the feelings and affections, is living, active, and real existence. . . . This is religion," he concluded. "All the rest is machinery."

We do not base our theology on emotions or on experience, but we make a great mistake if we completely divorce our theology from our emotions and experience. If worship is a response of the whole person to God, then we cannot ignore emotions. We express emotions at practically every other event in life; why not in worship? It makes no sense, and it is not biblical. Obviously, there must be doctrinal truth at the core of worship. Unless enthusiasm and emotion are inseparably linked to the truth, they are meaningless, even dangerous. The perfect blend is emotion regulated by understanding and enthusiasm directed by the Word of God. It is wrong to artificially manipulate people, working them into some emotional frenzy, but it is just as wrong to make a conscious effort to squelch people's emotions. If there is never laughter, never a sigh, never a tear, never a smile, never a joyful "amen," never a burden or a release from some burden, if there is only a stone-faced, passionless exercise of the routines and rituals of worship, then spiritual rigor mortis has overtaken the entire process.

Scripture is written for the heart as well as the head, and we must balance both. Emotionalism is the tendency to overindulge the emotions or to be too much influenced by them. However, *emotionalism* is different from the genuine expression of true *emotion*. God made us to experience many emotions: happiness and sadness, elation and depression, security and fear. Practically every emotion is expressed in Scripture, especially in the Psalms. The characteristic notes of biblical worship are exhilaration, celebration and joy (Ps. 89:15-16; 100:1-4; 122:1; Acts 2:46-47; 5:41; 8:39; 13:48). We must take our emotions out of the freezer and expose them to the warm glow of God's passionate love. Too many people go to the assembly to be scolded rather than to experience the joy of their salvation. Let the words of Hebrews 12:22-23 soak in, "But you have come to Mount Zion, to the heavenly Jerusalem, the city of the living God. You have come to thousands upon thousands of angels in *joyful assembly*, to the church of the firstborn, whose names are written in heaven." Worship must always be reverent and orderly, and there are times for us to be still, quiet, solemn, and penitent. We must approach worship with all the seriousness that God's holiness demands, but we must not be lifelessly dismal about it, never smiling, always with long and somber frowns. Our hearts and our faces need reminding that we are saved. If we cannot feel enthusiastic about that, we are in trouble. And if we are to rejoice in our hearts, we also are to rejoice in our physical and emotional expressions.

God-Centered Worship

This joy is not based in a self-centered approach to worship. Rather, it is a joy that comes from worship that is God-centered and Christ-centered. Although one of the purposes of worship is to edify one another, we human beings are not the primary focus of worship. People are not worthy of praise, but God is. When we assemble for worship, we must not be so preoccupied with one another that we forget that it is God whom we have come to praise. The chief aim of worship is to please God, to adore and honor him.

This means we must not come to worship with a me-centered agenda. We live in a consumer-oriented culture. If something does not seem immediately useful to us, our society tends to reject it. Sadly, many people approach life's choices with an attitude which asks, "What do I get out of this?" When applied to worship, such an attitude pridefully devalues the Lord and treats him as if he exists primarily to meet our selfish needs. It must offend the Father when we are more concerned about what we want, what we would like to do in worship, what makes us feel good, than we are about what God wants, what would honor him and what would give him the most pleasure in worship. We must worship God with an attitude that asks, "What can I offer up to the Lord?" Paul urged Christians "to offer your bodies as living sacrifices, holy and pleasing to God — this is your spiritual act of worship" (Rom. 12:1).

We are to seek to glorify God before we seek to gain anything for ourselves. The Lord is not our servant (although, in his goodness he chooses to serve us); he is Almighty God. We must serve him simply and purely because he is God. We worship him because he is worthy of worship whether we get anything out of it or not. The purpose of worship is to encounter the Living God. Whatever personal rewards (i.e. feelings, fellowship with brethren, etc.) we might receive from worship are secondary to our worship of God. However, God, in his goodness, sees to it that when we put him first and at the center of our worship, we also benefit greatly.

The word "worship" in the original languages of Scripture points out this "God-centered" nature of worship. The Hebrew and Greek words that appear most frequently in the Bible are ones that literally mean "to bow down" and "to kiss toward" in reverence and humility before God, to prostrate oneself before the God of all splendor, to show submissive lowliness and deep respect (Gen.

18:2; Rev. 5:14). Another frequently used word means "to serve." It is the same root word in Hebrew as the term "slave" or "servant." This is an important point to understand, for the Jew could think of no higher privilege than to be called a servant of God. (Exod. 3:12; Deut. 10:12-13; Heb. 9:14; Rom. 12:1).

There are two clear impressions from the meaning of these words. First, they indicate a submission of the human will to God. No one can worship God acceptably who comes before him with a prideful heart and a stubborn, unyielding will. We must come in genuine reverence and humility, with our hearts bowed low, our spirits laid prostrate before him, and our lives given in grateful service to the Majesty on high. Second, these words clearly indicate a physical response. People are not to come to worship like spectators at a theater, watching the preacher and worship leaders do their performance on stage. There is no place in worship to sit passively as an audience who merely listens and watches, but does nothing to participate actively.

Worship as Response

What should be our answer to all that God has done and continues to do for us? The only adequate response is worship and adoration and a life which strives to bring honor and glory to God. The key word is "response." God is the initiator, and we are the responders. "We love because God *first* loved us" (1 John 4:19). We do not worship God in order to be loved by God. He already loves us. Our worship of God takes place within God's love. Worship is not an effort to get God's attention. Rather, it is a response to the God who has already invited us to worship him (John 4:23).

C. Welton Gaddy says that worship is a gift between lovers. Our worship is a love gift to the love-giving God. Worship is a gift between lovers who keep on giving to each other. This is the kind of giving and receiving that forms a circular pattern between God and his people which defies comprehension and lasts forever. Gaddy writes, "Worship is not a tactic calculated to win God's grace. Worship occurs because of God's grace. Worshipers gather within God's grace. Worship is a celebration of God's grace." God wants us to worship him not because he is narcissistic, but because he knows we need to worship so that we will be like him. He gives. In worship we give back, thus becoming like God in his giving nature.

214

There are commands present in worship: repent, believe, go, and do. But the commands never come first. The New Testament clearly teaches that God's gifts always precede his demands. So many of our churches get this backwards in worship. We push demands and try to create a sense of guilt in people. We hope this approach will lead them to love and serve and worship God. It seldom works that way. What we need to do first is what God does first, tell people of God's love and what he has done for them. Then allow God's love to be the motivating force that leads them to respond in obedient faith. The question in worship is not "What can I give to the One who already *has* everything?" Rather, it is "What can I give to the One who *gives* everything?" God will still be God even if we never worship him. But if we do not worship him, we become the losers. Not only is it unnatural for us not to respond with worship, it is sinful.

We cannot worship God acceptably unless our response wholly captures our attitudes and engages our hearts. There is a great difference between what I will call "institutional" worship and worship that is a natural response to what God has done. Institutional worship is a system in which people worship because they feel forced to or in which they merely go through the motions. They think if they carry out certain rituals and follow a prescribed set of forms, they have worshiped God acceptably. However, we can worship this way without ever engaging our hearts. We can go through all the right motions and carry out all the right forms and be as cold and lifeless as a corpse. Such a checklist mentality must pain God's heart.

The early chapters of Isaiah describe how God's people had a correct form of worship, but were displeasing to him because their lives were full of injustice and their hearts were not right (Isa. 1:11-17; see also Amos 5:21-24). They went through the proper motions, but there was no meaning in them. In Matthew 15:1-9 we read how Jesus condemned some Pharisees and teachers of the law because they were careful to practice their traditions of worship while not fulfilling the moral obligations which God had clearly laid upon them. To that group of hypocrites Jesus applied the words of the prophet Isaiah:

> These people honor me with their lips,
> but their hearts are far from me.
> They worship me in vain;
> their teachings are but rules taught by men.

God wants in worship what he has always wanted, submissive lives and genuine hearts. King David's words in Ps. 51:16-17 ring as true today as they did 3,000 years ago:

> You do not delight in sacrifice, or I would bring it;
> you do not take pleasure in burnt offerings.
> The sacrifices of God are a broken spirit;
> a broken and contrite heart,
> O God, you will not despise.

It is not that God did not want Israel's sacrifices. God himself had commanded them to make sacrifice in worship. However, God did not want their worship unless their lives reflected righteousness and their hearts were given to him. That is true of our worship still. Going through the motions without engagement of heart and a life of discipleship is completely unacceptable to God, a sheer waste of his time and ours!

Norman Bales writes:

> Worship renewal requires us to focus more on the internal condition of our hearts than the external structure of the service. The corporate worship of the church will never be a satisfactory experience until we develop a quality relationship with God in the privacy of our closets. . . . Little doubt exists as to the need for worship renewal in most churches, but the renewal we need involves inward change more than it does outward modification.

The deepest joys of worship come only to those who throw all their hearts and energies into it, never to those who leave their hearts behind, no matter how many prayers they pray or how accurately they carry out the proper forms of worship. Ultimately, our worship depends on how much of our hearts we bring into it.

Worship and Ministry

In one sense, worship encompasses all of life. We tend to divide life into secular and sacred. However, that is a false dichotomy. In the total life of Israel there was a fusion between the spheres of secular and religious. Israel was to be "a kingdom of priests and a holy nation" (Exod. 19:6). Their total life was a service (worship) before the Lord. Paul wrote, "And whatever you do, whether in word or deed, do it all in the name of the Lord Jesus, giving thanks to God the Father through him" (Col. 3:17). If we take that verse seriously, we cannot restrict worship to that realm we typically call "sacred." Everything we do is to be dedicated to the glory of God. As Christians we are God's priests, and our bodies are his temple. As such, our entire lives — not only certain days and hours in the week — are to offer glory to God. Technically, it is not biblical to say we are "going to worship," since all we do, both in and outside the assembly, is to be done to the glory of God (1 Cor. 10:31). Our whole lives should offer up glory and praise to the Father. Our Sunday assembly is to be the corporate overflow of that daily worship.

The church exists to accomplish many different things. The church is to teach and baptize the lost, to educate and train its own people in the ways of God, to serve our fellow human beings, to build up and support fellow believers, to spur one another on toward love and good deeds. But the most important thing the assembled church does is worship God. Without worship, a congregation ceases to be a church. If worship is not the fundamental activity of the church, every aspect of its ministry will be adversely affected. When the church fails to worship, it ultimately fails in every other area as well. John MacArthur says, "Worship is to the Christian life what the mainspring is to a watch, what the engine is to a car. It is the very core, the most essential element."

Worship is the source of the church's power to carry out its mission in the world. It is the foundation of everything else the church is doing. Worship is fundamental. Timothy J. Christenson writes, "If worship is just one thing we do, everything becomes mundane. If worship is *the* one thing we do, everything takes on eternal significance." Olando Costas said it this way, "Worship is not a mere function of the church, it is the *ultimate* purpose." If the church does not worship, it does not live. Years ago, A.W. Tozer called worship "the missing jewel of the church." Praise God for the renewed interest in worship. More and more churches are striving to improve their worship, and as they do, they are finding that the worship of God is the dynamic behind every other area of service.

Sometimes we forget this fundamental truth and get things backwards. Ann Ortlund, in her excellent little book *Up With Worship*, uses a rather startling illustration to make her point. She says that worship plays a similar role in our relationship with God to the role that sexual intimacy does in a relationship between a husband and wife. A wife may insist that she loves her husband and offers as proof the fact that she cooks his meals, washes his clothes, and manages his household. But if she seldom makes time for sexual intimacy with him, if she seldom stops from her busy schedule to look him tenderly in the eyes and tell him how precious he is to her, he will soon begin to wonder if she really loves him at all. Without that intimate bond, the relationship becomes sterile, dry, and unsatisfying. God ordained intercourse in marriage as a ritual that bonds two partners together, and he says, "Do not deprive each other" (1 Cor. 7:5). We may teach a Bible school class, visit the sick and imprisoned, and provide shelter for the homeless. We may exclaim that we are busy doing any number of good things in God's Kingdom, but if we seldom give full attention to worship, God may wonder if we really love *him*. If we seldom seek God's face to tell him, "Dearest Father, I adore you more than life itself. You are truly precious to me," our relationship with him becomes dry and lifeless. Worship, both private and corporate, is a ritual which God ordained to bind us experientially to him, and he says, "Do not forsake the assembly" (Heb. 10:25).

Through the years I have read scores of definitions of worship that have touched me, but none have inspired me as much as this one from the pen of William Temple:

> Worship is the submission of all our nature to God. It is the quickening of conscience by his holiness; the nourishment of mind with his truth; the purifying of imagination by his beauty; the opening of the heart to his love; the surrender of will to his purpose — and all of this gathered up in adoration, the most selfless emotion of which our nature is capable . . . .

Of the more than 7,200 hymns written by Charles Wesley, one of the best loved is a prayer set to music. The last stanza of *Love Divine, All Love Excelling* reads:

> Finish then Thy new creation,
> Pure, unspotted, may we be;
> Let us see our whole salvation
> Perfectly secured by Thee;
> Changed from glory into glory,
> Till in heav'n we take our place,
> Till we cast our crowns before Thee,
> Lost in wonder, love, and praise.

In heaven we will be able to pray and praise him without ceasing. There we will be able to fully glory in God's perfect love. Then we will realize our whole salvation as we see him face to face. But until we get there, let us worship him with all our hearts. Let us, even now, earthbound though we are, find ourselves "lost in wonder, love, and praise!"

Chapter Eighteen

What kinds of songs best praise God?

Kenneth V. Neller
Harding University
Searcy, Arkansas

What kind of songs best praise God? The kind that please him.

This answer is deceptively simple, but it is absolutely true. There are available to Christians today a multitude of worship songs, with various styles of music and degrees of poetic beauty, and virtually every Christian has a personal preference. But in worship, personal preference is not the primary issue. The foremost concern of any Christian worshiper must be, what pleases GOD? He is the only one who is worthy of worship, he is the one who calls us to worship, and he is the one whose pleasure we should seek. As Ralph Martin observes,

> It is God who takes the first step in proposing the way in which he is to be approached, and it is His promised presence to an obedient people which ensures the communion. Worship which is man-devised and conducted according to human dictates and whims, however impressive and aesthetic it may appear, is not acceptable.[1]

Unfortunately, human emotions, man-made traditions, selfishness and pride often obscure the primacy of pleasing God in our worship.

Praising God Starts with the Heart

We *must* remember that God is Spirit and that he seeks spiritual worshipers (John 4:23, 24). When we sing our "psalms, hymns, and spiritual songs," the first thing he hears, and what he listens for, is not the music, not even the words, but our hearts (spirits). Songs that best praise God are songs which express, or attempt to express, the yearnings and confessions of the human spirit to *the* Spirit. Richard Foster correctly asserts, "We have not worshipped the Lord until Spirit touches spirit."[2] Songs that best praise God facilitate *spiritual* worship.

Moreover, for our songs to be pleasing to God, our hearts and lives must reflect the love and praise our lips sing (see Heb. 13:15, 16). If they do not, no song of any type or style will be pleasing to God (see Isa. 1:10-17; 58:1-14; Amos 5:21-24; 6:1-7). Paul admonishes Christians to "sing and make music in (with) your *heart* to the Lord" (Eph. 5:19).

Now, often we hear Christians say that God does not want singing with musical accompaniment. Certainly a careful study of what the Bible and history teach regarding singing, and a thoughtful reflection upon the nature of God, will surely lead one to conclude that man-made instruments accompanying Christian singing were not used for centuries by the church and do not facilitate the spiritual worship sought by God (John 4:23).[3] But to say that God does not desire our singing to be accompanied by *any* instrument is to overstate the case and is to be in danger of misunderstanding Paul in Ephesians 5:19. God *does* want singing accompanied by a musical instrument, his favorite musical instrument, the heart! As the Psalmist says, "*My heart and my flesh* sing for joy to the living God (Ps. 84:2 NASB, NRSV). But God can *never* be pleased with the words of *any* song if they are accompanied by the discordant sounds of an insincere heart or disobedient spirit. Songs that best praise God are accompanied by the music of a pure heart.

Having reminded ourselves that the primary concern of our singing is to please *God*, and that to please God our singing must be accompanied by a pure heart, we must also ask *why* God wants his people to sing. As with all forms of worship, we sing to praise God for who he is and to thank him for what he has done (Ps. 47:6-7; 105:1-3; Col. 3:16-17). We gather as Christians in assemblies so we can sing his praises and be heard by God's people, and so we in turn can hear other worshipers voice the praises of our God. We also sing together in order to express our joy in the Lord (Ps. 95:1; Jas. 5:13) and to teach and encourage one another (Col. 3:16; Eph. 5:19). Songs that best praise God are songs which accomplish one or more of these purposes: to praise, to thank, to express joy, to encourage, to teach.

There are a variety of types of songs with which to praise God. The categories given in the New Testament are psalms (*psalmoi*), hymns (*hymnoi*) and "spiritual" songs (*odai pneumatikai*) (Eph. 5:19; Col. 3:16). Psalms seem to refer to the psalms of the Old Testament or songs written in a similar style. Hymns are songs of praise. In New Testament times, hymns were usually sung in honor of a deity. Songs (or odes) in ancient times were any type of song. Perhaps this is why Paul says that Christians should sing "spiritual" songs (and psalms and hymns), songs that are sacred and designed to praise God and edify other Christians.[4] Though Paul uses three words to describe the songs that Christians should sing to God, they are basically synonymous words, and most scholars would not make too fine a distinction among them.[5] It is sufficient to say that whatever types of songs a Christian sings in worship, they should be sung to the praise and glory of God with a pure heart.

Selecting Songs Which Best Praise God

With these things in mind, it may be helpful to suggest a few guidelines regarding song selection. There are many songs from which to choose, both those published in standard song books (sometimes called "traditional" songs) and those written in the last few decades (sometimes called "contemporary" songs). Some recently published song books incorporate a sampling of the newer songs, but new worship songs are being written at such an astounding rate that no publisher can possibly publish them all, and no congregation can possibly learn and sing even a majority of them. In the midst of this seemingly endless variety, the following are some suggestions that may guide a worship leader when selecting songs to lead in a congregational setting:

(1) Songs should express praise or thanks to God and give encouragement to fellow Christians in a *biblical* way. No worshiper seeking to please God would want to offer him a song with lyrics that are contrary to his revealed Word. Moreover, music is an extremely influential teacher,[6] and great care must be taken to ensure that what is taught in song is first taught in Scripture. Both traditional and contemporary songs at times include inaccuracies regarding the names or character of God or Christ, or regarding salvation, heaven, etc. One must make allowances for the poetry of the lyrics, but most song writers do not have much theological

training, and songs can, unfortunately, sometimes teach error or foster misconceptions about spiritual things. The editors of songbooks do a good job of weeding out almost all biblically incorrect lyrics. Congregations that use contemporary songs, however, do not have the benefit of an editorial committee. Consequently, we must continuously remind ourselves that just because a song is recorded on a CD and people pay money to hear it, this is no guarantee that the song is pleasing to God!

(2) Songs should express praise or thanks to God or give encouragement to fellow worshipers in a *spiritual* way. This may be a somewhat subjective call, but since God seeks worship on a spiritual level, songs should help lift the spirit, or express the longings of the spirit, or turn our eyes toward spiritual themes or goals. Some songs are fun to sing because they have a good beat; some songs are enjoyable to sing because musically they are beautiful. While neither a good beat nor beauty is objectionable in and of itself, if the music simply appeals to the senses or distracts from the spiritual message of the lyrics, then it does not encourage the kind of worship God desires.

(3) Songs should be singable *congregationally*. Some songs, though beautiful, were written to be sung by skilled musicians, not by an assembly of ordinary folk. If the tune or the harmony is so difficult that many in the congregation cannot sing the song, then the song prevents participation and becomes more frustrating than inspiring. Once again, if the music does not enhance the words, or if it distracts from the words, then the spiritual significance of the song is lost. This is a matter of mature judgment, but the worship leader should be in tune with his congregation's abilities and with their propensity to be distracted by the music.

(4) When praising God, songs should be preferred which are written in the *first person* (using "I" or "we"). Certainly there are many good songs which exhort the congregation to "praise the Lord," and many of the biblical psalms are written in the second person imperative ("Shout with joy to God," Ps. 66) or even in the third person ("The heavens declare the glory of God," Ps. 19). These songs have been used by God's people for centuries and can obviously be sung with benefit. Yet a spiritual worshiper has a strong desire to speak not only *about* God, but also *to* him. A survey of the book of Psalms will also reveal a great many psalms written in the first person ("I will extol the Lord at all times," Ps. 34; "We

give thanks to you, O God," Ps. 75). Traditional songs include a significant number of songs that address God directly in prayer, but very few which address him directly in praise and in joyful thanksgiving. Many newer songs fill this void, and this, no doubt, largely accounts for their popularity in some circles.[7]

(5) Songs should take our *eyes off of ourselves* and direct them (primarily) toward God and also toward one another. Certainly there is a valuable place for personal "testimony" songs such as "Love Lifted Me" and "I Want to Be a Worker for the Lord." Such songs can cement our faith and encourage others. But the majority of the songs we sing in assembly should be directed away from ourselves and toward God and other worshipers. We assemble primarily not to receive, but to *GIVE*, both praise and thanks to God and encouragement to our fellow worshipers.

(6) Songs (and worship leaders!) should *use repetition judiciously.* Repetition is not always bad. In Revelation 4:8, the four living creatures in heaven around God's throne never stop saying, "Holy, holy, holy." In the Sermon on the Mount, Jesus repeats, "Blessed are . . ." and "You have heard that it was said . . . but I say to you . . . ." Likewise, many songs use repetition to advantage, such as "I Know that My Redeemer Lives" and "We Bow Down." Repetition can emphasize a concept, drive a point home, or create a worshipful mood. Nevertheless, some repetition can be trivial and tedious and thus distracting. Such repetition should be avoided.

(7) Finally, the songs we sing must be *intelligible.* Paul stresses how important it is that both the worshiper and those who hear him or her understand what is being said (1 Cor. 14:6-19). Likewise, if we sing words we do not comprehend, our worship will not be pleasing to God. If we ourselves do not understand the words, it is unlikely our fellow worshipers will understand them, so that what we sing will be edifying neither to them nor to us. To give one example, as beautiful as the song is, the lyrics "Night, with ebon pinion brooded o'er the vale" simply do not communicate a coherent concept to most modern worshipers; the lyrics must be explained. And, a one-time explanation is not sufficient, there will always be visitors, new members, and growing children in the congregation, so repeated explanations become necessary. As painful to some of us as it may be, we may have to sing a song with "difficult" lyrics only "to our self and to God," in order that the songs we sing in assembly might be intelligible to all, and thus pleasing to the Lord.

Putting the Songs Together

Perhaps it would be helpful here to discuss briefly the concept of constructing a worship service. Although it is becoming (thankfully!) less and less the rule, all too often a song leader will select songs which he or the congregation enjoys singing and will string them together almost randomly, without careful thought of what the worship service is about or what needs to be accomplished in the assembly. When a spiritual worshiper comes to the assembly, he or she comes desiring

- to come into the presence of God (Ps. 27:4,8; 42:1-2; 63:1; 73:25)
- to experience forgiveness (Ps. 32:1-5; 51:10-12; Isa. 6:1-7)
- to give God a gift (Ps. 51:15-17; 69:30-31; 107:21-22; Jonah 2:7-9; Heb. 13:15)
- to promise God something (Ps. 17:1-3; 116:1-2,12-14,17-19; 119:57-64)
- to be encouraged to keep his/her promises (Ps. 22:25; Heb. 3:12-13; 10:25).

An attuned worship leader will select songs (and perhaps Scriptures) which seek to facilitate these goals.

Moreover, the worship leader must be aware of the "flow" of a worship service. In addition to setting the proper tone for the sharing of the Lord's Supper, he must ask such questions as: Is it best to begin the service quietly, perhaps confessionally? Or, should we begin with loud, joyous praise? What is the theme of the sermon (or worship service)? Would it be most appropriate to close by praising God for his faithfulness, or by encouraging the congregation to be evangelistic? When the worship leader gives consideration to questions like these, the resulting selection of songs will make "sense" to the worshiper, who in turn will appreciate, concentrate better on, and assimilate the words he or she is singing.

Barry Liesch has written a most helpful and practical article for structuring a worship service entitled "A Structure Runs Through It" (*Leadership* [Summer 1993] 100-104). He, following others, suggests that we think of a worship service as having five phases (based on Psalm 95):

1) *Invitation*, "Come, let us sing for joy to the Lord . . ." This is not the invitation to respond to the gospel at the end of a sermon, but the "call to worship," the inviting of fellow worshipers to join

together in praise to God. This phase would begin the worship service and could include such songs as:

> Come, We that Love the Lord
> Come, Join Our Hearts
> O Come, Let Us Adore Him
> O, Worship the King
> We Bring the Sacrifice of Praise
> We Have Come into His House

2) *Engagement*, "Let us come before him with thanksgiving . . ." Here the service begins to turn from the worshipers to God. It would include songs which sing *about* God, his greatness, love, faithfulness, etc., and which praise and thank him. These would be songs like:

> Awesome God
> Come, Let Us All Unite to Sing
> Hallelujah, Praise Jehovah
> Holy, Holy, Holy
> Our God, He Is Alive
> Thank You, Lord

3) *Exaltation*, "For the Lord is the great God, the great King . . ." This phase is similar to "engagement," but it focuses on God's (or Christ's) greatness and "places" him on his throne, proclaiming him Lord. This phase could use songs such as:

> All Hail the Power of Jesus' Name
> Crown Him with Many Crowns
> How Great Thou Art
> Majesty
> Mighty Is Our God
> We Exalt Thee

4) *Adoration*, "Come, let us bow down in worship, let us kneel . . ." In the adoration phase, the mood is generally quieter, slower. Songs are almost exclusively in the first person, directly addressing God with "I" or "we." Possible songs would be:

> Christ, We Do All Adore Thee
> Fairest Lord Jesus
> Glorify Thy Name
> Joyful, Joyful We Adore Thee
> On Bended Knee
> We Bow Down

5) *Intimacy*, "For we are the people of his pasture, the flock under his care." Here worshipers express their love for God, their longing and desire to do his will, to be with him. Moving from this phase to the Lord's Supper flows very naturally. Songs for this phase could include:

> Abide with Me
> As the Deer
> I Need Thee Every Hour
> I Love You, Lord
> I Want to Be Where You Are
> O Master, Let Me Walk with Thee

Of course, not every service in every congregation must follow this pattern to be pleasing to God and a blessing to the worshipers. This is just a suggested format. Obviously, other "phases" of the worship service include preparation for the Lord's Supper, the "invitation" song after the sermon, and a closing song (preferably one which is upbeat and positive, emphasizing the point of the sermon, pledging faithfulness on the part of the worshiper, or reminding the worshiper of some duty or the "goal," heaven).

Another way of approaching format is that the worship leader might want to visualize the congregation at the beginning of a worship service as a crowd of worshipers walking up the mountain to the temple in Jerusalem to worship. (Imagine the excitement, the anticipation, the camaraderie!) Next, the worshipers arrive in the court of the temple. (We are approaching the holy God; how great is he! how worthy of praise!) Then, we enter the temple itself and stand in his presence before his throne. (He is awesome, we are unworthy; he is wonderful, we love him and are thrilled to be in his presence; we lay before him as an offering our gift, our lives.) Songs selected to create this succession of moods, punctuated by Scripture readings and prayers, may be very beneficial to the worshipers.

Alternatively, the worship leader may consider it inappropriate to begin the service loudly and joyously. After all, we are sinners; God is holy (remember Isaiah's reaction to being in the presence of a holy God, Isaiah 6:5-7). Who are we simply to barge into his presence? True, we are his children and he welcomes us, but he *is* HOLY. Perhaps we should begin quietly, reverently, confessing our sins. After this, we can celebrate God and what he has done for us in Christ.

Whatever structure a worship leader uses for organizing the songs and the other activities of a service, it is critical that the structure be one derived from prayerful planning, not a haphazard selection of songs in order to fill up space. God is too holy, and our time in his presence is too important for us to give him less than our very best.

Congregations of God's people have different personalities just like the personalities of people differ from one individual to the next. Churches are variously influenced by their spiritual heritage and by their culture. Consequently, songs and worship formats suitable for one congregation might not be suitable for another.[8] Nevertheless, so long as the focus is on doing what *God* desires and what pleases him, spiritual worshipers of any age, culture, or musical preference can find (or write!) spiritual songs which can express their praise, thanks and desires and which are edifying to others. And worshipers may be certain that when they sing such songs accompanied by a pure heart, God is pleased.

Endnotes

[1] Ralph Martin, *Worship in the Early Church* (London: Marshall, Morgan and Scott, 1964), 13.

[2] Richard J. Foster, *Celebration of Discipline* (San Francisco: Harper and Row, 1978), 138.

[3] Helpful studies on this topic are Everett Ferguson, *A Cappella Music in the Public Worship of the Church*, 2nd ed. (Abilene, TX: ACU Press, 1988); and Rubel Shelly, *Sing His Praise! A Case for A Cappella Music as Worship Today* (Nashville: 20th Century Christian, 1987).

[4] There are those, however, who understand "spiritual" as referring to songs "inspired by the Spirit." See Martin, *Worship*, 43, 47; and A.T. Lincoln, *Ephesians*, Word Biblical Commentary 42 (Dallas: Word, 1990), 345-346.

[5] See Ferguson, *A Cappella Music*, 15; F.F. Bruce, *The Epistles to the Colossians, to Philemon, and to the Ephesians*, NICNT (Grand Rapids, MI: Eerdmans, 1984), 158-159; and Lincoln, *Ephesians*, 345-346.

[6] See Dan Dozier, *Come Let Us Adore Him* (Joplin, MO: College Press, 1994), 154-158.

[7] The value of this "vertical" aspect of many of the contemporary worship songs can be seen even by one who stereotypes and vilifies contemporary-style worship services: see Dan Chambers, *Showtime! Worship in the Age of Show Business* (Nashville: 21st Century Christian, 1997), 104.

[8] For an enlightening discussion of culture and how it influences musical styles and taste, see Dozier, *Come Let Us Adore Him*, 147ff.

Chapter Nineteen

How can we have a deeper understanding of baptism and the Lord's Supper?

Randy Harris
Lipscomb University
Nashville, Tennessee

Change is in the air and, more significantly, in our churches. These changes, of course, will be of great delight to some and of even greater distress to others. I suppose that it is inevitable (and not altogether unhealthy) that talk of change would eventually touch such hallowed doctrines as baptism and the Lord's Supper. And so it has. Some old questions are being revisited, and some new ones are being asked.

For instance, in light of the increasing involvement of Churches of Christ with other evangelical groups and movements like Promise Keepers, which emphasize tearing down walls between "brothers" of different religious persuasions, many are again asking the question about the essentiality of baptism to be a Christian ("Surely the good brother I met from the Presbyterian Church at the Promise Keepers rally isn't lost!")

Or, to cite another example, many members of Churches of Christ are inquiring about the appropriateness of the Lord's Supper at times other than Sunday, for instance at Wednesdays or in the midst of the deep and intimate Christian fellowship of a Thursday night prayer group. This last question is somewhat new to me, the old issue being the necessity of every Sunday observance.

As intriguing and important as these questions are, they are not the focus of this essay. The title of this chapter properly conveys its direction. It is not a call for doctrinal innovation or a repudiation of the positions historically taken within Churches of Christ about the frequency of the Lord's Supper or the essentiality of believer's immersion. Rather it is a call for a deeper understanding and a correspondingly richer practice of these sacred rites. While I am not here calling for wholesale theological revision, I am convinced that there are aspects of these doctrines that we have neglected and, could they be recovered, would greatly enhance our participation.

Baptism

Is baptism essential to salvation? Is the mode of baptism crucial to its validity? How much must a person know (for instance, that it is for the remission of sins) for his baptism to be valid? What is the destiny of the pious unimmersed or those whose only baptism was infant sprinkling, which was then followed by living the life of faith?

Just to show that theologians can engage in plain talk, my answers are yes, yes, very little and I don't know. (For those who want additional commentary on question three, I think one must know enough to profess faith in Christ and repent in obedience to God). I suppose my orthodoxy on these questions may surprise some, but for the most part I believe our positions appear sound. But before returning to all the difficult questions that can be asked, let me make a few points about the theology of baptism that I believe need greater emphasis.

Baptism as an Act of God

I believe at the level of popular theology in Churches of Christ, the biggest problem in baptismal theology is on what we emphasize. Far too frequently the focus is on what the convert is doing rather than on what God is doing.

Due in large part to our revivalist heritage, my impression from attendance at countless gospel meetings is that the climactic moment of the service is the invitation song, and thus the moment at which the sinner makes the crucial decision to turn to God in Christ. The whole service is pointed toward bringing a person to make a decision (too often under considerable emotional duress) and not focused on what God is doing. The baptism itself, while crucial (essential), is virtually anticlimactic. Equally strange is the aftermath of the baptismal service in which the recipient is congratulated for what he has done.

Baptism is not portrayed in Scripture as a work one does. Baptism is more something done to the subject than by him. Thus, the focus of a baptismal scene is not what the subject does but what the passive subject has done to him by God. This passivity of the subject is no accidental feature of baptism, but is central to the ritual. Baptism is not self-administered, but involves surrendering to another's power over him. Just as one's body is given over to another and put in peril under the water, so one's life is being handed over to God and put at whatever risk is necessary for doing the divine will from now on. To be sure, baptism requires human activity, but the phrase "active passivity" comes closer to the reality. The human being's role is to present himself as available to the movements of God's grace. If this adjustment could be made, this might also allow us to think of baptism as the *place* where something happens rather than as a work one does.

Baptism as Place

It is almost a given that baptism is an act or, more perilously put, a work. Thus, the accusation is leveled against us of "water salvation" or "works righteousness." But I wonder if there is another way of thinking about it.

Perhaps thinking about baptism as the *place* where something happens rather than always thinking about it as the *means* would provide assistance. There is no question about the importance of the place of God's action throughout Scripture. The human being's role becomes the very modest one of being where God is acting.

Baptism no more washes away sin than the Jordan River cures leprosy or the pool cures blindness. God is always the active agent, and the human being merely places himself at God's behest. "It [baptism] saves you *by the resurrection* of Jesus Christ" (1 Pet. 3:21). But this leads us to the next point.

Baptism: Sign vs. Symbol

One will frequently hear a question framed like this, "Does anything *really* happen in baptism or is it only a symbol?" I think this suggests a misunderstanding of what a symbol is and does.

I think it is helpful to distinguish between signs and symbols (though theologians are by no means consistent in their usage of these terms). A sign is merely a pointer, while a symbol participates in the reality to which it points. For example, traffic signs invoke no emotional investment, while the American flag, which is not just a sign, but a symbol, creates a deep bond for the person to whom the symbol speaks. Baptism and the Lord's Supper are symbols to be sure, but they are not mere signs.

The Lord's Supper and Passover are reenactments that intend to make the partaker a participant in the events they memorialize. There is no violation of the once-for-all character of the original event; yet, the symbol is not a mere memory prod but the vehicle by which one becomes a part of the reality.

In like manner, baptism adds nothing to the one-of-a kind work of the death and resurrection of Christ, but is the means by which a person *participates* in that reality. Symbols participate in the reality to which they point. Our doctrine of baptism would be healthier if placed in the broader context of how symbols function throughout Scripture.

Baptism as Response

Let me quote briefly from a "teaching position" document of a local church:

> Once a person admits his sin and turns to Christ for salvation, some step must be taken to proclaim to heaven and earth that he is a follower of Christ. Baptism is that step. Baptism is the initial and immediate step of obedience by one who has declared his faith to others. So important was this step that, as far as we know, every single convert in the New Testament was baptized. . . . Baptism separates the tire kickers from the car buyers. Would you feel comfortable marrying someone who wanted to keep the marriage a secret? Neither does God. It's one thing to say in the privacy of your own heart that you are a sinner in need of a savior. But its quite another to walk out of the shadows and stand before family, friends, and colleagues to state publicly that Christ is your forgiver and master. This step raises the ante. Jesus commanded all his followers to prove it, to make the pledge, by public demonstration in baptism (Oak Hills Church of Christ, San Antonio, Texas, position paper).

Here is an eloquent reminder that baptism is *the* response of the human being to God's saving work in Christ. Apart from the work of Christ there is no baptism. But baptism as response to God's action in the cross must be combined with the idea of baptism as the place of God's action in the *present*. Baptism is both the human being's response of faith and the place where God actually does something to the human subject: cleanse them from sin, bestow the Holy Spirit, etc. The above statement also reminds us that baptism is not just a personal act, but a communal one. We declare our faith in the community.

It is precisely at this point that our baptismal theology is confused. Baptism is a public declaration of faith in God's saving work in Christ, but that is not all that it is. It is also the place where God cleanses us from sin and bestows the Holy Spirit upon us (that is, in the normal course of events, there are exceptional cases in Acts). Here is the heart of the matter, baptism is both our response and the occasion for God's action.

Rebaptism?

I close this section with some reflections on what has become a new controversy in Churches of Christ but is actually only a revival of an old one. What of those who are immersed without a fully correct understanding of baptism? Should they be reimmersed? On this point I join David Lipscomb who contended that God would not reject service done in obedience to God's law simply because one did not wait to learn all the blessings and promises connected with obedience[1]. He pointed out that it made no sense for a person who had begun a journey and gone a long way on the right road, upon taking a wrong turn, to return all the way to where he or she began. So it was with those who had been scripturally baptized, yet found themselves in sectarian establishments. Such a subsequent wrong turn did not undo their faith, repentance, or baptism. Such a person should keep all that he had which was true and right, and simply get off the wrong road and back on the right one. "We only return to the point at which we erred and there begin aright."[2]

I think I understand baptism better than I did ten years ago and much better than I did when it was actually done to me. But I do not need to be rebaptized every time I learn something new. My response of faith to God's work in Christ was genuine, and what God did in my behalf was not dependent on my full understanding of it. But this is why I would take a different tack on the question of infant baptism, for in this action there is no act of faithful response on the part of the one baptized.

Salvation without Baptism?

This always seems to be the point at which we conclude. Can one be saved without being baptized as an adult believer? Of course, we should all take care not to tell God what he can or cannot do. We can only teach what we understand Scripture to say. I would close this section with a quote from J.W. McGarvey who more eloquently says what I would say on this point:[3]

> Dear Bro.:
> Replying to yours of the 15th, I have no doubt there are pious persons who have never been immersed. It would be absurd and ridiculous to deny it in the face of what we see and know of thousands of persons living and dead who have exhibited self-sacrificing love of God and man, which puts to shame all common disciples. I have as little doubt that many unimmersed persons will be saved in the final day. It is not necessary in order to contend for scripture teaching on the subject of baptism to take the ground that God has tied his hands and put it out of his power to grant mercy to any who have been misled in regard to that ordinance. He has bound us, but he has not bound himself; except that he is bound to do what he has promised. He has not bound himself to do no more than he has promised. Don't injure the cause of truth by taking positions which rob God of the power to be merciful.
> Yours fraternally,
> J.W. McGarvey

The Lord's Supper

Those of us who have participated in the Lord's Supper every week for years are prone to believe that we have seen and heard every possible variation of the communion devotional even though the Lord's Supper is a many-faceted jewel, the beauty of which is reflected from many different perspectives. Where there are many directions we could pursue to enrich our understanding and participation in the Supper, I will suggest only one.

A common approach to the meditation on the Supper is something like the following: "Now as we come to the observance of the Lord's Supper, try to block everything around you out of your mind and concentrate fully on Jesus dying on the cross." But is this the correct approach or the only approach?

Consider the following passage from 1 Corinthians 11:17-34:

In the following directives I have no praise for you, for your meetings do more harm than good. In the first place, I hear that when you come together as a church, there are divisions among you, and to some extent I believe it. No doubt there have to be differences among you to show which of you have God's approval. When you come together, it is not the Lord's Supper you eat, for as you eat, each of you goes ahead without waiting for anybody else. One remains hungry, another gets drunk. Don't you have homes to eat and drink in? Or do you despise the church of God and humiliate those who have nothing? What shall I say to you? Shall I praise you for this? Certainly not!

For I received from the Lord what I also passed on to you: The Lord Jesus, on the night he was betrayed, took bread, and when he had given thanks, he broke it and said, "This is my body, which is for you; do this in remembrance of me." In the same way, after supper he took the cup, saying, "This cup is the new covenant in my blood; do this, whenever you drink it, in remembrance of me." For whenever you eat this bread and drink this cup, you proclaim the Lord's death until he comes.

Therefore, whoever eats the bread or drinks the cup of the Lord in an unworthy manner will be guilty of sinning against the body and blood of the Lord. A man ought to examine himself before he eats of the bread and drinks of the cup. For anyone who eats and drinks without recognizing the body of the Lord eats and drinks judgment on himself. That is why many among you are weak and sick, and a number of you have fallen asleep. But if we judged ourselves, we would not come under judgment. When we are judged by the Lord, we are being disciplined so that we will not be condemned with the world.

So then, my brothers, when you come together to eat, wait for each other. If anyone is hungry, he should eat at home, so that when you meet together it may not result in judgment.

And when I come I will give further directions.

While I cannot fully exegete this section in the confines of this paper, we can summarize the section as follows. The Lord's Supper in Corinth is within the context of communal meals which were common not just in Christian communities but throughout the ancient world. The Corinthian assembly seems to be a symposium setting rather than a structured worship. But the communal meal is being abused in Corinth, and the conflict seems to be between rich and poor. The rich are starting early and eating more and better food. This is not surprising since the problem of social status was common at communal meals and in many contexts a social ranking was accepted practice. The Corinthians apparently see no conflict between these practices and participating in the Lord's Supper.

Paul, however, finds their practice intolerable and censures them for it. Why? Because the church is the body of Christ, and the Lord's Supper is not only a communion with the Lord but a *communion with the body* as well. By their lack of fellowship in the meal, they despise the church and miss the point of the Lord's Supper. His demand is that a person discern the body (church, v. 29) when he participates. That is, the Lord's Supper is to be an experience of the community, not an isolated, individual act. The failure to participate in this way will result in divine punishment.

What does this mean to us today? We may insist that there is no discrimination between rich and poor in our observance of the Lord's Supper, and certainly no one is getting drunk in our assemblies. In fact, there is no real meal associated with the Lord's to be the occasion for these abuses, and we seldom have our worship services in homes.

But let us think a little deeper. The Lord's Supper originated at a meal (the Passover of Jesus and the apostles) and takes place in the context of a meal at Corinth. The aim of these meals is the fellowship of the participants with one another. Thus, the Lord's Supper is always in the context of Christian fellowship with one another. It is *not* an individual act of piety but a collective celebration. We recognize not just what Jesus had done for us but how he has brought us together.

Think about some of the things we do in our practice of the Lord's Supper.

1. We sit on pews looking at the back of each other's heads.
2. We drink from tiny individual communion cups.
3. We are perfectly quiet; there is no interaction with each other.
4. On Sunday night, we usher those who have not taken communion into a separate room for a hurried Lord's Supper service.
5. We see how quickly and efficiently we can pass the Lord's Supper in our Sunday morning assemblies to avoid a "dead time."
6. One poor deacon takes the Lord's Supper to shut-ins with rushed prayer (and without participating himself) so he can get around to all his stops.

All of this suggests to me that we may well be neglecting the horizontal, "one another" dimension that is precisely Paul's point in the above passage. The Lord's Supper is never about just me and Jesus. It is always about *us*!

But here we come to a truly difficult problem of practical theology. How can we recover the fellowship dimension of the Lord's Supper in our formal worship services and especially in our large churches? It is impractical to think that we will have a fellowship meal every Sunday and put the Lord's Supper there instead of in the worship.

It is little wonder that some have advocated the return to house churches or at least small groups for the purpose of restoring the fellowship aspect to the Lord's Supper. But for those who are not drawn to so radical a solution, the problem remains. It should be clear that this is not just a Lord's Supper problem. One cannot create fellowship at the Lord's Supper that is not already present. As our congregations become larger, there is a tendency for us to become a congregation of strangers. As this happens, something crucial to our church life and the Lord's Supper is lost.

I have found the reactions of people to the preaching of this 1 Corinthians passage interesting. Several times members have come to me afterwards saying that they did not mean to be sinning all these years by sitting on the pew, blocking everybody else out, and thinking about the suffering of Jesus on the cross. Of course I do not want to discourage such devoted focus. But to have church members of thirty to forty years be totally unaware of the fellowship dimension of the Lord's Supper is problematic to say the least.

So why not give some serious thought about how to incorporate this into the observance of the Lord's Supper at your congregation? Here are a few things others have tried (You may have better ideas!).

1. Partake together rather than one at a time as communion is passed.
2. Have a Sunday dedicated to the Lord's Supper as the center of worship and preach or teach on this aspect.
3. Have people share spiritual matters and pray for one another prior to communing with one another.
4. Experiment occasionally with small group communion in settings where it is appropriate and feasible.
5. Sing a song of unity and fellowship in the context of the Supper.

Not all approaches will work in all settings, but whatever the mechanics of the Lord's Supper, the "one another" theology must be recovered.

While we still listen to Paul, on another level the social implications he saw in the Lord's Supper go unheeded. Isn't it ironic that differing understandings of the Lord's Supper not only contributed to the separation of the Roman Catholic Church and Protestantism, but have provided a splintering force within Protestantism as well, from the sixteenth century forward? What Paul saw as a reason for unity has become a cause of division. But as the ecumenical movement goes sputtering into the future, a resolution hardly seems eminent.

However, by adopting the more modest (yet still challenging) goal of improvement at the congregational level, progress can surely be made. With the separation of fellowship meal and Lord's Supper and even the use of individual communion cups, the fellowship aspects of the Lord's Supper have surely suffered. Perhaps a reemphasis on this aspect of the Lord's Supper in our preaching and teaching is in order. Not only would it reintroduce an aspect that Paul thought was crucial, but it would also serve to make each person more aware of his relationship with, and responsibility to the people with whom he worships. Do we despise the church of God by our observance of the Lord's Supper?

Endnotes

[1]*Gospel Advocate* 49 (25 April 1907): 265.
[2]*Gospel Advocate* 12 (15 Dec. 1870): 1161.
[3]*Gospel Advocate* 37 (12 Dec. 1895): 790.

SECTION SEVEN
QUESTIONS ABOUT EVANGELISM

To say that evangelism is dead in Churches of Christ certainly says too much, for there are many signs in many places of the continuing power of the gospel to transform lives. This is especially true in the inner cities and around the world. Yet, statistics show that in the United States, the church is experiencing little or no growth. Thus the importance of this section. But the authors here offer no simple "how-to" manual to teach unbelievers (of which there are many available). Rather they ask us to consider more basic questions.

Evertt Huffard asks us to think about how our theology influences evangelism. If we are right in our initial contention in this book that doctrine affects all of life, we would expect our evangelism to be influenced deeply by our understanding of certain doctrines. Thus we cannot just forget about theology and go preach. Theology affects why, how, and what we preach.

Carson Reed and Jim Baird remind us that the evangelistic talk takes place in a changing world. Reed's article emphasizes the pluralism of our culture. That is, the day when we can assume that our neighbor is some brand of Christian is over. Our neighbor might be Muslim, Buddhist or Atheist. We cannot assume people share our basic worldview. In a pluralistic world such as this where the dominant virtue has become tolerance of others, how should we view the evangelistic task?

Baird points us to the relativism of postmodern culture. How can we talk about Jesus "the way, the truth and the life" to people who not only do not believe he is the truth but also further believe that there is no truth? Such is our task.

As inheritors of Jesus' mission to seek and save the lost, we must take our calling and our world seriously.

Chapter Twenty

How does theology influence evangelism?

Evertt W. Huffard
Harding Graduate School of Religion
Memphis, Tennessee

For several decades scholarly opinions have assumed and argued that the causes of growth in the Christian movement were more contextual than institutional. For example, one might argue that the church in the first century grew because of the Roman roads more than the power of the preaching of Paul.[1] Or, the contrast between the rapid rates of church growth in nineteenth century America compared to the flat growth in the latter part of the twentieth century can be attributed to very different contextual factors. One cannot deny the relationship between context and receptivity, but the church, as the individual, still bears some responsibility for the extent of evangelism and maturity of the church.

Michael Green attributes the growth of the early church to three contextual factors: the Roman peace, Greek language, and the Jewish religion.[2] None of these are significant factors for evangelism in the twenty-first century. However, there are some interesting parallels. The expansion of the world through Roman peace and roads may have been as mind-boggling as the sudden opening of millions of new worlds through the worldwide web and the "information superhighway." The Greek culture provided a universal language for the gospel and the Scriptures, but no more universal than English is today. The Jewish religion provided so many theological starting points for the growth of the church. The Jewish Christians of the Diaspora became a powerful force for revival and renewal. Evangelists in the twenty-first century might also find reaching the churched (not just the unchurched) with the gospel as necessary a starting point as evangelism in the synagogues of the first century.

Evangelism should function as a natural institutional concern of any church, regardless of contextual factors. The intent to evangelize may have more to do with kingdom growth than the receptivity of the community. The contextual factors may influence the rate of growth more than the fact of it. We can find people in any community who are searching for a way to be right with God or seeking his blessings. Churches have grown as much in times of war and persecution as in times of peace and prosperity. The context has influence, but not enough to excuse commitment to the growth of the kingdom. We need to balance understanding of demographic realities and receptivity with a spiritual commitment and witness to the transforming power and presence of God in the world.

Research by Kirk Hadaway concluded that evangelism is of value in discriminating between growing and nongrowing churches. "In fact, evangelism appears to be the only programmatic activity that retains a meaningful relationship to church growth when statistical controls are in effect."[3]

Although few would deny the role of contextual factors, I would not give them priority over the faithful, consistent proclamation of the good news of the kingdom of God at any time in history. Theologically speaking, God cannot be limited by context even though he incarnationally works within context. Nor can God's purposes of bringing believers into his kingdom be evaluated on pragmatic grounds. Something is terribly wrong when the unseen is measured by the seen. While rapid growth of the kingdom may tempt us to play a "numbers game" with evangelism, the ultimate goal is to glorify God. The goal is obviously more theological than methodological or programmatic.

Jesus Set a Theological Criterion for Evangelism

The history of the expansion of Christianity vividly illustrates what can happen when evangelism functions without theological criteria. The battle for the expansion of the church among Gentiles began as a cultural battle, but the victory took place on theological grounds. In the Jerusalem Conference, both Peter and James brought the "mind of God" into the discussion. Peter observed that "God made the choice" to accept the Roman Centurion; "God showed . . . that he accepted them;" and the whole issue could really "test God" (Acts 15:7-8,10). James argued that God was the first to show his concern for the Gentiles and implied that they have no choice but to follow God's leadership (Acts 15:14,19). The rationale for the Gentile mission had nothing to do with how many of them were lost or poor; it had everything to do with what God did and expected. That is, theology was fundamental to the expanding mission of the church.

However, within centuries, cultural and geopolitical power eroded the biblical theology that led to the conversion of Romans everywhere. Forced baptisms of people conquered by the Byzantine Empire rendered evangelism a servant of political ambitions. The Theodosian code (A.D. 478) authorized the death penalty for anyone who was circumcised or performed the operation, rendering evangelism as much a servant of cultural ambitions as circumcision had been in the first century. Five hundred years later, the Crusaders forced Muslims to be baptized as a sign of military defeat and cultural domination.

There was a time in Africa when missionaries required converts to Christianity to change their names to "Christian" (Western) names, rejecting their family and cultural heritage. Modern mutations include national evangelists who seek fortune and promise earthly blessings, rendering evangelism the servant of an American dream. Evangelism in Europe after World War II or in Eastern Europe after the fall of communism has served individualistic Western values more than create communities of believers in Jesus as Lord of all.

We can only hope that this dark side of the history of evangelism really represents the exception. Thousands of Christian martyrs, countless long-term missionaries, missionaries who gave a lifetime to planting indigenous churches, and the churches that survived years of persecution all bear witness to the presence of a spiritual criterion for initiation and participation in the Kingdom of God. Evangelism without the theological criterion becomes a servant of man and his culture, an abuse of God's promises and gift of life.

Jesus had very strong feelings about the process of bringing people into the Kingdom of God. With the force of a "temple cleanser," he challenged the lack of theological criteria for Jewish proselytizing of his own day. In the context of open condemnation for closing the doors of the kingdom through legalistic rituals and codes, Jesus calls the scribes and Pharisees hypocrites, children of hell, blind guides, fools, and serpents.

> Woe to you, scribes and Pharisees, hypocrites! for you traverse sea and land to make a single proselyte, and when he becomes a proselyte, you make him twice as much a child of hell as yourselves (Matt. 23:15, RSV).

The critique Jesus had for Jewish evangelism had nothing to do with how many responded. He was concerned with what it transformed people into. How one proclaims the message of the Kingdom of God was obviously a serious matter to Jesus. As DeRidder concluded, "Jesus' words in Matthew 23:15 also show that the test of a mission is not the zeal with which one pursues others to join him in his faith, but rather what he makes of them after they have been won."[4] Translated into the challenges of evangelism today, our task is not completed with a decision to be baptized. Jesus understood evangelism to be a process.

Christ's mission in the world defines the church's mission in the world. A theological criterion for evangelism is necessary to maintain a proper direction and balance. Three theological issues generate a criterion for evangelism that will be addressed in this essay: the purpose of the church, expectations of God for kingdom growth, and tensions of the kingdom.

Evangelism and a Theology of the Church

Without a clear theological purpose, evangelists tend to use their gifts to bring individuals to a commitment to Christ, but fail to develop a community of believers. God gave his body many different spiritual gifts for this specific reason (Rom. 12:3-8). The evangelist can use gifts to initiate people into the kingdom while other members of the body develop leadership and nurture persistence in faith.

A healthy theology of the church would not limit evangelism to baptism nor assume that any one person had all the gifts. Evangelism is the process of making disciples, which includes taking the initiative to go to the lost, baptizing those who believe, and teaching all the commands of Christ (Matt. 28:18-20). New Christians in Jerusalem naturally devoted themselves to teaching and fellowship (Acts 2:42). To say we are reaching the lost anywhere in the world without a biblical theology of the church falls far short of the teachings of Christ and the example of the early church.

Some efforts to evangelize Europe in the 1950s and Eastern Europe in the 1990s illustrate the consequences of a very weak functional theology of the church. It seems so easy to ignore the fundamentals of making disciples in cross-cultural settings, possibly because it requires proficiency in the language and an understanding of both cultures (their own and the host culture). We often seek shortcuts in the wrong places. Kingdom growth, like raising children, has very few shortcuts. When I have confronted this problem, I have been told that someone has to go, and even feeble efforts are better than nothing. I cannot agree.

My experience in several countries has convinced me that these feeble efforts did much more harm than good. For when trained long-term missionaries finally arrived on the scene, the church had developed such a reputation of shallowness and foreignness in the community that little could be done to turn it into a healthy, indigenous church.

So, you will hear exciting, unbelievable reports of many baptisms on some of these campaigns — but try to find the "converts" a few months later. How did the kingdom grow if after so many baptisms no healthy church or spiritual leaders exist five or ten years later? In such a setting, evangelism functioned outside the church and failed to fulfill the purposes of God through the church. The evangelists were not accountable to the church that sent them nor were they able to leave churches behind.

Evangelistic campaigns have served a valuable function in the growth of the church. They are most effective when they are invited by the local church and work in partnership with the local church. If a church does not exist, then they will plan to place a teacher/evangelist in the city, before the campaign starts, with intentions of developing fellowship and faithfulness in the lives of those who respond to the preaching of the Gospel. These campaigns have the immediate value of finding seekers, but they have also been the primary source of new missionaries.

Consider a problem much closer to home, where a biblical theology of the church relates to evangelism. Older established churches seldom develop a reputation for evangelistic zeal. They need a theological challenge that defines their very reason to exist. In fact, the strongest argument for new church planting is that they have a clear purpose to exist and have the best record for making new disciples. Few churches over twenty years old are evangelistic. Evangelists or preachers with a commitment to evangelism will find ministry in this context very frustrating. The church may give financial support to a mission effort but develop a status quo posture at home. The loss of evangelistic activity might explain why most of these churches tend to grow old and die. When the purpose of the church shifts to self-preservation, it loses a theologically valid reason to exist and dies spiritually long before it dies physically.

Recent studies also show that large churches are not as evangelistic as smaller churches. Based on the diagnostic analysis of 112 Churches of Christ, John Ellas discovered that growing churches tend to baptize more people than declining churches, except for churches with more than 700 in Sunday morning worship attendance. As churches grew larger, they declined in evangelistic effectiveness.[5] Should this not raise a theological question? Would God equate bigger churches to kingdom growth?

Although I would not argue that smaller churches are more spiritual, a strong case could be made for the need to define the purpose of the church, large or small, or it will be distracted by a survival mindset if it is small or a self-sufficiency mindset if it is large. Both problems can only be corrected by a theological rationale for existence and commitment to the purpose of God for the church in a specific community at a given time in history.

Paul spells out the purpose of the church for Christians in Ephesus. God's plan assumed a spiritual war in which the church would manifest the wisdom of God — to the end that God would be glorified (Eph. 3:10-21). This theological principle connects with reality for any church, especially the older or larger ones, at the point of evangelism. To go months or even years without a baptism in a local church will leave many without the slightest evidence that God's power is at work in the church. The primary evidence of divine victory comes from the hearts and lives that are being transformed into his glory.

Historically, restoration or unity of Christianized populations might be an important task but not greater than witnessing to the power of God to the lost. Disunity is an evil thing but a church without witness is irresponsible with both the message and mission of Christ.

Since transformation is a process, no church can point to any moment in history when it reached perfection or fully satisfied God's will. Christians cannot separate the benefits of the gospel (salvation) from the responsibility of the gospel (evangelism, witness, and service).[6] Without a theological foundation, churches slip into a competitive spirit of denominationalism rather than proclaim hope in Christ to all. This leads to unnecessary confusion for the multitudes of lost souls that should only have to decide whether to follow Christ or not, rather than which church is right.

To summarize, our understanding of the nature and purpose of the church will directly affect our understanding and participation in evangelism.

Evangelism and a Theology of Growth

The biblical narratives leave little doubt that God works in and through his people. The point at which that becomes most obvious is in evangelism. Therefore, the loss of evangelism in a church can lead to a secularization process that excludes God from the history of that church as well as from life in general. Evangelistic churches constantly praise God for the evidence they have each week of his work in transforming hopeless people into a holy nation.

It is no coincidence that when Churches of Christ were more evangelistic, one heard more about the providence of God. Without evangelism, the work of God fades into a glorious past. The church is left with the future, somewhat abstract, expectation of salvation. Man's ultimate destiny becomes the object of the process rather than the glory of God. As a result, the converts are misled by a simplified message of salvation without the faintest understanding of the demands of service, fellowship, and submission to the will of God.

This theological anemia directly impacts evangelism. When God is not considered a part of the process, the means of evangelism shift from the providential presence and working of God in life to human skill, knowledge, and salesmanship. Missionaries and evangelists have engaged in heated debate over methods as if the product were totally dependent on them. Churches, with a commitment to reach their neighborhoods, may be tempted to give up theological integrity to satisfy a consumer appetite with a good show on Sunday and a convenient Christianity. Marketing, although it is a valuable tool, could become the criterion for evangelism and upstage basic theological demands.

For example, can a theological issue be raised regarding the location of the church building or the target group the church is trying to reach? Did God lead the church to that location, or did it simply happen? Does God really want one kind of people in the church? As demographics change, would God expect the church to change or to move to another part of town so it could avoid change? If we begin with marketing values, it would be easy to confirm that there would be such cultural differences between the community people and the church, that the church should move to where it can best reach "their own kind." What this is saying is that pragmatic factors are beyond theological scrutiny.

The move from the farms to the city changed evangelism in America, contextually and institutionally. The tent meetings lost their impact on the city after a few decades. The message no longer seemed relevant. The rapid ethnic migration overwhelmed the churches among the urban majority. These changes just might be from God. It is possible that since we sent so few missionaries in the past, God might be bringing the world to us with the expectation that we will praise and honor him among the nations.

The move from the city to the suburbs placed evangelism on the endangered species list. As Christians climbed the social ladder, more basic needs were met and God became an option. Work and recreation consumed more time, and the church no longer held center stage. The higher the social status of a suburb, the higher the proportion of its residents who were members of religious institutions. However, when asked if we should try to make all men Christian, an evangelistic question, Protestants and Catholics in "new town" and "country club estates" were much more likely to disagree than those living further into the city.[7]

It is possible to argue that where one lives in America influences one's attitude toward evangelism. Since 1970 the nation has been suburbanized, and the resulting suburbanization of churches made theological issues subservient to budgets, buildings, location, and ministries to the churched. Gallup surveys identified a shift in motives for attending church from keeping religious loyalty to meeting individual needs. The increase of religious consumerism as a form of cultural individualism could be the most significant change in the religious world in the late 1980s.[8]

248

The reality is that the majority of the members of the Churches of Christ are suburban. Suburban churches have turned against the cities of America, assuming they are without hope and condemned. They have abandoned the cities in record numbers, seldom leaving any ministry behind.[9] If the evangelization of the nation and world were dependent on suburban churches (where most of the people, wealth, and resources are located), then we could expect a bleak future, given the current status of evangelism in these churches.

Nothing short of a theological awakening will return any church to the mission God has always had for it. That is, churches will not be motivated to plant churches among the poor in inner-city America or in their own part of town or elsewhere in the world just because there are so many lost with enormous spiritual needs. Although these needs can tug at some heartstrings, they are not adequate to pull a whole church of overfed, satisfied people into evangelism. Human motivation cannot do what spiritual motivation can. Churches are more likely to return to transforming cities and communities when they rediscover God's plan for all humankind, including their own neighbors in the city. When they go where God leads, they will discover that God is at work in the city. God's plan for the growth of the kingdom may not be limited to larger suburban churches but may include powerful evangelistic witness and ministry to the poor, homeless, jobless, or aliens of the city. The issue I am raising is not whether a church should move out of the city, for I have seen times when it was the best thing to do and times when it was not the best move. My concern is that leaders start with seeking God's will and direction before the pragmatic issues and congregational preferences prevail.

Significant institutional challenges would be necessary for most suburban or older established churches to change direction and appreciate their divine purpose. A tightly controlled budget may find just enough resources to meet the needs of their own members because they are there to make those needs known. Outside needs, such as evangelism and missions, might be viewed as necessary if the money were there. Decades could pass before they start to fulfill God's purpose for the church. Such churches would have to shift philosophy from being budget-driven to being purpose-driven churches if they intend to contribute much to the growth of the kingdom.[10] In other words, they will first seek what they think God wants them to do rather than allow the confines of a budget to determine what they can do. In response to the challenges God may place before them, they bring their budget up to fit the purpose. It can still be well managed but more in line with the divine purpose of the church. Depending on age and size, it would take several years to bring a vision to reality. You will know when it happens. Popular professional preachers would not be the only keynote speakers on lectureships. Recognition would also be given to evangelists and church planters.

Evangelism and the Tensions of the Kingdom

As we speed further into history, the image of the first-century Christian movement might dim through the passing of time and generations. The very powerful presence of the written Word and continued work of the Holy Spirit awaken seekers to restore the heart and soul of first-century Christianity. The revival or restoration movement in the United States of America experienced phenomenal growth in the nineteenth century and plateaued in the twentieth century. There may be little value in contrasting the early growth of the Christian movement with the apparent stagnation of our day and time. However, timeless theological issues may make the exercise worthwhile, for it reveals the value of integrating theology and practice in ministry today. Theological themes will motivate the church to face practical challenges and grow in any era of history. Theology without practice may leave the church without a future, but practice without theology leaves us without a valid mission. This tension is felt at various levels.

Motives for evangelism have experienced more change than the context. Green limits his discussion of the motives for evangelism in the first century to gratitude, responsibility, and concern for the lost.[11]

The rediscovery of praise in "contemporary" worship is but one indication of an effort to return a posture of gratitude to corporate worship. The suburbanization of the church, beginning in the 1970s, shifted the mission of the church from the individual witness, like first-century martyrs, to a form of cultural individualism that privatized the gospel. Some have even concluded that the most significant change in the religious world in the late 1980s was the increasing dominance of religious consumerism.[12] As churches suburbanized, evangelism shifted from a public proclamation to a private experience; thus, the larger suburban churches have proven themselves much less evangelistic, as Ellas discovered in his study of church growth.[13]

Based on the letters of Paul and first-century literature, Green concluded that the early Christians were very serious about their responsibility to live every day in the light of eternity, "conscious that their every action was subject to the scrutiny of the one God, their Savior, who would judge the quick and the dead."[14] The Enlightenment might be our first target of blame for the loss of the presence of God in daily life. The secular values that forced religious faith into a private world also stripped the gospel of the power of eternal life. The good news shifted to joining churches, church "shopping," and church hopping. As Lesslie Newbigin struggled with the task of evangelizing the modern Western world, he concluded that the first thing needed is the "recovery and firm grasp of a true doctrine of the last things, of eschatology."[15] The concern for the plight and condition of lost humanity motivated Jesus, Paul, and the church to evangelize the world.

A postmodern society will not accept the premise that the lost are really lost. If everything is to be viewed as arbitrary and constructed, then it will be difficult to see good news in the message and demands of the cross. When surface images displace substance, then the depth of reflection and repentance is lost in declaration and celebration. The resulting fragmentation and meaninglessness create a new demand for theological reflection.[16]

The democratization and business management style adopted in so many churches will challenge the existence and exercising of spiritual authority. There will be times when doing God's will would not "make sense" financially or pragmatically. From my experiences in missions and evangelism, there have been times that I had to conclude that if it makes sense, it probably did not come from God. If God is able to do immeasurably more than we ask or imagine, then I assume his power can never be limited to a budget (Eph. 3:20). This is not an argument for financial irresponsibility, just a plea to keep priorities straight and allow God to challenge the church to stretch out enough to serve the world.

Peter appreciated and expected these tensions of the kingdom. He challenged churches to remember who they were and interpret their presence in the world from a theological perspective.

Dear friends, I urge you, as aliens and strangers in the world, to abstain from sinful desires, which war against your soul. Live such good lives among the pagans that, though they accuse you of doing wrong, they may see your good deeds and glorify God on the day he visits us (1 Pet. 2:11-12).

Peter writes from a clear understanding of the difference between a believer and a nonbeliever, the same clear-cut distinction that necessitates evangelism. However, he also notes the tension within the Christian between the "natural desires" for survival and acceptance in a Roman society and the demands of the kingdom.[17] Out of this one reference flow theological themes of spiritual identity, sanctification, mission, spiritual warfare, ministry, and eschatology that naturally define the purpose of the church, means of its growth, and tensions with a lost world. Only a church deeply grounded in a biblical theology will maintain the intent and motivation for evangelism till the Lord comes again.

Endnotes

[1]James H. Smylie, "Church Growth and Decline in Historical Perspective," in *Understanding Church Growth and Decline, 1950-1978*, Dean R. Hoge and David A. Roozen, eds. (New York: Pilgrim Press, 1979), 67-68; note, for example, the 13 summary statements regarding church participation focus primarily on contextual factors, with no mention of evangelism or spiritual factors. Carl Holladay, "Church Growth in the New Testament," *Restoration Quarterly* 26 (1983): 85-102; argues that political and social factors of the Roman Empire may have had more to do with growth than methods (91).

[2]Michael Green, *Evangelism in the Early Church* (Grand Rapids: Eerdmans, 1970), 13-28.

[3]C. Kirk Hadaway, "Is Evangelistic Activity Related to Church Growth?" In *Church and Denominational Growth*, David Roozen and Kirk Hadaway, eds. (Nashville: Abingdon, 1993), 185.

[4]Richard DeRidder, *Discipling the Nations* (Grand Rapids: Baker, 1971), 122.

[5]John W. Ellas, *Measuring Church Growth* (Houston: Center For Church Growth, 1997), 105.

[6]Darrell L. Guder, *Be My Witnesses* (Grand Rapids: Eerdmans, 1985), 11, 91-95.

[7]W. Widick Schroeder and Victor Obenhaus, *Suburban Religion* (Chicago: Center for the Scientific Study of Religion, 1974), 38, 185.

[8]Penny Long Marler and David A. Roozen, "From Church Tradition to Consumer Choice: The Gallup Surveys of the Unchurched American," *Church and Denominational Growth*, David Roozen and C. Kirk Hadaway, eds. (Nashville: Abingdon, 1993), 267.

[9]Harvie Conn, *The American City and the Evangelical Church* (Grand Rapids: Baker, 1994), 139-150.

[10]Rick Warren, *The Purpose-Driven Church* (Grand Rapids: Zondervan, 1995), 95-109.

[11]Green, *Evangelism in the Early Church*, 236-255.

[12]Marler and Roozen, "Church Tradition," *Church Growth*, 267.

[13]Ellas, *Measuring Church Growth*, 105.

[14]Green, *Evangelism in the Early Church*, 248; examples of a daily awareness of eternity can be found in 1 Cor. 4:11-15; 2 Cor. 5:9-11; and 2 Tim. 4:8,17.

[15]Lesslie Newbigin, *Foolishness to the Greeks* (Grand Rapids: Eerdmans, 1986), 134.

[16]Craig Van Gelder, "Mission in the Emerging Postmodern Condition," in *Church Between Gospel and Culture*, George R. Hunsberger and Craig Van Gelder, eds. (Grand Rapids: Eerdmans, 1996), 134-138.

[17]J. Ramsey Michaels, *1 Peter*, Word Biblical Commentary (Waco: Word, 1988), 120.

Chapter Twenty-one

Will the church proclaim the gospel in a pluralistic culture?

Carson E. Reed
Westlake Church of Christ
Indianapolis, Indiana

Contemporary culture finds the search for truth to be increasingly subjective and personal. Though a deep longing for spiritual truth exists, American culture suggests that there are many roads that lead to that end. As Jewel, a leading voice of popular culture proclaims, "So we pray to as many different gods as there are flowers, but we call religion our friend. We're so worried about saving our souls, afraid that God will take His toll."

Pluralism, relativity, global awareness, and an increasing polarization in American culture set the context for the church at the dawn of the twenty-first century. Of particular import are the church's distinctive claims about the truth, the truth of the gospel. Can truth claims be made in a culture that affirms relativity? Can the historical claims of Jesus' ministry, including his death and resurrection continue to have the distinctive place in the church's message? If so, how can the church speak of the unique role of Jesus in matters of salvific faith in a culture that gives an increased hearing to alternative visions of spirituality? Is it possible, or desirable, for the church to maintain her historical witness to the message and claims of the gospel and still be a "neighbor" to other faith communities?

Such questions are important for the church. They loom large on the horizon as the church considers worship, mission, and public witness. Does the church have anything to say to the culture? Does the church have anything to say to itself to shape morals and faith?

What follows is an exploration and challenge of two ideas that, I believe, leave us without voice or witness to the larger world. The first of those ideas is the privatization of religious values and truth claims. I want to present a case for reaffirming Christianity's case for speaking in the public square. A second idea that has limited our evangelistic vision is an understanding of mission defined by a narrow understanding of salvation. Can we speak of evangelism, making claims about Jesus, in a pluralistic world? I believe that we can; but those claims must be shaped by the gospel, not by human needs. These two ideas — a privatized truth system and an exclusivistic mission mindset — often cross-pollinate and leave us with an infertile hybrid, stunting our witness and growth. Can we find fertility and life again?

A Starting Place

Deciding where to begin asking questions can make a huge difference on the answers we find. With the influx of media and the increasing presence of pluralism in our lives, the first impulse may be to begin with the reality of diversity in American culture. Those addressing pluralism from a pluralistic vantage point generally acknowledge the vitality and spirituality of various religious traditions.[1] Furthermore, they urge the necessity for worldwide unity and a corresponding inability of any particular faith tradition to provide the basis for such a unity.

However, the context of pluralism results in abdicating any claim to absolute truth. Clear truth claims become spurious and insupportable from this posture. However, to do so, distorts the Christian faith's historic claims about itself. Should not the church begin with the claims that are made upon us by the gospel of Jesus?

I would suggest that a more proper place to begin is within the claims of Scripture.

- We affirm the sovereignty of God and the completeness of his plan for all humanity.
- We affirm that Jesus Christ is the definitive disclosure of God's heart and will.
- We affirm that the church knows no other way to salvation than through the work of Christ.

Such declarations set the stage for an exploration of the church's message and witness to a pluralistic world. We cannot relinquish our biblical and historical heritage without losing our own identity.

255

Denying the historicity of Jesus' death and resurrection or mini-mizing the evangelistic nature of the gospel is like ordering a meat pie without cheese or tomato sauce at the local Italian restaurant. It may be a pie, but no longer is it pizza. Likewise, one may have a faith system that has Christian elements in it, but that does not make it Christian. Simply put, exclusive claims of the Christian faith cannot be negotiated for the church. The church's identity rests on those claims.

Pluralism and the Truth

However, this commitment to the unique and exclusive claims of Christianity should not make us timid about approaching plu-ralism. We must remember that any truth claim is exclusivistic. If I say that the house is red, that excludes all other colors. Intrinsic to the nature of truth claims is the notion of exclusivity. For various reasons, Christianity receives the particular scorn of popular cul-ture regarding this notion of absolute truth. How dare one ideolo-gy or faith system claim to be superior to another? Indeed!

Thus, in a postmodern world, any claim to truth generally is met with scorn or criticism. The work of noted philosophers and acade-mics Michel Foucault and Richard Rorty demonstrate the rejection of any absolute truth. All that remains is what an individual or a political entity accepts as "true" for themselves. As Foucault states:

> Each society has its regime of truth, its "general politics" of truth: that is, the types of discourse which it accepts and makes function as true; the mechanisms and instances which enable one to distinguish true and false statements, the means by which each is sanctioned; the techniques and procedures accorded value in the acquisition of truth; the status of those who are charged with saying what counts as true.[2]

This conviction, according to philosopher Rorty, results in anyone thinking that he or she can locate reality or truth being regarded as a "real live metaphysical prig."[3]

Yet such thinking itself reflects some notion of absolute truth. Does the conclusion that there is no absolute truth reflect a literary device, or is it not a truth claim being made? Or, to bring us back to the question of various religions, does not the claim that all reli-gions are the same reflect some notion of truth? To say that Islam, Buddhism, and Christianity are merely different ways of getting at the same thing is a truth claim. Such a truth claim does conflict with the claims of any one of the world's major religious traditions. That should not surprise us. That simply is the way that truth claims function.

This brings me back to where we began a little earlier. The place we begin makes a big difference on where we end up. Though not often recognized in discussions of pluralism, the claims of all religions come with claims of exclusivity. If the Qu'ran is a true revelation from God, then the New Testament texts have become so corrupted that Jesus has evolved from prophet to the Son of God and Allah from an indivisible oneness into Trinitarian expressions of God. If Hinduism or Buddhism is true, then perfect bliss involves dissolution into nothingness rather than personal, conscious existence for eternity. Even the Baha'i faith, with its efforts to combine the best of all the world's religions, finds itself excluding more "narrow" faith traditions.

The Christian faith is doing no more nor no less than any other religion or ideology when it makes a claim. Whenever anyone speaks about ultimate realities, it is speech that attempts to speak truth. In that sense, all people, whether Christian, Jewish, or neopagan, speak with the limitation and the freedom that their particular truth claims allow. What must be made perfectly clear is that the Christian makes no greater claim to truth than the Moslem or the practitioner of New Age philosophy. And the one who suggests that all religions are the same, or are simply descriptions of different parts of humanity's struggle to understand our ultimate destiny are particularly deluded. Listen to Lesslie Newbigin:

> In the famous story of the blind men and the elephant, so often quoted in the interests of religious agnosticism, the real point of the story is constantly overlooked. The story is told from the point of view of the king and his courtiers, who are not blind but can see that the blind men are unable to grasp the full reality of the elephant and are only able to get hold of part of the truth. The story is constantly told in order to neutralize the affirmation of the great religions, to suggest that they learn humility and recognize that none of them can have more than one aspect of the truth. But, of course, the real point of the story is exactly the opposite. If the king were also blind there would be no story. The king tells the story, and it is the immensely arrogant claim of one who sees the full truth that all the world's religions are only groping after. It embodies the claim to know the full reality which relativizes all the claims of the religions and philosophies.[4]

Everyone who comes into the public sphere comes with a set of assumptions. The question is whether those assumptions are true. That is to say, are the assumptions that Christians work with cogent, logically consistent, historically verifiable, and do they address the needs of humanity? If they are, then Christianity must speak in the public sphere, addressing the popular culture. The church speaks not merely because she holds good news, but because the good news she holds is true.

Getting Along in the Marketplace

Perhaps the biggest problem Christianity faces in the pluralistic culture of contemporary society is one of confidence. Frankly, I believe that many Christians have begun to believe culture's assessment of Christian faith. Since Christianity is dated, irrelevant, and incompatible with present day experience, then the best thing is to lay low and not speak out. This sort of reasoning leaves the Christian message often unstated in public dialogue and debate.

So how does the church speak in the public sphere? Is it possible to evangelistically articulate the message of Jesus? To do so, we must become aware of the dimensions and limitations of pluralism.

Pluralism needs to be defined and Lesslie Newbigin, quoted earlier, is helpful again. Newbigin, noted for his long missionary career in India, takes care to understand the nuance of pluralism. He suggests that we recognize that pluralism can refer to the variety of cultures and lifestyles within any given society. This notion, cultural pluralism, is a verifiable reality and often brings enrichment and color to a society. Newbigin wisely warns that cultural pluralism is not morally neutral; cultures can practice destructive things. Nevertheless, cultural pluralism is a given reality in Western culture. It is the context of the church's present ministry and life — as it was for the earliest church. Michael Green, a long-time scholar on evangelism comments:

> I find it ironic that people object to the proclamation of the Christian gospel these days because so many other faiths jostle on the doorstep of our global village. What's new? The variety of faiths in antiquity was even greater than it is today. And the early Christians, making as they did ultimate claims for Jesus, met the problem of other faith head-on from the very outset. . . . They did not denounce

other faiths. They simply proclaimed Jesus with all the power and persuasiveness at their disposal.[5]

But cultural pluralism does not adequately describe another form of pluralism that exists in our society. "Religious pluralism, on the other hand, is the belief that the differences between the religions are not a matter of truth but of different perceptions of the one truth; that to speak of religious beliefs as true or false is inadmissible."[6] Religious pluralism is dangerous and just plain wrongheaded. The effects of religious pluralism flow into American culture by reducing religious belief to something held in private. "You can think and believe what you want, and I will think and believe what I want. Neither of us will bring our faith into public discussion since we are both right on matters of religion."

This nonsense manner of reasoning has spawned a paucity of religious and value-based dialogue in American public life for over thirty years. Since we differ on beliefs, we must be silent. On the other hand, when we discover "facts," everyone is supposed to agree. Yet fact-finding becomes increasingly suspect in an environment where competing ideas are not allowed to be clearly heard and evaluated. Indeed, as Richard Neuhaus has stated, "Pluralism is a jealous god. When pluralism is established as dogma, there is no room for other dogmas. The assertion of other points of reference in moral discourse becomes, by definition, a violation of pluralism."[7]

The irony of pluralism's inability to be tolerant of anything but itself reveals the fallacy of contemporary culture's strictures on faith-language in the marketplace. In an effort to diminish intolerance and to maximize civilization, only those things that could pass the muster of reason could be proclaimed as public facts. The vision of John Locke, unfortunately, has given rise to the nightmares of Nietzsche. Within our postmodern frameworks, nothing seems certain. The hopes of modern rationalism have been dashed upon the rocks of individuality and pluralistic notions.

Thus, I would argue that persons of faith have much to offer to the public square. That in the name of civilized values and hope and tolerance, faith systems can and ought to speak. In fact, as Ian Markham argues in his work *Plurality and Christian Ethics*, the Christian realist has a stronger basis to articulate tolerance in a culturally pluralistic world than what he calls the secular antirealist.[8]

Markham suggests three distinct ways in which the Christian offers a decidedly stronger position for rational public dialogue than a person who denies the existence of God and must, by necessity wrestle with nihilistic implications of postmodernity. I would like to suggest that these three ways mark a trail for the Christian to follow in public dialogue and prepare the way to speak evangelistically.

First, the Christian is committed to truth. Truth, as noted earlier, is often given a bad rap these days. And though there might be some debate among realists about how much truth we can know, the criticisms of Richard Rorty and others who suggest that truth is unknowable is really quite absurd. If truth is unknowable, then the only thing left for public discussion is ideas and viewpoints.

Markham helpfully suggests that truth has to do with a certain correspondence between an assertion and observation with reality. To speak about sin, for example, as being true means looking at the reality of human experience and thus offering some corresponding acknowledgment. Obviously, absolute truth can only be grasped from the limitations of human finiteness. But such limitations do not imply that absolute truth does not exist. If no truth can be discovered, no correspondence between reality and conclusions be drawn, then we are left with no common ground on which to base ethics, values, or public discourse. Such a conclusion means that nihilism, or a meaninglessness to life, is a more accurate description of reality than the pluralistic and individual claims for meaning given by popular culture. Either there is something true to base public discourse and ethics upon or there is not. The Christian point of view suggests that there is and by doing so offers to the public square a more substantial and helpful line of thinking.

Second, since the Christian point of view affirms the existence of absolute truth and that we are in search of comprehending it, the idea of dialogue and discussion with other religions and with the secular atheist is a welcome one. Dialogue becomes a necessary and significant means to an end. However, for the person rooted in a pluralistic mindset, real dialogue is impossible. As Markham states:

> Dialogue for the secular anti-realist is more of a problem. At best, dialogue will be justified in terms of curiosity about the other positions in the market place. We can be informed, but not enhanced. We can listen, but not share. No synthesis of opposing positions can be

discovered. Dialogue with a view to a better understanding of our world is considered impossible. The irrational secularist is offering us a very impoverished view of the world.[9]

Third, not only does the pursuit of truth open up the possibilities for vigorous dialogue, but the affirmation of truth leads the way for real respect and tolerance to other postures in a pluralistic culture. Since the secularist reduces differences between religions as merely different cultural possibilities of understanding reality, the real differences over what is real, factual, and true are simply brushed off the table. Facts do not exist for the secularist; only a person's projections have any viability. This attempt to create mutuality and tolerance, in reality, has an opposite effect. It completely fails to give credit and understanding to the unique and powerful claims that different religious traditions have.

The Christian realist suggests that the truth claims of different religious traditions (including Marxism and New Age thinking) really do make claims to truth. These claims to truth do, at times, come into direct conflict with each other. And rather than dismiss this conflict and diminish the claim, the realist would argue that those claims should be heard in the public square. Honesty and mutual respect requires it.

The question as to whether the Christian has anything meaningful to say in the public square and how it should be said is answered in this way. Yes, the Christian does have something meaningful to say. The Christian has a truth claim, just as others in public dialogue have truth claims. In fact, I would argue that the realism that the Christian brings to such public spaces is considerably more reasonable and constructive than the false foundations of pluralism. By seeking after truth, by being committed to open dialogue, and by offering mutual respect, the Christian models a position of civility and tolerance.[10]

The Message

Once we recognize the need and value of the Christian message in our culture, we turn to ask what sort of message we bring. Is the message rooted in a God of love and thus our message is one of simply affirming the truth found in other faith traditions? Or, to move to the other side of the spectrum, is the message rooted in texts that speak exclusively of salvation being found in Jesus alone and thus pronounce a solemn damnation on all persons located outside of our particular expression of Christianity? Could our message find some mediating position?

To understand the context of various contemporary responses to the nature of the Christian message, Alan Race's work *Christians and Religious Pluralism* initiated a model that set the stage for many ongoing discussions.[11] In its simplest form, the model offers three distinct points of view. The first of those points would be exclusivism. In its classical expression, exclusivism does not recognize any saving activity outside of Christ and the confession of Christ as Savior. Sitting on the opposite pole is a second posture, pluralism. Pluralism suggests that all religions are equally promising paths to the one God. Pluralism accepts Christianity as one of many religions offering salvation; Christianity is not necessarily superior to any other faith. The third, mediating, point of view is described as inclusivism. This posture accepts God as being present in other faiths insofar as any truth contained in them has salvific value. Ultimately, anything true and good originates with Christ and points the way back to him. Inclusivism recognizes salvation outside of Christ, salvation that is ultimately to be completed in Christ in some way or another.

This threefold model dominates much of the literature on nature and character of the church's message in a pluralistic culture. Indeed, such a model can provide a helpful description in understanding some of the dimensions of the question.[12] However, having said all that, I feel that such discussions are ultimately unfruitful and inadequate to offer a clear foundation for the church's message. They ultimately fall prey to a false beginning point addressed earlier. Do we begin with our relationship to our culture, allowing the culture to define the formation of the message? Or do we allow the gospel to define the formation of the message?

Certainly, the answer is clear. But I must insist that all three options in the model above, including exclusivism, begin with the culture, not the gospel. They are attempts to understand the church's role in relationship to elements and ideas present in the culture. I would submit that the church's role is not to assimilate into the culture (pluralism), or to create a new system of understanding God's plan (inclusivism), or even to stand in judgment against the culture (exclusivism). Rather the church's call is to be faithful to the proclamation of Jesus in our message and in our life.

By limiting our message to the confines of this threefold model, we limit the questions we ask. Simply put, we find ourselves responding to such questions as "who can be saved?" or "can the good non-Christian be saved?" Ignoring the answer that Jesus gave to that question in his own ministry ("It's impossible for anybody to be saved!" [Mark 10:27, paraphrase]), we resolutely pick up the question and continue with our wrestling.

This question rests in our attempts to resolve our relationship to the culture and to others. But if we are after truth, then we need to reshape the question. The question leads in wrong directions. First, it is an attempt to respond to something that only God has the right to answer. If Jesus has warned his followers about anything, it was about making claims about the end of time and the judgments of God. Second, the question places emphasis on afterlife, not present existence. In the New Testament, the verb "to save" finds expression in three tenses: past, present, and future. Being saved has to do with both the "now" and the "future." Salvation as a present experience calls the church's moral and ethical life into account and offers promising dialogue with others.

A third objection that needs to be raised regarding the "who can be saved" question is the focus on the human as the center of dialogue and the center of history instead of God. The inevitable human assertion to place human experience as the center of life prompts this question. Yet, the witness of Scripture speaks of God as the center of history. Newbigin states it in this way:

> The gospel, the story of the astonishing act of God himself in coming down to be part of our alienated world, to endure the full horror of our rebellion against love, to take the whole burden of our guilt and shame, and to lift us up into communion and fellowship with himself, breaks into this self-centered search for our own happiness, shifts the center from the self and its desires to God and his glory. It is true, God forgive us, that Christians have turned even this into something that they thought they could possess for themselves; that they have privatized this mighty work of grace and talked as if the whole cosmic drama of salvation culminated in the words "For me; for me"; as if the one question is "How can I be saved?" leading inevitably to the question, "How can anyone be saved?" But this is a perversion of the gospel.[13]

What is a better question and a better model to shape our message? The better question and model rests on the proclamation of

Jesus as Lord and Head of the church. Hopefully, I stated the case above for Christianity to be heard in the public square, for the sake of culture. Here I am presenting the deep reason for us to speak at all. That reason rests on the conviction that the church has been called to speak and to live the message of Jesus. We believe Jesus to be truth; thus, we live out the natural corollary of that truth.

Should we engage the culture? Yes, we engage the culture because we believe we have truth that will shape and transform culture. Should we engage in mission? Yes, we have been given a message to speak, and we can do no less. Dialogue, ministry, evangelism, and mission all rest on the ultimate claim that the gospel has on the church. We speak, serve, evangelize, and engage in mission because we are commissioned to do so. We do so because we are called to do so. We do so to bring glory to God.

What of our secondary questions? What about our concerns about Muslims and Jews, Buddhists, Brahmins, and those who simply like Bud Lites? Maybe the apostle Paul's discussion in Romans 9–11 still bears witness to us. Why have the Jews rejected Jesus? What is God up to? Will they be saved? Paul responds to such questions by reminding his readers and us that God is sovereignly working out salvation and will do what He will do. "For God has consigned all men to disobedience, that he may have mercy on all" (Rom. 11:32, RSV). We must relinquish such questions, bowing to "the depth of the riches and wisdom and knowledge of God! How unsearchable are his judgments and how inscrutable his ways (Rom. 11:33, RSV)!

Does that mean that we stand without a calling? As we relinquish the secondary questions, we become free to ask the primary questions. The primary questions call the church into asking about her faithfulness to living and speaking the message of Jesus in a world broken and confused about its perceptions of reality. Will the church be faithful to her calling? Will she articulate the claims of Jesus? These are the productive, primary questions for the church. Leaving behind the guessing and the speculation about matters that belong to God, may the church take up her call to be the "body," the visible witness of Christ in a pluralistic, broken world.

Endnotes

[1] Of particular import are the works of Paul Knitter, *No Other Name?* (Maryknoll, NY: Orbis Books, 1985); Paul Knitter and John Hick, *The Myth of Christian Uniqueness.*

[2] Michel Foulcault, *Power/Knowledge, Selected Interviews and Other Writings 1972-1977*, Colin Gordon, ed. (NewYork: Pantheon, 1980), 52.

[3] As quoted by Ravi Zacharias, *Can Man Live Without God* (Dallas: Word, 1994), 123.

[4] Lesslie Newbigin, *The Gospel in a Pluralist Society* (Grand Rapids: Eerdmans, 1989), 9-10.

[5] Michael Green, *Acts for Today: First-Century Christianity for Twentieth-Century Christians* (London: Hodder & Stoughton, 1993), 38.

[6] Newbigin, *Pluralist Society*, 14.

[7] Richard J. Neuhaus, *The Naked Public Square* (Grand Rapids: Eerdmans, 1984), 150.

[8] Ian S. Markham, *Plurality and Christian Ethics* (Cambridge: Cambridge University Press, 1994).

[9] Markham, *Plurality*, 159.

[10] I am aware that someone could quickly state that Christianity has plenty of examples of incivility and intolerance. I do not deny that. History is filled with many travesties done in the name of Jesus (and I might add in the name of many different religious traditions). I speak here of the community of God in its ideal, biblical sense. That sort of community can be found within the annals of history as well. For example, we would be blessed richly by rediscovering the work of second century apologists and the practice of the pre-Constantine church.

[11] Alan Race, *Christians and Religious Pluralism* (Maryknoll, NY: Orbis Books, 1982); Paul Knitter picked up this paradigm in a well-known work, *No Other Name?*

[12] For one such helpful discussion see Dennis L. Okholm and Timothy Phillips, eds., *More Than One Way?* (Grand Rapids: Zondervan, 1995). This volume has a fourfold version of the model articulated by persons holding to those various positions with critiques presented following each presentation. Authors include John Hick, Clark Pinnock, and Alister McGrath.

[13] Newbigin, *Pluralist Society*, 179.

Chapter Twenty-two

How do we tell the truth to a culture that no longer believes in truth?

Jim Baird
Oklahoma Christian University
Oklahoma City, Oklahoma

> Yet he has not left himself without testimony: He has shown kindness
> by giving you rain from heaven and crops in their seasons; he provides
> you with plenty of food and fills your hearts with joy (Acts 14:17).

Marduk and Metopes

Two Septembers ago in the British Museum in London, I had the privilege of showing my sons the Elgin Marbles. The boys, then ten and thirteen, were especially taken with the metope panels showing the Battle of the Centaurs and Lapiths. Each panel is individual, showing a muscular human figure engaged in some stage of hand-to-hand combat with a powerful horse-man. In the story on which the panels are based, the centaurs were invited to the wedding of Pirithous and Hippodame. In the middle of the celebration, the centaurs repay the hospitality of their civilized hosts by trying to abduct the bride and other women. In the battle that follows, many are killed on each side, but the humans are victorious over their barbarous enemies.

These panels adorned the roofline of the Parthenon in Athens, and we imagine that the Athenians saw themselves in the story. They were congratulating themselves and their goddess, Athena, on their victory over the barbarous Persians. Again, order had been preserved from the chaos that threatened to engulf it.

The conflict between order and chaos is a theme that is frequently explored in ancient culture. Those who forged the first civilizations were keenly aware of this struggle. For the Babylonians, it

266

became the story of Marduk defeating the chaotic monster/ocean Tiamet. For the Egyptians, it became the story of the creator Ptah commanding the first land to rise out of the uninhabitable sea. For the Aztecs, it came to be expressed, tragically, in an offering of human blood to insure that the god of the Sun would continue to give life to the land. The ancients sensed that order was unnatural and precious. Chaos always threatened and had to be held at bay.

We need not seek far to discover why this theme was so important. Humans who lived so close to nature realized that their civilizing exertions were insufficient to guarantee the order of the world. They could organize themselves for defense against human enemies. They could plant the crops and dredge the canals that irrigated them. By their own efforts they could create small bits of order. But these same efforts showed them how dependent they were on the far greater order of the world in which they lived. What force was it that kept the sun in the sky? What created the grain in their fields and offspring in their cattle? What prevented the winter from lasting forever? Why didn't the sea rise and cover the land? Repeatedly, the ancients were made to realize that they survived only because of an order that they were powerless to maintain.

Rediscovering Chaos

What exactly does the old problem of chaos have to do with the Christian task of telling the truth to a culture that no longer believes in truth? Simply this. The postmodern truth-crisis can be seen as a rediscovery of our vulnerability to chaos. The ancients, who lived in a world saturated with nature, realized that they could not guarantee that nature would remain orderly. We are largely insulated from nature, but we live in a world saturated by human truth claims. Our anxiety arises from the realization, forced upon us by experience as much as by analysis, that we are powerless to guarantee truth.

I say this because our culture is just now emerging from a three-hundred-year search for guaranteed truth. Guaranteed truth would be truth which not only reflects the way the world really is, but could be clearly demonstrated to do so. Another way of putting it is to say that many western thinkers of what we call the Enlightenment were searching for the one truth-finding procedure that would eliminate all the possible sources of error.

The story of this search is a fascinating one, with many twists and turns. But it ended in failure. Postmodern scholars delight in pointing out that none of our modern paths to knowledge achieve guaranteed truth. Such scholars sometimes suggest that these failures stem from carelessness, prejudice, or malice. But the real culprit is human finitude. We cannot achieve guaranteed truth because to do so would be to jump out of our human limitations.

The Vulnerability of Science

Let us see how this argument might work in practice. In the popular mind as well as in the academy, science is often viewed as the pinnacle of human truth-finding achievement. Most would believe that if there is any area where human ingenuity and effort generate truth, it is in the realm of science. For this reason, postmodern scholars have delighted in pointing out the many ways in which even the hardest of the hard sciences are not self-guaranteeing.

"The world is both orderly and knowable" proclaims the paleontologist, Stephen Jay Gould, in his recent book *Full House*. In saying this, Gould is articulating two fundamental assumptions without which science would be pointless. In the case of each, if ultimate reality is chaos, the assumption fails and science fails with it.

Let's take the first assumption, that the universe is orderly. Science requires order because the essence of science is explanation by law. That which cannot be explained in terms of law cannot be grasped by science. To see why, simply try to imagine a world in which natural laws break down at random. In the lab yesterday, your sample of oxygen combined with hydrogen in a ratio of one to two to form water, but today's sample turns into a nice tuna sandwich. When you come back tomorrow, the entire tank of oxygen starts doing a fair imitation of Bill Clinton's 1996 Inaugural Address. You might have a nightclub act, but science is pretty well out of the question.

Of course, we do not expect oxygen to behave in this way, and we have a deep and well-supported theory that connects the lawful behavior of oxygen with the lawful behavior of many other aspects of the world. Nevertheless, our deepest theories are only theories of what has been observed in the past, and they give us no guarantees about the behavior of oxygen or anything else in the future. Science can describe orderly behavior if it occurs, but there is *absolutely nothing* in science that guarantees order in the first place. Nothing in science prevents the little bursts of chaos we imagined, or far larger bursts of chaos which could invalidate all our sciences.

What this means is that we have to assume an orderly universe even to take the first step in science. We have to assume order because any evidence we could have to prove that the universe is orderly would work only if we already knew the universe was orderly. The assumption of order is the assumption that the future will resemble the past. It would clearly get us nowhere to argue for that assumption by saying, "Look, we can count on the assumption of order in the future, because it has always worked in the past." All of us, scientists and nonscientists alike, are just stuck with the assumption of order. It is an assumption that we can neither prove nor guarantee.

"The Answers Are Out There"

The same could be said of Gould's second assumption, that the universe is knowable. This assumption is essential for science, especially because the actual work of science often involves years of fruitless searching in the dark. Only a faith that "the answers are out there" can sustain that kind of effort. Albert Einstein is a good example of this absolute faith. He published his work on Special Relativity in 1905, but was unable to extend his ideas to include gravity. For eleven long years he labored without success at this problem. In *Pythagoras' Trousers*, Margaret Werthem records his note to a friend during this period, "One thing is certain: that in all my life, I have not worked this hard . . . . Compared with this problem, the original theory of relativity was child's play." In the end, with the help of some friends who showed him the mathematical tricks that could express his insights, he published the results for which he is now most famous, the General Theory of Relativity. His faith in the knowability of the universe clearly sustained him. Without it, he would have failed.

Einstein was later quoted as saying, "God is subtle, but not malicious." He meant that although God might make the order of the universe a very deep order requiring enormous effort to uncover, He would not hide it completely from us. Einstein's use of God in this context is not merely rhetorical, as some have suggested. While his view of God is radically different from that of Judeo-Christian religions, he recognized that without some fundamental principle of rational order that grounded all of reality, science's basic trust in the knowability of the universe is just wrong.

The fact is that human science depends on too many factors that are out of human hands. We have already seen that the universe would be scientifically unknowable if it were fundamentally chaotic. But even an orderly universe might have had such a complex order that human beings could never even make the first steps in science. Or the fundamental processes of nature might have been radically nonlocal, so that simple events on earth would be fundamentally determined by variables in other galaxies. In such a universe, key pieces of information would be beyond all our means of gathering information.

Further, an entirely different kind of doubt arises if we consider the frailty of the human mind. The human intellect might be so deeply flawed that it is unable to recognize the true processes of nature. It might be just barely able to manage the tasks of survival and reproduction, but be doomed to failure in its attempts to come to any correct picture of the way the world works. In this case, our best scientists would be destined to spin one illusory theory after another, with no hope of coming to the truth. In any of these cases, and many others we can think of, the universe would be unknowable, and science would be hopeless. As it is with order, so it is with the knowability of the universe. Science is great at discovering what can be known about the universe, but there is *absolutely nothing* in science that guarantees that the universe is knowable.

The problems of order and knowability are just two of the fundamental ways in which our best knowledge is vulnerable to chaos. Indeed, they are not even the ones that are most commonly trumpeted by postmodern scholars. But the point is that the Enlightenment hope of guaranteed knowledge is doomed. We are what we are. In the end, we are stuck with our particular human tools of knowing about the world. There is no way we can independently check those tools to see if they are working. The bravest among us realize that if the forces that formed our tools are chaotic, then our deepest truths do not even deserve to be called false. They are absurd. For all our civilization we now stand shoulder to shoulder with the ancients, powerless and shivering before chaos.

Can We Do without Truth?

What should our response be, facing this rush-lit end of the Enlightenment? Some advocate despair because the only kind of truth is guaranteed truth. We know now that we cannot get that, so there must be no truth at all.

This is the approach of much postmodern thinking. According to this view, we must simply learn to get along without truth, in science or anywhere else. Rather than seek the one true view of the world, we should multiply the number of incompatible world-views, and be enriched by the competitive discourse that arises between them. Our goal should not be truth, which is unattainable in any case, but diverse and stimulating discussions. Richard Rorty suggests that the new cultural value should be edification rather than knowledge. The French deconstructionists propose that all views be equally privileged, so that no view can become politically oppressive. Paul Feyerabend suggests that we can maximize diversity by giving witchcraft the same privileges as particle physics. In essence, postmodernism says that since we are doomed to live in the dark, we might as well strike up an interesting conversation.

These proposals are worth looking into more deeply than is possible here. But let us be blunt. Postmodernism is already passing away. It suffers from the very weakness that it uncovered in modernism, in that it imagines a human capacity that does not exist. Human beings cannot jump outside their own limitations to achieve the self-guaranteeing truth that fascinated modernism. But humans are equally incapable of remaking themselves sufficiently to do without truth and meaning, as the postmodernists propose.

Just to take one example, it is on the face of it absurd to imagine that Einstein would have spent eleven agonizing years trying for a rigorous description of General Relativity if he had thought that the end result would be nothing more than an interesting addition to the cultural conversation. Einstein was obviously driven by the quest for truth. I think the same could be said of almost all scientists, at least when they are in their working clothes. Scientists actually doing their science think that their theories are getting closer to the truth, whatever they may say when the Philosophy Department starts heckling them.

Furthermore, postmodernists themselves seem quite clearly driven by an absolute as solid as the Ten Commandments; namely, intellectual freedom. But those who sacrificed in the past to make our current climate of intellectual freedom a reality would not have done so if they thought that the result would be merely *interesting*. The architects of the modern university believed that freedom would most readily lead to truth, and it is unlikely that intellectual freedom can survive without that conviction. The ugly fact is that the kind of intellectual freedom we enjoy today has its enemies. Consequently, it is costly to maintain. As a culture, we are not going to pay that price for long unless we have a powerful vision of the continuing pursuit of truth.

For these and a host of other reasons, I am convinced that postmodernism has a limited future. Human beings will continue to act as if the universe has meaning. We will continue to act as if truth is a real possibility. We will continue to act as if the fundamental reality is orderly and knowable rather than chaotic, even when we recognize that we lack the power to create or even uncover the nature of that reality.

This last paragraph reveals our current dilemma. Our worldview tells us the universe is devoid of truth or meaning, but we cannot help living as if truth and meaning are real. We live in unresolved tension. To use older language, we are broken.

Telling the Truth about Truth

It is at this point that Christianity has something difficult, but wonderful, to say. Jesus Christ can do today what he has always done. He can heal brokenness. His method is to help us see the painful truth and then offer himself as the solution.

The painful truth in this instance is that human beings really are utterly dependent on truth and meaning, yet we are utterly powerless to reach them. The messengers of Christ need to pronounce this truth tirelessly. We should be more persistent than the postmodernists in proclaiming the absurdity of human efforts in science, philosophy, politics, and even theology to the extent that they are attempts to guarantee truth or meaning by human power alone.

But unlike postmodernism, the followers of Christ do not preach despair. Postmodern despair comes from seeing only two alternatives: either we can guarantee truth and meaning for ourselves, or we must do without. But there is an obvious third alternative: Truth and meaning can be given to us by Another. Christian teaching is that the fundamental reality of the universe is not chaos, but Mind. Human minds are able to grasp some truth, and human lives are able to exhibit some meaning. But this is only because we are the creations of an absolute Mind who sustains these capacities within us. The Mind who sustains our minds has a name. He is Jesus the Christ.

Proclaiming the Jesus Everyone Already Knows

The coming collapse of postmodernism calls us Christians to a bolder proclamation of John 1:1-18 and Colossians 1:15-20. For too long, we have spoken of Jesus almost exclusively in his atoning role. As great as that is, it is only a part of his overall ministry to us. Jesus is the complete mediator between the Father and humanity (Col. 1:15 & 19). The Father, as his name implies, is the source of all. He is absolute and beyond our capacity to know (John 1:18a). His untranslated reality could never serve as the basis for our minds. But the reality of the Father is mediated to us by the Son. The Son takes the transcendent reality of heaven and translates it into this lawful simplification which we call the universe. He is thus the creator of our tiny cosmos (John 1:3; Col. 1:16), and the one who enlightens our minds, giving us the capacity to recognize the truth in our cosmos (John 1:4, 9).

In this way, we can see that Jesus offers himself as the mediator to heal our postmodern brokenness over truth, just as he is the mediator to heal our broken fellowship with the Father. As the followers of Jesus, we can proclaim good news: Jesus can make sense of what is otherwise senseless, just as surely as he can justify what is otherwise under judgment.

This approach puts us in the position of Paul in Athens, making known the unknown god. We share the culture with people who depend on Jesus, but do not recognize him or give him honor. Every scientist who searches confidently for a lawful explanation for some phenomena is depending on Jesus to sustain the universe against chaos. Everyone who assumes that nature will open itself to persistent investigation is trusting that Jesus, the Logos, has made the world simple enough for the human intellect to understand. Everyone who ever chooses to act nobly rather than dishonorably is depending on the meaning that only Jesus, the mediator, can supply. Jesus has been supporting us all along.

In this sense, we all already know Jesus. We know him as intimately as we know our own deepest values. Whatever we say, none of us can really convince ourselves that those values are nothing more than the random splutterings of chaos. In the coming decades, as postmodernism collapses under the weight of this simple human fact, we will have many more opportunities to help our friends recognize their utter dependence on whatever power it is that imposes order and meaning on chaos. That recognition creates shock, and in that moment of shock, we evangelists will do little more than give this power a name, Jesus. Those who allow themselves to be led by the Spirit will come to recognize that the Jesus we preach is not some stranger. He has always been as close as their own hearts.

That is how we will begin to tell the truth to a culture that no longer believes in truth.

SECTION EIGHT
QUESTIONS ABOUT CHRISTIAN LIVING

The recurring theme throughout this book is the relationship of doctrine and life. In this section the writers directly focus on four questions of Christian ethics. All become pressing issues due to various developments in contemporary culture and none look like they will go away any time soon.

The disintegration of the American family is well documented. Spousal abuse, child abuse, divorce, blended families, multigenerational households, one-parent households and a myriad of other issues challenge the church which would minister to families in trouble or crises. Mike Matheny asks us to consider what the church can do to help our families under fire.

Harold Shank reminds us of the poor that are always with us. As we have become an upwardly mobile fellowship, have we forgotten our duty to those in poverty? What is the church's responsibility in this regard and how shall we accomplish the task? What are the implications of the teaching of Jesus on wealth and poverty for those of us who have so much?

The third article addresses issues raised by the rapid advancement of medical technology. We can now keep the human organism alive much longer than has ever been possible before. As a result, how to deal with the terminally ill with a declining quality of life is an issue every family will likely face. Rubel Shelly encourages us to look at these issues from a Christian perspective.

Finally, in an age when environmental awareness has finally become fashionable what is the Christian's responsibility in this area? Do we have a responsibility for a world that is passing away?

All four articles remind us that as the world changes around us, we must constantly ask what the *Christian* response is, lest we find ourselves drifting into either faddishness or irrelevance.

Chapter Twenty-three

What can the church do to help the family?

Mike Matheny
Lipscomb University
Nashville, Tennessee

I received a phone call recently. The news was sad but common. Friends who had been married for several years were divorcing. The issues were complex, and children were involved. I hear this kind of news too often.

Over the last twenty to thirty years, the struggles of the modern American family have become a burning issue for churches, as well as for schools and the government. Troubled marriages and troubled children are evident everywhere. We have heard the painful stories of adultery and neglect. We know of families where there has been physical and sexual abuse. We know families that struggle with children who are involved in drugs and alcohol.

Many disagree on how to interpret today's family problems. Some claim that we need to return to the idea of the "traditional family" of the 1950's, a golden age for family stability. Others disagree, saying that there was never a golden era for the family. They call for us to change our notion of the "traditional family" to fit better today's situation.

It is hard to know for sure how healthy the American family used to be. We have much more information about today's families than the families of earlier times. We know more now about incest and abuse, alcoholism, divorce, and other family problems. We cannot compare today's family with the families of yesterday. Our culture is different; times are different. In some ways, our families today are better off; in other ways, family life is harder.

We can't turn the clock back. What we can do is turn to God for help. We should determine what God intended the family to be and then interpret what that means now in our troubled times. God's church can play a key role in helping families do this.

False Assumptions

The church reacted slowly when it began to hear about family struggles in our society. The mental health community reacted much more quickly. Churches initially buried their heads in the sand. We felt as though these problems that we were hearing about were only "out there." If people would only be Christians, we claimed, all these problems would fade away.

However, the problems in society began to appear in the church community also. Now *our* kids were struggling with drugs; *our* marriages were breaking up. Our initial response was to preach at people. We were confident that if people would study the Bible and learn the facts and information contained there, then they could straighten out their lives. When that didn't work, we concluded that those families must not have been serious about their faith. These families quietly left the church, and we breathed a sigh of regret but felt as though we had done our best.

I think our response was inadequate. We made three false assumptions. One, we assumed that people who had accurate Bible knowledge and correct Bible doctrine could then figure out how to apply it to their family struggles. In other words, we assumed that knowing the truth meant that we knew how it related to our family situations. We underestimated the complexity of family problems and the difficulty in knowing how Scripture applies to them.

Second, we assumed that if people knew the truth and had figured out how it related to family problems, that they would then do something about it. We assumed that they could take what they knew and translate it into action. The church continued to teach the truth; we expected the people to obey what we had taught them. We underestimated our need to motivate and encourage obedience, since obedience often requires courage.

Third, we assumed that those who were motivated to carry out the truth had the skills to do so effectively. Husbands and wives knew they needed to communicate better and tried to do so, but they needed help with their skills of communication. They tried to do right, but they may have made the situation worse. They needed Christian families who could model and coach.

The church can no longer afford these assumptions. We must figure out how God's Word applies to our world and our families. We must no longer be content with sowing the seeds; we must also be concerned about watering and fertilizing and weeding. Healthy families don't happen just because a person has good information. Attending church and hearing sermons are not enough. People need much more help. The church needs to model what it teaches. We need personal involvement with struggling families so that we can teach, encourage, and coach. And we need to rely on God's power to work wonders in tragic situations.

God's Purpose for the Family

So what did God intend the family to be? Why did God create the family? This is a foundational question that we must answer first. I will answer this question by discussing five purposes that I see revealed in Scripture.

First, God intended that marriage would provide companionship for people. In Genesis 2:18 God says, "It is not good for the man to be alone. I will make a helper . . . for him." God called this part of his creation "not good" because God designed human beings to be in relationships. It reflects the nature of God himself. Genesis 1:26 says, "Let us make man in our image, in our likeness . . . ." While this idea of "us" as applied to God is difficult to grasp, nevertheless there is a sense in which God is not alone. We usually call this the Trinity: God the Father, God the Son, and God the Spirit. In other words, it reflects the nature of God to be in relationship. So people, who are made in God's image, are created with a need for relationships.

We see this need for relationships reflected in many ways in Scripture. When God made a covenant with Abraham, he made a covenant with Abraham's family, not just one individual. God promised to work through Abraham's descendants, who later became the children of Israel. God's relationship was to a community of people, not only to individuals. In the New Testament, we read of God's church. Again, God did not choose to relate to people only as individuals, but through a community of faith. God knew that we needed other people in our lives to encourage, support, and care for us. He knew that it would be difficult for us to be faithful on our own, so he created communities of faith to help us.

The family functions in this way also. We need relationships to help us. Psalm 68:6 says that "God sets the lonely in families . . . ." It is when we feel lonely and out of touch with others that we are very vulnerable to doubt and discouragement. Satan can use loneliness to tempt us.

A major element of this companionship is communication. One problem that Adam encountered was that no other being was suitable for him. Other created beings could not talk with Adam, making it impossible for him to draw close to them in companionship. When we have impaired or strained communication, intimacy disappears. Lack of communication creates distance. Communication is essential if companionship is to be effective and strong.

Another major element of this companionship is commitment. God intended the marriage bond to be a permanent one. Divorce has become so commonly accepted in our society that we need to be reminded of the original ideal. God intended marriages to stay together. It is this kind of stability that allows a relationship to grow. It is in a committed relationship that trust and love can flourish. This was the original intention of God, and the church needs to continue to teach it.

The goal of this companionship and friendship in marriage is that the two people strive toward being one. Genesis 2:24 discusses the process of leaving one's own parents to join another and form a new relationship. Leaving parents and cleaving to a spouse produces "one flesh." This refers to more than sexuality. "One flesh" implies a unity of spirit and purpose, common caring and love, and a sexual bond. Marriage can produce the deepest unity possible between man and woman. The oneness shared by a married couple is a powerful bond that influences who we are as people. This intimacy shapes and molds us toward a more Christlike life.

Marriage is the place for the legitimate expression of sexual desire. God made us sexual creatures; sex is not evil. Yet sexual desire is strong, and it can lead to all sorts of problems if it is not expressed in the appropriate context. Paul warned about withholding sexual relations from one's mate (1 Cor. 7:2-6). The sexual relationship of marriage not only makes children possible, but it also brings much joy and unity to the marriage. Sex within marriage is healthy and "good" in God's eyes.

Second, God intended that families would produce children. Genesis 1:28 records God's telling the first man and woman to "be fruitful and increase in number; fill the earth. . . ." We do not sense as strong a need to populate the earth today as they would have then. Nevertheless, one of the main purposes of the marriage relationship is the creation of the next generation. We generally perceive children as a blessing to parents. They are seen as a sign of God's favor in the Old Testament, and this has been true throughout most of history. The birth of a child is usually a time of rejoicing.

Third, God intended that families nurture and educate their young (Prov. 22:6; Eph. 6:4). It is not enough to bring children into the world. We must also nurture and teach them. Parents have tremendous responsibility in this area. Our responsibility to nurture and care for our children begins when they are babies and continues for many years, even into adulthood. My parents still provide advice and guidance to me, but mostly they provide strong emotional support.

We live in a time when many children are not wanted. Many abortions are done because having a child would be "inconvenient." Children are abandoned, left to fend for themselves. People engage in sexual relations with no thought of the possible consequences and then are unwilling to bear those consequences. Caring for children begins before conception. We should have sexual relations with full knowledge of the possible outcome and full willingness to accept the responsibility of parenthood. One need of all children is to have parents that love them.

Children also need parents to discipline them. We need discipline to learn how to live in this world. Discipline teaches us to respect boundaries. Discipline shields us from things that would otherwise harm us. Discipline is actually an expression of love. Proverbs 3:11-12 tells us that the Lord disciplines those he loves. Lack of discipline is a lack of love. The more mature must guide the less mature, and discipline is one means of doing this. Of course, some forms of discipline are destructive. Parents need to understand the difference between proper discipline done out of love and abuse done out of anger. Paul tells fathers not to "exasperate your children" (Eph. 6:4). One means of frustrating our children is to discipline them out of proportion to the deed. As a parent, I have learned that discipline is not easy. The old saying, "this is going to hurt me more than it hurts you," has much truth in it if parents truly love their children.

Parents must pass on their faith to their children. In Deuteronomy 6:4-9 Moses discusses the responsibility parents have to educate their children in the faith. Parents are the first educators of their children although they may not be conscious of it. Children learn much about God, love, faith, kindness, forgiveness, honesty, etc., from living with their parents. We reflect what we really believe in how we live. Children pick up on this, even if we do not verbalize it to them. Sadly, this is a problem in many Christian homes because the lack of faith will shine through as well as faith. Parents who tell their children to pray but do not pray are sending mixed messages. Parents who tell their children not to lie but cheat on their income taxes are sending mixed messages. We need to be conscious of how we teach in both formal and informal ways.

Parents should also verbally teach their children. The passage in Deuteronomy suggests that this should be done in the normal course of everyday life. As we drive to the supermarket, as we wash clothes, cook supper, mow the grass, etc., we will have opportunities to teach our children. When we read to them (one of the best things parents can do for their children — it reaps many benefits), we can take opportunities suggested by the story to explain our faith. Of course, some reading we do with them can be from the Bible or based on the Bible. Children need to be instructed about Daniel, Jonah, Jesus, David, and the many other "heroes" of the faith.

The ideal is that both mother and father participate in verbally instructing their children about their faith. Unfortunately, this responsibility usually falls on the women. We men neglect this area of parenting far too often. I have two sons. I already see much room for improvement in my modeling and instructing my boys about my faith. Spiritual training is both my and my wife's responsibility, not the church's. The church should be a supplement to the home, not a replacement.

Scripture says that if we parents do our job, our children will be faithful (Prov. 22:6). This is not an absolute promise; our children have the responsibility to cooperate. Still, most of the time, children will follow the lead of their parents in matters of faith. Our children may not duplicate our faith and beliefs exactly, but they usually do turn out to be much like us.

Fourth, God intended the family to work. In Genesis 1:28 God instructs the man and the woman to "subdue" the earth. This implies that from the beginning, even before sin entered the world, God had work for people to do. The Garden of Eden was not going to be a life of complete rest and recreation. God has given people the responsibility of being the caretakers of his creation: developing it, harnessing its power, nurturing its growth. In fact, when God created woman to be man's helper, one implication was that man alone could not do all that God intended. God intended the team of husband and wife to work together, making it possible for them to accomplish more than a single person could. As the writer of Ecclesiastes says, "Two are better than one, because they have a good return for their work" (Eccl. 4:9).

Finally, God intended the family to serve others. Many passages of Scripture mention our duties to those around us. Jesus said that to love your neighbor was one of the two greatest commandments. One main purpose of the church in the New Testament was to reach out to a watching world and serve it. Serving others is one way we show God's love to others. God calls each individual Christian to a life of service, and God calls the church to serve others. He also expects the family to serve others. Yet we often forget others and focus on meeting only the needs of our own families. This family-centeredness can become selfish, hoarding up wealth and possessions, never sharing or giving. Not only is this a bad example for our children to see, it denies the people around us of the help we could provide. Families should look for opportunities to help neighbors, schoolmates, inner-city residents, the elderly, and others so that we can spread God's love and increase God's kingdom. This will call us to sacrifice some of our time and money that otherwise would have been spent on self or on family. We need a proper balance between taking care of our own and taking care of others, but *both* are essential for the Christian family.

Jesus' Attitude about the Family

As a conclusion to this analysis of what God intended the family to be, learning Jesus' attitude toward the family is very important. Jesus grew up in a family with a mother, a father, several brothers and sisters. However, some of Jesus' words appear very negative toward family life. For example, in Matthew 10:34-39, Jesus said that he would bring family division and strife, setting son against father and daughter against mother. Jesus declared that "a man's enemies will be the members of his own household." He also said that "anyone who loves his father or mother more than me is not worthy of me; anyone who loves his son or daughter more than me is not worthy of me . . . ." In Luke's account of this teaching (Luke 14:25-27), Jesus said a person must "hate his father and mother, his wife and children, his brothers and sisters. . . ."

Once during Jesus' ministry, his family came to see him. They stood outside a house waiting to speak with him, and he replied, "Who is my mother, and who are my brothers? . . . For whoever does the will of my Father in heaven is my brother and sister and mother" (Matt. 12:46-50). Once, a follower of Jesus asked permission to go bury his father. Jesus refused him permission, telling him to "let the dead bury their own dead, but you go and proclaim the kingdom of God." Another would-be disciple asked permission to go say goodbye to his family. Jesus again refused permission, telling the man "no one who puts his hand to the plow and looks back is fit for service in the kingdom of God" (Luke 9:59-62). And, of course, Jesus never married. He even implied that singleness was better, although he admitted that not everyone could accept this (Matt. 19:10-12).

So, did Jesus see the family as a roadblock to discipleship? Before we make a conclusion, we need to see other passages that bring some balance to the picture. First, Jesus did care about his family. In a very tender scene when Jesus was on the cross, he told the apostle John to care for his mother's needs (John 19:25-27). This proves that Jesus cared deeply about his mother and her pain and confusion at that moment. We also note that Jesus' relationship with his family must have been generally positive because we see his mother and brothers numbered among the original group of disciples in Jerusalem just before Pentecost Day (Acts 1:12-14). Following Jesus did not prevent Peter and several others from maintaining their marriages, since their wives went with their husbands on missionary journeys (1 Cor. 9:5). Jesus assumed that marriage was the normal course for most people. He referred his followers to the teachings of Genesis chapter 2 so they would understand God's original plan (Matt. 19:1-9). Jesus attended a wedding in Cana, which shows his acceptance of the marriage relationship. The early church taught about the importance of marriage and the taking care of one's family (for example, Eph. 5:21–6:4; 1 Tim. 5:8). How could the early church have taught these family responsibilities if they were against what Jesus taught? Too many eyewitnesses of Jesus were around to allow for such radical departures from Jesus' teachings, if it is true that he saw the family as a hindrance to the life of discipleship.

So how do we reconcile these negative statements of Jesus about the family with the traditional Christian understandings of the importance of the family? We should recognize two factors. First, Jesus and some of his early followers must be considered exceptional cases. Jesus' purpose on this earth was to establish the kingdom of God with power and to provide salvation for all people. He, like Paul, had dedicated his life to a cause that would have made normal family life impossible. I am convinced that Jesus loved his family, but he could not live a normal life because of what God had sent him to do.

Second, some of Jesus' statements mentioned above are about loyalty. It is true that no other loyalty can come before our loyalty to God. If our family becomes more important to us than obeying God, then we are idolaters of the family. Loyalty to God must be first; we must see everything else, even family, as less important. This is the meaning Jesus intended when he said that we must "hate" our parents (Luke 14:25-27).

If we understand these two factors, Jesus' teachings about the family are in harmony with the teachings of the early church. It is true that some will be called to serve God by being single. Nevertheless, it seems also true that most will serve God while being married and having children. While we can never put family in the place of God, we are called to love our families and to serve God in our families. The family is one arena of life where we can live out our loyalty to God. It is not the only arena of life where we must live out our faith; God also calls us to serve our church family and to serve in our communities. Still, it is one legitimate means by which we show our loyalty to God.

What are the general guidelines for how we should conduct ourselves in our families? Besides what we have already said, the biblical guidelines concerning family relationships are much like all other relationships in Christ. An easy way to summarize how we relate to each other in our biological families and in the family of God is to study the "one another" passages in the New Testament. Scripture teaches us to forgive, to be patient, to love, to serve, to respect, to submit, to comfort, to warn, to be gentle, and so on.

These commands on how to conduct ourselves serve equally well as guidelines for family living and guidelines for church fellowship because both are a sharing of life together in service to God.

Conclusion

The above principles are some things that the church should be teaching and modeling today so that we can be of help to families. If we teach, model, encourage, and coach families to live out these ideals, we can help them be more faithful to God's original intent for the family. We will also help them avoid the pain and struggles that are so common in families today.

To be effective in doing this, we cannot preach at them from a distance and hope they hear. We must stand alongside them and help them walk through their struggles, repent of their sins, and cope with their pain so that they remain faithful to God. Our goal is to help families be faithful to God and to each other.

I am optimistic about the possibilities of the church helping families today. My optimism is not based on our human ability to construct the perfect ministry program, to bring about political change to favor biblical morality, or to untangle the complexity of problems that are present in society. My optimism is based on the following four reasons.

First, I believe in the power of God. I believe that his power is still at work in the world. I believe that no greater power than his exists. I am convinced that he wants to help families. I believe his power can save a failing marriage. I believe his power can restore tense parent-child relationships. In Ezekiel 37, God asked the prophet, "Can these bones live?" God proved to Ezekiel that he could do things that no man thought possible. It might be the rational thing today to accept the failure of many families as evidence that we need to lower our expectations for family happiness and stability. Some are calling for trial marriages. Many want us to accept the inevitability of divorce. However, to do these things is an admission that we have lost hope. If God intended families to work, he can make them work if families will allow Him. The church can never lose sight of this. We must continue to trust in God and his power. The apostle Paul reminds us that we serve a God "who is able to do immeasurably more than all we ask or imagine, according to his power that is at work within us . . . ."

(Eph. 3:20). My confidence that the church can help families lies primarily in the power of God.

A second reason that I am confident that the church can help families today is the widespread awareness of the need for help. Families of all kinds are begging for help. Families are hurting so badly that they are open to anyone who offers help, religious or not. The church has an unparalleled opportunity to minister to many people in our society. These hurting people are crying out. Will we answer? Family problems are not easily solved. Do we have the love and the courage to respond? I am optimistic because so many recognize their need and are looking for answers.

Third, I am optimistic because of our human capacity to make choices. I believe that God has given us much freedom in life. Our lives are not predetermined; people can change, and families can change. Certainly, people need encouragement and guidance. Who better to offer it than God's people? Many family problems are caused by poor choices. We can teach people to make better choices, better choices regarding marital partners and parenting. We can choose to listen to God; we can choose to go our own way. But we can choose. Satan's power is not so strong that we have no ability to choose (1 Cor. 10:13).

A fourth and final reason for my optimism concerning the church's ability to help families comes from resiliency, our human capacity to cope with less than perfect situations. I am amazed at the coping ability of some individuals in tragic and difficult circumstances. We cannot resolve our family problems so that all the pain and struggles are gone. It is likely that some pain and struggle will remain even in the best of cases. Yet if our focus is on God, I believe that we can help people find the strength to cope, especially if we can give them some support and encouragement. Who is better equipped to do this than the church? Facing family problems is not easy if done alone. Families need the support of the community of faith. I am confident of the church's ability to help people cope with less than perfect family situations.

I have tried in this chapter to set out a vision for what the church can do to help families today. I am well aware of how complex the problems are and how imperfect the church is. Nevertheless, we must continue to proclaim the ideal lest we lose sight of it. Let us all pray that God grant us the wisdom we need and the strength we need to do what he wants done in this world.

Chapter Twenty-four

What should we do about benevolence?

Harold Shank
Highland Street Church of Christ
Memphis, Tennessee

One church leader put it this way, "The deacon who draws the shortest straw gets benevolence."

We know what he meant. A family in a fifteen-year-old, rusted-out station wagon knocks at the church door asking for gasoline money to the next city. Or later that evening, our home telephone rings. It's a stranded traveler at the local bus station, needing funds to get back for a beloved uncle's funeral. Or a poor mother comes up after the service with a complicated story about needing money to satisfy an impatient landlord. The general reaction among preachers and church leaders is, "I don't like doing this." At the next business meeting, the deacon with the shortest straw gets benevolence.

It doesn't stop there. An area childcare agency preempts the Sunday night sermon to show their slide presentation. A widow asks for a ride to the doctor. A shut-in needs her storm windows changed. The preacher thinks, "I studied Greek and Hebrew so that I can be PR man for orphans, run a taxi service for widows, and do handy-man tasks for shut-ins? Why can't we get the deacons to do these tasks?" The deacon with the shortest straw gets benevolence.

I've felt the same way. In planting a new mission church, I believed helping the poor would sap the young church's strength. A call from a stranded traveler or a man wanting help with his utility bill irritated me. What few times I actually took food to a poor family, I celebrated when the task was over. I was delighted that we had only one widow in the entire church and could concentrate on "real" ministry. Since we were miles away from most of the child care agencies and were a new, largely unknown congregation, they never called. My greatest regret was that the church was too young to have deacons. As the preacher, I drew the benevolence straw.

Not only did I despise handling the benevolence tasks, I had little room in my theology for any concern about the needy. I presented several lessons on Amos that totally sidestepped benevolence. I never preached on James 1:27. I saw no theological reason for benevolence. Since I had overcome my own poverty, I believed others could do the same.

One day, while driving through Memphis, God enabled me to see through the grand southern oaks lining each side of the freeway to the squalor of the shotgun houses that packed the nearby neighborhoods. At that moment, I felt the inconsistency between what I saw and the upper middle class church that I served, a stark contrast between the comfortable life I lived and the bare subsistence of people across town. That experience drove me back into the Bible where I discovered, for the first time in my long career of academic study and church work, that God had amazing things to say about *my* responsibility to the poor. My life, and my ministry, have not been quite the same since, for I found that every section of the Bible talked about the poor, that benevolence connected to the rest of the church's ministry, and that it did not take too much to bring my misguided concepts about benevolence into line with what God wanted all along.

Biblical Teaching about the Poor

In each section of the Bible, God's people are called to help the poor. The call first appears in the Law, continues in the Prophets and Psalms, and then resurfaces in the Gospels, Acts, and the Epistles.[1]

Deuteronomy 15 states God's highest expectation, "There will be no poor among you (Deut. 15:4, RSV).[2] To ensure that the Israelite society could achieve this goal, the text first listed laws which protected the poor (15:1-3), and then called for a community of people who would go beyond the laws:

> If there is among you a poor man, one of your brethren, in any of your towns within your land which the LORD your God gives you,

you shall not harden your heart or shut your hand against your poor
brother, but you shall open your hand to him (Deut. 15:7-8, RSV).

The text adds, "Your heart shall not be grudging when you give to
him" (Deut. 15:10, RSV). Deuteronomy 15 reflects both the laws protecting the poor and God's concern that the Israelite community go
beyond the law to protect the orphan, the widow, and the needy.

The prophets called for adherence to those laws. Isaiah typifies
the prophetic protest when God's people failed the poor. In Isaiah
1, God rejects Israelite worship because of the iniquities of the people, which included mistreatment of the poor.[3] The people are
warned, "Learn to do good; seek justice, correct oppression; defend
the fatherless, plead for the widow" (Isa. 1:17, RSV). The prophet
calls for no new laws, just adherence to those already on the books.
The standards of God regarding the poor were clear; Israel had
turned its head another way.

The psalmists continued the call to God's people. In Psalm 82,
God charged the people to help the poor:

> Give justice to the weak and the fatherless;
> maintain the right of the afflicted and the destitute.
> Rescue the weak and the needy;
> deliver them from the hand of the wicked (Ps. 82:3-4, RSV).

The psalmist sounds prophetic in his demand that justice be served
and rescue planned. Concern for the poor permeates the Psalms,
both in proclaiming God's special interest in the poor and Israel's
responsibility to the disadvantaged.

God's standard for how his people treat the poor is upheld in
the ministry of Jesus. Before his birth, the Song of Mary predicted,
"He has put down the mighty from their thrones, and exalted those
of low degree; he has filled the hungry with good things" (Luke
1:52-53a). Jesus accepted that challenge in the programmatic
description of his ministry in Luke 4:

> The Spirit of the Lord is upon me,
> because he has anointed me to preach good news to the poor.
> he has sent me to proclaim release to the captives
> and recovering of sight to the blind,
> to set at liberty those who are oppressed (Luke 4:18, RSV).

By quoting Isaiah 58 and 61, Jesus fully aligns himself with God's
demands about the poor in the Old Testament and makes it charac-

teristic of his ministry. Jesus does exactly what he sets out to do, as revealed in this message to the imprisoned John the Baptist:

> Go and tell John what you have seen and heard: the blind receive their sight, the lame walk, lepers are cleansed, and the deaf hear, the dead are raised up, the poor have good news preached to them (Luke 7:22, RSV).[4]

Jesus' own ministry report overflows with concern expressed to the disadvantaged of his society. As Deuteronomy demanded, Jesus went beyond the law to help those who faced the difficulties of life. Additionally, he called for the same response from his followers:

> When you give a dinner or a banquet, do not invite your friends or your brothers or your kinsmen or rich neighbors, lest they also invite you in return, and you be repaid. But when you give a feast, invite the poor, the maimed, the lame, the blind (Luke 14:12-13, RSV).

The presence of poor people presented an opportunity for the people of God to open their homes and tables (Luke 14:12-13) or their hearts and hands (Deut. 15:8-9) to the less fortunate. Jesus not only continued the standards of the Law, but he demanded that his followers do the same.

According to the book of Acts, they did. The early church attracted both the rich and the poor. Those who had shared with those who did not. Luke summarizes the benevolent program of the early church:

> There was not a needy person among them, for as many as were possessors of lands or houses sold them, and brought the proceeds of what was sold and laid it at the apostles' feet; and distribution was made to each as any had need (Acts 4:34-35, RSV).

The early Christians accepted the responsibility for taking care of the disadvantaged in a remarkable way.

The Epistles continue the expectation that God's people will care about the poor. At the Jerusalem council, Paul mentions one point of consensus, "Only they would have us remember the poor, which very thing I was eager to do" (Gal. 2:10, RSV). Paul participated in a fund raising effort among European believers to help poor Christians in Palestine. The two most often quoted texts about church contribution, 1 Corinthians 16:1-4 with its "lay by in store"

(KJV) and 2 Corinthians 8–9 with its "God loves a cheerful giver," which are often used in our services prior to the giving, do not reflect money raised for local church budgets but funds needed for famine-stricken church members in Jerusalem (Rom. 15:25-26). These two "giving texts" are Scriptures about benevolence.

James includes two long sections about the treatment of the poor (Jas. 2:1-13; 5:1-6), but summarizes the heart of God's expectation for his people in the oft-cited words, "Religion that is pure and undefiled before God and the Father is this: to visit orphans and widows in their affliction, and to keep oneself unstained from the world" (Jas. 1:27, RSV).

From the Law to the Epistles, from the Psalms to the Gospels, the Bible calls God's people to a special concern for benevolence. The Bible also makes benevolence central to how Jesus saw ministry.

The Biblical Links between Benevolence and Ministry

One way to characterize the ministry of Jesus is to focus on three key statements he made about ministry in Luke 6:36, Mark 10:45, and Luke 19:10. These three texts indicate that his ministry was characterized by showing mercy, being a servant, and seeking the lost. Each aspect of ministry has clear connections with helping the poor.

1. **Mercy.** In the first text, Jesus characterized ministry by calling his followers to mercy. The Sermon on the Plain climaxes with this statement, "Be merciful, even as your Father is merciful" (Luke 6:36, RSV). Jesus practiced a ministry of mercy. Jesus had compassion on the large, hungry crowd of four thousand people (Matt. 15:32). When Jesus asked the lawyer which passerby had been neighbor to the robbery victim, the man pointed to the Samaritan as the one who had shown mercy (Luke 10:37).

Benevolence demands mercy. As early as Deuteronomy 15, the mere presence of laws protecting the poor was insufficient, so God called his people to open their hearts. Jesus' ministry to the needy satisfied a law about justice to the poor and reflected his heart of compassion and mercy. John saw the truth of this connection in these pointed words, "But if any one has the world's goods and sees his brother in need, yet closes his heart against him, how does God's love abide in him?" (1 John 3:17, RSV). Benevolence emerges out of a merciful heart. Jesus' call for his followers to be merciful has close links to benevolence. We show our love for God and for each other by the way we share with those who do not have. Failure to share our goods with the needy is tantamount to not having any love in our hearts at all.

2. **Service.** In the second text, Jesus characterized ministry by calling his followers to service. Jesus came as a servant, "For the Son of man came . . . not to be served but to serve, and to give his life as a ransom for many" (Mark 10:45, RSV). Just after Jesus states his servant agenda, blind Bartimaeus calls for his attention, but the people try to silence him. Keeping his promise to be a servant, Jesus tends to the man's blindness (Mark 10:46-52). Later, when Jesus washes the disciples' feet in John 13, he again emphasizes his servant role. There and elsewhere, Jesus demanded the same of his followers.

Benevolence is a service ministry. Jesus fed the poor, made the blind see, let the lame walk, and helped the deaf to hear. It was servant work. Kings and the rich may pay little attention to such tasks, but Jesus made them a priority. Helping the poor provides clear opportunities for God's people to serve those around them. The haunting parable in Matthew 25 cements the link between service and the poor:

> Then they also will answer, "Lord, when did we see thee hungry or thirsty or a stranger or naked or sick or in prison and did not minister to thee?" Then he will answer them, "Truly, I say to you, as you did it not to one of the least of these, you did it not to me." (Matt. 25:44-45, RSV)

According to Jesus, service to the poor will serve as a key factor in the decisions of Judgment Day.

3. **Seeking the lost.** The third text calls attention to Jesus' concern to bring lost people to God. As he visited with Zacchaeus, he stated this critical goal, "For the Son of man came to seek and to save the lost" (Luke 19:10). The three parables in Luke 15 about the lost sheep, the lost coin, and the two lost sons affirm his mission to the lost.

His mission statement in Luke 4 links the lost and poor when he sets out to "preach good news to the poor." When he summarizes his ministry to John the Baptist in Luke 7:22, he says, "The poor have good news preached to them" (RSV). Because of his own mission, the tasks of evangelism and benevolence can never be separated.

Jesus never insisted that anyone listen to him preach before he would offer help. He never demanded that those who were healed or fed stay for his sermon. "Soup and sermon" has become a common description of those who reduce the links between evangelism and benevolence to the rule, "If you don't let us give you food for your soul, we will not give you food for your body."

Jesus used both evangelistic and benevolent opportunities. His work among the needy attracted attention to his message. His compassion gave his message a certain credibility by showing that he focused on their eternal destiny, and he cared about their current existence. The American proverb, "People don't care how much you know until they know how much you care" reflects the linked agenda of benevolence and evangelism in the ministry of Jesus.

Jesus describes ministry in terms of showing mercy, being a servant, and seeking the lost. Each aspect of ministry has strong connections to how God's people respond to the poor.

Bringing Benevolence into Line with Biblical Teaching

The notion that "the deacon who draws the shortest straw gets benevolence" seems at odds with the consistent biblical teaching about the poor and the close links that benevolence has with ministry. How do we move from a church where benevolence takes a back seat to other ministries to a congregation where work among the poor is valued in a biblical way? How can preachers and church leaders make benevolence central to the church's work? These three suggestions may be helpful to those who want to bring benevolence in line with biblical teaching.

1. **Practice aggressive benevolence, not just defensive benevolence.** Defensive benevolence waits for the poor to come begging. Defensive benevolence waits for the calls that come at the end of the month when the poor families have exhausted their money. Aggressive benevolence seeks out the poor before they have a chance to call. Aggressive benevolence builds relationships with those in need before problems reach a critical stage. Aggressive benevolence provides opportunities for displays of mercy, for service, and for seeking the lost that are typically absent in cases of defensive benevolence.

A ministry worker at the Inner City Nashville Church of Christ called on a woman who visited their Sunday assembly. He noted on the visitation report that her apartment had no furniture. One of the ministers, alerted to this situation, paid a second visit, and confirmed the visitation worker's observation. He asked the woman if the church truck could drop by with a couch, some chairs, and a bedroom set. The request overwhelmed the poor woman. Used to begging and pleading, she seldom encountered people who sought to help her before she asked. It allowed her to maintain dignity and raised questions in her mind about the church she had visited. Later she requested a Bible study and was baptized.

Christian child care agencies are another clear example of aggressive benevolence. Unwed, expectant mothers who find themselves in poverty often see an advertisement or hear on the street that the child care agency associated with Churches of Christ is ready to help. Their calls are expected. Workers anticipate the opportunity to sit down with the troubled, expectant mother to explain how they can serve her at such a critical time.

Aggressive benevolence complies with God's expectation that we help the poor. Seeking out the poor rather than reluctantly waiting for them to come to us creates opportunities to show mercy, to be servants, and to seek the lost. Churches that practice aggressive benevolence will find that such a ministry becomes a source of joy and fulfillment, far different from the church where the deacon with the shortest straw gets benevolence.

2. **Make benevolence central, not an add-on ministry.** Helping the poor is not an afterthought in the Bible, but central to God and the call to his people. He is a God of justice, love, and mercy. The poor are close to his heart. Our churches should reflect that centrality.

Benevolence should be central to the leaders in terms of where they give their time, money, and leadership. Concern about the poor must be a regular piece of the preaching ministry of the church. Churches that never hear sermons about the poor will seldom rise to God's standard. The numerous texts on the poor must be carefully considered in Sunday School classes. Christians who remain unaware of the biblical call to benevolence are unlikely to become concerned about making benevolence a central ministry of the church.

Churches have typically trained members for the works of ministry. Training programs for personal evangelism, Bible school teachers, young men and women abound. Colleges and special schools train ministers and missionaries. Training Christians to help the poor will move benevolence to a central position in church life. The annual Urban Ministry Conference held in Churches of Christ is devoted to providing basic training in the wide array of benevolence ministries. Several of the Christian colleges now offer programs in Urban Ministry which emphasize benevolence.

3. **Practice incarnational benevolence.** God took on human form, spoke human language, died a human death in order to communicate the salvation of God. God did not expect us to come to him, rather he came to us.

Under the banner of incarnational theology, evangelistic efforts have tried to make the gospel available in the culture and setting of the receiver. The Hebrew and Greek Bible is translated into the spoken language of the target population. Each person should hear God's word in his own language. At distant mission points, we train native Christians to be ministers because the local people who hear the gospel presented by a native speaker respond more positively than when presented by a person foreign to their culture. Church buildings, Bible study classes, evangelistic strategy all take the local culture into account so that a church building in Arkansas differs radically from a church building in the highlands of Papua New Guinea.

Benevolence must also follow the incarnational model. Rather than conducting benevolence based on the decisions of people who are not poor and perhaps have never been poor, the incarnational model suggests that the aid be delivered in ways that are most helpful to the people who are poor. Deciding to feed people under a freeway bridge when the people who live there already have food but no place to sleep, fails to present the benevolent aid in an incarnational way. An adage in benevolent ministry says, "It is one thing to give a man a fish. It is another thing to teach him to fish. It is quite another matter to give him access to a lake where he can fish." Each additional step delivers benevolence in a way that reflects the poor person's own setting and culture, which is what Christ did when he spoke Aramaic from a human body in Roman Palestine.

As people in poverty come to Christ, the incarnational model leads to starting churches of poor people who can then lead in shaping the ways aid is delivered to their setting, so that the benevolent help speaks their own language. Benevolence provides the giver with the satisfaction of giving and also helps those who need.

Just as the native speaker on the mission field guides the foreign missionary in presenting the gospel in the best way, so the poor person from an inner city church can provide guidance to ensure an incarnational benevolent ministry.

Benevolence in Action

Many Churches of Christ have practiced aggressive, centralized, incarnational benevolence. Stories of David Lipscomb caring for the poor victims of yellow fever in the late nineteenth century, the medical facility for the poor operated during World War I by the Russell Street Church of Christ in Nashville, the free noon meal and medical-dental clinic of Nashville's Central Church of Christ during the Great Depression, and the efforts beginning in the 1950s by the Madison Church of Christ to care for children all stand out as models for congregations.[5] Currently, churches such as White's Ferry Road Church of Christ in West Monroe, Louisiana, and Redwood City Church of Christ in Redwood City, California, provide leadership for international benevolence. Inner City Church of Christ in Nashville, Richland Hills Church of Christ in Fort Worth, and Impact Church of Christ in Houston are congregations that have done consistent and innovative benevolent work in their cities. Many other congregations have excelled in benevolent work.

The Highland Street Church of Christ in Memphis has tried to respond to God's call with regard to the poor. Located in one of the poorest cities in the United States, the church has participated in several ministries to the hurting and weak people of the city. They provide a free Friday night child care service for the parents of handicapped children. Each week, these special parents have four hours when they can rest and recreate, knowing that their children are well cared for.

Along with other Churches of Christ in the city, Highland supports the Life Skills Lab, a thirteen-week series of classes in which homeless and chronically unemployed people are taught the basic skills needed for finding, securing, and keeping a job. About seventy percent of the Lab graduates fully support themselves after graduation. About ten percent become Christians.

Joining with other Churches of Christ, Highland has embarked on the goal of starting a series of inner-city congregations that can lead in evangelizing and serving the city's poor. The first of several envisioned churches was started in 1994. That congregation continues to evangelize in the inner city and lead the other churches in benevolent activity.

Each August, Highland sponsors a store which provides school supplies for elementary grade students. During the first eight years of the School Store ministry, nearly 40,000 children received free supplies. In June, a Workcamp of five hundred area teenagers paints the homes of poor inner-city residents. Nearly two hundred houses have been painted in the past six years.

These ministries to the poor represent the kind of activity that can characterize aggressive benevolence when helping the poor is kept central to the church ministry. In many cases, the poor people who have been won to Christ now take a leading role in guiding the benevolent activity, and leadership in inner-city churches helps better target benevolent activity.

Conclusion

Abraham Heschel wrote, "Justice is scarce, injustice exceedingly common."[6] More people ignore the poor and oppress the weak than those who show concern for them. While we seek to do the right thing, it is much easier to do the wrong thing. Justice is uncommon.

Heschel goes on to remind us that most Americans associate justice with the blindfolded woman holding a scale. She often has a sword in hand. The image suggests that each person should get their fair share, that the scales should be balanced. The sword represents the power of the state to enforce such equality.

Such an image never appears in Scripture. We in Churches of Christ are not guided by the sword-wielding, scale-holding woman. Rather the picture in Scripture is that of an ever-flowing river. Amos gave us the God-approved image when he said, "Let justice roll down like waters, And righteousness like a mighty stream" (Amos 5:24, RSV). In God's dream for the world, his concern is that the poor not just have enough, but that the rivers of justice flow down continually, that his people make righteousness toward rich and poor as endless as a mighty stream.

Endnotes

[1]The Scriptures cited here are only representative texts. Ron Sider's *Cry Justice!* (New York: Paulist Press, 1980) contains a more comprehensive listing of biblical texts on the poor.

[2]For a fuller treatment of this text, see Harold Shank and Wayne Reed, "A Challenge to Suburban Evangelical Churches: Theological Perspectives on Poverty in America," *Journal of Interdisciplinary Studies* 7.1/2 (1995): 119-134.

[3]The relationship between worship and benevolence is explored more fully in Harold Shank, "The Other Six Days: Worship and Ethics," in *In Search of Wonder*, Lynn Anderson, ed. (West Monroe, LA: Howard Publishing, 1995), 95-117.

[4]On the connection of the Luke 4 and 7 texts with Deuteronomy 15, see Shank and Reed, "A Challenge."

[5]For more complete descriptions of these programs, see Anthony Dunnavant, "David Lipscomb on the Church and the Poor" *Restoration Quarterly* 33.2 (1991): 75-85; Paul Brown, "Evangelism by Mass Benevolence" (Florence, AL: International Bible College Lectures, 1988); Harold Shank, "Aggressive Grace: Central Church of Christ in Action," *Wineskins* (August 1992): 7-9; Jimmie Moore Mankin, "The Role of Social Service in the Life and Growth of the Madison Church" (D.Min. Diss., Fuller Theological Seminary, 1987).

[6]Abraham J. Heschel, *The Prophets*, Vol. 1 (New York: Harper & Row, 1962), 204.

Chapter Twenty-five

What about euthanasia?

Rubel Shelly
Woodmont Hills Church of Christ
Nashville, Tennessee

As of the spring of 1998, Oregon is the only state in the nation with a law permitting physician-assisted suicide. Voters first passed that state's Death with Dignity Act in 1994 by a narrow margin. Because of legal challenges, the measure did not go into effect and continued to be debated. The Oregon Legislature sent the law back to voters in November of 1997, and it passed by a significant majority.

An unidentified woman in her mid-eighties became the first person to die under that law on March 24, 1998.[1] Having suffered from breast cancer for twenty years, she died about half an hour after taking a lethal dose of barbiturates washed down with a glass of brandy. In a tape she made before taking the drugs, she said she had been given only two months to live. She said she was "looking forward" to dying "because being I was always active, I cannot comfortably see myself living out two more months like this."[2]

Since 1995, approximately fifty bills have been introduced in more than twenty states to legalize physician-assisted suicide. In no state outside Oregon has one passed. To the contrary, sixteen states have adopted laws that expressly criminalize assisted suicide. That brings the total to thirty-five states that explicitly outlaw it, and nine others make the practice illegal through case law or common law. In 1998 alone, nine states have introduced bills in their legislatures to allow assisted suicide; nine others have introduced bills that would either explicitly criminalize it or increase the penalties under existing law.[3]

I am opposed to suicide. Whether a physician, family member, friend, or stranger is involved to assist is essentially irrelevant. On the other hand, I do not believe that foregoing or withdrawing life-sustaining treatment is necessarily a form of suicide. This very important distinction often is not made in discussions of this topic.

Polls show a majority of Americans support euthanasia. My strong sense is that they do so on the basis of a nonarticulated sense of distinction between *active* and *passive* euthanasia. The distinction between the two is very important, and I suspect many of the polls about euthanasia do not frame their questions to differentiate them.

Do all patients have the right to know the truth about their terminal diagnoses? Is life, however painful or tenuous, always preferable to death? Should death always be deferred by whatever means? May some forms of treatment be denied to patients without being unethical or "playing God"? *Should* some forms of treatment be denied to patients without being unethical or "playing God"? Is it permissible to administer medications for intractable suffering in such quantities that we know they are likely to induce anesthesia-like sedation and hasten death? On what basis should decisions about terminating treatment be made? Cost? Allocation of resources? Quality of life? Emotional-financial strain on the patient's family?

In this paper, it will be argued that some of us need to reconsider the place of death both in the natural world and in our ethical systems. It is a common mistake within our health care establishment to view death as the ultimate evil. It will also be argued that it is sometimes unethical to resist death. In the course of this discussion of some of the ethical issues related to death and dying, some criticisms will be offered not only of the materialist-physicalist point of view but also of a widespread interpretation within the Christian tradition which sees death only and always as an evil thing.

Elaborate and worthwhile medical technology makes possible the artificial prolongation of physical existence in cases where people are already brain dead.[4] Thus, individuals who have suffered massive brain damage from trauma to the head, massive spontaneous hemorrhage into the brain (CVA), or anoxic damage from cardiac or respiratory arrest can be kept alive for months or years. But the issue addressed in this paper is whether ethically sensitive persons should do such a thing.

Perception and Posture

One's ultimate position on many death-and-dying issues is contained within his or her initial assumptions about the nature and value of human life; it may also be carried within his or her initial assumptions about death. The former thesis is more generally appreciated and more easily illustrated than the latter. We need to make sense of both before going further.

How may one's conclusion be shaped by an initial assumption about the nature and value of human life? In a well-known article in which he argues for active euthanasia (i.e., intervention designed to bring about a patient's death) in cases where newborn children suffer "from gross deformities or from severe physical, emotional, or intellectual handicaps," Michael Tooley insists that there is no morally relevant distinction which society should make between unwanted kittens and unwanted human infants.

> Why should it be seriously wrong to kill an unborn member of the species Homo sapiens but not seriously wrong to kill an unborn kitten? Difference in species is not *per se* a morally relevant difference.[5]

Tooley accepts the implications of his abortion position for infanticide in a straightforward and honest manner.

> If this view of the matter [that both unborn and newborn members of the species Homo sapiens have no serious claim to the rights which belong to human beings — RS] is roughly correct, there are two worries that one is left with at the level of practical moral decisions, one of which may turn out to be deeply disturbing. The lesser worry is where the line is to be drawn in the case of infanticide. It is not troubling because there is no serious need to know the exact point at which a human infant acquires a right to life. For in the vast majority of cases in which infanticide is desirable, its desirability will be apparent within a short time after birth. . . . The practical moral problem can thus be satisfactorily handled by choosing some short period, such as a week after birth, as the interval during which infanticide will be permitted.[6]

As a general rule, Christian ethicists have disavowed Tooley's position as altogether inconsistent with their view that members of species Homo sapiens have greater intrinsic value than animal life in general due to the *imago dei* borne by humanity. Tooley and John Paul II would have very different suggestions about the treatment of a Down's syndrome infant with obvious physical anomalies but capable of surviving with only routine and normal neonatal care.

But how might one's conclusion be shaped by an initial assumption about death? Suppose that someone values life, enjoys life, and feels a strong responsibility to preserve his life. Then, at age forty-four, he is diagnosed with lymphoma. He undergoes chemotherapy for several months and experiences remission. Two years later, however, his disease recurs with a vengeance. He undergoes a bone marrow transplant. The first posthospitalization exam is ambiguous, and he has to be put back in the hospital within six days due to severe breathing difficulties. X-rays show massive lung involvement, and the prognosis is bleak. As he gets weaker and his breathing more difficult, he suddenly has to be put on a ventilator and soon loses consciousness. It is now apparent to physicians and family that all hope of recovery is gone. Within a week, he is unable to respond to any external stimulus and is clearly hopeless by all clinical standards.

In this case, it is the family, principally a wife of eighteen years, who must make some hard decisions. If that wife believes that her husband's ultimate and only hope is the recovery of his physical health, it is conceivable that she will insist that "everything possible" be done. With nourishment, fluids, and antibiotics, it might be possible to prolong his existence by several days or even a few weeks. On the other hand, if she believes that his ultimate and greater hope is "to depart and be with Christ,"[7] she may make the decision to allow him to die without further treatment or life support.[8]

The common theme in practically all our judgments about death is that it is always and only an enemy. Indeed, that is the way practically all cultures of the world perceive it. So we personify death as the "Grim Reaper" and perpetuate the idea that it is always evil in human experience.

At a practical level, public expectation of the medical profession is less likely to be the alleviation of unnecessary suffering and untimely death than simply the elimination of suffering and death. Thus, medical professionals are expected to defy death at all costs, no holds barred. The extension of physical life becomes the chief end. Thus some things are done for injured, comatose, and terminally ill patients which hold no prospect of restoring them to health and which can, at best, prolong their existence — and possibly increase their suffering. In the meanwhile, the individual's personal resources are exhausted, costs to society through taxes and insurance rates rise, and treatment which could be of real benefit to others may be denied them by virtue of diversion to a hopeless case.

As an additional complication, physicians are trained to use the latest technology and, when in doubt, to extend life as energetically as possible.

At the level of untested assumptions, today's secular person in a secular culture is prone to give life (i.e., keeping the organism breathing) the same unqualified devotion his counterpart from a time gone by would have offered God. In fact, if the thing that one values above any other and for which he will sacrifice all else is his life, then life has become his or her god.

Exceptions to the Rule

I believe the general rule in making ethical decisions concerning any organism that has a human genetic code must be in favor of its preservation.[9] But it is a quantum leap, which some regard only as a logical next step, to insist that such a presumption demands that nothing be spared to keep someone breathing. There are surely exceptions to the general rule I have stated.

Take the case of Louis D. as a paradigm instance of what I take to be such an exception. Louis was seventy-two years old and suffered from cancer of the urinary bladder which had been treated with radiation. The therapy was unsuccessful and created the complication of severely burning his bladder, creating perpetual bleeding with the complications involved with clot-blocked catheters, several emergency trips to the hospital from home in the middle of the night for treatment when irrigation at home was inadequate to keep the catheter functional, severe pain, and frequent transfusions. Surgical procedures were ruled out by Louis's physicians because of heart disease (i.e., he had suffered two serious heart attacks within the three years previous) and chronic respiratory failure. He was dying, and there was no reasonable hope of recovery for him.

In what proved to be his final admission to the hospital, he was given more than a dozen units of blood over a three-day period because of severe bleeding. His primary physician and I counseled with him, his wife, and his son about the course of future treatment.

The family chose to stop the transfusions on the basis that (a) his condition was hopeless as to recovery from his disease, (b) his suffering was intense, and (c) the blood being given him could make the difference in life or death for an accident victim or surgical patient.

Less than everything that could have been done to extend his life was done. Did he commit suicide? Did his family murder him? Did his physician fail to function ethically in caring for him? Did I give his family irresponsible and unethical counsel relative to the management of his care? I believe the correct answer to all these questions is in the negative. In fact, I believe the immoral choice here would have been to prolong the agony of a man's death.[10]

What shall we say, however, about hydration and nourishment as opposed to antibiotics, transfusions, and respirators? In one of the early cases of its kind to reach the courts, Roman Catholic Bishop Louis Gelineau gave his judgment that it was "morally permissible to withhold food and water" in the case of forty-eight-year-old Marcia Gray.[11] Following a stroke two years before, Mrs. Gray had been in a coma. Eight surgical procedures had been performed on her, and her condition was unimproved. Glenn Gray, her husband, petitioned in federal court to order that the hospital remove his wife's feeding tube and allow her to die.

This case is not unique. It is estimated that between 12,000 and 15,000 patients are in health care facilities across the United States at any given time who have no higher brain function but whose brain stem maintains such functions as heartbeat and breathing. Sometimes termed a "persistent vegetative state," this condition can be maintained for years. In the celebrated Karen Ann Quinlan case, for example, she lay comatose for nine years after being removed from a respirator and died in 1985.

I do not disagree with Bishop Gelineau, although many of his fellow Catholics took angry exception to his position. Is there not a time when families have the right to decide enough is enough? Is it unreasonable for ethical and religious people to support persons like Mr. Gray in making decisions to allow death to occur?

Since such cases as those of Quinlan and Gray, a rather substantial body of law has evolved in right-to-die cases.[12] The courts have consistently affirmed a patient's right to refuse life-sustaining treatment. They have concluded that no rational distinction is to be made between competent and incompetent patients, withholding or withdrawing treatment, and ordinary versus extraordinary treatment. The single distinction that has been upheld in several court cases is the distinction between the withdrawal or withholding of life-sustaining treatment (i.e., passive euthanasia) on the one hand and physician-assisted suicide (i.e. active euthanasia) on the other. In light of the Oregon law cited at the beginning of this paper, it is doubtful that such a distinction can long be maintained without court challenge.

The 1990 term of the United States Supreme Court took a significant step beyond the Quinlan case in the Cruzan case. Nancy Cruzan, a 32-year-old factory worker had been in a coma since being in an automobile accident in 1983. Her parents petitioned for the right to remove feeding tubes that were keeping her alive. The state resisted, saying that it had an "unqualified interest" in maintaining her life. The Missouri Supreme Court ruled that the state did have the responsibility to keep Ms. Cruzan alive. The United States Supreme Court disagreed with that ruling and permitted the removal of feeding tubes. Since that case, courts have even been willing to rule that a hospital can remove a brain-dead person's life support over the objection of that patient's family.[13]

With constant care involving antibiotics and tube feeding, many terminally ill and hopeless persons are not likely to die soon. People who object to allowing such patients to die raise the fear that the decision to forego the routine medical intervention of tube feeding and hydration for these people could be expanded to include not only the truly hopeless cases of the sort involving Louis D., Marcia Gray, or Nancy Cruzan but also the physically handicapped or mentally impaired. While the articulation of that fear is proper and serves as a safeguard to our process of making ethical decisions, the slippery slope reasoning employed in such an argument is not particularly persuasive. The line between terminal illness/injury on the one hand and physical/mental handicap on the other is clear enough for us to recognize and respect.

A Critical Distinction

There is an important distinction one can make between extending life with reasonable hope of recovery and extending the death process without adequate justification. The former can be argued for as ethically obligatory, whereas a good case can be made that the latter is ethically repulsive. If this thesis is granted, then it follows that a physician sometimes does more for his or her patient by doing less.

Again, however, the obscuring of this distinction between extending life with hope and extending the process of dying without adequate grounds results from one's initial assumptions about the nature of human life and/or one's assumptions about death.

If physical life is an absolute rather than relative value for an individual, then nothing short of everything possible to extend it must be done. Whether materialist or dualist, whether believing that death is the final act in the human drama or a transition from one form of life to another, whether atheist or Christian, the view of life as an absolute value commits one to doing everything necessary to preserve physical existence for as long as possible.

Yet, few people hold life to be an absolute value. Upon reflection, practically everyone admits that there are some fates worse than death. For the physicalist, such a fate might be horrible pain or the loss of "quality" to her life. For the dualist, death in some noble cause that grants the union of his spirit with God (i.e., martyrdom) would be an option preferred to the forfeiture of spiritual well being through apostasy. At the heart of the Christian faith is the belief that Jesus of Nazareth went to his death by consent for the sake of others. Within any such system, the preservation of physical existence cannot be regarded as an absolute good and the choice to forego its continuation as an absolute evil.

As to one's initial assumptions about death, most seem tempted to regard it as always and only evil. But is that so? Let us grant that it is often an enemy. We may even stipulate that it is almost always an enemy. But is it always and only The Enemy?

From a physicalist point of view, death is natural and necessary rather than evil. The cycles of nature require death in order for life to be preserved. From a religious point of view, death also seems natural and necessary rather than intrinsically evil. Within the Judeo-Christian tradition, for example, man's creation to have dominion over the earth and with permission to sustain himself on earth requires the death of plants and animals. Neither is there good reason for thinking that the death of human beings would have been forestalled without the Fall. On a traditional understanding of the Fall, sin introduced the necessity of physical death by virtue of denying man access to the Tree of Life, but not the possibility of physical death from such things as drowning or work-related accidents.

Final Considerations Relative to "Active" and "Passive" Euthanasia

Death, then, needs to be reconsidered. It is not an absolute evil. It is sometimes an instrumental good for those who have no hope of recovery from illness. Sometimes the real evil may lie in forcing someone to resist it.

Active euthanasia, however, is a very different matter. It is intervention designed to terminate life. It is popularly called "mercy killing." Both ethically and practically, this is easily distinguishable from simply permitting the death of a hopelessly ill woman or man. Morally sensitive people should oppose it in every possible way.

First, it is in direct conflict with our tradition of upholding the sanctity of human life. Whether preserved in the Ten Commandments or the Hippocratic Oath, that tradition says we are to affirm, nurture, and give aid to people in pain. The antithesis of that heritage is to destroy troublesome or traumatic life.

Second, active euthanasia creates a world of hopeless moral ambiguity. Impatient heirs can make their wishes known to ill parents in none-too-subtle ways, and anyone who is weary of a family nuisance can positively intimidate that person to death. Does anyone think it impossible that an individual or small group could put someone to death and swear they only aided the deceased to carry out his own wish to die?

Third, the swinging of the pendulum toward tolerance for active euthanasia will communicate the message that terminally ill persons have a duty to get out of the way of the living. For example, suppose a cancer patient for whom treatment has been ineffective tells his or her family, "I know I'm a terrible burden to you, and I wonder if I shouldn't just end my own life!" I can imagine two responses with very clear and contrasting messages.

"What do you mean!" says one family. "You are central to our lives. We love you, and you could never be a burden to us. Never!" That answer communicates a relationship within the group that inspires a will to live for one and affirms compassion and support by the others.

"Perhaps we should think about that," replies another family. "You might suffer toward the end, and we're not really rich enough to hire nurses so you can be cared for while we stay at our jobs." With such openness to the idea of helping her die, what feelings are likely to go through the mind of that patient?

I know of no one who comes onto Planet Earth with an exemption from suffering. Patient-assisted suicide is not the moral or practical solution to pain. Companionship and support, loyalty and compassion, love and kindness: these are better answers to the problem of suffering than carbon monoxide, lethal injection, or a prescription for death-dealing drugs.

Our call is not to become executioners. Instead, it is to provide humane, morally responsible, and palliative care for sufferers. We can only hope that Measure 16 and laws of its kind are systematically blocked from becoming American physicians' licenses to kill.

Conclusion

There are certainly cases when the artificial extension of physical existence without hope of recovery is an ethical good. There have been several cases, for example, in which a woman has been kept alive for weeks after being declared brain dead and has given birth to healthy children. Following the delivery of the child, her life-support systems were removed. More commonly, of course, these life-support systems are used to keep accident victims or patients who have had heart attacks alive until they can be treated successfully.

Nothing that I have argued in this paper should be interpreted to be critical of these uses of artificial prolongation of physical life. It is their use in cases which are without reasonable hope of recovery and which result in dehumanized and inordinately expensive continuation of physical existence that needs to be questioned.

In 1976, California became the first state to authorize living wills. Now all fifty states provide some form of statutory authority for some form of advance directive that allows a patient to specify circumstances under which he or she would choose to decline or discontinue life-sustaining treatment. In addition to the living will, also a durable power of attorney permits a person to name an agent or proxy to make health care decisions for him or her. Forty-six states and the District of Columbia authorize both living wills and durable powers of attorney. Alaska recognizes only living wills. Massachusetts, Michigan, and New York recognize only the appointment of health-care agents.

The relatively quick adoption of such legislation was prompted by the Patient Self-determination Act that Congress enacted in 1990. This act requires hospitals and other health-care entities to distribute written information at the time of admission about a patient's rights under state law to refuse medical treatment and to formulate advance directives.

In spite of these laws, much more still needs to be done than has been to date to educate the public about its rights and responsibilities in such decisions. And physicians need to exercise responsible caution in initiating intravenous lines or feeding tubes with certain patients. For, while there is no ethical distinction between failure to initiate such therapy and its discontinuation once begun, there seems to be an obvious psychological distinction between the two.

Sensitive physicians — assisted by family ministers, medical ethicists, social workers, and others — will have to deal with situations on a case-by-case basis without the luxury of rigid guidelines. And, yes, there are legal questions, inconsistent policy statements at a federal and local level, and emotional demands made by family members that have no underpinnings in reason.

In cases where counsel, discussion, and rational decisions are sought, however, the rule of thumb seems to lie within the physician's awareness of the difference between protecting, enhancing, and enabling living and simply prolonging dying. Skill and technology that do the former are admirable and ethical; the same skill and technology used for the latter are unnecessary and ill advised.

Death is not always The Enemy and is not always to be resisted. The real enemies to the patient are trauma, disease, degeneration, and unnecessary pain. The real enemies to the family are anxiety, stress, and pointless financial drain. The real enemies to the health care profession are an insensitivity which fails to see that what is best for a patient is not always the most that is possible, a fear of ever accepting death as an ally in doing what is best for a patient, and the failure to face up to the emotional-spiritual pain which is involved in these cases.

Finally, a postscript about such cases as the one in Oregon with which this essay began. What is the best way to deal with the growing movement toward physician-assisted suicide in the

United States? While some will undoubtedly insist on legislative solutions, I think the best practical solution has to do with the training of physicians, a broader provision for hospice care, and spiritual engagement by families and friends of dying persons.

More physicians need to be trained in the effective management of pain and depression in their patients. Even Dr. Pieter Admiraal, the Dutch anesthesiologist and pharmacologist who pioneered active euthanasia in the Netherlands, now insists that all pain can be treated and that euthanasia for pain can be treated. He further says that euthanasia for patient pain is social and medical malpractice.[14] Quality hospice care that takes significant financial and emotional stress off families with terminally ill patients should be covered by insurance providers. Very few carriers do so now, and yet they complain about the high cost of in-hospital medical services. Finally, we need to help families deal with the incredible stress of providing patient care for dying family members at the level of their own emotional, physical, and spiritual reserves. Otherwise, I should not be surprised to see more dying patients press for their own deaths for the sake of the "burden" they are imposing on their families.

Who knows? It just might happen yet that the best thing to come from our societal debate over euthanasia will be the willingness on the part of some of us to grapple with our fears, learn to face death in courage that arises from faith, practice love and support of others in their grappling with the same issue, and experience God's presence in the process.

Endnotes

[1]"First known suicide under Ore. Law revealed," *USA Today* (26 March 1998), 1A.

[2]Ibid.

[3]"States approach to assisted suicide emerging as a study in contrasts," *Dallas Morning News* (30 March 1998), 8A.

[4]Brain death is defined anatomically as the destruction or irreversible dysfunction of all neural tissue above the first cervical vertebra. The two basic criteria for a determination of brain death are the absence of all cerebral and brainstem functions and irreversibility.

[5]Michael Tooley, "Abortion and Infanticide," *The Rights and Wrongs of Abortion*, Marshall Cohen, Thomas Nagel, and Thomas Scanlon, eds. (Princeton, NJ: Princeton University Press, 1974), 66.

⁶Ibid., 79. Note: Tooley's second and (to him) greater worry is "whether adult animals belonging to species other than Homo sapiens may not also possess a serious right to life" (p. 79). If this line of reasoning is correct, he insists, "one may find himself driven to conclude that our everyday treatment of animals is morally indefensible, and that we are in fact murdering innocent persons" (p. 80).

⁷Language used by Paul the Apostle when speaking of the prospect of his own death in Philippians 1:23.

⁸This is not meant to suggest that all or most people who believe in an afterlife would forego measures designed to keep a terminally ill patient alive indefinitely or that all or most people without such a belief would insist on such measures. The former might insist on life support and hope for a miracle in response to prayer, and the latter might discontinue life support in favor of a quicker and more merciful death. The case studies presented in this section are designed only to construct plausible rationales for making decisions about death and dying.

⁹This is admittedly a conservative principle for determining what constitutes human life and therefore a conservative guideline for those who should be regarded as having a *prima facie* right to life. This identifies my position on the side of protecting fetal life, imperfect newborns, brain-injured teens, terminally ill adults, or the very elderly.

¹⁰A similar case that received far more publicity involved the death of James A. Michener, the novelist who died at age 90. A week before his death at his home in Austin, Texas, he ordered physicians to disconnect him from life-sustaining kidney dialysis. "James Michener, who opened worlds to readers, dies," *USA Today* (17 October 1997), 4A.

¹¹"R.I. right-to-death case splits Catholics," *USA Today* (12 January 1988), 3A.

¹²For a summary of this legislation, see Lawrence O. Gostin, "Deciding Life and Death in the Courtroom," *Journal of the American Medical Association* 278:18 (12 November 1997): 1523-1529.

¹³"Patient removed from life support, despite family's objections," *AP/Cable News Network* (20 February 1998).

¹⁴Quoted in Robin Bernhoft, "Don't kill the patient, train the doctor," *Citizen* (20 September 1993): 1-4.

Chapter Twenty-six

Is ecological responsibility a part of the gospel?

David Jackson
Meadowbrook Church of Christ
Jackson, Mississippi

In the fall of 1997, representatives of the nations of the world assembled in Kyoto, Japan. The purpose of their meeting was to address the increasing problem of world pollution. Special attention was given to "greenhouse gases" which threatened to warm the earth. The fears included melting polar icecaps, flooding coastal plains, spreading deserts, and other causes of untold suffering. Leading countries of the industrialized world were identified as the main sources of the problem, and they were expected to come forth with a solution.

While these international discussions were dealing with technological, economic, and political issues, other voices were raising questions from a different area of concern. What about the role of Christian faith in addressing individual responsibility for the state of our environment? Ought people of faith to have a sense of responsibility in the care and keeping of our environment?

Tony Campolo, in *How to Rescue the Earth without Worshipping Nature,* offers a word of caution to Christians who may become serious about preserving or restoring nature. In response to his efforts to promote ecological awareness, some have charged that he is becoming associated with "new agers" and other extremists. While he insists that his activism is a necessary extension of his Christian faith, the critics are not so sure.

Is the concern about ecology merely a passing fad? True, these days our own culture frequently reminds us to recycle, prevent waste, and avoid sources of environmental pollution. Is this matter also a question of faith? As a Christian, do concerns for ecology have a place in my faithful response to my acceptance of Jesus as Lord?

A Recent Concern

As a college student at the end of the decade of the sixties, I can recall the increasing expressions of concern as the earth's resources were measured and found wanting. The alarm was sounded that we were rapidly depleting our supplies of essential elements for human life. Minerals, arable land, petroleum, even water: all were measured in terms of years of supply. The Arab oil embargo in 1973 seemed only to underscore the truth of the predictions of doom.

The statements of anxiety made sense in view of three specific areas of study: world population growth, acknowledged depletion of essential natural resources, and the "shock" of change caused by the explosion in technological development. Who could argue with the numbers? Earth's population reached one billion for the first time somewhere around 1800 AD. Within one hundred years that number had doubled, to two billion. Only eighty years were needed to reach 4 billion, and roughly one fifth of them lived in true poverty.[1]

The measuring of resources demanded the acknowledgment that many of them were nonrenewable. In addition to the concern over materials under the earth's surface, observable changes in climate were also attributed to human activity. Russell Chandler has reported the extent of the problem:

> On the land, deforestation and desertification are the two prime enemies. Forest destruction has brought on widespread flooding and loss of topsoil, contributing to global warming, and speeded the extinction of plants and animals. Every year huge expanses of tropical forests — the equivalent of one football field per second — fall to the chainsaw and the torch.[2]

A more recent summary includes these amazing statistics:

> By the year's end, the numbers are staggering. The total loss of rain forest will equal an area the size of the state of Washington; expanding deserts will equal an area the size of the state of West Virginia; and the global population will have risen by more than 90,000,000. By the year 2000 perhaps as much as 20 percent of the life forms extant on the planet in the year 1900 will be extinct.[3]

Alvin Toffler was one of the first to signal the dangers of rapidly expanding technology. He wrote about the stress caused by our trying to adapt to the rapid pace of change in 1970 in *Future Shock*. He had coined the term, he wrote, "to describe the shattering stress and disorientation that we induce in individuals by subjecting them to too much change in too short a time."[4] In a similar vein, Neil Postman has warned that technology changes the way we view life: "Technology is ideology."[5] He continues:

> It would have been excusable in 1905 for us to be unprepared for the cultural changes the automobile would bring . . . . But it is much later in the game now, and ignorance of the score is inexcusable. To be unaware that a technology comes equipped with a program for social change, to maintain that technology is neutral, to make the assumption that technology is always a friend to culture is, at this late hour, stupidity plain and simple.[6]

To be sure, our culture has changed since the early '70s. New words — such as ecology, pollution, ecosystem and recycling — have appeared in our everyday conversations. We think and act differently as the result of our heightened concerns. A research group called the Club of Rome, in 1972 published a summary of warnings based on computer models of future conditions. The title was *The Limits to Growth*, and for the first time decision-makers began to consider how to bring about changes in the course of progress toward environmental catastrophe. The government even began to exercise influence through a new agency, the Environmental Protection Agency.

A Christian Concern?

Even though our society as a whole is much more aware of the need for environmental responsibility, does Christian faith play any role in these concerns? The question is not rhetorical. Most of us can recall hearing few sermons on the topic in the last twenty-five years. In many churches preaching has included ecological concerns only as a subpoint in larger discussions.

The cautious answer to the question is "Yes," or perhaps better, "Yes, but . . . ." Most responses to questions of ecology which take a biblical perspective begin with the consideration of creation in Genesis. While any approach will ultimately be based in God's intention for his created order, followers of Christ must first seek for guidance from Jesus, since he is our example in all things.

In the Sermon on the Mount Jesus points to the Father's care for "birds of the air" and "lilies of the field" (Matt. 6:25-30). God feeds the common birds, which are less valuable than human beings, and he clothes the ordinary grass of the field in splendor greater than that of Solomon. The fact that he pays such attention to these unremarkable elements in nature is taken as assurance that his care for us will assuage our anxiety concerning the necessities of life. God did not cease his active relationship with his creation at the end of the sixth day of creation.

Jesus made a similar point regarding sparrows and the assurance of God's provision for his people. Two of these common birds might be bought for a penny, but the Father takes note of every one of them (Matt. 10:29-31). Since his human creatures are more valuable, it follows that he will be even more vigilant in providing for their needs. If Jesus can speak with certainty of God's continuing involvement with the created, physical, nonhuman order, then the followers of Jesus must also reflect such a caring perspective.

Many of the parables of Jesus reveal a detailed knowledge of the natural cycles and, thus, a respect for the physical order made by God. In the parable of the farmer sowing his seed (Matt. 13:3-9), he used a variety of soil conditions to reflect attitudes of the human heart. Pulling weeds too soon from a field of wheat might result in damage to the crop (vv. 24-30). Therefore, judgment in the kingdom is reserved for the appointed Judge at the proper day (vv. 36-43). The fruit produced by a specific plant, by which it was useful or harmful to human purposes, easily reflected the relationship of the human heart to the true nature of an individual (Luke 6:43-45). Only a buried seed is able to produce a harvest of many seeds (John 12:24).

Respect for the physical world as reflected in the ministry of Jesus provides a ready connection with the account of creation found in Genesis. As the divine Creator spoke the words, all parts of the universe came to be, just as he intended. Six times God declared that his handiwork was "good" (1:4, 10, 12, 18, 21, 25), and finally that it was "very good" (v. 31). The modern reader has the impression of a master craftsman standing by to survey with admiration his completed work.

Then the great God handed his creation over to human caretakers. His instructions were, "Be fruitful and increase in number; fill the earth and subdue it. Rule over the fish of the sea and the birds of the air and over every living creature that moves on the ground" (Gen. 1:28). One of the first tasks that God gave to Adam was to name everything else in the created order (2:19-20). Man and woman together thus stood in creation in a position of dominion over the rest of God's creation.

Certainly the exploration of the earth, the seas, and more recently the stars — the innate curiosity to know what lies over the next hill, is a reflection of the role of human beings in their God-given capacity as rulers over creation. Science and technology, research and discovery, studies in chemistry and physics are all legitimate pursuits of this divinely intended role. I have always benefited greatly from Christian professors of various sciences who speak of the ways in which their deeper knowledge of the structures and functions of our universe serves to deepen their faith in the God who is author of all.

Virginia Stem Owens suggested some years ago that it is believers, even more than skeptical scientists, who stand to profit from an awakened sense of the importance of nature:

> . . . That thousands of blurry-eyed, nature loving Christians will shake themselves, blink, and begin to take a hard, intimate, respectful look at the handiwork of their Creator. That they will sit down on a stump or a rock somewhere silent and feel the listening, watching, thrumming sense of separation that makes it painfully impossible for human beings to live like lilies and the desire that makes it equally impossible to stop trying.[7]

A Stated Reservation

At this point a reservation must be addressed. The "yes, but" part of the answer recognizes two reasons for hesitation. The first is to realize that ecological concerns are not essentially part of "the gospel," if that term describes the good news of the significance of the death, burial, and resurrection of Jesus Christ. While we may reasonably argue that environmental sensitivity is a logical extension of loyal submission to the things of God, our position on recycling or the use of pesticides is not essential to salvation.

The second caution addresses two limits that we must recognize. The first one requires moderation in our exploitation of nature. As Stott puts it, "Our dominion is a delegated, and therefore a responsible, dominion."[8] God has entrusted the care of his physical creation to us, and we may expect an accounting for our treatment of it. Psalm 24 reminds us, "The earth is the LORD's, and everything in it." Our possession of anything as our own is, therefore, illusory. The biblical image of stewardship (Matt. 25:14-30; Luke 16:10-12) is appropriately chosen for this very reason. Our role is correctly expressed by the words in another Psalm, "The highest heavens belong to the LORD, but the earth he has given to man" (115:16).

Even our worship ought properly to reflect the understanding of giving back to God that which is already his, "I have no need of a bull from your stall or of goats from your pens, for every animal of the forest is mine, and the cattle on a thousand hills" (Ps. 50:9-10). He will declare to us either "well done, good and faithful servant," or "you wicked, lazy servant," based on our recognition of the role we must fill.

In keeping with this qualification of our role as stewards, then, we are responsible for using the earth's resources properly. Christians may perceive recycling as a response to their faith-based conviction that our God is honored when we behave responsibly toward our environment. Our use of nonrenewable resources may likewise reflect our efforts to honor the Father.

Such a view is encouraged also by consideration of the motives for much of the harm caused by technology and human consumerism. Greed, money-lust, and abuse of power are always condemned in the Bible. To the extent that these same evils drive the ruin of earth's natural resources, environmental destruction is sinful. This condition is just one more way that the suffering of the sinful world is reflected in nature (Rom. 8:18-25).

Another author who reflects this same thesis is Ronald Higgins. In 1978, he published a book entitled *The Seventh Enemy: The Human Factor in the Global Crisis*. His first six enemies were listed as overpopulation, the global shortage of food, dwindling resources, environmental crises, the nuclear threat, and the spread of technology. As you may guess, the "seventh enemy" is we, human beings.

This approach effectively counters those who would lay the responsibility for our environmental woes at the feet of biblical faith. An example is provided by the following attack on "three horrifying lines" from Genesis 1:28:

If you want to find one text of compounded horror which will guarantee that the relationship of man to nature can only be destruction,
which will atrophy any creative skill, . . . which will explain all of the
destruction and all of the despoliation accomplished by western
man for at least these 2,000 years, then you do not have to look any
further than this ghastly, calamitous text.[9]

Nature Is Not God

The second limitation is necessary if we are to recognize properly the distinctions made in the biblical version of creation. While
nature must be honored as God's handiwork, it must not be worshiped as divine. "The heavens declare the glory of God; the skies
proclaim the work of his hands" (Ps. 19:1). Our admiration of
nature ought to propel us to glorify the author of nature, rather
than to cause us to worship creation. "Since the creation of the
world God's invisible qualities — his eternal power and divine
nature — have been clearly seen, being understood from what has
been made, so that men are without excuse" (Rom. 1:20).

Furthermore, human beings stand as created beings, but on a
different and higher level than all the rest. Only the crown of God's
creation is made in his image. Dominion over the rest of creation is
the specifically designated role of human beings in God's order.
Therefore, human life is to be treated as more valuable than other
creatures because God considers it so (Matt. 10:31; 12:12).

This difference in evaluating human life versus nonhuman provides the justification for raising animals for food, keeping them as
pets, and conducting medical experimentation on them, while
abhorring such practices toward humans. While cruelty is always
evil, animals may be used as the means to a benevolent end. Human
beings, however, are always infinitely valuable in themselves and
must never be used instrumentally. One writer has suggested that
those who fail to recognize this distinction are not really closer to
nature, but alienated from it. "We don't even know enough about
nature to see the differences within it."[10] The same author criticizes
the glaringly erroneous "leap of logic" committed by some envi-
ronmentalists and animal rights activists:

They fail to see that the rights endowed to animals are not identical
with the rights of human beings. Yes, we are an animal species, but
we, by our ability to think and reason, are also different from the
wolf, the deer, the cow and the rest of creation. To deny this reality is

to run from the responsibilities it carries. No other species can alter its habitat with the deliberation that the human species can. And human beings are the only species capable of self-determination; we do not function solely out of instinct.[11]

While it is true that all of nature declares the praises of the Creator, and any part of nature may stimulate our thoughts of God, neither nature nor any of its parts are divine. Genesis presents a chronicle of activity in which God's powerful word brings instantly into existence everything that we know as a part of life on this planet. Specifically, every object of worship in the ancient world that is less than God is revealed to have been created by God. The earth itself is not "Mother" to all the rest. The waters, the great "deep" of ancient mythology, are not divine. All of the plant kingdom, including the sacred trees of pagan worship, were made by God's command. The sun, moon, and stars did not control human life on the earth, but were intended instead to serve humankind as "signs to mark the seasons and days and years." Wild animals, creeping creatures, and domestic stock were all created by the infinite desire of God. That line must never be crossed!

The Songs We Sing

Our hymns indicate an abiding awareness and appreciation of the natural world. In this instance at least, our hymnology has outpaced our practice. Stuart K. Hine's words to "How Great Thou Art" provide a good example, as they speak of our "awesome wonder" at God's works. The bird song in the "woods and forest glades" and the view "from lofty mountain grandeur" all combine to convince us of how great God is.

Equally familiar are Maltbie Babcock's words to "My Father's World," that God "speaks to me everywhere," if we have "list'ning ears" to hear it. An older hymn from Isaac Watts includes these words: "There's not a plant or flow'r below/But makes thy glories known . . . ."

A more recent hymn, "God Who Stretched the Spangled Heavens," by Catherine Cameron, gives expression to the responsibility we must shoulder in our technological age, with the plea, "Show us what we yet may do." This prayer is further articulated in the words, "Great Creator, give us guidance/Till our goals and Yours are one."

Conclusion

At the beginning of *How to Rescue the Earth*, Tony Campolo cites several Christian writers as saying that environmental concerns are the most important issues for the church in the next century. Whether or not they are correct, it does seem obvious that the way we treat the world and our environment has spiritual implications. In the first place, our respect for the things of God must surely extend to include his physical creation. In addition, whether or not those around us will give credence to the gospel we preach may depend, in some part, on how sensitive we appear to be to the welfare of the created world around us. They may not be able to see how we handle spiritual concerns, but they can understand from observation how we deal with the world God made us. Concern means very little if it does not become translated into action. To the extent that we show respect for the natural world around us, we also honor the Creator of the world.

Endnotes

[1]See John R. W. Stott, *Involvement: Being a Responsible Christian in a Non-Christian Society*, Vol. 1 (Old Tappan, NJ: Revell, 1984: reprint, 1985), 151-153.

[2]Russell Chandler, *Racing Toward 2001: The Forces Shaping America's Religious Future* (Grand Rapids: Zondervan, 1992): 73.

[3]David Orr, quoted in James M. Wall, "In Jeopardy: Sustaining the Earth," *Christian Century* (December 3, 1997): 1115.

[4]Alvin Toffler, *Future Shock* (New York: Random House, 1970), 2.

[5]Neil; Postman, *Amusing Ourselves to Death* (New York: Penguin Books, 1986), 157.

[6]Ibid.

[7]Virginia Stem Owens, "Consider the Fingerprints of God," *Christianity Today* (Nov. 17, 1978): 17.

[8]Stott, *Involvement*, 157.

[9]Ronald Higgins, *The Seventh Enemy: The Human Factor in the Global Crisis* (New York: McGraw-Hill), 162.

[10]Julia Ahlers, "Thinking Like a Mountain: Toward a Sensible Land Ethic," *Christian Century* (April 25, 1990): 434.

[11]Ibid.

SECTION NINE
QUESTIONS ABOUT ESCHATOLOGY

As this book goes to press, the change of the millennium is upon us. (Whether it is in 2000 or 2001 is quite beside the point.) And with it goes all the hope to which late twentieth century Americans have become so accustomed. Concerns about how our computers will handle the century shift are accompanied by predictions of doom and the end of the earth.

Of course this is not entirely new. There have always been those eccentrics who have confidently predicted the day of the return of Jesus, only to see the day pass and then be forced to recalculate. But even apart from these people, it has become fashionable in the Christian community to see in the chaos and evil of our world the grounds for the imminent return of Christ.

Theologically, these concerns fall under the category eschatology, a study of the last things. It is with eschatology that these last two articles are concerned, although in quite different ways.

Cecil May's article directly addresses the question of whether there really are observable signs that show Jesus is coming soon. He does this by examining the passages most often thought to give guidance on these matters.

The second article by James Walters takes a different tack, asking what difference it makes to how we live in the here and now if we truly accept the biblical point of view on eschatology. This is an altogether appropriate place to end, for it reminds us of where we began, with the conviction that doctrine is not just about what we believe; it is about how we live.

Chapter Twenty-seven

Are there signs that Jesus is coming soon?

Cecil May Jr.
Faulkner University
Montgomery, Alabama

Some of the most popular preachers on television and many best selling religious books proclaim enthusiastically and often, "Jesus is coming soon! This very generation will see the Lord's return."

From a variety of biblical contexts they cite "signs" that, they say, signify that. What are these signs? Do they really mean Christ is coming soon?

The Establishment of the Modern State of Israel

A full page advertisement in *Christianity Today* includes the statement,

> In May of 1948, after almost 2000 years of wandering, the modern state of Israel was born. Jesus said the generation that sees this will not pass away before his return.[1]

In 1970, in what became one of the best selling books of the decade, Hal Lindsay noted Jesus' words in Matthew 24:34, "Assuredly, I say to you, this generation will by no means pass away till all these things take place" (NKJV). Then he asked,

> What generation? Obviously, in context, the generation that would see the signs — chief among them the rebirth of Israel. A generation in the Bible is something like 40 years. If this is a correct deduction, then within forty years or so of 1948, all these things could take place.[2]

It is now fifty years since the modern state of Israel began. Is it certain that Jesus will return while at least some of the people who were living in 1948 are still alive? Did Jesus say anything that implies that?

Those who believe the establishment of Israel in 1948 is a sign Jesus will return within this generation may be misreading both Jesus' statement about "this generation" and the significance of the present Israeli State.

This Generation

Jesus told the Pharisees that because they and their fathers had rejected, persecuted, scourged, and killed every prophet God had sent to them, "All the righteous blood shed on the earth" would be avenged on them. Then he added, "Assuredly, I say to you, all these things will come on this generation" (Matt. 23:35-36, NKJV).

Jesus' words were true. Just a little over forty years later, Roman armies under Vespasian and Titus sacked and destroyed Jerusalem with a terrible slaughter of the Jews still there.

As the disciples and Jesus were leaving the temple grounds where these words were spoken, the disciples commented on the size and majesty of the temple buildings. Jesus responded, saying,

> Do you not see all these things? Assuredly, I say to you, not one stone shall be left here upon another that shall not be thrown down (Matt. 24:2, NKJV).

> The disciples came to Him privately, saying,
> Tell us, when will these things be? (Matt. 24:3, NKJV).

"These things" are the destruction of the temple and the city of Jerusalem. So Jesus elicited from them a question as to when that will occur, and he then proceeded to answer it. His answer culminated in the words,

> Assuredly, I say to you, this generation will by no means pass away till all these things take place (Matt. 24:34, NKJV).

The expression "this generation," in both Matthew 23 and 24, means "the sum total of people now living."

Not everyone, of course, thinks so. Most advocates of the premillennial scheme of things believe "this generation" means the Jewish race.[3] They base this view on the idea that the Greek word *genea* (generation) really means race or family. So the promise is that the Jewish race will endure until the Lord returns.

There is reason to question whether *genea* is ever used in the New Testament to mean race or family. The most common meaning is "the sum total of those born at the same time, expanded to include all those living at a given time,"[4] and that meaning fits, every time *genea* occurs. However, when not just the word "generation" but the phrase "this generation" is considered, New Testament usage makes the meaning unmistakable. Look at just two passages typical of many.

But to what shall I liken this generation? (Matt. 11:16, NKJV).

An evil and adulterous generation seeks after a sign, and no sign will be given to it except the sign of the prophet Jonah. . . . The men of Nineveh will rise in the judgment with this generation and condemn it, because they repented at the preaching of Jonah; and indeed a greater than Jonah is here" (Matt. 12:39, 41, NKJV).

"This generation" is the generation living when Jesus said that. It is the one characterized as "evil and adulterous." It is the one to whom the "sign of the prophet Jonah," which is Jesus' resurrection on the third day after his death, was given. The generation to whom Jesus spoke was the one compared to the one to whom Jonah spoke. This is so in all the New Testament usages of the phrase.

Jesus was saying, then, in Matthew 24:34, "The sum total of the people now living will not die until 'these things,' the destruction of their city and temple, are accomplished."

Hal Lindsay, and those responsible for the *Christianity Today* advertisement, recognize that "this generation" means the total of people living at a particular time. To them, Jesus is saying, "Once 'these things' begin to occur, all of them will happen within one generation." And they think "these things" include the Second Coming of Christ.

However, if that had been Jesus' meaning, he should have said "that generation" rather than "this generation." "This generation" is the people living at the time Jesus used the expression.

The Restoration of Israel and the Modern Israeli State

Prior to the Assyrians capturing and scattering the Kingdom of Israel (about 722 B.C.) and the Babylonians carrying the Kingdom of Judah into exile (about 597 B.C.), the prophets, who were prophesying the Jews would be scattered among the nations, also prophesied that the Lord would visit them in mercy and restore them to the land God had given their fathers.

There are many such promises, but they were all fulfilled following the Babylonian captivity. God did restore them to their nation. They returned under the leadership of Zerubbabel, Ezra and Nehemiah and rebuilt the walls of Jerusalem and the temple. After that return, no further promise of reestablishment of the nation is given.

In the New Testament, Old Testament promises made to Israel are fulfilled in the church, "the Israel of God" (Gal. 6:16). "They are not all Israel who are of Israel" (Rom. 9:6, NKJV). "And if you are Christ's, then you are Abraham's seed, and heirs according to the promise" (Gal. 3:29, NKJV).

The Signs of Matthew 24

A series of signs and prophecies Jesus gave in Matthew 24 is said to include some elements that have not yet occurred, or that did not occur until this generation, including the restoration of Israel to the promised land and the Second Coming of Christ. These signs of Matthew 24 are the signs usually cited in the attempt to prove Jesus' Second Coming will occur very soon.

However, the clearest and most consistent thing said by the New Testament about the Second Coming and the end of the world is that no one knows when it will occur (Mark 13:32).

Jesus warns there are no signs to announce the time is approaching, no notices in advance (Matt. 24:43). He will come "like a thief in the night" (1 Thess. 5:2; 2 Pet. 3:10). "But know this, that if the master of the house had known what hour the thief would come, he would have watched and not allowed his house to be broken into" (Matt. 24:43, NKJV).

Precise Signs of the Destruction of Jerusalem

The "signs" of Matthew 24 (and parallels in Mark 13 and Luke 21) are signs Jesus gave for the destruction of the temple and city of Jerusalem.

In this discourse Jesus is replying to the disciples' question concerning the temple, when will it be that "not one stone shall be left here upon another?" (Matt. 24:1-3, Mark 13:1-4 and Luke 21:5-7).

Jesus' response is to give his disciples a detailed series of signs in chronological order, leading up to a particular one they could recognize precisely, so they could flee Jerusalem when the destruction of the city was imminent.

The first signs mentioned are the ones so often cited today: "wars, rumors of wars, famines, earthquakes." When these occur, Jesus said, "the end is not yet" (Matt. 24:6, NKJV). "All these are the beginning of sorrows" (v. 8, NKJV).

What "end" is "not yet"? Obviously the one they had just asked about, the destruction of Jerusalem and the temple.

These signs, however, do not signify that even that end is here. Jesus says they are but preliminary signs. He is telling his disciples not to be prematurely frightened when they hear of them.

Indeed, these signs were characteristic of the generation to whom Jesus spoke, and of nearly every generation since that time, including this one. And in nearly every generation someone has read them and declared their generation, therefore, to be the last.

Jesus then says there are further signs to be noted: persecution, betrayal, apostasy on the part of many, and the gospel preached throughout the world. "Then the end will come" (Matt. 24:9-14).

There were, of course, persecutions, betrayals, and apostasies within the generation to whom Jesus was speaking, including several recorded in Acts, and, contrary again to much popular preaching, God is not still waiting for the gospel to be preached worldwide so he can bring about the end (Matt. 24:9-14). The gospel was preached to the whole world in the generation to which Jesus spoke.

Before A.D. 65 the apostle Paul wrote to the church at Colossae concerning "the gospel, which has come to you, as it has also in all the world," and, "the gospel which you have heard, which was preached to every creature under heaven" (Col. 1:6,23, NKJV). The destruction of the city and temple which Jesus was predicting occurred about five years later in A.D. 70.

If one feels limitations must be put on Paul's statements that the gospel had been preached "in all the world" and "to every creature under heaven," the same limitations can be put with equal validity on Jesus' statement that "this gospel of the kingdom will be preached in all the world."

Then, since that brings us to the point in the predicted series of signs at which "the end will come," Jesus gives a final sign which signifies time for immediate flight.

> "Therefore when you see the *'abomination of desolation,'* spoken of by Daniel the prophet, standing in the holy place" (whoever reads, let him understand), "then let those who are in Judea flee to the mountains" (Matt. 24:15-16, NKJV).

The New Testament tells us what this "abomination of desolation" is. In Luke's parallel account of this discourse, it is "Jerusalem surrounded by armies" (Luke 21:20).

The flight counseled is urgent. If they are not in their house, they are not to take time to go in to get anything. That makes a great deal of sense if, as the context indicates, Jesus is talking about the destruction of Jerusalem, and the Roman armies are already on the scene. It makes no sense at all, if he is talking about the Second Coming. Where would one go to flee the Second Coming (Rev. 6:13-14)?

"All of these things," Jesus said, would be fulfilled before "this generation" passes away (Matt. 24:34). The destruction of Jerusalem did occur within the lifetime of those to whom Jesus spoke these words.

Many generations have since come and gone, and Christ's Second Coming has still not occurred. Jesus was not giving signs of the Second Coming. He was giving signs for the destruction of the temple and city.

Admittedly, there are images in this section that sound at first reading as if they were referring to the Second Coming. Jesus says, "The sun will be darkened, and the moon will not give its light," "the stars will fall from the sky," "they will see the Son of Man coming on the clouds of the sky with power and great glory," and "he will send his angels with a loud trumpet call, and they will gather his elect from the four winds, from one end of the heavens to the other" (Matt. 24:29-31).

While our minds, hearing such language, jump to the end of time and the Second Coming, the minds of Jews in Jesus' day, steeped in the language and imagery of the Old Testament, would go back to the prophets and the kind of events they so often used imagery like this to predict.

There, this imagery (called apocalyptic language) is used to predict the fall of nations, especially when their fall is being described as a judgment of God.

Isaiah 13:10 (NKJV), for example, says,

> For the stars of heaven and their constellations
> Will not give their light;
> The sun will be darkened in its going forth,
> And the moon will not cause its light to shine.

But the context shows that the destruction of Babylon by the Medes is what is being talked about (Isa. 13:1,17).

Isaiah 19:1 says, "The LORD rides on a swift cloud, and is coming to Egypt." The rest of the chapter shows that the coming defeat of Egypt by the Assyrian army is what is being prophesied by this apocalyptic figure of the Lord riding on the clouds to judge them.

The "gathering of the elect" is signaled by a trumpet, just as it is in Isaiah 27:13 (NKJV):

> So it shall be in that day:
> The great trumpet will be blown;
> They will come,
>> who are about to perish in the land of Assyria,
>> And they who are outcasts in the land of Egypt,
>> And shall worship the Lord
>> in the holy mount at Jerusalem.

In Isaiah this gathering is the return of the people of God after the exile. In Matthew 24 it is the calling of the elect through the gospel as it is proclaimed by God's messengers.

The Greek word *angeloi* is only translated "angels" when the translators decide on the basis of context that "heavenly messengers" are meant. Otherwise it is translated by its generic meaning, "messengers." John the Baptist (Matt. 11:10), John's disciples sent by the imprisoned John to inquire if Jesus were really the Messiah (Luke 7:24), Jesus' disciples sent ahead into Samaria (Luke 9:52), and the spies received by Rahab in Jericho (Jas. 2:25) are all called *angeloi*.

Jesus said, "They will come from the east and from the west, and from the north and from the south, and sit down in the kingdom of God" (Luke 13:29, NKJV). There he was speaking of the Christian dispensation, and that is not significantly different from saying they will gather his elect from one end of heaven to the other. If Luke 13:29 is not speaking of the Second Coming, then Matthew 24:31 need not be so understood either.

Space does not permit a discussion here of every expression in the section, but they all have similar Old Testament parallels relating to God's judgments in history as he uses other nations as his instrument of punishment. Here it is his own chosen people, and the city and temple he had promised them, on whom his judgment is to be visited. No wonder the imagery is stark and strong!

No Signs of Second Coming

After relating "history in advance" to his disciples on this occasion, leading them to recognize the precise last moment they could flee the city before being trapped and destroyed with the temple, and saying all of it would happen in their generation, Jesus then turns his attention to another matter, his return.

"Of that day and hour no one knows" (Matt. 24:36, NKJV).

Mark (13:4) and Luke (21:7) both record only that the disciples asked about the destruction of the temple. Matthew, however, records that, after they asked about the temple, they also asked, "And what will be the sign of Your coming, and of the end of the age" (Matt. 24:3, NKJV). In the second section of this discourse, Jesus answers the disciples' second question.

The contrast between the two sections is striking.

In the first, a series of signs leads up to the exact moment when the end of the city is near, culminating in a final sign, the appearance of the Roman armies, when they should immediately leave the city.

History records that the Jerusalem church did obey their Lord's command to flee, and they did not, therefore, perish in the siege.[5] They understood the word of Jesus and what these signs meant.

In the section concerning the Second Coming, however, the emphasis is on the fact that no one knows the time when the Lord will come; there are no signs, no warnings. It will be like in the "days of Noah" when they "did not know until the flood came and took them all away" (Matt. 24:37-39, NKJV), like the master of a house who had no idea when a thief would come (Matt. 24:43).

The lesson is often repeated, "Therefore you also be ready, for the Son of Man is coming at an hour when you do not expect Him" (Matt. 24:44, NKJV).

This stark contrast, exact signs in their generation leading to the destruction of Jerusalem, and no signs as to the time of the Second Coming, guards against two mistakes often made concerning this passage.

Some take the whole passage to refer to the Second Coming. That is the mistake of those who cite these "signs of the end" as applying to today's generation. Some, on the other hand, take the whole passage to refer to the destruction of Jerusalem, and see no reference even in the latter part to the Second Coming.

The contrast between the two parts shows Jesus could not be talking about the same event in both parts.

The Approaching New Millennium

As we approach the day when our calendars will change from 1999 to 2000, excitement about the "new millennium" is in the air. It is no surprise that some of that excitement spills over into the religious realm and adds to the spirit of anticipation of those expecting the Lord's return in this generation.

In a colorful magazine beautifully printed on slick-finish paper, "the 6000 year period from Adam to the second advent of Jesus Christ," it is said, will be immediately followed by "the Millennial Era, the 1000 year reign of Jesus Christ."[6]

The prospect of a six-thousand-year period from creation to the Second Coming is based on six days of creation, followed by the seventh day when God rested.

> If we apply the Bible rule for prophetic time and allow a thousand years for each day (2 Pet. 3:8), this makes six thousand years of creating time, six thousand years during which the Creator is working. At the end of the six days, God sends his Son to take over the governing of the earth.[7]

Careful Bible students reading 2 Peter 3:8 in context will be surprised to note that, when Peter said, "With the Lord a day is like a thousand years, and a thousand years is like a day," he was "giving a Bible rule for prophetic time." Actually he was simply reminding us that "soon" or "a long time," when it relates to when the day of the Lord will come, is not the same with God as it may seem to us it should be.

Moreover, there are more calendar problems than seem to be recognized by those who predict the Lord's return on the basis of the change of millennia on our calendar.

For one, there is not sufficient biblical data for calculating the exact time of Adam's creation at four thousand years before the birth of Christ.

Secondly, if there were a biblical significance to the changing of the millennia on our calendar, it would likely stem from it being two thousand years from the birth of Christ. However, a monk by the name of Dionysius (6th century A.D.) calculated what he thought was the year of Christ's birth, named it A.D. 1, and designated all years according to how long before or after that event they were. The problem is, he missed it.

From circumstances recorded by Josephus, we know that Herod, called the Great, died in 4 B.C. But Herod, of course, was alive when Jesus was born. So Jesus has to have been born before 4 B.C., probably about 6 B.C. (That makes for an interesting calendar quirk; Christ was born six years "Before Christ.")

So if something of significance was supposed to occur at the beginning of the 2000th year from the birth of Jesus, it would have already happened, probably January 1, 1995! (A corollary fact: the church was established thirty-three years after the birth of Christ, but that was not A.D. 33. It was about A.D. 27.)

The approach of A.D. 1000. also gave rise to much speculation about the end, even hysteria. But it passed, and the world did not end. Will the year 2000 be the same?

For certain, the Lord will come sometime. This world will end, and resurrection and judgment will follow. But the one thing we know about its timing is that no one knows when it will be. "Of that day and hour no one knows" (Matt. 24:36, NKJV).

Some suggest that the very fact so many expect some end-of-the-world event at the dawn of the new millennium may make it less likely to occur then. But then that becomes "the hour you least expect"!

"Watch therefore, for you do not know what hour your Lord is coming" (Matt. 24:42, NKJV).

In all the speculation and discussion about millennia and signs, let us remember the most important thing: Jesus is coming again.

To trusting Christians, that is truly a "blessed hope and glorious appearing" (Titus 2:13, NKJV). To the rebellious and stubbornly disobedient, it is "a certain fearful expectation of judgment, and fiery indignation" (Heb. 10:27, NKJV).

"And what I say to you, I say to all: 'Watch'" (Mark 13:37, NKJV).

Endnotes

[1] Christianity Today (Feb. 9, 1998), 17.
[2] Hal Lindsey, *The Late Great Planet Earth*, 54.

[3]For example, C.I. Scofield, *The Scofield Reference Bible* (1945 ed.), 1034.
[4]Arndt and Gingrich, *Lexicon*, 1957, 153.
[5]Eusebius, *Ecclesiastical History*, III, 5.
[6]*Megiddo Message*, Vol. 85, No 1, January, 1998, p. 11.
[7]Ibid.

Chapter Twenty-eight

How should we live
in light of the Second Coming?

James Walters
Heartbeat Ministry
Hanover, New Hampshire

If asked the question, "What does the Second Coming have to do with ethics?" most Christians would think first of the last judgment and how its expectation, either fear of punishment or anticipation of reward, might affect one's behavior. This is certainly an important aspect of Paul's moral reasoning (See for example, 2 Cor. 5:9-11; Rom. 14:10-12; 1 Thess. 5:1-11), however, it is not the dominant feature. In order to identify and understand the dominant feature, we must explore the framework of Paul's ethical or moral reasoning.

Paul and Moral Reasoning

The letters of the Apostle Paul provide a unique window through which we may observe his moral reasoning in action. Paul was a church planter whose mission was to preach Christ where Christ had not already been named (Rom. 15:20) rather than to build on the foundations others had laid. Inevitably, therefore, he left immature churches behind. He continued to nurture these churches by return visits, the visits of coworkers, and letters. Because he was not available to be consulted on a day-to-day basis, he sought to address behavioral issues by inviting believers to engage in moral reasoning. In other words, he taught them to think like Christians. His letters, therefore, contain not only, or simply, instructions about what to do in a given situation, but an invitation to participate in all the complexities of moral reasoning that go into Christian decision-making. That Paul invites his readers to engage in moral reasoning is apparent in 1 Corinthians 10:14-22. In the introduction to this discussion, he writes, "Therefore, my dear friends, flee from the worship of idols. *I speak as to sensible people; judge for yourselves what I say*" (10:14, NRSV). He then proceeds to build an argument based on the Christian's union with Christ and the incompatibility of a contemporaneous union with an idol/demon (10:15-22).

The moral reasoning evidenced in Paul's letters includes a variety of interconnected factors which bear on decision-making in very discrete ways: the cross, traditions, the community, the measure of one's faith, judgment, spiritual gifts, Scripture, the Holy Spirit, etc.[1] By focusing in this essay on the Second Coming, we are asking more narrowly how *time* figures into Paul's moral reasoning. This is what scholars call "eschatology" (from the Greek word *eschatos*), popularly defined as the study of "last things." I prefer something like "how Christians set their watches" or "knowing what time it is" because the concern is not nearly so much with what will happen at the end as it is with knowing where one stands currently in light of the development of God's purposes in the world. This essay has two main parts. First, we will look at the Second Coming as a "reference point" in Paul's moral thought world by surveying Romans 5–8; Then we will see how Paul uses this reference point in moral reasoning by briefly analyzing texts in two of his letters, 1 Corinthians and Colossians.

The Second Coming as a Reference Point

Paul conceives of the future (the reign of Christ) as having broken into the present with the death and resurrection of Christ. This event ushered in the opportunity for those "in Christ" already to participate with Christ in the new age, though not fully. Full participation must wait until the Second Coming. This combination of participation and anticipation is reflected countless times in Paul's letters and is marked off by two reference points, the death/resurrection of Christ and the Second Coming. The Christian life has an eschatological shape because it is lived between these events. Both reference points are underscored in Paul's commentary on the Lord's Supper tradition, "For as often as you eat this bread and drink the cup, you proclaim the Lord's death until he comes" (1 Cor. 11:26, NRSV). The phrase "until he comes" is clearly a reference point that speaks volumes about the nature of the believer's experience of the present: The present is viewed as an "interim time." Instead of trying to explain this in an abstract way, I will survey Paul's most detailed introduction to this eschatological perspective.

Romans 5–8 and the Framework of Paul's Eschatology

In Romans, Paul addresses house churches in Rome that were experiencing tensions over certain Jew-Gentile issues. Consequently, in the letter he attempts to create as much common ground as possible between Jews and Gentiles. This requires undercutting the boasting of the Gentile Christian majority as well as censoring the ethnic exclusivity of some Jews.[2] After demonstrating the impartiality of God in chapters 1–4 — God is shown to be impartial both by the way he saves (Jews and Gentiles alike are saved by faith) and by the way he judges (Jews and Gentiles alike will be judged by their deeds) — he moves on to a discussion of the believer's life of faith in a manner that transcends the categories of "Jew" and "Gentile." In Romans 5 Paul sets up the argument by grouping all human beings, whether Jew or Gentile, in Adam or in Christ so that the question of where one stands in relation to the Law of Moses could be transcended by a larger question.

Notice how the first eleven verses of chapter 5 shift the previous discussion from the question of *how God saves* to *how God sanctifies* the saved. Because of Christ's redemptive work, God is no longer an enemy. This, however, does not mean the end of conflict for believers, but it does underscore that God is an ally in the believers' struggles, not a foe.

Paul clarifies the nature of the struggle Christians face in 5:12-21 by introducing two rival solidarities or dominions, Adam and Christ. Sin reigns over all human beings because they have shared in Adam's sin by following his example of disobedience. Notice how Paul speaks here of "sin" as a power that reigns rather than "sins" as individual misdeeds. This power reigned even before Moses gave the Law and individual misdeeds could be counted. Against this reigning power of sin, typified by Adam, Paul places the (even more potent) reigning power of grace, typified by Christ. Associated with Adam are sin, death, trespass, condemnation and disobedience while their opposites — grace, life, righteousness, justification and obedience — are associated with Christ.

Not surprisingly, Paul's discussion of Christian behavior in chapter six fits the frame Paul constructed in chapter 5. The gist of Paul's argument in chapter 6 is that since Christians are no longer "in Adam" but are "in Christ," their new identities must be reflected in their lives. Since Christians have shared in Christ's death by their baptism and have been raised to walk in "newness of life," while awaiting their own "resurrection like his," any continuation of a life reflecting Adam is unthinkable. Christians no longer live under the dominion or reign of sin (Adam) and must not, therefore, permit sin to regain a foothold in their lives.

Although this language is by now familiar to many Christians, the eschatological assumptions that stand behind it are not. Notice how Paul assumes that the reign of Adam/sin predated the reign of Christ/grace, but now they are concurrent dominions. Their concurrent status is what explains the continuing struggle Christians face. Sin continues to look for an opportunity in the lives of Christians to reestablish Adam's dominion. The remainder of the argument in chapter six drives home Paul's point that those "in Christ" must not permit sin to reign in their bodies.

In chapter 7 Paul makes it clear at the outset that Christians are no longer "bound" to the Law; however, he spends the bulk of the chapter shifting responsibility for the problem human beings face from the Law to sin. The Law is "holy," "just," "good," and "spiritual" (cf. 7:12,14). Although the Law was open to exploitation (cf. 7:8,11), the actual culprit was sin. In terms so graphic that many scholars conclude that Paul could only have been writing about his pre-Christian experience, the Apostle describes the conflict one encounters with sin while one is in Christ but not yet completely free from Adam (7:15-25).

The limits of these concurrent dominions (Adam/Christ) are clarified in chapter 8 as Paul explains how the Holy Spirit assists believers in their struggles with sin. Those who are in Christ have their minds set on the Spirit and walk according to the Spirit. Consequently, they fulfill the "just requirement of the Law" (vv. 1-8, NRSV). The Spirit dwelling in Christians bears witness that they belong to God even while they await their ultimate resurrection through the Spirit of him "who raised Christ from the dead" (vv. 9-11). In the meantime they reject the power of the flesh, putting to death the deeds of the body by the power of the indwelling Spirit (vv. 12-17).

Verses 18-25 are the critical time setting verses. This paragraph describes Christians, even the whole creation, living in hope of final redemption. The sufferings of the "present time" are contrasted with the "glory that is to be revealed." The creation was "subjected to futility" and since that time has been in "bondage to decay," a clear reference to the cursing of the ground in the Genesis story of Adam's fall. Those in Christ who have the "first fruits of the Spirit," as well as the creation itself, groan like a woman in childbirth awaiting freedom. Clearly the "glorious liberty of the children of God" is to be realized at the "redemption of our bodies" (8:21b,23b, RSV). This is when the reign of Adam is finally ended. Human beings no longer possessing bodies like Adam are no longer under the threat of sin exploiting them through their kinship with him. Even the creation is no longer under the curse of Adam's transgression.

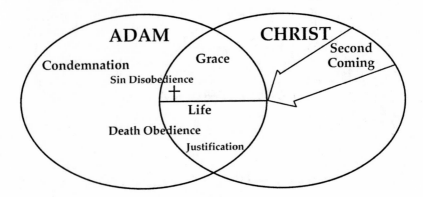

Now a fuller diagram is possible. This time by using overlapping ellipses to represent the concurrent dominions we will be able to depict more clearly the limits of the dominions.

For Paul, God's future reign has already broken into the present with the death and resurrection of Christ. Those who are in Christ already participate in that reign while still having bodies like Adam. Consequently, although they are no longer under the dominion of sin, they are vulnerable to the power of sin, which is ever seeking to reestablish its reign in their lives. Christians are able to resist this assault, however, by keeping their minds set on the Spirit and enlisting the aid of the Spirit in "putting to death the deeds of the body." They live in hope, anticipating the redemption of their bodies and freedom from the struggle that now challenges them.

Those who are "in Christ" were *formerly* slaves of sin, but are *now* slaves of righteousness; nevertheless, they have *not yet* experienced the redemption of their bodies though they have *already* received the first fruit of the Spirit, the Spirit of him who raised Christ's body from the dead and will raise their bodies as well. You can see why Paul Sampley uses the phrase "Walking Between the Times" as shorthand for Paul's moral reasoning.

We have used Romans 5–8 to explore the eschatological framework of Paul's moral reasoning. Next we will observe how Paul used eschatology to address behavioral issues in two other letters, 1 Corinthians and Colossians. Seeing how these ideas function is the best way to understand what the Second Coming has to do with ethics in Paul. Let's turn our attention now to 1 Corinthians, a letter where Paul does more "clock setting" than in any other letter.

Eschatology and Moral Reasoning in 1 Corinthians

The Corinthians tended to view themselves as somewhat independent of their physical bodies as if the final redemption of their bodies had already occurred. This resulted in an overspiritualized existence in which moral issues associated with the body seemed irrelevant or unspiritual. Thus, inappropriate actions resulted from mistaken views of their bodies, which were in turn the result of mistaken eschatological views. Consequently, Paul repeatedly attempts to "reset their clocks" so that their views of their bodies would be corrected. Scholars call the Corinthian viewpoint an "over-realized eschatology" because it assumes that realities belonging to the future are already being experienced or "realized" in the present.

In the first four chapters of 1 Corinthians Paul addresses the problem of the Corinthians' misplaced allegiance to teachers and the schisms that resulted. In the conclusion of Paul's remarks on this problem, he challenges the frame of reference the Corinthians use when they evaluate teachers by sarcastically contrasting their views of themselves with the experience of the apostles. Notice the "clock-setting" references in Paul's remarks:

> *Already* you are filled! *Already* you have become rich! Without us you have become kings! And would that you did reign, so that we might

share the rule with you! For I think that God has exhibited us apostles as last of all, like men sentenced to death; because we have become a spectacle to the world, to angels and to men. We are fools for Christ's sake, but you are wise in Christ. We are weak, but you are strong. You are held in honor, but we in disrepute. *To the present hour* we hunger and thirst, we are ill clad and buffeted and homeless, and we labor, working with our own hands. When reviled, we bless; when persecuted, we endure; when slandered, we try to conciliate; *we have become, and are now,* as the refuse of the world, the offscouring of all things (1 Cor. 4:8-13, RSV).

If the Corinthians view themselves as "already reigning," they are apt to view Paul's sufferings as an indication of weakness, a spiritual deficiency of some sort. That they drew this conclusion is apparent in 2 Corinthians where Paul has to defend his apparent weakness (cf. esp. 2 Cor. 11:16–12:10). How one responds to suffering and difficulties of various kinds is determined largely by one's eschatological views. This is clear in a text we already discussed, Romans 8:18 (RSV): "The sufferings of this present time are not worth comparing with the glory that is to be revealed." Note how "sufferings" are *now* and "glory" is *not yet.* The Corinthians are mixed up about what is *now* and what is *not yet.*

Related to this is also the elaborate "clock-setting" Paul does in 1 Corinthians 15. In this chapter Paul responds primarily to Corinthians who believed they had already experienced the resurrection, making any future resurrection of the body irrelevant. Paul argues that a future resurrection is certain, and any claim to the contrary undermines belief in Christ's resurrection (15:12-14). Furthermore, he is adamant that the future resurrection of Christians is a bodily resurrection, though he admits that the body will be changed. Note how this supports a worldview wherein Christians are more connected to their bodies. What one does in one's body has more profound implications since the body, at least in its transformed state — is eternal.

In this same chapter, Paul uses the Adam-Christ typology we saw earlier in Romans and associates the body with Adam and the spirit with Christ. The tension between the two, however, is not resolved until the Second Coming. Notice again the clock setting. Christ has *already* been raised; Christians have *not yet* been raised; at the *present time* Christians share the body of Adam; the reign of Christ has *already* broken into the present; however, Christ's enemies have *not yet* been defeated completely; death has *not yet* been destroyed; those in Christ *now* live during a time of struggle; at the Second Coming, when all the enemies of Christ are defeated, the Kingdom will be given back to God; God will be everything to everyone; Adam will be nothing to anyone.

The ethical implications of Paul's reasoning come to the surface when he argues that if the opposite view were true, one should "eat and drink" and be merry (1 Cor. 15:32). Moreover, his final exhortation in the chapter calls the Corinthians to a productive stewardship of their bodies since their actions are "not in vain" (15:58).

As you can see, Paul's view of the body is informed by eschatology. Because believers know that their bodies will inherit eternal life, changed though they may be, they treat them as sacred temples of the Holy Spirit. In fact, Paul uses this very terminology in the conclusion of a discussion of sexual morality in 1 Corinthians 5–6. Paul rejects the view that sexual intercourse is merely an animal appetite without moral implications. Instead, he argues, on the basis of the Christian's union with Christ, that to have sexual relations with a prostitute would be to join Christ to a prostitute. Moreover, because the body will be raised, it cannot be treated as spiritually irrelevant (cf. 5:12-20). The very notion that a temple can be defiled assumes a connection between the spiritual and material that Paul aims to underscore for the Corinthians.

Because Christians are "walking between the times," they can neither be world denying (ascetic) nor world embracing (libertine). This ambiguous status is reflected most clearly in 1 Corinthians 7. In this chapter Paul takes being "in the world" very seriously as he responds to what appear to be "world denying" approaches to marriage and sexual relations on the part of some at Corinth. It is clear that Paul takes sexual appetites seriously when he cautions married Christians against practicing sexual abstinence in marriage. The same viewpoint is reflected in his disclaimer that not all have the "gift" to remain unmarried (7:7).

On the other hand, he exhorts those who are considering marriage to remain single, or direct their daughters to do so, and gives an eschatological reason. Paul's instructions, ". . . let those who have wives be as though they had none, and those who mourn as though they were not mourning, and those who rejoice as though they were not rejoicing, and those who buy as though they had no goods, and those who deal with the world as though they had no dealings with it" (7:29, RSV), are bracketed by clear eschatological references. This ambiguous posture is to be observed because the "time has grown short" (7:29, RSV), and "the present form of this world is passing away" (7:31, NRSV).

It should be apparent that to the Corinthians, with their "over-realized" eschatology, Paul shouted, "Not yet! Not yet!" However, it is interesting that to the Colossians, who had an "under-realized eschatology," he shouted, "Already! Already!" This contrast will further clarify how eschatology figures into Paul's moral reasoning.

Eschatology and Moral Reasoning in Colossians

The Colossian Christians had fallen under the influence of false teachers who questioned the gospel they were taught by Epaphras and challenged the approach to regulating behavior they had been following. These teachers offered an alternative approach that required a number of Jewish observances along with a world-denying approach to regulating behavior. They managed to exert their authority over the Colossian Christians by exploiting their fears, fear that they had *not yet* been delivered from the guilt of their sins and fear that they were *still* in danger from spiritual powers.

Paul claims that these teachers were hawking a message that was based on "philosophy and empty deceit, according to human tradition, according to the elemental spirits of the universe, and not according to Christ" (2:8, NRSV). He tells the Colossians that they have *already* come to "fullness" in Christ. Consequently, they did not need what the false teachers offered. He specifies two benefits associated with the cross that seem especially directed toward undermining the false teachers' appeals to fear. In verses 11-14 he emphasizes that by their baptism the Colossian Christians have already experienced a "spiritual circumcision" that erased the debt that stood against them (i.e. the guilt of their sins) by virtue of what Christ did on the Cross. In verse 15 he adds that the Cross also marks the "disarming of the rulers and authorities." These are not human political leaders, but rather spiritual forces (cf. Eph. 6:10ff).

After Paul explains that the Colossians have nothing to fear, because their debt of sin has been removed and the spiritual powers have been disarmed, he begins to deal directly with the ways in which the false teachers have attempted to regulate their behavior on the basis of these fears. In verses 16-20 he exhorts the Colossians not to allow the false teachers to condemn or judge them any longer for failing to observe certain Jewish practices. His rationale for rejecting their approach to behavior regulation comes, however, in verses 20-23, and it is here that the eschatological dimensions of his thought come to the surface. By submitting to regulations like "Do not handle, Do not taste, Do not touch," they were acting as if they *still* belonged to the world and were needing to free themselves from the world by following these world-denying regulations. If they did not follow these regulations, they were apparently told they would be in danger from spiritual powers. Paul says in effect, "Not so!" You have *already* died with Christ to the elemental spirits of the universe. You should not be living as though you *still* belonged to the world.

I hope the eschatological diagram presented above is coming back to your mind. If you put "elemental spirits of the universe" and the "debt of sins" in the domain of Adam, you can see the problem. They have an "under-realized" eschatology. If they have adopted a "handle not, taste not, touch not" approach to getting out of their bondage to the world they need to be told that they have *already* been delivered from bondage to the world. The regulations for behavior modification the false teachers have offered have "an appearance of wisdom in promoting self-imposed piety, humility, and severe treatment of the body, but they are of no value in checking self-indulgence" (2:23, NRSV). Rather, those who are *already* in Christ set their minds on things above and put off what belonged to their old self/Adam (3:1-11).

Conclusion

For Paul, the Second Coming is not simply Judgment Day. Rather, it is the climactic wrapping up of God's purposes, which has already entered its final phase with the death and resurrection of Christ. It is not enough to know what actions will be considered acceptable or unacceptable at the Last Judgment so they can be enforced in anticipation. Imagine for a moment what a disaster it would have been if the Colossian letter had been sent mistakenly to the Corinthians or vice-versa. Shouting *not yet* to the Colossians or *already* to the Corinthians would have been a spiritual and moral disaster. When we understand that, we are beginning to understand what the Second Coming has to do with ethics in Paul's writings.

And, most important, we might know in our own churches when we should say *not yet* and when we should say *already.*

Endnotes

[1]In my judgment the best explanation of how these interconnecting factors play out in Paul's moral reasoning is found in Paul Sampley's book, *Walking Between the Times: Paul's Moral Reasoning* (Minneapolis: Fortress, 1991).

[2]For a detailed analysis of the context of these issues, cf. James C. Walters, *Ethnic Issues in Paul's Letter to the Romans* (Valley Forge, PA: Trinity Press International, 1993).

$\Diamond$

Dr. Harold Hazelip — a short sketch

$\Diamond$

Don L. Meredith
Harding Graduate School of Religion
Memphis, Tennessee

Herbert Harold Hazelip, the son of Herbert and Maggie (Ferguson) Hazelip, was born in Asphalt, Kentucky, on August 3, 1930. His eight siblings were Raymond (deceased), Lawrence (of Pasadena, TX), Woodrow (deceased), Edna Lewis (of Asphalt, Kentucky), Ruth Duvall (of Louisville, Kentucky), Charlotte Willison (of Nashville), Eva Douglas (of Nashville), and Marie, who died as a result of an accident at the age of fourteen. He married Helen Frances Royalty on March 23, 1956. They have two sons, Pat and Jeff, and five grandchildren.

Harold was baptized on August 10, 1944, and graduated from high school before his sixteenth birthday. He attended Freed-Hardeman College and graduated with a B.A. in Bible from David Lipscomb College in 1950. He received a B.D. from Southern Baptist Theological Seminary in 1958 and in 1967 completed a Ph.D. at the University of Iowa, with a major in religion and a minor in speech. In addition to his degree studies was a study tour of England and Scotland in 1966 and a leave the first six months of 1983 to do research in Cambridge, England, in the area of ethics, with an emphasis on biomedical ethics.

Dr. Hazelip's first sermon in Asphalt, Kentucky, on January 26, 1947, began a thirty-five year preaching career. He preached at the following three congregations while obtaining his education: Central Church of Christ in Owensboro, Kentucky, 1949–53; Taylor Boulevard Church of Christ in Louisville, Kentucky, 1954–64, and the Central Church of Christ in Cedar Rapids, Iowa, 1964–67. He served as pulpit minister at the Highland Street Church of Christ in Memphis, November 1967–May 1982, during his years at the Harding Graduate School of Religion. He is an outstanding communicator who can present a challenging message in an average of only twenty-three minutes (according to the Highland Street members).

Dr. Hazelip has traveled widely and been a popular speaker throughout the United States. He has lectured at all the lectureships of the colleges and universities associated with the Churches of Christ, at a number of these several times. He has been a frequent speaker at other lectureships, retreats, encampments, seminars, and workshops throughout his career. He has preached in at least twenty-five states, Canada, New Zealand, Australia, Singapore, Pakistan, Israel, France, and Russia. He made a sixteen-nation tour of mission work among Churches of Christ in 1963, a mission tour of Germany and Spain in 1975, and in the summer of 1986 lectured to members of a Holy Land tour on the biblical importance of the sites on their itinerary.

Dr. Hazelip's national reputation is probably the result of his mass media ministry, which began in the early days of his career with the first two congregations he served. He conducted a daily radio program in Owensboro, Kentucky, for three years and a weekly radio program in Louisville, Kentucky, for five years, but is most well known for his work with the *Herald of Truth*. He began with the *Herald of Truth* as a scriptwriter for the programs in 1971, was a guest speaker on the radio program in the summers of 1973 and 1974, and a co-speaker in 1975. He began as a guest speaker on the television program in 1972 and in January 1975 joined Batsell Barrett Baxter on a regular basis on the TV program. After twenty-two successful years as a featured speaker, he terminated his work with the *Herald of Truth* on December 31, 1992.

Dr. Hazelip has also written extensively for the publications associated with the Churches of Christ. He served on the editorial board of the *20th Century Christian*, *Alternative*, and *Restoration Quarterly*. He served as editor of *UpReach*, May 1982–February 1989; senior editor, March 1989–March 1993; and editor-at-large since April 1993. He wrote an article in every issue of the first twelve volumes of *UpReach* and published seventy-five articles in its first thirteen years of publication. His practical articles on ethical issues, faith building, spiritual development, and marriage and the family have made valuable contributions to our literature.

Through his teaching and administrative roles, Dr. Hazelip has also played a significant role in the Churches of Christ. He came to the Harding Graduate School of Religion as associate professor of doctrine in September 1967 and became the school's second dean in fall 1972. Students appreciated his classes in preaching, Christian doctrine, philosophy of religion, and Christian ethics, and he continued to teach part-time while serving as dean. The school thrived during his tenure as dean. In December 1972 the school received its regional accreditation from the Southern Association of Colleges and Schools. The school's physical plant was greatly improved. Both a new classroom building and an addition to the library were completed in 1978, and the E.H. Ijams Administration Building was later refurbished. Among the changes in the degree programs was the redesigning of the Master of Theology curriculum in 1974, which significantly changed enrollment patterns. While Dr. Hazelip was dean, enrollment increased from 167 in fall 1972 to a school record fall enrollment of 282 in 1982 and spring enrollment of 286 in 1978. In spring 1986 Dr. Hazelip resigned to become president of Lipscomb University.

During Dr. Hazelip's eleven years as president, there were many positive changes at Lipscomb University. He worked hard to increase mission awareness among students and faculty. He made annual trips to foreign mission sites at his own expense and spoke in thirty to sixty congregations annually to promote mission emphasis. As a result hundreds of students are now involved in missions in some way. The university also began its overseas program in Vienna, Austria, and has enjoyed record enrollments during several of his years.

In 1988 the University achieved Level III accreditation by the Southern Association of Colleges and Schools. The name was changed to Lipscomb University, and the business administration, music, and social work programs received professional accreditation. The university completed two major fund raising campaigns, and more than $20 million in construction and renovation were completed on the campus. Among these additions were a new university library and the installation of a computer system, which included a campus-wide fiber optic network with Internet connections in each dormitory room and faculty office. Faculty teaching loads were reduced, and a faculty sabbatical program was instituted.

Dr. Hazelip retired as president of Lipscomb University on May 31, 1997. He serves as chancellor of the university and continues to work in fund raising. He taught the Bible component in the overseas program in Vienna in fall 1997 and teaches two courses in doctrine in the Bible department each semester.

Bibliography of written works of Dr. Harold Hazelip

◇

Compiled by Don L. Meredith
Harding Graduate School of Religion
Memphis, Tennessee

1962

The Truth about Taylor Boulevard. Louisville, KY: Taylor Boulevard Church of Christ, 1962.

1966

"How to Interpret the Bible." *Abilene Christian College Lectures* (1966): 73-82.

1967

"The Challenge of the 'Death of God.'" In *The Church, the Campus, the Challenge.* John F. Wilson, ed., 42-53. Bible Chair Lectures, 1967 [Springfield, MO, 1967].
"The Challenge of the New Morality." In *The Church, the Campus, the Challenge.* John F. Wilson, ed., 17-29. Bible Chair Lectures, 1967. [Springfield, MO, 1967].
"Stephen Marshall: Preacher to the Long Parliament." Ph.D. diss., University of Iowa, 1967.

1968

"Baptism and the Believers' Church." *Mission* 1 (Jan. 1968): 7-10.
"The Inspired Word." *Harding College Lectures* (1968): 93-101.
"What About the Signs of Matthew 24?" *Fort Worth Christian College Lectures* (1968): 105-118.

1969

"The Local Minister." *Harding of Memphis Graduate School Bulletin* 8 (Sept. 1969): 2-3; reprinted in *Minister's Monthly* 15 (Oct. 1969): 53-55.

"The Ethical Standard in the Bible." *The Spiritual Sword* 1 (Jan. 1970): 45-46.

Review of *Fundamentals of Faith*, by Carl F. H. Henry. *Restoration Quarterly* 13 (1970): 182-183.

1970

"A Time for Faith in a Day of Unbelief." *Fort Worth Christian College Lectures* (1970): 256-286.

"Today's Protestantism." *Abilene Christian College Lectures* (1970): 260-268.

1971

"A First Century Faith in the Twentieth Century." *Harding College Lectures* (1971): 127-134.

"Jesus' Attitude toward Scripture." *Harding Graduate School of Religion Lectures* (1971): 106-114.

Review of *The Protest of a Troubled Protestant*, by Harold O. J. Brown. *Restoration Quarterly* 14 (1971): 60.

"The Wonderful Word in Worship." *Fort Worth Christian College Lectures* (1971): 112-122.

1972

"Choosing One's Niche — Under God." *Harding of Memphis Graduate School Bulletin* 11 (Dec. 1972): 2.

"In the Image of God (Genesis 1:26,27)." *Lubbock Christian College Lectures* (1972): 9-14; reprinted in *UpReach* 2 (Mar./Apr. 1980): 24-27, 30.

"Jesus, Lord and Savior." *Harding College Lectures* (1972): 280-288.

"The Message of the Church." *Abilene Christian College Lectures* (1972): 46-55.

"The Search for Meaning in Life." In *Spiritual Power*, edited by J.D. Thomas, 99-108. Abilene: Biblical Research Press, 1972.

"Why Has Christianity Failed?" In *Spiritual Power*, edited by J.D. Thomas, 109-119. Abilene: Biblical Research Press, 1972.

1973

"Futalgia." *Harding of Memphis Graduate School Bulletin* 12 (May 1973): 2.

"Habits, Schedules and Semesters." *Harding of Memphis Graduate School Bulletin* 12 (Aug. 1973): 2.

"Harding Graduate School Fully Accredited." *Harding of Memphis Graduate School Bulletin* 11 (Jan. 1973): 2

"Image and Influence." *20th Century Christian* 35 (Sept. 1973): 36-37.

"An Impossible Dream." *Opportunity Magazine* 4 (Summer 1973): 6-7.

"Nothing Gold Can Stay." *Harding of Memphis Graduate School Bulletin* 12 (Apr. 1973): 2; reprinted in *20th Century Christian* 42 (Mar. 1980): 4-5.

"Of Seagulls and Graduate Study." *Harding of Memphis Graduate School Bulletin* 12 (July 1973): 2.

"The Peter Principle and You." *Harding of Memphis Graduate School Bulletin* 12 (Nov. 1973): 2.

"Scholarship or Evangelism?" *Harding of Memphis Graduate School Bulletin* 11 (Feb. 1973): 2.

"Should Preachers Study Theology?" *Harding of Memphis Graduate School Bulletin* 12 (Apr. 1973): 3.

1974

"Be Happy." *Power for Today* 20 (July/Aug. 1974): 32.

"Be Perfect." *Power for Today* 20 (July/Aug. 1974): 25.

"Be Reconciled." *Power for Today* 20 (July/Aug. 1974): 62.

"Be Thankful." *Power for Today* 20 (July/Aug. 1974): 45.

"Burial of Christ." *Lubbock Christian College Lectures* (1974): 55-62.

"Graduate Study and Missions." *Harding of Memphis Graduate School Bulletin* 13 (Dec. 1974): 2.

"On Developing Leadership." *Harding of Memphis Graduate School Bulletin* 13 (Nov. 1974): 2.

"Pursuing the Ideal." In *What Lack We Yet?* edited by J.D. Thomas, 299-301. Abilene: Biblical Research Press, 1974.

"Revelation 20 and the Millennium." *Harding College Lectures* (1974): 207-216; reprinted in *Restoration Quarterly* 18 (1975): 229-235 and *Magnolia Bible College Lectures* (1984): 56-62.

"To School or Not to School." *Harding of Memphis Graduate School Bulletin* 13 (April 1974): 2.

1975

The Bible Answers. Abilene: Herald of Truth, 1975.

"Fall Semester at Harding Graduate School." *Gospel Advocate* 117 (21 Aug. 1975): 538.

"Lifelong Learning." *Harding of Memphis Graduate School Bulletin* 14 (Dec. 1975): 2.

The Lord Reigns: A Survey of the Book of Revelation. Abilene: Herald of Truth, 1975.

"A Quiet Storage Space." *Harding of Memphis Graduate School Bulletin* 14 (April 1975): 1; reprinted with a few changes in *20th Century Christian* 38 (Feb. 1976): 15.

The Voyage of Life. Abilene: Herald of Truth, 1977. Based on sermons preached on the Herald of Truth, Nov. 1975.

1976

"But One Thing." *Harding of Memphis Graduate School Bulletin* 15 (May 1976): 2.

"The Christian and the Revolution." *20th Century Christian* 38 (Jan. 1976): 20-21.

"Getting Ready for Ministry." *Harding of Memphis Graduate School Bulletin* 15 (Nov. 1976): 2.

I Believe. Abilene: Herald of Truth, 1976. Transcripts of Herald of Truth radio sermons aired Sept. 5-Nov. 28, 1976. Published by Herald of Truth in 1982 as *Becoming What You Believe: Practicing the Christian Lifestyle*.

"The Joy of Forgiveness." *Harding College Lectures* (1976): 303-310.

"One Person Makes the Difference." *20th Century Christian* 39 (Dec. 1976): 12-13.

"The Role of Women in the Church." *Harding College Lectures* (1976): 51-55.

"Till Death Do Us Part." *20th Century Christian* 39 (Oct. 1976). 19-20, 31.

"Total Fitness." *Harding of Memphis Graduate School Bulletin* 14 (Jan. 1976): 2; reprinted in *20th Century Christian* 41 (May 1979): 15-17.

"What to Do with Our World?" *Harding of Memphis Graduate School Bulletin* 15 (April 1976): 2.

1977

"The Creating Word." *20th Century Christian* 39 (Sept. 1977): 5-6.

Discipleship. 20th Century Sermon series, v. 9. Abilene: Biblical Research Press, 1977.

"The Latest Thing in the Religious Scene Today." *Freed-Hardeman College Lectures* (1977): 202-204.

"The Library Is the Hub." *Harding of Memphis Graduate School Bulletin* 15 (Feb. 1977): 1-2.

"Preaching on the Future." *Harding of Memphis Graduate School Bulletin* 15 (Mar. 1977): 2.

"Read Again the Conversions in Acts." *Gospel Light* 47 (Sept. 1977): 139.

"Reading the Future." *Harding Graduate School of Religion Bulletin* 16 (Aug. 1977): 2.

"Receiving and Giving: The Rhythm of the Christian Life." *Firm Foundation* 94 (1 Feb. 1977): 68.

"Seated with Christ." *Lubbock Christian College Lectures* (1977): 58-66.

"Spiritual Strength and Encouragement." *Christian Woman* 45 (Oct. 1977): 23-24.

"Where Are the Heroes?" *Harding Graduate School of Religion Bulletin* 16 (Nov. 1977): 2; reprinted in *20th Century Christian* 41 (May 1979): 14-15.

1978

"Awesome Power of a Young Man's Vision." *Christian Chronicle* 35 (21 Feb. 1978): 1, 4; reprinted in *Gospel Herald* 44 (Mar. 1978): 17.

"Depression." *HGSR Bulletin* 18 (Oct. 1978): 1-2.

"Developing Spirituality." *Abilene Christian University Lectures* (1978): 11-17.

"God Is My Fuhrer." *20th Century Christian* 40 (Apr. 1978): 11-13.

"I Am the Resurrection." *20th Century Christian* 40 (Mar. 1978): 11-13.

"In God We Trust." *Harding Graduate School of Religion Bulletin* 18 (Aug. 1978): 1-2.

"'Marriage' — Its Meaning." In *Your Marriage Can Be Great*, edited
    by Thomas B. Warren, 94-97. Jonesboro, AR: National
    Christian Press, 1978.
"Restoring the Ideal." *20th Century Christian* 40 (May 1978): 6-7.
"You Make a Difference." *Harding Graduate School of Religion
    Bulletin* 18 (Dec. 1978): 3.

1979

"Because He Came." *UpReach* 1 (Nov./Dec. 1979): 4-7.
"Believe the Years, Not the Hours." *Harding Graduate School of
    Religion Bulletin* 19 (Aug. 1979): 2.
"Calm in the Middle of the Storm." *UpReach* 1 (June 1979): 7-8.
"The Christian Graduate School As a Dean Sees It." *Tri-State
    Christian Observer* 12 (May 1979): 2-3.
"The Church Today." *20th Century Christian* 41 (Feb. 1979): 31-33.
"*Devotional Guide to Bible Lands* (with Batsell Barrett Baxter). Grand
    Rapids, Baker Book House, 1979.
"The God Who Revealed Himself." *UpReach* 1 (Aug. 1979): 12-14.
"The God Who Wouldn't Give Up." *UpReach* 1 (Oct. 1979): 8-11;
    reprinted in *UpReach* 4 (Sept./Oct. 1982): 21-23 and pub-
    lished as "Will God's Love Ever Give Up?" In *Discover
    God's Love in Your Life*, 1-13. Fort Worth: Sweet Publishing
    Company, 1985.
"The Greeks Had a Word for It." *UpReach* 1 (Feb. 1979): 15-17.
"Matthew 19:3-12: an Exegesis." *Abilene Christian University
    Lectures* (1979): 162-170.
"Shall We Call the Bible Inerrant?" *Alternative* 5 (Spring 1979): 9-14.
"Sit Right Down." *Harding Graduate School of Religion Bulletin* 19
    (Nov. 1979): 2; reprinted in *Gospel Herald* 46 (Sept. 1980): 7.
What God Wants Most: A Study of the Ten Commandments. Abilene:
    Herald of Truth, 1979. Presented as Herald of Truth radio
    programs Feb. 4-Apr. 8, 1979.
"When We Cease to Be Good." *UpReach* 1 (Apr. 1979): 6-8.

1980

"Barriers to Fellowship." *20th Century Christian* 43 (Oct. 1980): 7-8.
"Enough Is Enough!" *Harding Graduate School of Religion Bulletin* 20
    (Feb. 1980): 2; reprinted in *The Sower's Sourcebook* 2 (Feb.
    1986): 1,8.

"For Love of Family." *Christian Family* 6 (Aug. 1980): 13-14; reprinted in *Christian Family* 12 (Mar. 1986): 8-9. Published in a slightly different version in *UpReach* 3 (Sept./Oct. 1981): 16-19.

"Gifts of God's Grace." *UpReach* 2 (May/June 1980): 12-15, 28-29; reprinted in *UpReach* 3 (Mar./Apr. 1981): 20-23.

"Heralds of Hope." *Harding Graduate School of Religion Bulletin* 20 (Sept. 1980): 2.

"How to Find Peace with God." *UpReach* 2 (July/Aug. 1980): 16-19, 29-30; reprinted as AThe Search for Personal Peace." *UpReach* 16 (Jan.-Mar. 1994): 27-29.

"It Takes All Kinds." *UpReach* 2 (Nov./Dec. 1980): 21-23.

"The Last Third of Life." *UpReach* 2 (Sept./Oct. 1980): 8-11, 28.

"Power and Authority." *Harding Graduate School of Religion Bulletin* 20 (Mar. 1980): 1-2.

"Righteousness in the Home." *Alternative* 6 (Summer 1980): 20-24.

"A Steward Must Be Faithful." *Harding University Lectures* (1980): 70-75.

"Trapped by Uppers and Downers." *UpReach* 2 (Jan./Feb. 1980): 8-11, 28.

"We Give Thee but Thine Own." *Harding University Lectures* (1980): 1-9.

1981

Anchors in Troubled Waters: How to Survive the Crises in Your Life (with Batsell Barrett Baxter and Joe R. Barnett). Grand Rapids: Baker, 1981.

"But God Was at Work . . ." *20th Century Christian* 44 (Nov. 1981): 27-28.

"Can You Help Me Believe Again?" *UpReach* 3 (July/Aug. 1981): 16-19.

"The Church: Hierarchy or Family?" *UpReach* 3 (Nov./Dec. 1981): 21-23, 30.

"The Fatherhood of God." *Lubbock Christian College Lectures* (1981): 1-8.

"I Know It When I See It." *UpReach* 3 (Jan./Feb. 1981): 16-19.

"Living More Simply." *UpReach* 3 (May/June 1981): 8-11.

1982

"An Act of the Will." *UpReach* 4 (Mar./Apr. 1982): 15, 21-23.

"Church Discipline: The Neglected Commandment." *Harding University Lectures* (1982): 167-172.

"The Church in the 1980's." *Harding University Lectures* (1982): 161-166.

"The Committed Marriage." Abilene: *Herald of Truth*, 1977. Chapter one broadcast as *Herald of Truth* program No. 526 (Oct. 2, 1977) and reprinted as article in *UpReach* 4 (July/Aug. 1982): 17, 22-23, 30, and in two parts in *Teenage Christian* 24 (Feb. 1983): 19-22; (Mar. 1983): 8-11.

"A Faith for the Nations." In *The Man of the Messianic Reign and Other Essays: A Festschrift in Honor of Dr. Elza Huffard*, edited by Wil C. Goodheer, 52-59. Wichita Falls: Western Christian Foundation, 1982.

"The Fractured Family." *UpReach* 4 (May/June 1982): 19-22.

"Goals Worth Waiting for." *UpReach* 4 (Jan./Feb. 1982): 8-9, 21, 29-30.

"Listen to the Lord." *20th Century Christian* 44 (May 1982): 12-14.

"The Preacher and His Books." *Christian Chronicle* 39 (Feb. 1982): 15.

"Religious Scholarship among Us: Today and the Future." *Christian Scholars Conference* (1982): 13 p.

"Sunrise . . . Sunset." *Harding Graduate School of Religion Bulletin* 22 (Dec. 1982): 2.

"The Unity of the Spirit." *HGSR Bulletin* 22 (Mar. 1982): 2.

"Vocational Evangelism." *Harding Graduate School of Religion Bulletin* 22 (Oct. 1982): 2.

"The Word Became Flesh." *UpReach* 4 (Nov./Dec. 1982): 9-11, 30.

1983

"And Not Blink." *Harding Graduate School of Religion Bulletin* 24 (Dec. 1983): 2; reprinted in *Teenage Christian* 25 (July 1984): 30-31 and 26 (Nov. 1985): 10-11.

"A Burden Too Heavy." *UpReach* 5 (Nov./Dec. 1983): 4-7, 27.

"Concentrating on One Thing." *Harding Graduate School of Religion Bulletin* 24 (Nov. 1983): 2.

"Dealing with Stress." *UpReach* 5 (Sept./Oct. 1983): 4-7.

"Good News for the Poor." *UpReach* 5 (May/June 1983): 14-17, 29.

"Jesus and the Fractured Family." *UpReach* 5 (July/Aug. 1983): 8-11.

"What Lack I Yet?" *UpReach* 5 (Mar./Apr. 1983): 15-17. Published in Spanish as AQue me Falta?" *Nuestro Tiempo* 1 (May 1984): 6-7.

"Why Do Bad Things Happen to Good People?" *UpReach* 5 (Jan./Feb. 1983): 9, 28-29.

1984

"The City." *UpReach* 6 (Jan./Feb. 1984): 25-27.

"The Clergymen Speak." *Mid-South: The Commercial Appeal Magazine* (25 Nov. 1984): 8.

"Congratulations, *UpReach* Family!" *Herald of Truth International* (Jan./Feb. 1984): 1.

"Die before You're Through." *20th Century Christian* 45 (Oct. 1984): 15-16.

"Frail Vessels — Priceless Treasures." *Harding Graduate School of Religion Bulletin* 25 (Aug. 1984): 2.

"God's Forever Family." *UpReach* 6 (July/Aug. 1984): 4-7, 30.

I Want to Become. Abilene: Herald of Truth, 1984.

"I'm Not Good Enough to Be a Christian." *UpReach* 6 (Sept./Oct. 1984): 4-7, 17. An abridged version published in *UpReach* 16 (Jan.-Mar. 1994): 10-11.

Lord, Help Me When I'm Hurting. Grand Rapids: Baker, 1984.

"Matthew 19: 3-9." *Harding Graduate School of Religion Bulletin* 25 (Nov. 1984): 2; reprinted in *The Sower's Sourcebook* 2 (Jan. 1986): 3.

"The Mind of Christ." *20th Century Christian* 45 (Aug. 1984): 26-28.

"Missions at Harding Graduate School." *Harding Graduate School of Religion Bulletin* 25 (Sept. 1984): 1.

"Pushing Back the Walls. *Harding Graduate School of Religion Bulletin* 25 (Apr. 1984): 2.

"The Single Christian." *UpReach* 6 (May/June 1984): 5-7, 17.

"Thinking Like a Servant." *Abilene Christian University Lectures* (1984): 99-106.

"What Will You Do with Your Life?" *UpReach* 6 (Mar./Apr. 1984): 14-16, 30.

"Why Doesn't God Give Me What I Want?" *UpReach* 6 (Nov./Dec. 1984): 4-7, 30.

"Why Graduate School?" *Harding Graduate School of Religion Bulletin* 25 (July 1984): 1.

"The Will of God." *Harding Graduate School of Religion Bulletin* 25 (Oct. 1984): 2; reprinted in *Voice of Freedom* 33 (Jan. 1985): 14.

1985

"Abortion." *20th Century Christian* 46 (Aug. 1985): 20-22.

"Better to Reign in Hell?" *20th Century Christian* 46 (Feb. 1985): 34-36.

"Birth Control and Overpopulation." *20th Century Christian* 46 (Aug. 1985): 15-17.

"Creating Stronger Family Unity." *UpReach* 7 (Nov./Dec. 1985): 4-7, 17.

"The Family's Lifeblood: Encouragement." *UpReach* 7 (July/Aug. 1985): 4-7, 11.

Happiness in the Home: Guidelines for Spouses and Parents. Grand Rapids: Baker, 1985.

"The Heart of the Gospel." *Image* 1 (15 Dec.1985): 26-27.

"Hindrances to Unity." *Harding University Lectures* (1985): 236-244.

"Holistic Education for Ministers." *Harding Graduate School of Religion Bulletin* 26 (Mar. 1985): 2.

"How to Discuss God in Your Home." *UpReach* 7 (May/June 1985): 5-7, 30.

How to Make a Good Marriage Better. Abilene: Herald of Truth, 1985.

"I Love God but Will My Children?" In *Discover God's Love in Your Life*, 38-47. Fort Worth: Sweet Publishing Co., 1985.

"Jesus and Ethical Issues." *20th Century Christian* 46 (Aug. 1985): 8-10.

"Making Moral Decisions." *Harding Graduate School of Religion Bulletin* 26 (Jan. 1985): 2.

"New Technologies." *20th Century Christian* 46 (Aug. 1985): 26-29.

"The New Testament Is Full of Trouble." *20th Century Christian* 43 (June 1981): 7-9.

Review of *Classical Apologetics: A Rational Defense of the Christian Faith and a Critique of Presuppositional Apologetics,* by R. C. Sproul, John Gerstner, and Arthur Lindsley. *Harding Graduate School of Religion Bulletin* 26 (Apr. 1985): 2; reprinted in *The Sower's Sourcebook* 1 (Aug. 1985): 6.

"Right to Die?" *20th Century Christian* 46 (Aug. 1985): 30-32.

7 Ways God Can Help You Be Happier. Abilene: Herald of Truth, 1985.

"Training Ministers" *Harding Graduate School of Religion Bulletin* 26 (Feb. 1985): 2.

"Traits of a Happy Family." *UpReach* 7 (Jan./Feb. 1985): 5-7, 17. Published in Spanish as "Characteristicas de la Familia Feliz." *La Voz Eterna* 23 (Sept. 1985): 12-17.

"The Value of Life." *20th Century Christian* 46 (Aug. 1985): 12-14.

"What Is a Family?" *UpReach* 7 (Mar./Apr. 1985): 5-7, 17.

"What Makes a Christian Marriage Different?" *UpReach* 7 (Sept./ Oct. 1985): 4-7, 22.

"What the World Really Needs." *Harding University Lectures* (1985): 295-299.

"Why Do We Do What We Do?" *20th Century Christian* 46 (Aug. 1985): 4-7.

1986

"The Broken Heart." *Harding Graduate School of Religion Bulletin* 27 (Apr. 1986): 2.

"Calling on the Name of the Lord." *Gospel Advocate* 128 (16 Jan. 1986): 51.

"Can We Still Believe in Jesus?" *UpReach* 8 (May/June 1986): 4-7, 11. Revised version published in *UpReach* 19, no. 1 (1997): 4-7.

"The Christian Scholar's Task." *Gospel Advocate* 128 (21 Aug.1986): 489, 491.

"Don't Lose Heart." *UpReach* 8 (July/Aug.): 4-7, 20.

"Freedom of Worship." *Gospel Advocate* 128 (3 July 1986): 388.

"How Does One Say Goodby?" *Harding Graduate School of Religion Bulletin* 27 (June 1986): 2.

"In the Life of Christ." *20th Century Christian* 49 (Dec. 1986): 7-9.

"Is Apocalypse Now?" *UpReach* 8 (Jan./Feb. 1986): 4-7, 13.

"The Possible Dream." *UpReach* 8 (Nov./Dec. 1986): 4-7, 12-13; reprinted in *Gospel Advocate* 128 (18 Dec. 1986): 748, 750.

"Power for Our Mission." *Harding Graduate School of Religion Bulletin* 27 (Jan. 1986): 2.

Questions People Ask Ministers Most. Grand Rapids: Baker, 1986.

"A Reason for the Hope." *UpReach* 8 (Mar./Apr. 1986): 4-7, 13.

"Why Aren't Families Close Anymore?" *UpReach* 8 (Sept./Oct. 1986): 4-7, 11.

1987

"Ethical Matters Which Christians in a University Context Must Address in the Final Decade of the Twentieth Century." *Christian Scholars Conference Papers* (1987): 10 p.

"God's Counter Culture." *UpReach* 9 (May/June 1987): 4-7, 13.

"Great Words of Evangelism: Salvation." *Harding University Lectures* (1987): 21-25.

"Home: The Million Dollar Word." *UpReach* 9 (Nov./Dec. 1987): 4-7, 13; reprinted in *UpReach* 11 (May/June 1989): 4-7, 11.

"In Touch with the Past." *UpReach* 9 (Sept./Oct. 1987): 4-7, 27.

Jesus Our Mentor and Our Model: A Hero for Heroic Living (with Ken Durham). Grand Rapids: Baker, 1987.

"Man Does Not Stand Alone." *UpReach* 9 (Mar./Apr. 1987): 4-7, 23.

"A People under the Word." *UpReach* 9 (Jan./Feb. 1987): 4-7, 23.

"Priests to Each Other." *UpReach* 9 (July/Aug. 1987): 4-7.

"A Servant Death." *20th Century Christian* 50 (Dec. 1987): 20-22.

"Tomorrow's Opportunities for Evangelism." *Harding University Lectures* (1987): 132-136.

1988

"Becoming Persons of Integrity." *UpReach* 10 (Sept./Oct. 1988): 4-7, 13.

Becoming Persons of Integrity (with Ken Durham). Grand Rapids: Baker, 1988.

The Bible Land: Walking Where Jesus Walked (with Bill Humble). Nashville: Christian Communications, 1988.

"Finding Companionship." *UpReach* 10 (July/Aug. 1988): 4-7, 11.

"God-Given Life." *UpReach* 10 (Jan./Feb. 1988): 4-7, 10-11.

"The God Who Keeps His Promises." *UpReach* 10 (Nov./Dec. 1988): 4-6, 20.

"I Have Decided to Follow Jesus." *UpReach* 10 (Mar./Apr. 1988): 4-7, 11.

"The 20th Century Christian and Christian Education." *20th Century Christian* 51 (Oct. 1988): 12-16.

1989

Anchors for the Asking: Rediscovering a Secure Faith in a Shifting World (with Ken Durham). Grand Rapids: Baker, 1989.

"The Christ Who Transcends Culture." *Abilene Christian University Lectures* (1989): 66-74.

"Family Well-Being: The Bottom Line." *UpReach* 11 (Nov./Dec. 1989): 4-7, 17.

"God's Plan for Healthy Families." *UpReach* 11 (Sept./Oct. 1989): 4-7, 11.

"Healing Invisible Wounds." *UpReach* 11 (Jan./Feb. 1989): 4-7.

"The Quest for Wholeness." *UpReach* (Mar./Apr. 1989): 4-7, 11.

"Women and Christian Ministry." *20th Century Christian* 52 (Oct. 1989): 9-12.

1990

"Always Returning." *UpReach* 12 (Aug.-Oct. 1990): 18-21.

"Building the Affair-Proof Marriage." *UpReach* 12 (May-July 1990): 8-9.

"Curing the Critical Home." *UpReach* 12 (Nov./Dec. 1990): 12-15.

"Evangelizing Korea Today." *Gospel Advocate* 132 (July 1990): 60.

"Making a Marriage Work." *UpReach* 12 (Jan.-Apr. 1990): 8-9.

"The Word of the Cross (1 Corinthians 1:18-25)." *Harding University Lectures* (1990): 41-47.

1991

"The Adventure of Fathering." *UpReach* 13 (July-Sept. 1991): 25-27.

"If I Were Starting My Family Again." *UpReach* 13 (Apr.-June 1991): 11-13.

Review of *Christian Faith, Health, & Medical Practice*, by Hessell Bouma III, Douglas Diekema, Edward Langerak, Theodore Rottman, and Allen Verhey. *Restoration Quarterly* 33 (July 1991): 191-192.

"The Way of Faith." *UpReach* 13 (Oct.-Dec. 1991): 27-28; reprinted as AI Want to Believe." *UpReach* 16 (Jan.-Mar. 1994): 18-19.

"Who Is Jesus?" *UpReach* 13 (Jan.-Mar. 1991): 5-7.

1992

"Challenges to Christian Education." *Gospel Advocate* 134 (Apr. 1992): 23, 25.
"Generation to Generation: The Path of Faith." *UpReach* 14 (Apr.-June 1992): 19-21.
"Jesus: The Stranger from Galilee: Who Is This? *UpReach* 14 (Oct.-Dec. 1992): 21-22.
"Loving the Unborn." *UpReach* 14 (July-Sept. 1992): 16-18.
"What Does My Faith Allow Me to Be?" *UpReach* 14 (Jan.-Mar. 1992): 8-10.

1993

"Are You Living Your Baptism?" *21st Century Christian* 55 (Feb. 1993): 12-14.
"Directions for Life: Moral Education for Young Adults." *UpReach* 15 (Apr.-June 1993): 16-18.
"Gratitude for Our Past — Hope for Our Future." *UpReach* 15 (Oct.-Dec. 1993): 8-11.
"The Meaning of Salvation." *UpReach* 15 (July-Sept. 1993): 11-13.
"Servant Leader." *UpReach* 15 (Jan.-Mar. 1993): 6-7.

1994

"Can Jesus Save Even Me?" *UpReach* 16, no. 3 (1994): 2-3.
"The Christian World View." *UpReach* 16 (Apr.-June 1994): 27-29.
"Remember Each Other." *21st Century Christian* 56 (Feb. 1994): 19-21.

1995

"Whatever Happened to Responsibility?" *21st Century Christian* 57 (June 1995): 6-8.

About the Editors

Gary Holloway is Dean of the College of Bible and Ministry at Lipscomb University and preaches at the Natchez Trace Church in Nashville. Holding degrees from Freed-Hardeman, Harding, The University of Texas, and Emory University, he has recently published four books, *The NIV Commentary on James and Jude*, *A Miracle Named Jesus*, and *Unexpected Jesus* from College Press, and *The Main Thing* from ACU Press. He is married to Deb Rogers Holloway.

Randall J. Harris teaches at Lipscomb University in the College of Bible and Ministry and preaches for the Donelson church in Nashville, Tennessee. He holds degrees from Harding University, Harding Graduate School of Religion, and Syracuse University. His areas of expertise are modern theology and ethics. He is a member of the American Academy of Religion and Society of Biblical Literature. He received an outstanding teacher award from Lipscomb University in 1990.

Mark C. Black is Associate Professor of Bible at Lipscomb University, Nashville, Tennessee. He is also Associate Minister at the Donelson Church of Christ. Before coming to Lipscomb he was the preacher for the Okolona Church of Christ in Louisville, Kentucky. Mark received the B.A. from Freed-Hardeman University, the M.A. and M.Div. from Harding Graduate School of Religion, the Th.M. from Princeton Theological Seminary, and the Ph.D. from Emory University. Mark and his wife Margo have three daughters: Sara, Jessica, and Allison.

Printed in the United States
23197LVS00004B/121-141